Reason and Religious Belief

REASON AND RELIGIOUS BELIEF

*An Introduction to
the Philosophy of Religion*

Michael Peterson
William Hasker
Bruce Reichenbach
David Basinger

New York   Oxford
OXFORD UNIVERSITY PRESS
1991

Oxford University Press

Oxford   New York   Toronto
Delhi   Bombay   Calcutta   Madras   Karachi
Petaling   Jaya   Singapore   Hong Kong   Tokyo
Nairobi   Dar es Salaam   Cape Town
Melbourne   Auckland

and associated companies in
Berlin   Ibadan

Copyright © 1991 by Oxford University Press, Inc.

Published by Oxford University Press, Inc.,
200 Madison Avenue, New York, NY 10016

Oxford is a registered trademark of Oxford University Press

Library of Congress Cataloging-in-Publication Data
Reason and religious belief : an introduction to the philosophy of
religion / by Michael Peterson . . . [et al.].
p. cm.   Includes bibliographical references.
ISBN 0-19-506155-1
1. Religion — Philosophy.   2. Christianity — Philosophy.
I. Peterson, Michael L., 1950–
BL51.R326   1991
210 — dc20   89-48073

4 6 8 9 7 5 3

Printed in the United States of America
on acid-free paper

Preface

Reason and Religious Belief grows out of our many years of collective experience reflecting upon the issues in philosophy of religion and teaching them to undergraduate students. So, in our writing, we have been especially conscious of the need to communicate the issues in ways that students can understand.

Perhaps more than anything else, though, the book was born out of long-standing friendship and intellectual interaction among the four of us. We dare to hope that the enjoyment and even the excitement of the type of philosophical discussion that we have shared will show through these pages and become contagious. Our different interests and specializations within the philosophy of religion are welded together by our complete agreement on the nature of the philosophical task in general: to analyze important concepts and evaluate major arguments, with the overall aim of finding the most reasonable position on any issue.

No project of this magnitude can be successful without help from others. We wish to thank the Faculty Research and Development Committee of Asbury College for providing a small grant to defray the costs of producing this manuscript. We are grateful also to Robert Audi and George Mavrodes for reading and making valuable suggestions on earlier drafts of the manuscript.

Wilmore, Kentucky	M. P.
Huntington, Indiana	W. H.
Minneapolis, Minnesota	B. R.
Rochester, New York	D. B.
April 1990	

Contents

Introduction

Philosophy of religion is receiving more attention in recent years than it has for many decades. Professional philosophers are bringing new techniques to bear on traditional problems and are pioneering important new territory as well. In 1980 *Time* reported this resurgence of interest in the philosophical examination of religion, stating that "God is making a comeback." It is becoming increasingly obvious to more and more people that the issues surrounding belief in God are extremely significant. This text has been written as an introduction to the basic issues and options in the exciting field of philosophy of religion. We try to provide a very accessible, comprehensive text in the philosophy of religion — one that is as current as possible, historically informed, theologically sophisticated, and philosophically challenging.

The present text does not assume background in philosophy on the part of the reader, and thus should prove useful to undergraduate, graduate, and seminary students with no previous exposure to philosophy. Since no prior mastery of introductory terms and concepts is required, the text should be accessible even to thoughtful and diligent readers who study it apart from any formal course setting. While this text is designed as a basic presentation of matters in the philosophy of religion, it also contains a good deal of general philosophy that supplies helpful background about major philosophers and their ideas as the book develops.

The essential strategy of this introductory text is to distill and discuss the main issues in the field, extracting the intellectual dialogue with which the more complex and difficult primary literature is occupied. We invite students to participate in that great dialogue about religion which has occupied many historical and contemporary philosophers. Our primary emphasis is on the *structure* of the issues. We want students to understand precisely what each issue is, the shape of its logic, what is at stake, and the main options it presents. Our ultimate goal is to help students form reasonable opinions about the issues and acquire the ability to continue to think about them in meaningful and helpful ways.

Knowing the pedagogical advantage of finding a point of contact with students, we begin each chapter with a concrete story, example, or quotation and gradually develop the larger issue under discussion. We try to draw students naturally into the issues and encourage thoughtful response, striving throughout for clarity and accessibility in our presentation. For a number of years we have employed this technique in our own teaching and have confidence in its effectiveness.

Despite the broad logical order governing the sequence of the first several chapters, instructors using this text can assign chapters in almost any order, as the topics are somewhat independent. Obviously, supplementary readings, preferably of original works, can be coordinated with the individual chapters. Study questions are included at the end of each chapter in order to aid private review as well as classroom discussion. Suggested reading is included for each topic so that students can further pursue the issues. Indexes of names and selected topics enable students to trace efficiently the occurrence of particular concepts and viewpoints.

Since the long-standing interest among Western philosophers has been *theism*, this text is devoted largely to the issues related to the view that there exists a supreme spiritual Being, transcendent from the world, who is omnipotent, omniscient, and perfectly good. This, of course, is the view known more precisely as *classical theism*. The major theistic religions (Judaism, Christianity, and Islam) basically share this view of God. While focusing primarily on issues pertaining to classical theism, we do consider some issues or variations of issues that pertain more specifically to *Christian* theism, primarily because interest in Christian theism is quite common among contemporary Anglo-American philosophers of religion. At appropriate points we also indicate how the issues treated here apply to major nontheistic religions and theological conceptions, thus acquainting students to some degree with Hinduism, Buddhism, and other non-Western traditions. In fact, we believe that references to non-Western religious traditions can enhance the students' perspective on the central issues at hand.

Although a study of this sort almost inevitably assumes some familiarity with the religious tradition or theological concepts being examined, we try to make the most minimal assumptions along these lines. Ideally, our readers will be somewhat acquainted with Western religious faith and the sorts of beliefs characteristic of theistic religions generally. However, we supply enough description and exposition of these beliefs so that even the neophyte should be able to grasp quickly the religious concepts and doctrines under discussion. Beyond this, we do not assume that readers are theists or religious believers of any persuasion.

We cover all of the issues typically treated in standard philosophy-of-religion texts, and also a few rarely discussed topics that many instructors would like to see included. Chapter 1 begins by surveying the pervasive religiosity of the human race and defining exactly what a philosophical examination of religion would be. Chapter 2 examines what is perhaps for many people their most familiar and concrete contact with religion: religious experience. We examine such questions as whether there is a common core or structure to all religious experiences and whether these experiences can serve to justify religious beliefs. We move beyond experience in Chapter 3 and consider whether religious commitments are subject to rational evaluation. After looking at two extreme positions — hard rationalism and fideism — we adopt a posture that we call *critical rationalism*. Critical rationalism is committed to the analysis and evaluation of religious beliefs, but does not maintain that these beliefs are subject to conclusive proof or disproof. We devote Chapter 4 to the attributes traditionally associated with the theistic deity, attributes that define more precisely the Being who is the subject of further argument and debate. We do not neglect, however, the trenchant critique of the traditional concept of deity offered by process thinkers.

In the following two chapters, we are occupied with arguments for and against the existence of God, respectively the main fare of natural theology and natural atheology. In Chapter 5 we examine the classic arguments for the existence of God, arguments that still fascinate and challenge those who think about whether it is possible to provide rational support for theistic belief. Chapter 6 analyzes and discusses the problem of evil — widely recognized as the most serious rational objection to belief in God.

Although natural theology and atheology constitute a significant portion of traditional philosophy of religion, the aims and methods of these enterprises came under severe criticism during the 1980s. Recently, philosophers have argued that belief in God need not rest on rational argument, but can be "basic" in the framework of our beliefs. This position, known as "Reformed epistemology" and considered in Chapter 7, is so new that almost no other introductory text addresses it.

In the subsequent six chapters we proceed to a variety of enduring issues. Chapter 8 discusses the problem of religious language, of how human words can apply to God meaningfully. Although the day has just passed when this subject was at the very forefront of philosophy of religion, many of the issues involved are fundamental to progress in other areas of the field. In Chapter 9 we consider the problem of miracles. Since Christian theism has historically involved a belief in miracles, this chapter first probes the difficulty of definition; then it faces the problem of whether miracles are possible and, if so, whether they are identifiable. Chapter 10 focuses on the problem of life after death, allowing us to show that concepts of postmortem survival vary with views of the human self. We also scrutinize certain arguments for the reality of life after death.

In Chapter 11 we look closely at the relationship between religion and science. This topic is covered in only a small portion of texts in philosophy of religion, where it is usually developed in terms of current issues — say, the creation–evolution debate or the possibility of producing life from DNA — rather than in terms of some overall understanding of religion and science. We bring some guidance to various disputes by making vital conceptual distinctions between the natures of the two large human activities in question. In the succeeding chapter we take up the increasingly pressing problem of religious diversity. This issue alone is inspiring numerous new courses in colleges and universities. Here, in Chapter 12, we see that through modern communication and travel, people have become acutely conscious of the great differences between religious and cultural traditions, making us wonder how such divergent belief-systems can all be said to be true. In Chapter 13 we explore the connection between religion and ethics, raising such questions as whether ethical norms can originate in God and whether religion offers a distinctive vision of human moral fulfillment.

Coming near the end of our study, we recognize that one historically important way in which philosophy has intersected with religion has been the explication and analysis of theological doctrines. Therefore, we devote Chapter 14 to an examination of some representative contemporary efforts in this area. Current work on key doctrines in Christian theology, such as the Incarnation and the Atonement, provides rich material for reflection and discussion. Much of the work on these topics is quite fresh and only lately is emerging. The final chapter serves as a capstone to our study of the philosophy of religion, summarizing the main lessons that can be learned and inviting readers to continue exploring the issues in the fascinating field of philosophy of religion.

In an introductory treatment of intellectually significant issues, we are convinced that the impact on readers is determined not so much by *what* particular issues are selected for treatment as by *how* those issues are handled. Hence, the posture or stance of the authors is of major consequence. We have sought to strike a balance between pure neutrality on the one hand and outright advocacy on the other. While we attempt to be fair to various positions, we will sometimes indicate which one seems most reasonable to us among alternatives. This approach is more personal than "pure neutralism" and, we believe, helps enlist readers in the activity of critical thinking about the issues.

It is certainly true that undertaking the present study in the philosophy of religion can help those who are already believers to develop a deeper understanding of their faith as well as become aware of responsible objections to it. But it is equally true that those who do not have faith can gain a better understanding of the multitude of important issues to which religious faith gives rise.

Believing that a serious study of philosophy of religion offers both intellectual stimulation and personal rewards, we have designed this text toward these ends. If we have met our philosophical and pedagogical objectives in sufficient measure, we dare to hope that all our readers will find this exploration of the philosophy of religion genuinely worthwhile.

Reason and Religious Belief

1

Thinking about God:
The Search for the Ultimate

Religion is a powerful force in human life. . . .

- A Cro-Magnon society buries a fallen hunter in fetal position, surrounding him with useful objects — weapons, necklaces, and cooking utensils — as though he might experience another life.
- The members of an aboriginal tribe pray to the great spirit of the sky to regard them favorably and not withhold rain.
- In modern Japan, a Zen Buddhist meditates on the unity between the "I" and the "not-I."
- During the Islamic holy month of Ramadan, a devout Moroccan family practices fasting from dawn to sundown.
- On Easter Sunday, Christian believers all over the world celebrate the Resurrection of Jesus, just as Christians have done for two thousand years.

Evidence is abundant that human beings are incurably religious. Prehistoric and primitive tribes manifested their religious impulses in animistic and totemistic practices. From the dawn of civilization, a multitude of religions have developed, each very complex. More advanced world religions, for example, have highly sophisticated concepts of an Ultimate Reality: For Jews it is Yahweh, for Christians it is the Triune God, for Muslims it is Allah, for Hindus it is Śiva or Viṣṇu, for Theravāda Buddhists it is Nirvāṇa.[1] Even those who spend enormous energy repudiating religion — such as Madalyn Murray O'Hair and the Association of American Atheists[2] — witness in a peculiar way to its impact on human life.

Defining Religion

There are many definitions of religion.[3] C. P. Tiele (1830–1902) wrote that "religion is, in truth, that pure and reverential disposition or frame of mind

3

which we call piety." F. H. Bradley (1846–1924) stated that "religion is rather the attempt to express the complete reality of goodness through every aspect of our being." And James Martineau (1805–1900) claimed that "religion is the belief in an ever living God, that is, in a Divine Mind and Will ruling the Universe and holding moral relations with mankind." It is apparent that each of these definitions specifies a different characteristic: Tiele accents the attitude of piety, Bradley links religion with goodness, and Martineau focuses on belief in ethical monotheism.

Other definitions of religion touch upon additional traits, such as ritualistic acts, prayer, and communication with gods, and each definition seems to have some measure of validity. However, wisdom counsels that we not elevate any single feature to the status of a universal definition. Religions are too complex for that. There are primitive, shamanistic religions, for example, that seem not to involve feelings of genuine piety so much as they involve prudential or utilitarian acts of obeisance. Thus, Tiele's definition is not adequate. Likewise there are polytheistic religions (such as those of ancient Greece and Egypt) that do not recognize a single divine ruler of the universe. Therefore, the definition given by Martineau also fails to cover all religions.

These shortcomings suggest that religion is notoriously difficult to define. On the one hand, in speaking too generically about religion we risk being imprecise and may even distort the rich and complicated details of actual religions. For example, religion is usually but not always associated with the supernatural or the divine. The notion of a supernatural realm does not occur in the nontheistic schools of Buddhism and functions in very different ways, say, in Taoism, Hinduism, and Islam. The great differences among religions make it difficult to find a least common denominator or to talk at length of religion in general. On the other hand, focusing on just one specific religion often causes us to ignore or underestimate some of the very broad traits that religions seem to share. In light of the difficulties of defining and applying the term *religion*, we may feel as if a final and definitive solution will forever elude us. But a tentative, working definition is adequate for the present study. Being aware of pitfalls on both sides, we must proceed with caution. The fact remains that we will make no headway into the question of what makes a specific religion a religion if we do not seek some characteristics common to all religions.

We might attempt to formulate a working definition of religion by enumerating what seem to be the general structural traits of all religions. Ninian Smart takes this approach and lists six broad characteristics or "dimensions" that he believes are present in all actual religions: the ritual, the mythological, the doctrinal, the ethical, the social, and the experiential.[4] Smart's list is certainly helpful, but there are other ways of classifying the characteristics of religion. For present purposes, let us say that *religion is constituted by a set of beliefs, actions, and emotions, both personal and corporate, organized around the concept of an Ultimate Reality*. This Reality may be understood as a unity or a plurality, personal or nonpersonal, divine or not, and so forth, differing from religion to religion. Yet it seems that every cultural phenomenon that we call a religion fits this definition. The prescribed actions vary from ritualistic patterns to ethical living; the desired emotions vary from feelings of piety and humility to a sense of optimism about life and the universe. It is imperative, therefore, not to identify distinctively religious action or emotion with any specific cultural expression. There is latitude for some variation among cultures and religions.

As the title of this text suggests, our present study is directed at *beliefs*. Beliefs, for our purposes, are simply statements that are taken as true; they are truth-claims. Every religion rests on beliefs—beliefs about the nature of the Supreme Reality, the appropriate response to it, and a number of related matters. The beliefs of a given religion account for the particular actions it endorses and emotions it evokes. These beliefs may be made official and presented in the form of doctrine, or they may be somewhat implicit in the daily practice of the religion. It seems clear, though, that the numerous details of any religion are very much an extension of how the fundamental beliefs about the Ultimate are interpreted and expressed in real life. Such beliefs, as we shall say, are *religious beliefs*, and, like all beliefs, they may be examined for consistency, coherence, plausibility, and truth.

Now, in any given case, if we found a network of actions, emotions, and beliefs focusing on some Ultimate Reality, then our general definition would be satisfied to a sufficient degree and we would be justified in saying that we have an instance of religion. Obviously, some cultural phenomena embody all of the relevant features to a remarkable extent and thus provide clear and uncontroversial examples of a religion. Roman Catholicism and Orthodox Judaism are unmistakable instances of religion according to our definition. Other instances less obviously possess the set of relevant characteristics and are still arguably instances of religion, such as certain forms of Buddhism and even Unitarianism. Some people would even argue that secular humanism and communism are religions or at least strongly exhibit religious characteristics. After all, they focus respectively on human progress and the collectivist state as Ultimate Reality, approving the value systems and aspirations that accompany them.

Of course, we cannot fully understand a given religion—its preferred attitudes and emotions, its prescribed rituals, its important stories and myths, and its recommended way of life—simply by looking at it. A multitude of psychological, sociological, and historical factors that are not obvious to the untrained eye form the contours of every religion. That is why an expert, say, in the psychology or sociology of religion can reveal fascinating insights to those who are merely novices. Disciplines such as psychology, sociology, and anthropology provide helpful avenues into the complex realities of the religion. However, there is another major dimension of every religion: the *intellectual*. The intellectual dimension pertains to its central beliefs or truth-claims. Thus, it is the intellectual dimension—that aspect of religion dealing with beliefs—that gives meaning and point to the many actions and experiences of those who adhere to a given religion. Since philosophy is the discipline that raises considerations of consistency and truth in beliefs, philosophy can legitimately examine religious beliefs. Before we can fully understand the value and function of the philosophical scrutiny of religion, we must survey some of the other major ways of investigating religion.

The Manifold Study of Religion

There are indeed many ways of studying the complex reality of religion, giving rise to numerous academic disciplines that officially take religion as their subject matter. Although these disciplines sometimes overlap, it is helpful to differentiate them in terms of their characteristic methods and aims in order to place the philosophy of religion in sharper perspective.

In the *psychology of religion*, the psychologist investigates the effect that religious beliefs and practices have on the integration of personality. The *sociology of religion* is an academic field in which the sociologist is concerned to discover how the religious beliefs and practices of a given group function in society and how they contribute to social structure. The *anthropology of religion* leads the anthropologist to focus on the role of religion as an integral part of a cultural context, giving significance to its art, work, and tradition. In studying the *history of religions*, the historian examines the development of religion over time, as it interacts with political, economic, and social realities. In the *comparative study of religions*, the comparativist traces out the details of many religions, seeking to identify, where possible, themes that are similar or features that are common to most or all of them.

One problem with restricting the study of religion to these disciplines is that they do not permit questions about the reasonableness and truth of religious beliefs to be fully considered. It is actually within the domain of philosophy that such questions must be treated. Religious concepts must be examined for clarity and coherence, the rational basis of religious beliefs must be scrutinized, and the ramifications of religious perspectives must be carefully explored. After the other disciplines have completed their studies, this kind of truly philosophical investigation of religion remains to be performed.

What Is Philosophy of Religion?

The examination of the intellectual dimension of religion — that is, its key beliefs — is most beneficial when it is guided and informed. Since philosophy is that discipline which closely examines beliefs, we may rightly expect it to aid our study of religious beliefs. To seek to know whether given beliefs are meaningful, consistent, and reasonable is to engage in a distinctively philosophical activity. The academic discipline that examines the intellectual dimension of religion is known as the *philosophy of religion*. In one sense, philosophy of religion is an extension of our innate human drive to think hard about a multitude of important issues. As an academic subject, philosophy of religion refines this innate drive for questioning and understanding by bringing the techniques and insights of the formal discipline of philosophy to bear upon religious beliefs.

Philosophy has historically stressed several key factors in the investigation of any important topic, including religion. The first factor is the desire for *clarity*, which frequently leads philosophers to ask about the precise meaning of terms and concepts. Philosophers of religion, for instance, are deeply concerned about the definitions of such major terms as *God, miracle*, and *evil*.

The second factor generally stressed by philosophers is the need to be *critical*, to detect and scrutinize hidden assumptions, and to look at alternatives and objections to every position. That is why philosophers of religion are never content with mere exposition of a given theory, but delve more deeply into its positive and negative points.

Third, philosophers have always emphasized that responsible opinions must be based on *argument* rather than on private preference or group conviction. Even those who hold the position that there are beliefs for which we need no argument must provide an argument for their position. Furthermore, their opponents must also formulate arguments for why they disagree. Ideally, then, one will rest one's point of view on sound thinking and will be open to persuasion based on further careful reasoning. Many introductions to the philosophy of religion, for example, as a means of evaluating the rationality of religious belief, often devote a significant amount of space to arguments for and against the existence of God.

A fourth factor that is sometimes included as a function of philosophy is the *constructive* or *synthetic*, an aspect of the philosophic task that involves attempting to build a comprehensive point of view. The synthetic approach was taken to extreme in the nineteenth and early twentieth centuries by idealistic philosophers who deduced very elaborate and highly speculative systems of thought from a few principles that they took as certain. As a reaction, the synthetic approach has been in disrepute for many decades among narrowly analytic philosophers. A more realistic and balanced understanding of this aspect of the philosophic task is that it provides a way of putting together many specific conclusions of many related arguments into a unified perspective or position. Thinkers in the philosophy of religion, for example, might have some definite opinions about which, if any, of the traditional theistic arguments for the existence of God work, about the force of the problem of evil, about whether miracles are possible, about the meaning and import of religious experience, and the like. But it takes additional philosophical work to appraise the collective compatibility of the individual conclusions as well the overall helpfulness and viability of the position to which they give rise. This consideration reflects the constructive function of philosophy.

In addition to employing the basic methods or strategies of philosophizing, the philosophy of religion draws insights and themes for further investigation from other established areas of philosophical concern: *epistemology, metaphysics, ethics*, and so forth. For example, philosophers of religion might consider the epistemology of religious belief, pondering questions about the sources and justification of religious knowledge. Alternatively, they might analyze various metaphysical theories of the nature of God and the structure of the divine being, or the metaphysics of human free will in relation to divine sovereignty. They might even trace the connection between a given religious tradition and a certain ethical way of life.

Naturally, the particular approach we take to philosophy of religion depends on precisely how we conceive of the philosophical task in general. The *traditional* conception of philosophy, which was dominant throughout the history of Western thought, was that philosophy can investigate the content of our beliefs, including the truth or falsity of theological beliefs. The name *natural theology* came to be used as a label for the enterprise which presumed that belief in the existence of God and other religious beliefs could, and indeed should, be established by philosophical argument.

Since the early decades of the twentieth century, the *phenomenological* approach to religion has had its proponents — thinkers promising to provide a new method for describing and understanding phenomena as they really are.[5] It does this by "bracketing" (or suspending) preconceptions as well as critical questions about truth or falsity, in order to "disclose" or "lay bare" the essence of religion as actually experienced by its own adherents.[6]

Yet for most of the twentieth century, the principal philosophical approach among English-speaking philosophers has been *analytic*. Narrowly conceived, this approach restricts the task of philosophy to analyzing the logic of our ideas and elucidating the meaning of our concepts, and denies that philosophy can address questions of truth or falsity in our beliefs.[7] More broadly conceived, the analytic approach is seriously concerned with clear analysis and logical rigor, but as a prelude to more substantive considerations of truth and reasonableness.

The present study is basically analytic in its style, seeking to clarify and analyze important concepts and arguments. Yet it is not *narrowly* analytic in that it seeks to point out, where possible, those positions that seem most correct and fruitful. In this way, our current venture preserves much of the spirit of the traditional approach, without adopting wholesale the old model of natural theology. No sustained attempt is made in these pages to apply phenomenological techniques, since such an approach would be appropriate to an entirely different kind of study.

While the preceding explanation of the relationship in which philosophy stands to religion is somewhat loose and approximate, it is on equal footing with similar explanations regarding philosophy of art, philosophy of science, philosophy of history, and a number of other studies in which, again, philosophy thoroughly inspects a stated subject matter. Obviously, all such studies suffer from a double ambiguity in that both the nature of philosophy and the discipline under study can be conceived in a variety of ways. Here, however, we assume that the enterprise of philosophy is to be conducted according to our foregoing description. So, we are now in a position to propose a working definition: *Philosophy of religion is the attempt to analyze and critically evaluate religious beliefs.*

At this stage, philosophy of religion must still be distinguished from two other disciplines with closely related interests. It differs from *dogmatic* (or *confessional*) *theology*, which begins from the assumption that a certain religious tradition is authoritative, or that a specific creed is in fact true. A dogmatic theologian seeks to provide ways of elucidating and systematizing accepted doctrines, but does not challenge them. Philosophy of religion is also distinct from *apologetics*, which is concerned to defend a given religious position from intellectual objections. Apologetic projects may be either *negative* or *positive*: Negative apologetics seeks to show that certain criticisms of a specific religious position fail, whereas positive apologetics seeks to show that the position is reasonable or credible. Apologetics often has a very practical side, lending itself readily to the practical activity of persuasion. While philosophical awareness and logical skill are relevant to the enterprises of dogmatic theology and apologetics, these activities are not philosophical in the fundamental sense of beginning from a position of relative openness to alternative views and willingness to critique their own most basic commitments.

The God of Theism

Since religious systems merit serious philosophical investigation, worthwhile exercises in philosophy of religion can be conducted by inquiring into the specific beliefs of any religion or into certain types of beliefs shared by several religions. For the past twenty-five hundred years in Western culture, the chief interest of philosophers who study religion has been the theistic concept of deity. In theism, God is conceived as a spiritual being, transcendent from the world, who is omnipotent, omniscient, and perfectly good. We might call this view *classical theism*. Amid all of their differences, most traditions within three great historical religions—Judaism, Christianity, and Islam—share this basic view of God. Contemporary Anglo-American philosophers continue to be interested in issues surrounding *classical theism*, including nontraditional proposals for modifying it. The present study focuses primarily on the most significant issues related to *classical theism*, although at some points issues in other theistic religions and even nontheistic religions are given serious consideration. Much of our discourse in this book is drawn from historical Judeo-Christian beliefs about God, since those beliefs give shape to many past and present issues.

Some say that purely intellectual interest in God (in this case, the God of theism) misses the heart of true religion. They contend that the abstract analysis of religious concepts and the logical examination of theological beliefs fail to appreciate the intimate, personal involvement of religious faith. Contending that "the God of the philosophers" is not "the God of religion," they often argue that rigorous intellectual investigation has nothing to offer to devout faith. While intellectual interest—or, more precisely, philosophical interest—in religion is not the same thing as passionate religious commitment, it is extremely doubtful that faith can be totally divorced from reason.

Although religious faith certainly involves an element of personal trust in God, that trust is normally based on a number of *beliefs* about what God is like and how a person becomes properly related to him.[8] Now, having faith in God and living in a manner which manifests that attitude amount to *more* than intellectually adopting beliefs that God exists and that God is perfect in power, knowledge, and justice. But having faith in God is *at least* a matter of accepting such beliefs. In some cases, a religious believer may not have a clear and self-conscious understanding of his own beliefs, or may not be particularly adept at articulating them. However, this does not alter the fact that religious faith rests on beliefs about the kind of object in which one has faith.[9]

Besides, the instant the believer makes some sort of claim of faith, some statement about his relation to the God he worships, he has automatically entered the arena of rational discussion and dialogue. Wittingly or unwittingly, he has stated some intellectual beliefs — uttered truth-claims that are subject to being criticized and defended. Insofar as religious faith is a matter of holding certain beliefs, then, it is open to rational evaluation. Even the belief that faith is immune from critical examination must itself be rationally evaluated.

Actually, it is not just the outsider or critic who has the right to examine the belief component of religious faith. The believer himself may want to seek deeper understanding of his faith by probing its beliefs further — what St. Anselm (1033–1109) called "faith seeking understanding."[10] In fact, all major religions recognize their own intellectual dimension, or belief component, and contain self-critical elements; in addition, they recognize that they must confront criticism from outside and have reputable intellectual traditions that undertake this task. If religion in modern life is to have any relevance to people who are intellectually honest and morally sensitive, it must be open to continued scrutiny. Over the centuries, the classical theistic view of God has produced a rich legacy of dialogue and debate — an exciting ongoing discussion in which the reader of this text is invited to participate.

The Nature of Our Task

The task that lies before us is an important one: to think philosophically about particular issues in religion, specifically, the issues related to the theistic concept of God. Thoughtful and informed people are already aware of many of these issues which arise when they reflect on the events and experiences of ordinary life: "Does God exist?" "Are miracles possible?" "Why would a good God allow suffering?" "Among many religions, can only one be true?" Yet there are complexities in such issues that are not immediately obvious, but have been brought to light by centuries of intense and vigorous discussion in the philosophical community. Both historical and recent discussions benefit us most by allowing us to see clearly the structure of the issues — what exactly is at stake, where the burden of proof lies, and what options are open. Attaining an adequate degree of understanding is a prelude to forming a reasonable opinion and having some sense of how to pursue these and other philosophical issues in religion.

It is important, though, not simply to know the issues and options in philosophy of religion, but to adopt a certain stance toward them. Our posture or stance should be a balance between pure neutrality at one extreme and blind bias at the other. We cannot be completely neutral toward the issues, since they are part of the host of deep religious problems that relate to the search for our own humanity and our place in the universe. Neither can we allow prejudice to control how we evaluate the issues. While each of us may prefer a certain perspective, we must gain the ability to examine impartially both our own perspective and those opposing it. A kind of interested objectivity is what is needed, attempting both to be fair to various positions and to acknowledge when possible which one seems most reasonable among alternatives. It is in this spirit that this book has been written.

The present venture, then, is open to all who are seeking understanding and who are committed to subjecting all beliefs, religious or otherwise, to rigorous philosophical examination. The results of this process are hard to predict. For some, it will lead to the modification of certain views. For others, it could lead to either the acceptance or rejection of theism. And for still others, it may lead to deeper commitment.

STUDY QUESTIONS

1. Formulate your own definition of "religion." Test your definition to see if it applies to various cultural phenomena we would normally call by that name.

2. Try to define "philosophy."

3. What is philosophy of religion? Explain how approaches to philosophy of religion are influenced by different approaches to philosophy itself.

4. Discuss the importance of considering matters of consistency, coherence, plausibility, and truth with respect to religious beliefs.

5. Distinguish among the various academic studies of religion.

6. Is it possible to remain completely neutral in the study of religion? Is it desirable to remain neutral? What kind of objectivity should we seek in the investigation of religion (or any important subject)?

7. At the outset, what issues in religion would you identify for philosophical analysis and discussion? Prior to reading this book, have you ever read any material that subjects religious beliefs to rational scrutiny?

8. Try to state in your own words the basic position of classical theism. Discuss its relation to specific concrete religions.

9. Show how some major issues in philosophy of religion arise out of certain events and experiences in ordinary life.

10. Explore the objection that philosophical interest in religion misses the essence of religious faith. Do you think that religion or religious faith is subject in any way to rational investigation?

NOTES

1. For an excellent study of the religions of the world, past and present, see Ninian Smart, *The Religious Experience of Mankind*, 3rd ed. (New York: Scribners, 1984).
2. See, for example, *American Atheist* magazine which is published by O'Hair's group. Also see Robert G. Ingersoll, *Atheist Truth vs. Religion's Ghosts* (1900; reprint ed., Austin, TX: American Atheist Press, 1980). A general secularist view is expressed in P. Kurtz, ed., *Humanist Manifestos I and II* (Buffalo, NY: Prometheus Books, 1973).
3. The following definitions are cited in William Alston, "Religion," *The Encyclopedia of Philosophy* (New York: Macmillan, 1967), vol. 7, p. 140.
4. Ninian Smart, *The Religious Experience of Mankind*, 3rd ed. (New York: Scribners, 1984), pp. 6–12.
5. The father of this movement is Edmund Husserl. See his *The Idea of Phenomenology*, trans. W. Alston and G. Nakhnikian (The Hague: Nihoff, 1964).
6. Gerardus van der Leeuw's *Religion in Essence and Manifestation* (New York: Harper & Row, 1963) is a work that takes this approach.
7. One of the classic sources in the analytic tradition, which denies substantive content to philosophy, is A. J. Ayer, *Language, Truth and Logic* (New York: Dover, 1936). A classic source promoting philosophy as the enterprise of elucidation and not of advancing truth-claims is Ludwig Wittgenstein, *Philosophical Investigations*, trans. G. E. M. Anscombe (New York: Macmillan, 1953).
8. We follow tradition and the scriptures of all three theistic religions by using masculine pronouns to refer to God. It is not implied that God in any literal sense possesses gender or sexuality, and most thinkers in these traditions would insist that God is *not* a sexual being.
9. This point is elaborated in H. H. Price, "Belief 'In' and Belief 'That'," *Religious Studies* 1, no. 1 (1965): 1–27.
10. St. Anselm, *Proslogium*, in *St. Anselm, Basic Writings*, pt. 1, 2nd ed., trans. S. M. Deane (LaSalle, IL: Open Court, 1974).

SUGGESTED READING

Alston, William. "Problems of Philosophy of Religion." *The Encyclopedia of Philosophy*, New York: Macmillan, 1967, vol. 6, pp. 285–89.

Burtt, Edwin A. *Types of Religious Philosophy*, rev. ed. New York: Harper & Brothers, 1951.

Lewis, H. D. "History of Philosophy of Religion." *The Encyclopedia of Philosophy*, New York: Macmillan, 1967, vol. 6, pp. 276–85.

2

Religious Experience:
What Does It Mean
to Encounter The Divine?

People in many different religious traditions not only claim to experience God, Nirvāṇa, or Brahman, but feel that such experiences give meaning and direction to their lives. In the eighth century B.C., the Hebrew prophet Isaiah recorded his experience of God:

> In the year that King Uzziah died, I saw the Lord seated on a throne, high and exalted, and the train of his robe filled the temple. Above him were seraphs, each with six wings, . . . calling to one another: "Holy, holy, holy is the Lord Almighty; the whole earth is full of his glory." . . . "Woe to me!" I cried. "I am ruined! For I am a man of unclean lips, and I live among a people of unclean lips, and my eyes have seen the King, the Lord Almighty."[1]

One of the more famous experiences of the divine is found in the writings of the North African Christian theologian Augustine (354–430):

> I was asking myself these questions ["Why not make an end of my ugly sins at this moment?"], weeping all the while with the most bitter sorrow in my heart, when all at once I heard the sing-song voice of a child in a nearby house. Whether it was the voice of a boy or a girl I cannot say, but again and again it repeated the refrain "Take it and read, take it and read." At this I looked up, thinking hard whether there was any kind of game in which children used to chant words like these, but I could not remember ever hearing them before. I stemmed my flood of tears and stood up, telling myself that this could only be a divine command to open my book of Scripture and read the first passage on which my eyes should fall.[2]

Some experiences make less, or even no, appeal to sensory data but nonetheless provide focus to human life, as illustrated by the following description of an awareness of the universal Self:

> Not by sight is It grasped, not even by speech,
> Not by any other sense-organs, austerity, or work.
> By the peace of knowledge, one's nature purified—

In that way, however, by meditating, one does behold
Him who is without parts.[3]

How are we to understand such experiences? In this chapter we will explore
what a religious experience is, whether there is a common core to described
religious experiences, and whether we can use religious experience to justify our
religious beliefs.

Types of Religious Experience

An *experience* is an event that one lives through (either as a participant or an
observer) and about which one is conscious or aware. For example, to experience a World Series baseball game is to play in it, attend and watch the game,
or (in an extended or mediated sense) see or hear it via television or radio. We
have many different kinds of experiences, but it is religious experiences that
interest us here. *Religious experiences* are held to differ from ordinary experiences in that what is experienced is taken by the person to be some supernatural
being or presence (God either in himself or as manifest in some action), a being
related to God (a manifestation of God or personage such as the Virgin Mary),
or some indescribable Ultimate Reality (such as the non-dual Absolute
[Brahman] or Nirvāṇa).

It is important to distinguish having a religious experience from gaining a
religious insight. The former, as we are using it, requires an encounter with God
or Ultimate Reality, whereas the latter need not. For example, one might get an
insight into the way sin proliferates and conquers us by noting, when digging in
one's garden, that if the roots of a nearby tree are not continually removed
from the soil, they gradually spread and choke out the vegetable plants. Although some understanding of God is necessary to understand the concept of
sin (which is an offense against God), the gardener need not have experienced
God to achieve this religious insight. That is, some event in our ordinary
experience might trigger an insight into our spiritual condition or the relation
of God to the world without our ever experiencing God in that event. Of
course, a religious experience *can* be the source of religious insight. Both
Isaiah's and Augustine's experiences of God gave them understanding both
about the nature of God and about their own sinfulness. But experiencing God
is not essential to having religious insight, whereas to have a religious experience requires that God or Ultimate Reality be either the object of the experience or taken to be such.

We experience God or Ultimate Reality in a variety of ways. Richard Swinburne (1934–   ) suggests five types of religious experience, classified according
to how the experiences come about.[4] These types he considers to be mutually
exclusive and totally exhaustive of the possibilities.

1. *Experience of God or Ultimate Reality mediated through a common,
public, sensory object*. For example, one might see God in an icon, sunset, or
ocean. Icons or sunsets are not God, but that in and through which God or the
supernatural is encountered.

Crossing a bare common, in snow puddles, at twilight, under a clouded sky,
. . . I have enjoyed a perfect exhilaration. . . . In the wood, is perpetual

youth. Within these plantations of God, a decorum and sanctity reign, a perennial festival is dressed. . . . Standing on bare ground, — my head bathed by the blithe air, and uplifted into infinite space, — all mean egotism vanishes. I become a transparent eyeball; I am nothing; I see all; the currents of the Universal Being circulate through me; I am part or particle of God.[5]

2. *Experience of God or Ultimate Reality mediated through an unusual, public, sensory object*. For example, one might experience the supernatural through an appearance of the Virgin at Lourdes or in a bush that burned but was not consumed.

Now Moses was keeping the flock of his father-in-law, Jethro. . . . And the angel of the Lord appeared to him in a flame of fire out of the midst of a bush; and he looked, and lo, the bush was burning, yet it was not consumed. . . . God called to him out of the bush, "Moses, Moses!"[6]

The appearance would be public, in that many people present could (in theory) observe what is happening and experience God through it. However, it is unusual, for few claim to have seen the Virgin at Lourdes, and only Moses claimed to witness a burning bush that was not consumed.

3. *Experience of God or Ultimate Reality mediated through a private object that can be described in normal sensory language*. For example, a person might experience God in a dream or vision, as did Peter, who, in a trance, saw a cloth filled with nonkosher animals lowered from heaven.[7] Visions, dreams, locutions, and the like, despite being described in sensory language, are available only to one person.

I was sitting in a certain chapel, and while I was taking pleasure in the delight of some prayer or meditation, I suddenly felt within me an unwonted and pleasant fire. When I had for long doubted whence it came, I learned by experience that it came from the Creator and not from creature, since I found it ever more pleasing and full of heat.[8]

4. *Experience of God or Ultimate Reality mediated through a private object that cannot be described in normal sensory language*. Here one feels or sees something that is experienced as ineffable. For example, St. Teresa of Avila (1512–1582) relates the following experience:

I was at prayer on a festival of the glorious Saint Peter when I saw Christ at my side — or, to put it better, I was conscious of Him, for neither with the eyes of the body nor with those of the soul did I see anything. I thought He was quite close to me and I saw that it was He Who, as I thought, was speaking to me. . . . All the time Jesus Christ seemed to be beside me, but as this was not an imaginary vision, I could not discern in what form: what I felt very clearly was that all the time He was at my right hand, and a witness of everything that I was doing.[9]

5. *Experience of God or Ultimate Reality that is* not *mediated by any sensory object*. The person is intuitively and immediately aware of God or the One. A Western mystic, Nicholas of Cusa (1401–1464), writes,

> But I perceive, not with my fleshy eyes, which look on this icon of Thee, but with the eyes of my mind and understanding, the invisible truth of Thy face, which therein is signified, under a shadow and limitation. Thy true face is freed from any limitation, it hath neither quantity nor quality, nor is it of time or place, for it is the Absolute Form, the Face of faces.[10]

This type is most richly illustrated by the higher meditational states of Hinduism and Buddhism:

> Of one who has entered the first trance the voice has ceased; of one who has entered the second trance reasoning and reflection have ceased; of one who has entered the third trance joy has ceased; of one who has entered the fourth trance the inspirations and expirations have ceased; of one who has entered the realm of the infinity of space the perception of form has ceased; of one who has entered the realm of the infinity of consciousness the perception of the realm of the infinity of space has ceased; of one who has entered the realm of nothingness the perception of the realm of the infinity of consciousness has ceased.[11]

Perhaps few experiences fall cleanly into a given type. For example, Nicholas of Cusa commends beginning meditational experience with an icon, though the ultimate experience of God is nonsensory. Hence, it is less important to try to categorize each experience than to understand more generally the nature of religious experience. The important point is that religious experiences are diverse, and students of them must be careful not to ignore their diversity.

But that brings us to our next question: What is religious experience? More specifically, what kind of experience is it? Three possibilities have been suggested.

Religious Experience as a Feeling

In his influential nineteenth-century writings, Friedrich Schleiermacher (1768–1834) contended that religious experience is not an intellectual or cognitive experience, but "a feeling of absolute or total dependence upon a source or power that is distinct from the world."[12] It is self-authenticating, intuitive, and unmediated by concepts, ideas, beliefs, or practices. Since it is a feeling, preceding conceptual distinctions, we cannot describe it. It is an affective rather than a cognitive experience.

This view influenced many, including Rudolf Otto (1869–1937). There is, he agrees, a side of God that can be grasped by reason. By analogy we can ascribe to God attributes such as spirit, purpose, good will, omnipotence, and selfhood. "All these attributes constitute clear and definite *concepts*: they can be grasped by the intellect; they can be analyzed by thought; they even admit of definition."[13] Yet in respect to God's deeper nature — his holiness — God cannot be rationally known; he is ineffable. God's holiness we must apprehend by something that goes beyond the rational, namely, by feeling.

Religious experience is a feeling, or better, a complex of feelings. This feeling comes in many forms:

The feeling of [the *mysterium tremendum*] may at times come sweeping like a gentle tide, pervading the mind with a tranquil mood of deepest worship. It may pass over into a more set and lasting attitude of the soul, continuing, as it were, thrillingly vibrant and resonant. . . . It may burst in sudden eruption up from the depths of the soul with spasms and convulsions, or lead to the strangest excitements, to intoxicated frenzy, to transport, and to ecstasy.[14]

Otto finds the numinous manifested in three specific types of feeling. There is the feeling of dependence—that we are mere creatures, "submerged and overwhelmed by [our] own nothingness in contrast to that which is supreme above all creatures."[15] There is the feeling of religious dread (awe) and of being overpowered before the "*mysterium tremendum*." We shudder and quake at the "sight" of God. And finally, we have a feeling of longing for the transcendent being that fascinates us. There is built into us a restlessness, a longing for God.[16]

The claim that "feeling is the deeper source of religion"[17] implies that philosophical and theological reflection are secondary products, outgrowths of experience. Were there no religious experience, there would be no theologies or religious philosophies.

One problem with this analysis of religious experience is that it is hard to see how one can generate cognitive religious truth-claims, as found in theology and religious philosophy, out of noncognitive feelings. If both the experienced and the experience are ineffable, and if the latter is so fundamental that it precedes cognitive distinctions, what religious truths follow upon it? Even attempts to describe the experience by analogy presuppose that the event can be cognitively understood, so that one can appreciate which analogies are appropriate to the experience and which are not.

A second objection is that defenders of this view have misunderstood the nature of feelings and emotions. Emotions are not more fundamental than beliefs or behavior. Indeed, as do beliefs and acts, emotions depend on concepts. Emotions

are in part constituted by concepts and judgments. To say that a concept is constitutive of an emotion is to say that the emotion cannot be specified without reference to that concept. . . . In order to specify an emotion it is necessary to specify the quality of the feeling, the object of the emotion and the rational grounds by which the subject justifies the emotion. We can now see that among those grounds are the subject's beliefs about the causes of his state.[18]

But if concepts in part constitute emotions, religious experience cannot be completely divorced from the cognitive.

Religious Experience as Perceptual Experience

A second view is that religious experience is a type of perception. William Alston (1921–   ), for example, holds that it has the same structure as perception.[19] In our ordinary, sensory perception—as when seeing a cat—there are three elements: the person who sees the cat (the perceiver), the cat that is seen (the perceived object), and the appearance of the cat (the phenomenon). Similarly, it is held, there are three elements in religious experience: the religious experiencer, God who is experienced, and the appearance or presentation of God to the experiencer. There is much philosophical debate concerning precisely how perception is to be analyzed. In particular, questions are raised concerning the status of the phenomenon. But there is general agreement that in perception, objects present themselves to us in ways that enable us to know them. Similarly, in religious experience God presents himself in ways that enable us to know him and his actions.

Some might think it strange to understand religious experience as a kind of perception. There are, it seems, important differences between ordinary perceptual or sense experience and religious experience. Sense perception is a common experience, whereas religious experience is less common, perhaps even rare; sense perception yields a great deal of information about the world, whereas religious experience yields apparently little information about God; all humans have the capacity for sense perception, but many seem not to have the capacity for religious experience. These differences, however, do not show that religious experience has a structure unlike perception. For one thing, neither the frequency of an experience nor the amount of information it yields tells us anything about its structure. Further, there are many people, such as the blind or the deaf, who have limited sensory and hence perceptual capacities, but this fact casts no doubt on the claim that seeing or hearing is a form of perception. Similarly, the fact that many do not have religious experiences does not disprove this claim about its structure as a form of perception.

There is, however, one significant difference that is alleged to show the falsity of the thesis that religious experience is a type of perception. It concerns the nature of the perceptual appearance or presentation (the phenomenon). Ordinary perception is sensory; the perceived object presents itself as bearing certain sensory qualities. For example, the desk in front of me appears brown, hard, rectangular, and wooden. But those who have religious experiences report that what they perceive — namely, God — bears perceptual qualities that are *not* sensory. The qualities they experience in God are divine goodness, power, love, sovereignty, and giving strength. As we noted above, sometimes religious experience does have sensory content, but where it does, often that content comes from that which mediates the experience (for example, sunsets and icons) rather than the object of the experience (God).[20] But the characteristics of the sunset are not the characteristics of God. The problem, then, is this: If the characteristics of what is allegedly perceived (the phenomenon) are so different in the case of religious experience, is not its structure so different that it is a mistake to understand religious experience as a form of perception?

Alston admits that the perceived qualities of religious experiences of God — properties such as power, beauty, and goodness — are not sensory. Some of these, for example, concern God's dispositions or the attitudes behind his actions. However, for Alston that does not mean that they cannot be the content of a perception. He distinguishes between phenomenal qualities (the way something looks to me at the moment) and objective qualities (the disposition of an object to look in a certain way in certain circumstances). When we describe an experienced object, he claims, frequently our description refers to its objective and not its phenomenal properties. We do not describe the object by saying how the thing *appears* at the moment, listing the sense data we receive—for example, that my house appears to me dingy yellow and off-white, darker yellow in the shadows, trapezoidal beneath the roof, and so on. If we did this, the description of the object in each experience would be both indefinitely large (in order to reflect the quantities of received sensory data) and so unique (since, for example, I perceive my house under indefinitely many lighting conditions and from indefinitely many angles) that we could not construct usable concepts from such diverse patterns. Rather, we often speak about the thing's objective or dispositional qualities by using, for example, comparative concepts. That is, we describe the object of our experience by saying that it looks as we would expect it to look under normal conditions. In describing the house I see, I often do not delineate how it appears at this precise moment; rather I say that it looks just as my house would look under normal circumstances.

In a similar fashion, qualities such as power, goodness, and love are reported using not phenomenal or sensory concepts, but comparative concepts. They characterize how God could be expected to appear under certain conditions. If our experience of God is described using comparative concepts, there is a very distinct parallel between the way we report objects of sense perception and our perception of God. Just as we frequently report our perception of things not by using phenomenal concepts, but rather by using comparative concepts—for example, by saying that what we perceive looks like a dog, feels like a satin pillowcase, or tastes like candy; so our reports of our experience of God appeal to comparative rather than phenomenal concepts. Of course, there is still a question concerning which phenomenal qualities characterize our experience of the divine, but the religious experiencer need not determine this, for it is not uncommon for persons to have perceptual experiences of things without being able to specify what the constitutive phenomenal properties are or should be.

But, it might be objected, we know how houses, cars, and trees would appear in normal circumstances because we could, if pressed, provide the relevant phenomenal description. Ultimately the objective properties are also phenomenal. How do religious experiencers know how God would appear in normal circumstances, since they cannot provide a phenomenal description? Alston suggests that our experience with humans who are more or less good gives us some idea of what it is like to experience a good God showing his goodness. But does knowing how good people act give us an expectation of how we should experience God's goodness? Here again we would be moving from the one point of comparison that contains sensory information (how good people act) to a point that lacks it (how God acts). Further, would we not have to have some idea of the phenomenal conditions under which we were to experience God in order to anticipate how God would manifest his goodness under normal circumstances? These are precisely the grounds under which we know, for example, what a pillow looks like, when we say that this object in front of us looks like a pillow. In short, the absence of phenomenal concepts in experiences of God raises questions about whether religious experience is a kind of perceptual experience.

The question concerning how God would appear gives rise to a second problem. Whereas there is a general consistency regarding human sensory perception, so that we can check the accuracy of any particular perception by appealing to other perceptual experiences, religious experiences present a great diversity, so that the accuracy of any particular experience cannot be so easily confirmed. Religious experiences are conditioned by distinctive cultural and religious perspectives, so that what people in various religions perceive widely differs. The Ultimate Reality that a Hindu experiences is very different from the God a Christian experiences. But we cannot easily confirm which is correct independent of the distinctive religious systems.

This, of course, does not show necessarily that religious experience is not perceptual; it might only mean that religious experiences are more open to individual interpretation. We will return to this problem, both later in this chapter, when we explore the question of whether there is a common core to religious experiences, and in subsequent chapters.

Religious Experience as Giving a Supernatural Explanation

Defenders of a third view reject the thesis that religious experiences are perceptual experiences. To call an experience a perception entails a claim not only about the person's awareness of the event (something must have been presented to or appeared to the perceiver), but also about the cause of the experience. For our experiences really to be perceptions, the perceived object must be there and make a causal contribution (of the right sort) to our experience of it. For example, to say that a person sees a cat is to grant both that there is a cat and that the cat is the cause of that person's seeing it. If the cat does not exist and does not cause the perception, then we say, not that the person perceives or sees the cat, but rather that she hallucinates a cat or mistakes something else to be a cat.

If religious experience is a kind of perceptual experience, the same conditions must hold true for it. That is, if religious experience is a perceptual experience, what is perceived must exist and make a causal contribution (of the right sort) to our perception of it. Now, if we restrict our consideration to how persons *interpret* their experience (what might be called a *phenomenological description*), it would not be a problem to use the model of perception to understand religious experience. Embedded in the experiencers' understanding of the experience is a claim about its cause. Such persons believe that they actually have perceived God, his activity, or some being related to him. Encountering God or Ultimate Reality is, for them, part of what it is to have a religious experience.

However, to describe *objectively* religious experiences as perceptual experiences would be too restrictive in that, if we want to be liberal in allowing that people of diverse faiths have religious experiences, this formulation commits us to the belief that the objects or causes of those religious experiences really exist. That is, we could not admit that someone had a religious experience without admitting that God or Ultimate Reality exists. To avoid this unsatisfactory result, Wayne Proudfoot (1939–) holds that our characterization of religious experience must be broad enough to permit another person to admit that people have religious experiences that they describe in terms of believing that they have experienced something supernatural, without having to grant that there is any such supernatural object.

A religious experience, then, is an experience the person who has it *takes* as religious. To take an experience as religious means that experiencers believe that a naturalistic explanation of the experience is insufficient, and that it can be explained only in terms of religious doctrines.[21] For example, persons who claim to have experienced God will reject any attempt to locate the cause of the experience in their digestive processes, emotions, wish fulfillment, or subconscious. For them, it can be understood only as God speaking to or encountering them.

According to this view, then, it is important to distinguish the *description* of the experience from the *explanation* of the experience. In describing the experience, the perspective of the subject dominates. Religious experiences cannot be described apart from their experiencers' belief systems, including their belief that the experienced óbject exists. This means that a description of a religious experience will include a causal account of the event that invokes the existence of the supernatural. For example, one cannot describe the experience that Augustine had without reference to his belief that God exists and can communicate in this way. In this sense, religious experience cannot be reduced to any other kind of experience; to do so is to misidentify the experience. This being the case, scientific accounts (whether of the social or the natural sciences) are irrelevant to describing the experience, for whereas science attempts to explain the experience in terms of its natural causes, religious experience requires the supernatural explanation as part of its description.

However, the fact that experiencers understand the experience in terms of the supernatural does not mean that they really experienced the supernatural, or that there is no adequate natural *explanation* for their experience. It might have just happened that, apart from any divine activity or intention, a child nearby was playing a game in which that particular sing-song — "take it and read" — was a part. However, were this true, it would not make Augustine's experience any less religious. It simply means that what he took as its ultimate cause — God himself — might not be its cause. In other words, an experience can be a genuine religious experience because of its locus in a belief system while no supernatural object is perceived. All that is required is that the experiencers *interpret* their experience in terms of categories and beliefs about the supernatural.

All experience is mediated by concepts and beliefs and is shaped by language. When experiencers have an experience, they identify that experience under some set of concepts and rules. There is no uninterpreted datum that is experienced and then later interpreted. The experience itself is embedded both in some interpretation of the world and in some commitment to a certain set of religious beliefs and practices. Thus, for example, the mystics are committed to the belief that their religious experience of God is ineffable and yet communicates knowledge about God; should some experience not satisfy those criteria, it is simply not a mystical experience. This means that there will be no single description of religious experiences. There will be numerous accounts, each reflecting the belief structure of the perceiver.

But how can we evaluate whether a person had a veridical experience? If religious experience is shaped by each person's concepts and beliefs, how can we determine which account—the natural or the supernatural—provides the best explanation? Proudfoot is correct when he argues that, though the outside party (Jane) must describe the experience Joe has in terms of Joe's beliefs about the world and its cause, Jane need not endorse those beliefs. Let us suppose that Jane, as a strict naturalist, does not believe in God. Will not the imposition of Jane's own belief systems on her explanation of Joe's experience merely juxtapose belief structures, so that ultimately one cannot decide which explanation—naturalistic or supernaturalistic—is correct? This becomes clear when Proudfoot assigns the analyst the task of trying to ferret out why people who have had religious experiences understand them as they do and contends that "what we want is a historical or cultural explanation."[22] This assignment begs the question concerning which belief system provides the appropriate framework for explaining the events, for why should one assume that a historical or cultural explanation is more to the point than a supernatural or theistic one?

One response is that we can evaluate the veracity of religious experience-claims only within particular belief systems. That is, the explanation of the experience must be internally consistent with the set of beliefs and concepts that the experiencer uses. But then it becomes impossible for persons with a belief system different from that of the religious experiencer to evaluate the claim, for lacking the particular set of beliefs and concepts the experiencer uses, they are in no position to evaluate the explanation given by the experiencer.

Is There a Common Core to Religious Experience?

Differences over how to understand religious experience raise a fundamental issue, which is much disputed. On the one hand, there are those who argue that all religious experiences have something in common. This is particularly evident, according to some thinkers, in mystical experiences, which involve an immediate and noninferential consciousness of some Reality, prior to any subject-object differentiation. The mystic achieves union with Reality either epistemologically (when there is no experienced subject-object distinction) or ontologically (when there is no real distinction between experiencer and object). This experience can be interpreted only later through the use of rational concepts and categories, but to do so is already to depart from the ineffability of the original experience.

The view that there is a common core to religious experiences—a core that transcends the boundaries of different religions, denominations, and cultures—can be found in writers such as William James (1842-1910) and Walter T. Stace (1886-1967). Stace is concerned particularly about mystic experiences. His goal is to give a phenomenologically objective description of the mystic experience. He notes that one must be careful to distinguish between the experience and the interpretation of the experience. The interpretation is introduced in order to enable the person to understand and communicate the experience. Stace wants to ascertain the pure description of the experience itself. He lists seven distinctive features of the core mystic experience:

1. the Unitary Consciousness; the One, the Void; pure consciousness;
2. nonspatial, nontemporal;
3. sense of objectivity or reality;
4. blessedness, peace, and so forth;
5. feeling of the holy, sacred, or divine;
6. paradoxicality;
7. alleged by mystics to be ineffable.[23]

But, one might ask, does not this very classification invoke interpretation, especially when Stace speaks about the One or the Void (with capital letters) as fundamental to this experience? Stace replies that one must distinguish levels of interpretation.

> If a mystic speaks of the experience of "an undifferentiated distinctionless unity," this mere report or description using only classificatory words may be regarded as a low-level interpretation. But this is being more precise than is usually necessary, since for most purposes it is just a description. If a mystic says he experiences a "mystical union with the Creator of the universe," this is a high-level interpretation since it includes far more intellectual addition than a mere descriptive report.[24]

His point is that the above seven characteristics are purely descriptive. Interpretation enters later, in attempts to identify the One with, for example, the God of Christianity or Hinduism.

However, the admission that in a basic description there is interpretation, even if only of a low level, is fatal to the contention that one can discern a cross-cultural, universal core. This becomes clear when, in making the distinction between extrovertive and introvertive mystical experiences, Stace suggests that the introvertive kind is a more complete version of the extrovertive, since "consciousness or mind is a higher category than life."[25] To speak of categories and to evaluate them is to introduce interpretation into the most important of the alleged core elements.

Taking the opposite position, Steven Katz (1944–   ) argues that there is no experience that is unmediated by concepts and beliefs. All experience is processed through the beliefs, learned categories, and conceptual framework of the experiencer. Even self-consciousness—the paradigm of intuitive experience—is a product of inference. Consequently, religious and cultural beliefs condition religious experience, to the extent that persons in different religious traditions actually experience differently. There is not *one* religious experience, but a plurality of diverse experiences. Katz appeals to his own Jewish tradition to support his thesis:

> All these [Jewish] cultural-social beliefs and their attendant practices . . . clearly affect the way in which the Jewish mystic views the world, the God who created it, the way to approach this God, and what to expect when one does finally come to approach this God. That is to say, the entire life of the Jewish mystic is permeated from childhood up by images, concepts, symbols, ideological values, and ritual behavior which there is no reason to believe he leaves behind in his experience. Rather, these images, beliefs, symbols, and rituals define, *in advance*, what the experience *he wants to have*, and which he then does have, will be like.[26]

That is, our prior beliefs, formed by interaction with our religious tradition, shape our religious experience by preforming the schema in terms of which the experience is perceived and understood.

As confirmation of this position, note the role of gurus and teachers of the mystical tradition. The relevant wisdom is closely held by small groups of devotees, led by a master or teacher who instructs them in a specific method for achieving the desired goal. Hence, the mystic experience itself is conditioned by the methods and beliefs instilled by the teacher. The attainment of genuine mystic insight is sanctioned, if not determined, by the master.

How then does one account for the apparently similar descriptions of religious experience given by Stace? First, Katz holds that the similarity is only apparent. Although the descriptions of the experiences use the same terminology, there is no reason to think that the terms have the same meaning in all the reports. That two persons from different traditions, for example, describe their experience as paradoxical does not mean that it is paradoxical in the same way, or that the same content stands in the relationship of paradox. Indeed, the terms *paradox* and *ineffable* serve to "cloak the experience from investigation and to hold mysterious whatever ontological commitments one has," rather than to "provide *data* for comparability."[27] Second, the terms used to characterize the experience are too general and vague, so that they fail to carefully delineate the mystical experiences they purportedly characterize. When James suggests that every mystical experience is characterized by ineffability and noetic quality, it leaves open whether the ineffability is the same and whether the noetic quality has the same content. The truth-claims of Mādhyamika Buddhism, with its emphasis on the emptiness of Reality, differ markedly from the truth-claims of Christianity about God and his relation to his created world. The Realities in the two cases cannot be identified.

Henry Suso's "intoxication with the immeasurable abundance of the Divine House . . . entirely lost in God [of Christianity]," the *Upanishads* "sat [what is] . . . is expressed in the word *satyam*, the Real. It comprises this whole universe: Thou art this whole universe," as well as the Buddhist's "dimension of nothingness," all can be included under these broad phenomenological descriptions of "Reality," yet . . . it is clear that Suso's Christian God is not equivalent to the Buddhist's "nothingness," and that the experience of entering into the Divine House is not equivalent to losing oneself in Buddhist "nothingness." It becomes apparent on reflection that *different* metaphysical entities can be "described" by the same phrases if these phrases are *indefinite* enough.[28]

Katz's analysis has not gone unchallenged. One criticism is that his view cannot account for some fundamental features of mystical experience. Mystics claim to be able to achieve a state in which self-awareness and awareness of objects cease. Yogis, for example, meditate on various things, such as physical objects, invisible things, the self, and finally consciousness. Gradually they attain to *samādhi*, a form of inward concentration in which progressively all conscious content is removed — consciousness of all distinctions between perceptual objects, of inner states such as joy, of oneself as a distinct being, of objects of meditation as distinct from oneself, or ultimately of consciousness itself. In the final intuitive state, all — past, present, and future — are unified in pure consciousness.

The very attaining of pure consciousness defies Katz's analysis. To reach enlightenment, mystics often specify a path or a set of techniques by which they intentionally "forget" or bracket their previous experiences and categories of understanding. Yoga, for example, specifies eight methods or types of practice directed toward the realization of pure consciousness. These include a lifestyle of self-restraint and abstention (celibacy, no stealing, and no injury), moral observances (practicing contentment, penance, and study), practice of bodily postures, breath control, concentration on objects, and meditation. Adherents claim that following such a discipline ends their automatic perceptual and conceptual responses to what they experience. Ultimately, the yogi achieves pure consciousness, in which all categories, ideas, and external input are forgotten.

The methods used, such as concentration for extended periods on a particular object, or, in the case of some Zen Buddhists, wall meditation, have been duplicated in the laboratory. Experimentees whose eyes were exposed only to a patternless field (by taping halves of ping-pong balls over them or by mounting a tiny projector on a contact lens so that the same object always appears) did not report seeing nothing (which still involves making conceptual distinctions) but described an end of seeing, "a complete disappearance of the sense of vision for short periods."[29]

In short, if forgetting and the like are possible, and if the mystic can attain a state of pure consciousness in which there is neither object nor content of consciousness, then Katz's thesis must be reconsidered. Since all categories and experiences are transcended, there is nothing in the higher-stage mystical states to be conditioned by prior conceptual categories or experiences.

However the issue of a common core to religious experience is resolved, both views raise a further serious question about religious experience. If Katz is correct that the diversity of religious experience is not only so great, but conditioned by the prior beliefs of the experiencer, what does this tell us about what is experienced and the beliefs founded on such experiences? Can religious experience so conditioned by prior concepts provide a sound basis for religious beliefs? If the mystic is correct that pure consciousness provides an exception to this thesis, but if the very exceptions are contentless states, how can they provide any sound basis for religious beliefs? In short, should we look to religious experience to justify religious belief?

Can Religious Experience Justify Religious Belief?

Some have contended that religious experience plays a valuable role in that it justifies the religious beliefs people hold. As one bumper sticker puts it, "God is not dead—I talked with Him this morning!" But whether the alleged experience of God can be used to ground our beliefs depends, in part, upon how one characterizes religious experience.

First, suppose that religious experience is a feeling. Schleiermacher thought that he not only could generate the structure of religious belief by an appeal to these feelings, he also could justify it. But can feelings justify cognitive belief? The difficulty arises from the claim that both God (as transcendent) and our experience of God (as feeling, unstructured by concepts and beliefs) are ineffable. But for the experience to have cognitive significance, it must be mediated by rational beliefs and concepts.

Otto faces a similar problem. He grants that the conceptual descriptions of the numinous are not "genuine intellectual 'concepts,' but only a sort of illustrative substitute for a concept."[30] He calls the concepts used to describe the experience "ideograms"—imperfect analogies drawn from our ordinary experience. Yet he designates certain concepts as appropriate for marking the numinous. To distinguish what appropriately designates it from what does not implies that there is some conceptual system by which the numinous can be grasped. The experience of the numinous, therefore, must have some intellectual content.

In short, those who describe religious experience as feeling encounter a dilemma. If the religious experience is ineffable, then it cannot be used to ground beliefs, for there is no rational content to provide the grounding. If, however, the experience has conceptual content, then it cannot be independent of conceptual expression or immune from rational criticism. Those who make religious experience into mere feeling cannot have it both ways.

Next, suppose that one characterizes religious experience as in the third way above—namely, that it is experience which the experiencer believes cannot be explained by natural causes. Then the very designation of an experience as religious requires that experiencers have certain beliefs about what they take to be its cause. The identification of the cause is part of the description of the experience. But then religious experience cannot be used to justify belief in the existence of that cause. To do so would be to argue in a circle: The experience is religious because someone perceived it as being caused by God; and that person has good reason to believe God exists because of his religious experience.

The argument here is similar to the argument commonly given regarding what miracles can and cannot show. If miracles are defined as events brought about by God, they cannot be used as evidence for God's existence. God's very existence has been assumed in order to identify the experience as miraculous. Similarly, if religious experience is defined in terms of a supernatural cause, then the experience cannot be used to justify belief in that cause.

This means that religious experience is meaningful insofar as it finds its place within a particular religious world-view. The experience makes sense because a person already has a set of beliefs that includes the supernatural. The supernatural is not inferred from or grounded in the experience, but is part of the very description, and hence a presupposition, of the experience.

But perhaps this judgment is too hasty. On this view, an experience is held to be religious when the experiencer believes that one cannot understand or explain the experience apart from the supernatural. If this is so, then there is at least one explanation of the event that is both *prima facie* reasonable and requires the existence of God. This would not preclude the possibility that someone else might be able to provide a completely naturalistic explanation of the event. However, the more experiences that can be cogently explained by appeal to the supernatural, and the more these experiences fit in with a coherent belief structure, the more likely it is that this explanation is correct. That is, the more coherent the account, and the more the appeal to the supernatural explains certain experiences, the more the burden of proof would be on the person who denied the veridicality of the experience to show that God was not the cause.

In other words, if the fact that our experiences reflect our belief structure means that our experiences cannot be used to justify our beliefs, then none of our experiences can justify our beliefs, for on this view all experiences invoke our belief structures. This would mean that my experience of seeing a cat in the tree would not justify the belief that there is a cat in the tree, for it would presuppose that there are such things as cats, trees, and cats in trees. But what then would justify this belief? Such a view would leave all experiential beliefs unjustifiable.

Finally, those who hold that religious experience is a perceptual experience argue that religious experience can be used to justify religious beliefs. We commonly use our perceptions to justify our beliefs about the world. For example, we are justified in believing that there is a robin on the lawn when we see a robin on the lawn, and have no reason to think that the perceptual conditions are unusual. Similarly, religious persons are justified in believing that God exists, loves them, or answers their prayers on the basis of their religious experiences.

But cannot we be mistaken about our religious experiences, and if so, how can they provide evidence to justify religious belief? Of course, we can be mistaken, but this is neither contrary to our normal perceptual experience nor sufficient to deny that religious experience justifies religious belief. When a person says that she sees a robin outside, we ordinarily grant that there is a robin that she sees. Swinburne calls this the Principle of Credulity: When it seems to someone that something is the case, it probably is so, unless there are special considerations to mitigate the claim.[31] That is, the way things appear to be provides good grounds for believing that this is the way things are. We are justified in holding the belief until contrary considerations are introduced that would cast doubt upon either this particular perception or the accurate functioning of our perceptual apparatus in general. This does not mean we could not be mistaken about the experience, but it places the burden of proof on those who would claim that the experience was not genuine.

Similarly, in the absence of special considerations, religious experience should be taken by experiencers as providing good grounds for the belief that God or Ultimate Reality exists. This does not mean that experiencers could not be mistaken in their belief. But parallel to ordinary perceptions, persons are justified in maintaining their belief until they are given good reason to think that the belief conflicts with other justified beliefs (for example, about the nature and character of God) or that there is some shortcoming in their perceptual apparatus. The religious experience provides a *prima facie* justification for beliefs about God.

But can we accept the Principle of Credulity? One problem is that whereas there is a fundamental uniformity about the way we report both ordinary perceptual experiences and the beliefs about objects of those experiences, there is quite a diversity of reports about religious experiences and the claims based on them. As we noted above, persons give incompatible descriptions of the Reality experienced. For example, Christians describe the God they encounter as triune and really distinct from themselves, whereas Hindus characterize Brahman as the whole of reality and describe the relation of the self (*ātman*) to Brahman nondualistically.

Can all these religious perspectives be reconciled, particularly if they support radically contrary or contradictory beliefs? Perhaps they cannot, but this, it is argued, is not fatal to the Principle of Credulity. The principle does not entail that all perceptions should be veridical. Where perceptions yield conflicting testimony, we must turn to other experiences and rational arguments to determine the truth of the various claims. That is, where there are different accounts, additional considerations must be introduced to help decide which, if any, of the religious experiences are veridical. Although the reports provide a *prima facie* ground for their acceptance, not all beliefs based on such experiences are true. Just as we at times doubt perceptual claims for good reasons, we might do the same for claims based on religious experience. Consonance with other justified beliefs about God and religious practices might be one way to winnow out less reliable claims.

One might wonder, however, whether this response really does justice to the diversity of claims about the Reality that is allegedly perceived in religious experience. If persons in varying traditions report religious experiences, and if these traditions contain radically incompatible views of the world, what justification can religious experience provide for any particular belief?

Clearly many points need to be resolved if we are to accept the thesis that religious experience is a perceptual experience that justifies religious beliefs. The Principle of Credulity needs to be investigated; it might be asked, for example, whether this principle is to be applied in the same way to all perceptual claims. In addition, the significance of the diversity of reports about religious experience and the conflicting claims to which they give rise must be explored. This suggests that the justification of religious belief must be approached from a number of directions, something we will do in more detail in other chapters of this book.

STUDY QUESTIONS

1. What are the five types of religious experience suggested by Richard Swinburne? Find an example of two of them from some religious, philosophical, or devotional literature.

2. Compare and contrast the view of religious experience as perception with the view that it is what the experiencer takes as not subject to explanation by natural causes. How would each view explain the first three accounts in this chapter? In what ways would their explanations differ?

3. If you know people who have had a religious experience, ask them how they would describe the experience. Which of the three explanations of the nature of religious experience do their descriptions best illustrate, and why?

4. Compare and contrast the arguments that might be given for and against the thesis that there is a common core to religious experience. Which do you think is correct, and why? Might there be a common core to higher-state mystical experiences, but not to other types of religious experience?

5. Give an argument (either one from this chapter or one of your own) either for or against the thesis that religious experience can be used to justify religious beliefs. What view of religious experience have you presupposed? What objection might be raised against your argument?

6. If you are a religious believer, do you use religious experience to justify your religious beliefs? After reading this chapter, how do you think differently about your experience?

7. If you are a religious believer and do not use religious experience to justify your religious beliefs, to what do you appeal? Why do you think this provides good grounds for your beliefs?

NOTES

1. Isa. 6:1–3, 5 (NIV).
2. Augustine, *Confessions*, trans. R. S. Pine-Coffin (New York: Penguin Books, 1961), VIII, 12.
3. *Maṇḍukya Upaniṣad*, III, i, 8, in Sarvepalli Radhakrishnan and Charles A. Moore, eds., *Indian Philosophy* (Princeton, NJ: Princeton University Press, 1957), p. 54.
4. Richard Swinburne, *The Existence of God* (Oxford: Oxford University Press, 1979), pp. 249–52.
5. Ralph Waldo Emerson, "Nature," "Essays and Addresses," *Selected Writings of Ralph Waldo Emerson* (New York: New American Library, 1965), p. 189.
6. Exod. 3:1–4 (NIV).
7. Acts 10:10–16 (NIV).
8. Richard Rolle, *I Sleep and My Heart Wakes*, in Elmer O'Brien, ed., *Varieties of Mystic Experience* (New York: Holt, Rinehart and Winston, 1964), p. 161.
9. E. Allison Peers, ed., *The Life of Teresa of Jesus* (Garden City, NY: Image Books, 1960), p. 249.
10. Nicholas of Cusa, *The Vision of God* (New York: Frederick Ungar, 1960), p. 23.
11. *Saṁyutta-Nikāya*, XXXVI, 115, in Henry Clarke Warren, ed., *Buddhism in Translations* (New York: Atheneum, 1973), p. 384.
12. Friedrich Schleiermacher, *The Christian Faith* (Edinburgh: T. & T. Clark, 1928), p. 17.
13. Rudolf Otto, *The Idea of the Holy* (London: Oxford University Press, 1958), p. 1.
14. Otto, p. 12.
15. Otto, p. 10.
16. Augustine, I, 1; C. S. Lewis, *Pilgrim's Regress* (Grand Rapids, MI: William B. Eerdmans, 1958).
17. William James, *The Varieties of Religious Experience* (New York: New American Library, 1958), p. 329.
18. Wayne Proudfoot, *Religious Experience* (Berkeley: University of California Press, 1985), pp. 87, 108.
19. William Alston, "The Perception of God," *Topics in Philosophy* 16, no. 2 (Fall 1988).
20. If the religious experience is of an embodied personage such as Jesus or the Virgin Mary, the problems developed here do not arise, for presumably their appearances would have sensory content.
21. Proudfoot, pp. 176–88.
22. Proudfoot, p. 223.
23. W. T. Stace, *Mysticism and Philosophy* (New York: Macmillan, 1960), pp. 131–32. I have given the characteristics of his introvertive type. The extrovertive type differs slightly in items 1 and 2, but he considers this type to be a lower level, an "incomplete kind of experience."
24. Stace, p. 37.
25. Stace, p. 133.

26. Steven T. Katz, "Language, Epistemology, and Mysticism," in Steven T. Katz, ed., *Mysticism and Philosophical Analysis* (Oxford: Oxford University Press, 1978), p. 33.
27. Katz, p. 54.
28. Katz, p. 51 (brackets in original text).
29. Robert K. C. Forman, "A Construction of Mystical Experience," *Faith and Philosophy* 5, no. 3 (1988): 259–65.
30. Otto, p. 19.
31. Swinburne, p. 254.

SUGGESTED READING

Alston, William. "Christian Experience and Christian Belief." Alvin Plantinga and Nicholas Wolterstorff, eds., *Religion and Rationality*. Notre Dame, IN: University of Notre Dame Press, 1983.

James, William. *The Varieties of Religious Experience*. New York: New American Library, 1958.

Katz, Steven T., ed. *Mysticism and Philosophical Analysis*. Oxford: Oxford University Press, 1978.

Proudfoot, Wayne. *Religious Experience*. Berkeley: University of California Press, 1985.

Otto, Rudolf. *The Idea of the Holy*. London: Oxford University Press, 1958.

Stace, W. T. *Mysticism and Philosophy*. New York: Macmillan, 1960.

Swinburne, Richard. *The Existence of God*. London: Oxford University Press, 1979, chap. 13.

Underhill, Evelyn. *Mysticism*. Cleveland, OH: Meridian Books, 1955.

3

Faith and Reason:
How Are They Related?

A magazine article is headlined, JUDGE BANS TEXTBOOKS.[1] Reading on, we find that a group of parents in Mobile, Alabama, has brought suit against the school district because of the presence of "secular humanism" in the school curriculum. The parents are objecting not to such familiar sore points as sex education and the teaching of evolution, but to a wide range of state-approved textbooks in such fields as history, social studies, and home economics. The judge in the case, agreeing that the texts were infected with "humanism" (meaning mostly that people should rely on themselves rather than on God for the solution of problems), banned forty-four of them in a single ruling.

This little story is a contemporary illustration of the problem of *faith and reason*—the problem, that is, of what (if anything) reason has to do with religious faith. It is clear that a good many parents deeply mistrust the influence of "worldly learning" on their children—learning that at some points may contradict the teachings of the children's faith and may tend to lead them away from faith. The ultimate solution, for many of these parents, is to educate their children in special, religious schools where they will be taught only the "right" things.[2] But in a number of cases parents have also brought suit against the local school district on the grounds that, in violation of the Constitution, it has introduced a "religion"—namely, "secular humanism"—into the public school curriculum their children were required to study. In some cases, these pressures have led to removing from the school curriculum such classics as *The Old Man and the Sea*, *The Red Badge of Courage*, and *The Merchant of Venice*.

Can Reason Be Trusted?

While this legal case may be an extreme example, the relationship between faith and reason has seldom been tranquil or peaceful; rather, conflict and controversy appear at every turn. In fact, quite a few people, many of them serious religious thinkers, have said things which suggest that faith[3] and reason are not compatible *at all*—that their relationship is, and must be, one of mutual rejection and hostility. The apostle Paul (d. 62/68?) wrote, "See that no one makes a prey of you by philosophy and empty deceit" (Col. 2:8). The early Christian writer Tertullian (160–220) asked, "What has Athens to do with Jerusalem?" (By "Athens" he meant Greek philosophy, by "Jerusalem," the Christian church.) The implied answer is, "Nothing—faith and philosophy have nothing in common; they are totally opposed." Pascal (1623–1662) wrote, "The heart has its reasons which reason does not know," and he implied that some persons might have to take steps to dull their reasoning faculties in order to be able to believe![4]

Still, it is much harder to bring about a clear-cut separation of faith from reason than these statements might indicate. Those who stress faith and attack reason often place a great deal of emphasis on *religious experience*: recall the bumper sticker that says, "God is not dead—I talked with Him this morning!" However, as we saw in the previous chapter, religious experience is by no means a purely emotional "happening"; rather, it involves *concepts* and *beliefs* about the Being that is experienced. If we tried to separate religious experiences from such concepts and beliefs—from the *religious belief-system*, as we shall call it—then there would be no way of saying *who or what it is that is experienced*, or of explaining what sort of difference the experience ought to make to the person who has it. But such a religious belief-system needs to be *understood*, at least to some degree—and it is hard to see how understanding it is not going to involve the use of reason.

In fact, none of the religious thinkers mentioned above totally repudiates reason. It has been argued persuasively that the apostle Paul's warnings are directed only at a certain kind of reasoning, namely "worldly wisdom," which is the product of "human conceit that shuts itself up against the truth," and not against the use of reason as such.[5] Even a cursory reading of his letters will show that he frequently makes use of reasoning, analysis, and arguments in the course of his religious teaching.[6] Tertullian, in spite of his diatribe against philosophy, was himself trained in philosophy and can be shown to have made use of it in his explanations of Christian doctrines. And while Pascal, like Paul, was severely critical of a certain kind of reasoning, one of the major projects of his life was constructing an "apologetic" (a rational defense) for Christianity.

The real question, then, is not whether reason has any place in religion—the answer to that question is obviously yes—but what kind of place reason does and should have.[7] But here also, at least part of the answer is relatively uncontroversial. All religious communities do in fact make use of reason, and in effect sanction its use, in the process of *teaching* the religion's belief-system to children and new converts, and in enabling the faithful to *understand*, so far as possible, what their faith is about. Such uses of reason really do not need to be debated. The really controversial question is this: What role (if any) should reason play in the *validation* (or invalidation!) of religious belief-systems? Granted that we may have to make use of reason in understanding the faith, is it also true, in any sense, that having faith at all depends (or should depend) on *having good reasons to believe* that one's faith is *true*? That is the real core of the "problem of faith and reason," and that is the question to which the rest of this chapter is devoted.

Strong Rationalism

The first answer to our question[8] to be considered is that of *strong rationalism*, which holds that *in order for a religious belief-system to be properly and rationally accepted, it must be possible to prove that the belief-system is true.*[9] The word *prove*, to be sure, is somewhat ambiguous; for our present purposes we understand it to mean: to show that a belief is true in a way that should be convincing to any reasonable person.[10]

The central idea of strong rationalism was stated forcefully by the English mathematician W. K. Clifford (1845–1879), as follows:

> It is wrong always, everywhere, and for anyone, to believe anything upon insufficient evidence.
>
> If a man, holding a belief which he was taught in childhood or persuaded of afterwards, keeps down and pushes away any doubts which arise about it in his mind . . . and regards as impious those questions which cannot easily be asked without disturbing it — the life of that man is one long sin against mankind. . . .
>
> Inquiry into the evidence of a doctrine is not to be made once for all and then taken as finally settled. It is never lawful to stifle a doubt; for either it can be honestly answered by means of the inquiry already made, or else it proves that the inquiry was not complete.[11]

Why does Clifford set such high standards for religious belief? In answering this he emphasizes the serious consequences, for oneself and especially for others, that may result from accepting a belief without adequate evidence:

> A shipowner was about to send to sea an emigrant ship. . . . Doubts had been suggested to him that possibly she was not seaworthy. These doubts preyed upon his mind, and made him unhappy. . . . Before the ship sailed, however, he succeeded in overcoming these melancholy reflections. . . . He watched her departure with a light heart, and benevolent wishes . . . and he got his insurance money when she went down in mid-ocean and told no tales.
>
> What shall we say of him? Surely this, that he was verily guilty of the death of those men. It is admitted that he did sincerely believe in the soundness of his ship; but the sincerity of his conviction can in no wise help him, because *he had no right to believe on such evidence as was before him.*[12]

We will all sympathize with Clifford in his condemnation of the shipowner; he goes on to argue, as we have seen, that *any* belief held upon insufficient evidence is reprehensible.

One objection often raised against Clifford's kind of view is that there are many people, especially those who must work hard for a living and have little education, who simply do not have the time or, perhaps, the ability to do the kind of serious thinking he requires before one is entitled to have faith. Clifford takes note of this objection and rejects it: "'But,' says one, 'I am a busy man; I have no time for the long course of study which would be necessary to make me in any degree a competent judge of certain questions, or even able to understand the nature of the arguments.' Then he should have no time to believe."[13]

Clifford's opinion, very thinly concealed, is that *no* religious belief-system is capable of meeting the high standards of proof that should govern all of our believing, and so a reasonable (and moral) person must do without religious beliefs. But not all strong rationalists, by any means, have been hostile to religion. John Locke (1632–1704) was a Christian whose standards for proper belief were essentially the same as those later stated by Clifford; he thought, however, that Christianity, when properly understood and defended, could meet those standards.[14]

Thomas Aquinas (c. 1224–1274) differed in some of his views from Locke and Clifford, but he agreed with Locke in holding that by careful rational investigation it was possible to make a convincing case for the truth of Christianity.[15] A contemporary philosopher of religion whose position is very close to strong rationalism as defined here is Richard Swinburne (1934–).[16]

Now, the appeal of this perspective to those who wrestle with the problem of faith and reason is undeniable. Which of us has not felt frustrated, even angry, at the many things people (perhaps especially religious people) claim to "know" but are unable to give any good reasons for? In view of this frustration, the desire to have "real proof" for the things we believe is very understandable. The strong rationalist does not make any sloppy appeals to "faith"; she offers to *prove* that her view is correct — and challenges you to do the same for your view, if you disagree with her.

All the same, there are reasons to question whether strong rationalism is the right view to take. For one thing, it can be questioned whether the kind of rational guarantee upon which the strong rationalist insists is even *desirable* from the standpoint of religious faith. There is a very common and widespread view among religious people that in faith one "steps out beyond" what can be proved or rationally guaranteed, and that this "stepping out," with its attendant risk and uncertainty, is an important, even essential element in faith. (Kierkegaard, discussed in the next section of the chapter, expresses this very powerfully.) Of course this idea that faith must involve risk and uncertainty could be wrong, but it is common enough among religious people that it needs to be taken seriously. And if the idea is correct, then strong rationalism cannot be the right way to approach religious faith.

Another question about strong rationalism is this: Can it be made to work? That is, is it actually possible to do what the strong rationalist demands and show that a particular religious belief-system is true in a way that should be convincing to any reasonable person? The strong rationalist (if she is religious) thinks that it is, and is prepared to show you how it can be done. Against this stance, though, there is the undeniable fact that, in spite of centuries of argument by strong rationalists and others, no one religious belief-system shows any signs of being proved in a way that "satisfies all reasonable people." What is the problem here?

Now the mere fact that not everyone is convinced by her arguments is not immediately devastating to the strong rationalist. What she will say is that her arguments are sound and *ought* to be convincing to anyone, but something has gone wrong in this particular case. Perhaps the other person simply has not studied the arguments carefully enough, or has not understood them correctly. Alternatively, someone may lack the training or even the intellectual capacity to understand some arguments that in themselves are perfectly good. (This would be true of most of us in the case of some of the advanced arguments in mathematics, for instance.) Finally, the other person may be "blinded by prejudice," so that, even if he seems a reasonable fellow in most everyday situations, his prejudices simply do not allow him to see the truth in religious matters.

All the same, the way the discussions of religious arguments have actually gone is not very encouraging to the strong rationalist. If her perspective is correct, one would expect that in the case of at least some religious arguments the misunderstandings and resistances would gradually be overcome, and over a period of time more and more thinkers would recognize these arguments as sound and rationally compelling. What seems actually to happen is almost the reverse: Even philosophers who accept a particular argument as correct are likely, as they continue to study it, to find that it contains loopholes such that an intelligent person *could* refuse to accept the argument without being obviously unreasonable. Rather than moving in the direction of consensus, the trend seems to be toward a recognition that *no* such arguments are convincing for all reasonable persons.

It is important to realize that this lack of universally convincing arguments applies not only to religious belief-systems, but to *all* arguments supporting "world-views" — general, overall accounts of what reality is like. Sometimes the impression is given that if one wants to be religious one has to rely on "pure faith," but that if one's world-view is based on science one can have solid proof. This is a very serious mistake. It is true that many results in various branches of science are so firmly established that no reasonable person is likely to dissent from them. (A "flat-earther" is, after all, our favorite example of someone who sticks to his views in defiance of the evidence.) But science as a total world-view — the idea that science tells us everything there is to know about what reality consists of — enjoys no such overwhelming support. This world-view (often termed *scientific naturalism*) is just one theory among others, and is no more capable of being "proved to all reasonable people" than are religious belief-systems. To claim that the strong support enjoyed by, say, the periodic table of the elements transfers over to scientific naturalism as a world-view is highly confused if not deliberately misleading.

Yet another problem with strong rationalism arises: Strong rationalism assumes that "reason" exists in human beings as a faculty that is neutral as regards conflicting world-views, and thus can be used to prove things to everyone (prejudice aside) regardless of what world-views people are initially inclined to accept. But is reason really neutral in this way? It seems clear in everyday life that people's belief-systems — their world-views — *do* have a considerable impact on which sorts of arguments they find convincing and believable. Philosophers, aware of this fact, have invested immense effort in trying to establish a totally "pure" and "presuppositionless" approach to philosophy. The attempt of Descartes (1596–1650) to begin his philosophizing from a stance of "universal doubt" is a well-known example.[17] Perhaps not quite all the returns are in on this effort, but a large proportion of contemporary philosophers seem convinced that the thing cannot be done — that there is *no* pure, assumption-free standpoint on which our knowledge can be based in a way that is independent of "where we are coming from."[18] But if this is correct — if the goal of totally eliminating prior convictions and "prejudices" from our belief-systems is unattainable — then the approach of strong rationalism cannot be made to work.

Fideism

The second kind of view we must examine is commonly called *fideism*[19] — "faith-ism." Fideism is defined in a number of ways by different writers, but for our purposes we will define it as the view that *religious belief-systems are not subject to rational evaluation*. To say, for instance, that we have *faith* that God exists and that he loves us is to say that we accept this in a way that does *not* depend on any evidence or reasoning, and that we refuse to have anything to do with trying to prove or disprove God's love for us.

Is this just a stubborn rejection of reason on the fideist's part? Not necessarily. The fideist reminds us that an argument (*any* argument) must rest on premises or assumptions of some kind. If someone will not grant any assumptions to begin with, then it is impossible to argue with such a person. (This, in effect, is what the philosophical skeptic does — which is what makes it so frustrating to argue with a skeptic!) Now, what is assumed as a premise in one argument may be established as a conclusion in another argument, but this process cannot go on forever; somewhere along the line we must come to our *fundamental assumptions*, those things we accept without proof just because they are so absolutely basic that there is nothing more basic by which they could be proved.

Now the important point that needs to be seen, according to the fideist, is this: *For a sincere religious believer, the most fundamental assumptions are found in the religious belief-system itself.* Religious faith *itself* is the foundation of one's life — it is, in the phrase of Paul Tillich (1886–1965), one's "ultimate concern." But if this is so, then the idea of testing or evaluating one's faith by some external, rational standard represents a terrible mistake, which very likely reflects a lack of true faith. Thus it is sometimes said that if we test God's Word by logic, or science, we are really worshipping science or logic rather than God!

Now for some people the idea that religious faith must be accepted without any proof or evidence might seem uncomfortable — even frightening. But a true fideist sees no problem in lack of proof; rather, he revels in it. Søren Kierkegaard (1813–1885), a Danish thinker, heaps scorn on those who would seek the truth of religion in an objective, detached way through evidence and argument. They forget that what is at stake here is their own existence as human beings.

(In modern society, it would be almost comparable to selecting one's spouse on the basis of points scored in a beauty or body-building contest!) Furthermore, he points out, objective, rational inquiry is an "approximation-process" in which one comes closer and closer to the ultimate answer, but never quite reaches it; there is always one more bit of evidence to consider, one more book or article to read and evaluate. And this, of course, means that the decision for or against God is put off indefinitely. But the person truly concerned about his soul realizes that "every moment is wasted in which he does not have God."[20] In fact, if we could *prove* God's existence and his love for us it would then be impossible to have *faith* in God—so even if our inquiry were successful, it would frustrate rather than facilitate the goal of coming to know God! As Kierkegaard says,

> Without risk there is no faith. Faith is precisely the contradiction between the infinite passion of the individual's inwardness and the objective uncertainty. If I am capable of grasping God objectively, I do not believe, but precisely because I cannot do this I must believe. If I wish to preserve myself in faith I must constantly be intent upon holding fast the objective uncertainty, so as to remain out upon the deep, over seventy thousand fathoms of water, still preserving my faith.[21]

But if assembling arguments and evidence in favor of belief in God is useless, how *does* one come to have faith? The answer is simple: You must *commit* yourself, you must take the "leap of faith," believing without having (or wanting) any reasons or evidence to show that your belief is true. The idea of a leap of faith can be illustrated by the following story: You are attending an outdoor party with a group of friends. After a while the party gets a bit slow, and just to keep things moving one of your friends offers you a bet: He bets you fifty dollars that you will not dive into your host's swimming pool in total darkness. (The pool is down the hill, well away from the lighted patio where the party is going on.) You are a good diver, so you accept the bet, strip down to your cut-offs, and proceed to the pool. Naturally, the whole group trails along behind; the fact that nobody can see where he is going makes it all the more fun. Finally, you reach the bottom of the diving board and begin climbing the ladder, surrounded by cries of "Do you think he'll really do it?" "Wait and see—he'll chicken out!" But as you reach the top of the ladder, a horrible thought occurs to you. It is quite early in the spring, and the last time you saw the pool by daylight it had been drained for the winter. It is *very* dark, and strain as you will you cannot see whether the pool has any water in it or not. Furthermore, your host has something of a reputation as a practical joker; it just might appeal to him to let you jump into an empty pool. If you descend the ladder to check, everyone will say you copped out and you will lose the bet, and you really cannot afford to lose fifty dollars. So, you jump. . . .

When religious people are introduced to Kierkegaard's idea of faith, many of them find it very attractive. It seems to be closer to their own ideas, and perhaps experience, of faith than the "hard-nosed" logical approach recommended by strong rationalism. The idea that faith involves *commitment*, and *risk-taking*, seems to make a great deal of sense to many religious people. The extent of Kierkegaard's influence is seen in the fact that he is the primary inspiration of the philosophical movement known as existentialism, as well as of the "neo-orthodox" theology of such men as Karl Barth (1886-1968) and Rudolph Bultmann (1884-1976).

Still, there are some real problems with fideism. One problem is this: Given that faith is a leap, how does one decide *which* faith to "jump for"? To a person who already is committed, that may not seem to be a problem, but what about the person who is searching for a faith, and sees several alternatives that seem about equally plausible—say, Roman Catholicism, charismatic Protestantism, and Bahai? It would seem that a reasonable approach would be to examine the alternatives carefully and see which is most likely to be true—but that, of course, is precisely what the fideist says cannot be done. Surely it is essential, though, to have *some* reasonable way in which the claims of competing belief-systems can be assessed—otherwise, what basis would we have for rejecting even the most bizarre cults, Jim Jones's People's Temple, of the Jonestown massacre, being a well-known example?

The notion that religious belief-systems represent the believer's "most fundamental" assumptions and thus cannot be tested by anything else may involve an ambiguity in the word *fundamental*. The sincere believer's beliefs are "fundamental" in the sense that they provide the basic, overarching guidance for the way she lives her life; they establish her direction, her goals, and her reason for living. But it does not follow from this that these beliefs are "fundamental" in the sense of being *more evident*, and *more obviously true* than anything else she knows or believes. In fact, we all find that there are obvious facts in everyday life—things we perceive through sight and touch and hearing—that more or less force themselves upon us in a way that has very little to do with what religious belief-systems we accept or reject. Simple truths of arithmetic, too, seem to have a self-evidence about them that is apparent to people regardless of the world-views they embrace. Such truths as these are, in a way, "fundamental" *in our knowledge* ("epistemologically fundamental," as philosophers would say), though they by no means provide the sort of "fundamental guidance" for our living that is offered by religious beliefs. And in view of this, it may be feasible to use such epistemologically fundamental beliefs in order to *test* religious belief-systems.

Furthermore, it does not seem to be true that one cannot test one's faith by rational standards without losing the faith itself; on the contrary, there are many cases in which this has actually been done. Martin Luther (1483-1546) though that Copernican astronomy, with its view of the earth as moving through the heavens, was incompatible with faith: When the Hebrew leader Joshua wanted to prolong the daylight so his troops could complete their victory in a battle (Josh. 10:12-14), he commanded the *sun*, not the earth, to stand still—so, it must have been the sun, *not* the earth, which was moving in the first place! More recently, Christians (including Kierkegaard and other modern fideists) have found that the damage to one's faith from accepting modern astronomy is entirely negligible. And many believers have had the experience of coming to believe that some of their views concerning God involve logical contradictions. (For instance, one might conclude that one's belief in absolute divine control of everything that happens is inconsistent with one's belief in human free will.) As a consequence, such believers have sometimes modified their religious understanding of things, but few experience this modification as a "loss of faith." To the charge that testing one's faith by logic is placing logic above God, the retort might be that a really strong and sound faith involves the confidence that one's beliefs can *pass* any properly conducted test on the basis of logic and evidence.

Can we not, in fact, go even further than this, and say that in order to be taken seriously by a reasonable person, a religious belief-system *must* be subjected to the tests of logical consistency and factual correctness? What would we make of a religious person who, calmly and deliberately, tells us that she is well aware that some of her beliefs are logically contradictory or conflict with well-known facts, yet she finds this no obstacle to holding these beliefs? Would we not conclude that either (1) she is badly confused and does not know what she is saying, or (2) she is not seriously interested in the *truth* of her beliefs, but is determined to maintain them (perhaps for the comfort they give her) *whether they are true or not?*[22] In fact, even fideists usually avoid admitting, straight out, that their beliefs are logically contradictory or in conflict with established facts. Usually they will say that their beliefs contain *apparent* contradictions, thus holding out the hope that, from a more ultimate perspective, it would be seen that there is not a real contradiction after all.[23] Another possibility is that they will challenge the "secular" sources of the "alleged facts" that conflict with their beliefs — thus, "young-earth creationists" challenge the scientific credentials of "mainstream" astronomy and geology, which support the conclusion that the universe is many billions of years old. But in refusing to admit *real* conflicts between their own views and logic, or well-established facts, aren't these believers admitting, in effect, that it *is* valid to use logic and evidence to test the soundness of religious beliefs?

In fact, it is surprisingly difficult to avoid engaging in the rational evaluation of belief-systems. In conversations with religiously oriented persons, it sometimes seems that they are quite happy to use arguments as long as they think they have good arguments available; it is when they are stuck, or when the argument seems to be going against them, that appeals to "pure faith" begin to surface. Even sophisticated fideists are apt to be inconsistent here. They may not make any attempt to "prove" that their own faith is correct, but they are quite likely to begin pointing out flaws, inadequacies, and inconsistencies in other, competing religious belief-systems. In all fairness though, it must be admitted that if such logical flaws pointed out in another's belief-system tend to cast doubt on that system, then similar flaws in one's *own* belief-system, as pointed out by others, must tend to cast doubt on whether one's own beliefs are correct. Simply ignoring such challenges leaves one open to the suspicion that one is not really interested in what is *true*, but only in holding on to one's present beliefs regardless. What seems to be called for, then, is to *answer* the criticisms of one's convictions — to show that the objections to one's faith are mistaken or not serious, or can be met by a minor reformulation of one's beliefs that leaves the substance of the faith unchanged. But to do this, of course, is precisely to *engage in the rational evaluation of religious belief-systems*, which is what the fideist says cannot be done!

Critical Rationalism

Suppose we conclude, then, that both fideism and strong rationalism are mistaken. Unlike fideists, we will say that it *is* possible to rationally criticize and evaluate religious belief-systems, but in contrast with strong rationalists we will say that this evaluation can not be expected to result in a conclusive, universally convincing *proof* that some particular system is correct.

If we accept this, then we are in effect affirming *critical rationalism*,[24] here defined as the view that *religious belief-systems can and must be rationally criticized and evaluated although conclusive proof of such a system is impossible*. Like strong rationalism, critical rationalism tells us to *use* our rational capabilities, to the greatest extent possible, in assessing religious beliefs. This involves developing the best arguments we can—the best "case," so to speak—for a belief-system and then comparing this with the case made for alternative systems. (Such a case for theism is developed in Chapter 5.) It also involves considering the main *objections* to the belief-system in question. (A major objection to theism is discussed in Chapter 6.) And it may involve considering rational foundations for belief that do *not* take the form of arguments (for this see Chapter 7). Critical rationalism tells us to do all these things, but it warns us not to be overconfident or overoptimistic about the conclusiveness of such an investigation. This view is "critical" in two ways: It emphasizes the role of reason in criticizing, or critically evaluating, religious beliefs, as opposed to conclusively establishing such beliefs as true. The view is also "critical" with regard to the view of reason itself; it takes a more modest and limited view of reason's capabilities, in contrast with the excessively optimistic estimate of reason incorporated in strong rationalism.

Critical rationalism, as we have seen, emerges almost automatically if we reject both strong rationalism and fideism. All the same, it will be helpful to say a bit more about it, in order to get more of an idea about how it will work out in practice. Just how should we proceed, if we want to evaluate religious beliefs in the way critical rationalism recommends?

To begin with, we will select some particular belief, or limited group of beliefs, for investigation. (The limitation is of some importance here: If we try to study everything at once, our results will probably be too superficial to have much value.) The belief may be one we are ourselves inclined to accept, or one whose truth or falsity seems especially important to us—or, it could even be determined by a course assignment!

Having selected a belief for study, the next step is to make sure that we *understand* the belief as accurately as possible. This involves deciding on definitions of key terms and exploring the implications of the belief—determining what other beliefs are required, if this one is accepted, and what other beliefs are excluded by it. If the belief in question is one we are not personally inclined to accept, we shall need to pay careful attention to those who *do* accept it, so as to avoid misunderstandings resulting from our own lack of familiarity and possible prejudice. If on the contrary the belief is one we do accept, then we need to listen to the questions and criticisms of opponents so as to become aware of problems and ambiguities that we may have overlooked through familiarity.

Once we are fairly sure we understand the belief to be studied, the third step is to look at *reasons* for and against accepting the belief. At best, such reasons will fall short of conclusive, universally convincing proof, but that does not mean they have no value at all. It has been argued by George Mavrodes that, with regard to religious and world-view beliefs, we need not understand "proof" as meaning reasons that are or should be *universally convincing* (as was stipulated above in defining strong rationalism). Rather, the notion of "proof" may be understood as being "person-relative"—that is, something may be proved perfectly well to one person even though the very same reasoning might *not* constitute a proof for someone else.[25] That may seem strange at first, but it is not really. The reader of this chapter undoubtedly knows a great many things that the writer does not know (and vice versa, of course!). Now, suppose that a woman who knows the same things the reader knows might make some of those things the basis of an argument that, *for the reader*, would conclusively establish some further conclusion. But if the writer were to consider that same argument, it would not be a proof *for him*, because he would not know whether the basic premises of the argument were correct! So the limitations involved in critical rationalism do not even eliminate the possibility of *proofs* of religious doctrines, if "proof" is taken in this limited, person-relative sense.

Nevertheless, we will often have to settle for something less than this, and it cannot be denied that the study of religious beliefs according to the principles of critical rationalism will sometimes prove to be rather frustrating. In a sense, the critical rationalist is in a more exposed, more vulnerable position than either the fideist or the strong rationalist. The critical rationalist *is* committed to the task of rational evaluation of religious beliefs, unlike the fideist, who makes his "leap of faith" and is then able to ignore issues of rational justification. But the critical rationalist, unlike the strong rationalist, has no assurance that by proceeding properly she will be able to prove, conclusively, that one particular position is correct and that others are mistaken. So unlike the adherents of either of the other two views, the critical rationalist is *never* in the position of being able to decide, finally and for good, that the discussion concerning the truth and validity of her religious beliefs has reached its ultimate conclusion.

Broadly speaking, the approach taken throughout this text is that of critical rationalism. If we were fideists, then many of the arguments we put forward and discuss concerning the truth or falsity of religious beliefs would lose their point. If we were strong rationalists, the arguments might remain but they would be used in a different way, and we would be making stronger claims for their conclusiveness than we in fact find ourselves able to make. Critical rationalism fits together well, furthermore, with the emphasis on considering alternative religious views that is present throughout the text. In a sense, the critical rationalist *needs* alternative views and the proponents of these views, more than either the fideist or the strong rationalist. The strong rationalist *proves*, and *knows with certainty*, that her own view is right, so her concern with other views can be limited to studying them to determine their errors, as well as looking for the best way to persuade their proponents to embrace "the truth." And the fideist, once he has performed the "leap of faith," has very little need for alternative views; at most, they may be of use, by way of contrast, in displaying the excellence of the "chosen" view—which, judged by its own internal standards, will always emerge as superior in any comparison.[26] The critical rationalist, in contrast, has *no* absolute rational assurance that her own view is correct, so she needs the competing views both so as to assess their merits in comparison with her own, and for the sake of the penetrating criticism of her own view that is most likely to come from those who do not share it.

We have laid a good deal of stress on the continuing, open-ended nature of critical reflection as advocated by critical rationalism. But it may seem that this serves to show that Kierkegaard was right after all, in saying that those who try to judge faith by objective, critical reflection will go on forever that way, and will never reach the point of *having* faith and of *being* religious. Does not this emphasis on an open-ended, never final process simply confirm what he said?

Not necessarily. But it does show that Kierkegaard was right about something else: Religious faith often, perhaps always, involves a *commitment*, a "stepping out" and entrusting ourselves to something that goes beyond what we have conclusive proof of. And those who live the life of faith tell us that this commitment is *not* a tentative, partial, "fingers-crossed" sort of thing, carefully proportioned to the exact degree of rational evidence we may have for a particular conclusion. Some of the ancient Israelites were inclined to reason thus: "It seems pretty likely that our God, Yahweh, really is the one who is running the show, so by all means let's worship him, 'pay our dues,' make the appropriate sacrifices, and so on. Still, it is also true that Baal, the God of the Canaanites, has some pretty impressive credentials of his own. So, the smart thing to do is to hedge our bets a little—we will sacrifice to Yahweh, all right, but we will also do what we can to keep on the right side of Baal—just in case." According to the biblical text, Yahweh was not too happy about this approach to the matter—in fact, those who proceeded in this way were in deep trouble. Our commitment to God is supposed to be *total* commitment, even when we do not have total proof that our belief in God is correct! And critical rationalism in no way *speaks against* such total commitment. Rather, it tells us that we should not pretend to greater rational certainty than is in fact available, but neither should we fail to exercise our powers of reflection and rational thought while we are making the most important decision of our lives.

It is true enough that this combination of religious commitment to "total devotion" with a mental attitude that is rational, reflective, and open to alternatives is likely to create some inner tension. But this tension is not necessarily of the destructive, ultimately harmful kind—rather, it is one that is actually lived out, in a rewarding and productive way, in the lives of many reflective religious persons.[27]

STUDY QUESTIONS

1. In your own thinking about religious matters, do you have questions about the relation of faith and reason? If so, how would you articulate your questions?

2. Which of the viewpoints on faith and reason sketched in this chapter most closely matches the approach taken by most religious persons you know? Discuss.

3. Explain strong rationalism, and discuss the reasons making this plausible as a view of faith and reason.

4. Which of the objections against strong rationalism strikes you as most convincing? Discuss.

5. Explain fideism, and explain the fideist's reasons for saying that religious beliefs cannot be rationally evaluated.

6. What are some of the factors that make fideism attractive to many religious persons?

7. Have there been situations in which you, personally, have taken something like a "leap of faith"? If so, describe one of these situations.

8. Are the objections to fideism given in the text convincing or not? Discuss.

9. Is it possible to test religious beliefs by logic and evidence without ceasing to have *faith* in these beliefs? Discuss.

10. Explain critical rationalism, showing how it differs from strong rationalism and from fideism.

11. What do you see as the strong points of critical rationalism? What are its weaknesses?

12. Is it possible to be a critical rationalist, admitting that one's beliefs cannot be conclusively proved, without becoming "wishy-washy" in one's faith?

NOTES

1. *U.S. News and World Report*, March 16, 1987, pp. 10–11. (The verdict was later overturned on appeal.)
2. It should be said that many parents who send their children to religious schools do not do so for the negative, defensive kinds of reasons implied here.

3. The term *faith*, as used in religious contexts, is rather complex in its meaning. Faith usually involves a *cognitive* aspect; it involves *believing* that the doctrines of the religion are true. But it also is often thought of as involving, or implying, a *volitional* aspect, expressed in *commitment* to the object of faith and *obedience* to what is commanded; there may also be an *affective* aspect of *trust* or *love*. In this chapter we have in mind primarily the "belief" aspect of faith, but we in no way wish to minimize the importance of the other aspects.

4. See Blaise Pascal, *Pensées*, trans. W. F. Trotter, and *The Provincial Letters*, trans. Thomas M'Crie (New York: Random House, 1941), p. 83.

5. See Paul W. Gooch, *Partial Knowledge: Philosophical Studies in Paul* (Notre Dame, IN: University of Notre Dame Press, 1987), p. 42.

6. See, for example, I Cor. 15.

7. Note the difference between "does" and "should" – while it is clear that reason does in fact have *some* place in religion, we cannot automatically assume that the place it actually has in people's thinking about religion is the place it *should* have.

8. The three main positions discussed in this chapter result from a present-day analysis of the issues; they were not applied as self-descriptions by the historical philosophers mentioned. Some thinkers, indeed, may not be too easy to classify: Many of Pascal's statements, for example, sound like fideism, yet his position as a whole seems rather to be that of "critical rationalism." Somewhat similar analyses of the alternatives on the faith-reason issue have been put forward by William J. Abraham in *An Introduction to the Philosophy of Religion* (Englewood Cliffs, NJ: Prentice-Hall, 1985, chaps. 7, 8, 9, and 10) and by C. Stephen Evans in *Philosophy of Religion: Thinking About Faith* (Downers Grove, IL: InterVarsity Press, 1985, chap. 1).

9. *Rationalism*, as used here, contrasts with *irrationalism* or *fideism*; in general, rationalism in this sense implies a reliance on reason, or intelligence, in deciding our beliefs and actions. There is another use of rationalism in epistemology, in which it contrasts with *empiricism*; rationalism in this other sense is the view that the most important truths are known by "pure reason" without reliance on sense perception. That is *not* the way rationalism is used in this chapter.

10. It is not required, for "proof" as understood here, that a belief be shown with absolute certainty to be true. But it must at the very least be shown to be more likely to be true than false (its probability must exceed one-half) on the basis of evidence of a kind that is generally accessible.

11. William K. Clifford, "The Ethics of Belief," in George I. Mavrodes, ed., *The Rationality of Belief in God* (Englewood Cliffs, NJ: Prentice-Hall, 1970), pp. 159–60.

12. Clifford, pp. 152–53.

13. Clifford, p. 160.

14. For an excellent discussion of Locke's views, see Nicholas Wolterstorff, "The Migration of the Theistic Arguments: From Natural Theology to Evidentialist Apologetics," in Robert Audi and William J. Wainwright, eds., *Rationality, Religious Belief, and Moral Commitment* (Ithaca, NY: Cornell University Press, 1986), pp. 38–81.

15. An important difference is that Thomas, unlike Clifford and Locke, did not lay on *each individual believer* (or even on each *adult* believer) the responsibility for providing rational justification for his or her beliefs. For Thomas's views, see the article by Wolterstorff cited in n. 14, and also Ralph McInerny, "Analogy and Foundationalism in Thomas Aquinas," in Audi and Wainwright, pp. 271–88.

16. See Richard Swinburne, *The Existence of God* (Oxford: Oxford University Press, 1979), and *Faith and Reason* (Oxford: Oxford University Press, 1981).
17. More recent philosophers who have pursued this ideal include Edmund Husserl (1859–1938) and Bertrand Russell (1872–1970).
18. Among the important philosophers who argue against the ideal of "pure, presuppositionless reason" are Ludwig Wittgenstein (1889–1951) and Hans-Georg Gadamer (1900–   ).
19. FEE-day-ism; the word is derived from the Latin word *fides*, meaning "faith."
20. Søren A. Kierkegaard, *Concluding Unscientific Postscript*, trans. David F. Swenson and Walter Lowrie (Princeton, NJ: Princeton University Press, 1941), pp. 178–79.
21. Kierkegaard, p. 182.
22. It should be noted that many of us sometimes find ourselves in a position that is somewhat similar to this. That is to say: We may be aware that a set of beliefs contains or implies a contradiction, but we may have no idea *which* of the beliefs needs to be given up or modified—each of the beliefs, taken separately, seems to have strong evidence in its favor. In this case we may well decide, for the time being, to continue to accept all of the beliefs in question, since under the circumstances, giving up any one of them might well leave us worse off than we were originally. This situation, however, is quite different from that of the fideist described in the text. In the situation described, we are well aware that there *is* falsehood somewhere in our beliefs; we just don't know how to identify and correct it. The fideist in the text, on the other hand, is simply unconcerned about the presence of contradictions in his belief-system.
23. For an incisive criticism of this strategy, see David Basinger, "Biblical Paradox: Does Revelation Challenge Logic?" *Journal of the Evangelical Theological Society* 30 (1987): 205–13.
24. The term *critical rationalism* is found in the writings of Karl Popper [see *The Open Society and its Enemies, Volume II* (Princeton, NJ: Princeton University Press, 1971), p. 231], and the meaning given to this term here is broadly consistent with Popper's use of it.
25. See George I. Mavrodes, *Belief in God* (New York: Random House, 1970), pp. 17–48.
26. It must be said in fairness that fideists, and strong rationalists, sometimes exhibit in practice a more generous appreciation of conflicting views than these descriptions might suggest. Still, it is probably true in general that fideists and strong rationalists have *less* interest in the consideration of alternative views than do critical rationalists.
27. For an excellent depiction of this tension from the standpoint of evangelical Protestantism, see Daniel Taylor, *The Myth of Certainty* (Waco, TX: Word Books, 1986).

SUGGESTED READING

Abraham, William J. *An Introduction to the Philosophy of Religion*. Englewood Cliffs, NJ: Prentice-Hall, 1985, chaps. 7, 8, 9, and 10.
Evans, C. Stephen. *Philosophy of Religion: Thinking About Faith*. Downers Grove, IL: InterVarsity Press, 1985, chap. 1.

Hick, John. *Faith and Knowledge*. Ithaca, NY: Cornell University Press, 1957.

Mavrodes, George I. *Belief in God*. New York: Random House, 1970.

_____, ed. *The Rationality of Belief in God*. Englewood Cliffs, NJ: Prentice-Hall, 1970.

Mitchell, Basil. *The Justification of Religious Belief*. Oxford: Oxford University Press, 1981.

Pascal, Blaise. *Pensées*, trans. W. F. Trotter, and *The Provincial Letters*, trans. Thomas M'Crie. New York: Random House, 1941.

Swinburne, Richard. *The Existence of God*. Oxford: Oxford University press, 1979.

_____. *Faith and Reason*. Oxford: Oxford University Press, 1981.

(See also suggested reading for Chapter 7.)

4

The Divine Attributes:
What Is God Like?

"Put this piece of salt in the water and come to me tomorrow morning."

Shvetaketu did as he was told. Then his father said to him: "Do you remember that piece of salt you put in the water yesterday evening? Would you be good enough to bring it here?"

He groped for it but could not find it. It had completely dissolved.

"Would you please sip it at this end? What is it like?" he said.

"Salt."

"Sip it in the middle. What is it like?"

"Salt."

"Sip it at the far end. What is it like?"

"Salt."

"Throw it away, and then come to me."

He did as he was told but that did not stop the salt from remaining ever the same.

His father said to him: "My dear child, it is true that you cannot perceive Being here, but it is equally true that it *is* here.

"This finest essence,—the whole universe has it as its Self: That is the Real: That is the Self: That *you* are, Shvetaketu!" (*Chandoya Upanishad*)[1]

In this text from the sacred writings of India, Shvetaketu and his father are probing a topic of intense interest to religious people—they are considering the *nature of God*. The answer they arrive at, to state it all too simply, is that God is the Being that is the inner reality of everything whatever. The salt is imperceptible to touch or vision; nevertheless it pervades every drop of the water. Similarly, God, or Being, or Brahman, is imperceptible to human senses, yet nevertheless completely pervades all of reality, including the inquirer who raises the question concerning the nature of God: "That *you* are, Shvetaketu!"

This question concerning the nature or attributes of God will occupy us throughout the present chapter. We shall not, however, concern ourselves primarily with the specific answers found by Shvetaketu and his father, and by others in the Hindu religious tradition. Rather, we shall focus most of our attention on a view of God known as *classical theism*; this is the conception of God that has been held, with some variations, by the vast majority of thinkers in the great "theistic" religions of Judaism, Christianity, and Islam. But the view of God seen in the selection from the Upanishads, often termed *pantheism*, will not be neglected entirely; instead, it will be introduced from time to time as a contrast and an alternative to classical theism. And we shall also, from time to time, explain and comment an another sort of conception of God that has recently become popular in some Christian and Jewish circles, a view known as *process theism*.[2]

At this point, however, a question may be occurring to the reader. What is the point, it may be asked, of inquiring about the *nature* of God when, as yet, we have not even established whether there *is* any such being as God? Would it not make more sense, first to show that there *is* a God, and then to discuss his (or her, or its) attributes or characteristics?

There is certainly some point to this, but consider a counterquestion: If we have no idea *what* God is, then what sense is there in asking whether God *exists* or not? Lewis Carroll wrote a marvelous poem entitled "The Hunting of the Snark," but it would make little sense to ask whether there really are snarks, because Carroll never tells us clearly what sort of creature a snark is supposed to be. If we are similarly "in the dark" as to God's nature, what meaning can we attach to the question whether God exists or not?

It seems likely that the question of God's existence seems to most of us to make reasonably clear sense because we *do* have an idea of what God is like, and when we ask whether God exists it is *that kind* of being whose existence is being asked about. Most of us, furthermore, have a background in the theistic religious traditions, and the conception of God's nature we are presupposing is one that is at least fairly close to the classical theism we will be studying in this chapter. It therefore seems important to become as clear as we are able to about that conception of God, before we proceed with other matters.

The right way to understand the concerns of this chapter, then, is this: We do not at all mean to assert here that there *really is* a being, called God, with the various characteristics discussed throughout the chapter. Rather, we are *presenting a hypothesis* concerning the nature of a being whose existence will be investigated later on. The questions we will be asking are of two kinds: First, what *is* the conception of God's nature held by classical theism (and, from time to time, what are the conceptions held by pantheism and by process theism)? And second, is this conception one that is *coherent* and *logically consistent*? If it should develop that a certain idea of God suffers from unreconcilable internal contradictions, then with regard to that particular conception we need proceed no further: A "God" whose nature can be stated only in contradictions cannot possibly exist, and to suppose that there is such a God is nonsense.

How will we arrive at the characteristics we attribute to God? In part, the question is one of history and tradition: The attributes considered here are some of those that *in fact* have been ascribed to God by theistic thinkers. Many such thinkers, however, would assert that there is more to it than this; they would claim that the theistic concept of God possesses an *internal unity and coherence* going far beyond any list of characteristics that merely happen to be ascribed to God in a certain tradition. And an important source of this unity and coherence lies in the attributes considered in the next section.

Perfect and Worthy of Worship

In developing our conception of God, we would be foolish to overlook the fact that, above all, *God is a being who is the object of worship*. God's "worship-ability"—or, to use a word that is no longer very familiar, his "worshipful-ness"—is of primary religious importance, so that a conception of God that is lacking at this point is unacceptable regardless of other merits it may possess. Whatever else may be true of God, it must at least be said that *God is worthy of worship*.

But what sort of God is required, if God is to be worthy of our worship? The attitude or activity of worship is no doubt complex and difficult to de-scribe completely and accurately, but there can be no doubt that worship, in the full sense of the term, is supposed to involve *total devotion* of the worshipper to the one worshipped. In worship we totally dedicate ourselves to God; we place ourselves at God's disposal completely and without reservation. Any hint of "bargaining" with God—any mental reservation by which, however subtly, we "keep our options open" with respect to a possible shift of allegiance—detracts severely from the complete commitment that worship properly requires of us.

But if this is the case, we can ask, What must be true of God in order to make such unreserved devotion appropriate—in order, that is, for God to be "worthy of worship"? It is fairly clear, to begin with, that *God must be the greatest of all beings*. How could it be reasonable, or even plausible, to offer to God such total devotion if there exist other beings equally or even more worthy of our adulation, obedience, and so on? Under such circumstances as these, the response of a reasonable person would seem to be that God might, indeed, be entitled to a measure of honor and obedience because of his superi-ority to all others in the immediate vicinity, but not unreserved trust and honor and obedience, not *total devotion*. One would give to God his due, while keeping in mind the possibility that someone else might appear to whom even more was due. God would merit respect, honor, and a degree of obedience—but not worship.

God, then, must be the greatest of all beings. But we can go further than this. Suppose it is plain to us that, though God is *in fact* the greatest of all beings, it is entirely possible that there should have been a being *superior* to God in one or several ways: Would this not inevitably detract from the unre-served devotion required for worship? As a matter of fact, we are supposing, God is the greatest of all beings, and there is nothing else in existence that could supplant him in our esteem. But things perfectly well could have been different; there might very well have been some other being able to rival or even surpass the God whom we worship. This being so, then even in the midst of our worship, would we not occasionally find ourselves with a touch of regret for the greater things that might have been?[3]

With this line of thought in mind, we are ready to appreciate the point of a definition of God offered by the great medieval Christian thinker Anselm (1033–1109). Addressing God, he said, "We believe that thou art a being than which nothing greater can be conceived."[4] He was saying, in effect, that God is so great that *no being is conceivable that would surpass God in any way*. God, in other words is the *absolutely perfect being*. Not only is there in fact no other being equal or superior to God, but there could not be any such being, for God contains in himself all possible perfection and excellence.

This conception of God, as the absolutely perfect being, is one that, upon reflection, many religious persons have found to be deeply satisfying. It is, as we have seen, plausibly thought to be implied by the very idea of worship,[5] and it lays the foundation for a conception of God that it is very hard to challenge as inadequate.

"Perfect-being theology," (or, "Anselmian" theology, as it is also called[6]) becomes, then, the "binding thread" that ties together and unifies the discussion of the various attributes ascribed to God by classical theism.[7] Can we, indeed, go further and say that the notion of God as the perfect being gives us all the guidance we need in setting forth the divine attributes, so that our whole conception of God can be, as it were, woven in its entirety from this single thread?

Probably not, for several reasons. For one thing, although the idea of God as the perfect being has strong intuitive appeal, it is by no means the case that different theologians, even from the same religious tradition, will always agree on which conception of God's attributes has the effect of portraying God as "more perfect" than another. For example: It seemed clear to Anselm, as to Augustine (354–430) and most other ancient and medieval theologians, that in order to be perfect God must be *impassible*—that is, God must be incapable of emotion, and in particular incapable of feeling any sorrow or suffering as a result of the afflictions of his creatures. Since suffering is negative, a harm to the being that undergoes it, a perfect being must be *incapable* of suffering. Many more recent theologians, on the other hand, rebel against the notion of an "impassible" God, insisting that God's perfection, and in particular his attributes of love and sympathy, positively *require* that he be capable of suffering along with his creatures. Clearly, we have here a major disagreement, and one that will not readily be settled by further discussions about the meaning of the term *perfect* as applied to God.

It should also be realized that in setting forth God's attributes we cannot possibly ignore the religious and theological tradition within which any given theology operates. If, for instance, one were to offer to the Jewish religious community a conception of God radically at variance with that found in the Hebrew Bible and in Jewish tradition, that conception would not be warmly received no matter how plausible a case one could make for the "perfection" of God so conceived. An interesting historical example of this is presented by the philosopher Baruch de Spinoza (1632–1677). Born a Jew, he was excommunicated from the synagogue for his "heretical" conception of God, which was in fact closer to pantheism than to traditional Jewish theism. As we have noted, intuitions about perfection may vary, and a philosopher of *religion* who is seeking to apply that notion would do well to pay attention to the conception of God that actual religious communities have found to best represent perfection and worshipfulness.

A further consideration that must guide our application of the notion of divine perfection is that of *logical consistency and coherence*. As was already noted, any conception of God that is supposed to represent an actual being must at least meet the requirement of logical consistency. To be sure, a set of divine attributes that are logically inconsistent could not possibly be part of the description of a perfect being, so this criterion may already be included in the very idea of "perfect being" theology. But while this reasoning may be valid, it is also true that humans can be quite ingenious in imagining and ascribing to God seemingly marvelous characteristics that in fact are logically inconsistent. It is important, then, to carefully investigate the logical consistency of the various attributes we wish to ascribe to God.

Necessary and Self-Existent

We begin with a pair of attributes that at first may seem abstract and difficult to grasp, yet are important for pointing out the fundamental difference, according to classical theism, between God and everything else whatsoever. First, consider *self-existence*. It is a familiar thought to us that for many things, especially living creatures of all kinds, it may take energy and often effort simply for the thing to remain in existence. We live our lives "from within," and when the inner vitality needed to do this becomes weak we feel our own existence as imperiled and insecure. But we also depend on external beings and circumstances in various ways for our existence. Other beings brought us into existence, and we depend on food, water, air and so on to sustain us in existence. Furthermore, we are all too aware of various things that might damage or destroy our existence; in a sense, then, we are dependent on the *non*occurrence of these sorts of things for our continued life and well-being.

Now, consider the idea of a being that is dependent on other things in none of these ways. It owes nothing to any other being for its origin or sustenance, and it is entirely incapable of being threatened, harmed, or destroyed by anything else whatsoever. Such an entity would exist wholly "from within," entirely "on its own steam." It would be, in a word, *self-existent*.

Now we introduce two additional terms: *necessary* and *contingent*. To say something is contingent is to say that it depends on things or circumstances other than itself: Contingency plans are plans for what may or may not be done, depending on other things that may or may not happen. If on the other hand a being is *not* contingent in any way and it will exist regardless of anything that may happen to other things or circumstances, then its existence is inevitable, inescapable. It is, in other words, a *necessary being*, a being that *depends on nothing but itself, and, given that it exists, its nonexistence, either in the past or in the future, is absolutely impossible.*

Now it is very clear that God, as conceived by classical theism, is a necessary and self-existent being in the senses explained above. God is eternal; no other being is relevant to his coming into existence, since he never in fact came into existence, and nothing whatever can in any way threaten or endanger God's existence. We further note that God's necessity and self-existence is an essential element in his perfection; it seems clear that God is greater in depending on nothing outside himself than if he were so dependent. And these characteristics of necessity and self-existence fundamentally distinguish God from all other things in existence.[8]

There is however another, even stronger, sense in which something may be said to be "necessary." Some propositions are said to be *logically necessary*, meaning that it is logically impossible that they be false; the falsehood of such propositions would in some involve a contradiction. (For example, it would involve a contradiction to deny that "Every triangle has three angles"; this is a *logically necessary proposition*.) Picking up on this, we can say that a *logically necessary being* would be a being whose *existence* is logically necessary and whose *nonexistence* would be contradictory and logically impossible. It should be noted that if God's existence is logically necessary it will also be necessary in the sense previously explained, but the converse does not hold; God might be self-existent, and in *that* sense necessary, without being logically necessary.

Should God be understood as a logically necessary being? This question is highly controversial. A good many theistic philosophers and theologians — perhaps the majority — have asserted that God's existence *is* logically necessary, but many others have disagreed. On the face of it, "God exists" does not *seem* to be a logically necessary truth, and the proposition "There is no God" does not seem, at first glance, to be logically contradictory. This proposition has even been accepted as *true* by quite a few persons who are in general quite expert in the detection of contradictions. And Immanuel Kant (1724–1804) has persuaded many philosophers with his argument that *no* proposition asserting the *existence* of something can be logically necessary. (Thus, "Every triangle has three angles" is necessary, but "A triangle exists" is not necessary.)[9]

Still, it may be that none of these considerations is decisive. Kant's arguments, while impressive, have been strongly disputed, especially in recent years.[10] And we should not be misled by simple examples into thinking that it is always easy to determine whether a given proposition is either logically necessary or self-contradictory. Mathematics, for example, contains a great many necessary propositions whose necessity (and truth) are far from obvious, and some mathematical statements have resisted even the most intensive efforts of mathematicians to determine whether they are necessarily true or not.

The question of the logical necessity of God's existence will be pursued further in the next chapter, as part of the discussion of the ontological argument for God's existence. In closing this section, we note the following: If God's existence *is* logically necessary, then this will surely count as a "perfection" of God, one of the many excellences that set God apart from all lesser beings. If on the other hand God's existence is *not* logically necessary, it will also be the case that it is *impossible* that God's existence should be necessary. And in that case, "necessary existence" will *not* count as a perfection; rather it will just be another of the many logically incoherent attributes that we humans, in our confusion, have invented and ascribed to God.

Personal Creator and Sustainer

We now turn to some attributes that are more familiar to ordinary religious people. To say that God is *personal* is to say at least the following things: God has *knowledge and awareness*, God *performs actions*, God is *free* in the actions he performs, and God can *enter into relationships* with persons other than himself. These requirements seem minimal, in that a God lacking in any of them would seem *not* to be fully personal; on the other hand, if God does meet these requirements then it would seem appropriate to describe God as "personal" even though there may be many respects in which God is very different from the human persons we know.[11]

From the standpoint of theism it seems evident that personality, or personhood, should be considered as a perfection of God. Many of the finest things we know — love, intelligence, creativity, and moral goodness, for example — are attributes exclusively of persons, and if God were not personal he would be debarred from possessing any of these excellences. There is also the extremely important point that for theists, worship and the religious life generally are conceived in terms of a *personal relationship* with God; thus if God were *not* personal the theist's entire idea of the religious life would collapse.

God, according to classical theism, is also the *creator* of all things other than himself. The idea of creation is important in all the theistic faiths, and it seems essential to the idea of an absolutely perfect being that, if there are beings other than God in existence, God should be their creator. (Classical theists have usually asserted that it was not necessary for God to create — that it would have been perfectly possible for God to refrain from creating anything and to remain as the sole concrete being in existence.) God's status as creator ensures his superiority, mastery, and ownership over all the things he has created in a way that could hardly be done otherwise. God is said, furthermore, to have created "out of nothing" (Latin, *ex nihilo*). This is not to be understood as if "nothing" were the name of some sort of mysterious "stuff" out of which God created the universe. Rather, to say that creation is out of nothing means that there *was no* material out of which God created; rather, all things other than God exist solely because he wills them to exist and have no other basis at all for their existence. Creation out of nothing contrasts with and is superior to two other modes in which the production of things might be imagined. It is superior to production from preexisting materials, because in the latter case God's act of creating would be dependent upon, and probably to some extent limited by, the materials he had to work with. (There would also in that case be the problem of how to account for the existence of the materials.) And it is superior to creation *ex deo*—"out of God's own being"—because this would tend to compromise the absolute distinction between creator and creature that is the hallmark of theistic metaphysics.

God is not only the creator but also the *sustainer* of finite things. This is to say, that *created things are totally dependent on God for their existence from moment to moment*. A dramatic but not inaccurate way of putting this is to say that, were God for a single instant to completely forget about his creation, in that instant the entire creation would collapse into nothingness.

These attributes fundamentally distinguish the theistic God from God as conceived in pantheism. The Hindu Brahman, and other versions of the pantheistic deity, are *not* personal; rather, they constitute an ultimate, impersonal "power of being" that exists in all things whatever.[12] The God of pantheism is not the creator, for that implies a distinction between God and the universe that is alien to pantheism. The pantheistic God does, in a way, "sustain" the existence of all things, but this is in the manner of the *inner substance* of all things, rather than as one being maintaining others in existence.

The God of process theism is like the God of classical theism in being personal, but the relationship between God and the universe is considerably different: Process theism rejects both the idea of creation *ex nihilo*, and the radical distinction between God and the world posited by classical theism. Process theism's conception of God's relation to the world is best expressed by saying that the world is *God's body*, through which he lives his life as we live our lives through our bodies. This means that God and the universe are not wholly distinct from each other, as in classical theism; rather, all finite things, including human beings, are in a sense included in God's own being. Perhaps the best way of conceiving this is to imagine that each individual cell in a human body is possessed of its own consciousness and awareness, however limited, of what is happening to it and is going on around it. Then imagine that these individual "cell-consciousnesses" are, as it were, caught up and included in the *unified* consciousness that is the "mind" of the entire body—a consciousness that both transcends and includes each one of them. In some such way as this, each of us is a "cell" in the body of God, and because of this, God is able literally to *share*, in a most intimate way, in all of our experiences, our joys, and our sorrows. In the words of A. N. Whitehead (1861–1947), the philosopher whose works inspired process theism, "God is the great companion—the fellow-sufferer who understands."[13]

All of this means that the relationship between God and the universe is conceived very differently in process theism than in classical theism. In classical theism, there is a *one-sided dependence* of the universe upon God, whereas in process theism the relationship is better described as one of *interdependence and mutuality* between God and the universe. Whitehead went so far as to say, "It is as true to say that God transcends the World, as that the World transcends God. It is as true to say that God creates the World, as that the World creates God."[14] Since God needs his body through which to live, even as we need our bodies, it must be concluded that *God can never be without a body*—that is, without a universe. That does not necessarily mean that the present universe is, like God, without beginning and without end, though this is a possibility. But if, as scientific evidence seems to suggest, our present physical universe had a beginning in time, we may be assured that *before it* there was another universe, or perhaps an endless series of universes, so that God has never been without a body—without a world.

All-Powerful, All-Knowing, and Perfectly Good

God is *all-powerful*, or *omnipotent*; he is *all-knowing*, or *omniscient*; and he is *perfectly morally good*. All of these attributes are fundamental to the theistic view of God, and each of them involves difficulties in understanding and formulation.

Apparently, the natural way to understand God's omnipotence is simply to say that God can do anything whatever. But this quickly runs into difficulties. Can God create a square circle, or cause it to be true that $1+2=17$? At least since the time of Thomas Aquinas (c. 1224–1274), it has been recognized that the exercise of God's power must be limited to what is *logically possible*. The expression *square circle* is one that could not possibly apply (correctly) to anything, and so the fact that God cannot make one implies no defect in God's power. Other limitations on what God can do stem from God's own nature; God cannot do things that require embodiment (such as being hit in the face with a snowball), or imply limitations (such as, for instance, forgetting something). Perhaps more significant, it is generally held that God cannot do things that imply a moral fault, such as breaking one of his promises. In view of such considerations as these, we may say that God's omnipotence means that *God can perform any action the performance of which is logically consistent, and consistent with God's own nature.*[15]

Philosophers have devised a great many puzzles with which to test definitions of omnipotence; one of the most intriguing is the "paradox of the stone." Consider the following question: Can God create a stone that he cannot lift? If he cannot create such a stone, there is something he cannot do, and he is not omnipotent. (It is obvious that making something one is unable to lift is a logically possible thing to do—home builders, for example, do this all the time.) Suppose, on the other hand, that God *can* create a stone he cannot lift. So far, so good, but now there is *another* task that God cannot perform—namely, to lift the stone in question! So either way, God is not omnipotent. (So as not to cut short the reader's attempt to wrestle with this puzzle, the solution is relegated to an endnote.[16])

The most immediately obvious way of expressing God's *omniscience* is to say that God knows everything—or better (since only *true* propositions can be known), that God knows all true propositions. A difficulty arises, however, in that it seems there are propositions that are true at some times but not at others. Consider the proposition "Martha was married last Sunday." Assuming that Martha does indeed marry on a Sunday, this proposition is true for exactly one week, from midnight on the Sunday of the wedding to Sunday midnight one week later. God, presumably, *knows* this proposition for exactly as long as the proposition itself is true—though to be sure, he would know *after* the time-period in question that this proposition *had been true* during that period.[17] In view of this, we can modify our definition to say, that at any time God knows all the propositions which are true at that time.

But do we also need a clause, similar to the one in the definition of omnipotence, excluding true propositions which are such that it is *logically impossible* that God should know them? *Are* there any true propositions of this sort? One possible candidate consists of propositions about decisions God himself is going to make. It seems likely that it is not possible for anyone, including God, to be in the process of making a decision and also, while making it, already to know what the decision will be. So if God *does* make decisions (as theism says he does), there may be truths God logically cannot know while he is making those decisions. To be sure, it might be held that God does not decide things in time, but rather, in some peculiar way, before time or outside of time. But even if this is true, it does not entirely blunt the force of the point made: There would still be an "aspect" of God's life, even if not a period of time, in which he must operate without knowledge of certain true propositions. (Other candidates for true propositions that God logically cannot know will be discussed in the next section of this chapter.)

There is one further point to be made before we present our full definition of omniscience. We humans not only know things, we also believe things; some of the latter are true, and others are false. Now, it may be that God has *no* beliefs over and above his knowledge, and certainly he holds no false beliefs. But then our definition of omniscience needs to be crafted so as to explicitly exclude God's holding false beliefs.

With these considerations in mind, we can define God's omniscience as follows: *At any time, God knows all propositions that are true at that time and are such that God's knowing them at that time is logically possible, and God never believes anything that is false.* The most controversial element in this definition is the clause stating that God knows only what it is logically possible for him to know. But this really should not cause any difficulty: If there are no truths that it is logically impossible for God to know, then the clause in question will exclude nothing from God's knowledge, but that does not mean that the definition is incorrect or inadequate.

It is a matter of consensus among theists that God is *perfectly morally good*. Whatever character traits, principles of action, and so on it may take to qualify a being as morally perfect must definitely be held to characterize God. What needs to be clarified here mainly involves two things: What is the *content* of perfect moral goodness? And, what is the *relation* between moral goodness and God?

The specific content of moral goodness—whether, for instance, love is more important as a divine attribute than holiness and justice, or the reverse, or whether they are all equally important—is something theists find it hard to agree about. One's answers to these kinds of questions are apt to depend in important ways on particular theological views about the way in which God acts and deals with people, and so these matters are perhaps best left to be dealt with within the various theological traditions. In what follows we shall speak generally of God's "goodness," "love," "justice," and the like, without claiming to specify exactly what each of these means or how they are related to each other.[18]

With regard to the *relation* between goodness and God, an initial question is whether God is capable of acting contrary to moral goodness. A few philosophers have thought that, in order for God to be morally praiseworthy, he must be capable of doing evil, even though he never in fact does so.[19] The vast majority of theistic thinkers, however, have held that God is *essentially* morally perfect—that his very nature is such that it is impossible for him to act in a way that is morally wrong. This view was, in fact, anticipated in our discussion of omnipotence, when we assumed that God is *incapable* of breaking one of his promises.

Another question about the relation between goodness and God concerns the source of the standard of moral goodness. Does there exist, independently of God, a standard of goodness to which God, like all other persons, is morally obligated to conform? Or, on the other hand, do moral good and evil owe their existence entirely to the will and command of God? Or is there some further possibility for the relation between God and the standard of moral goodness? For the time being, this question will be deferred; it will be discussed in Chapter 13, "Religious Ethics."

None of the attributes discussed in this section can properly apply to God as conceived in pantheism. The pantheistic God can, to be sure, be said to possess "all power" and "all knowledge," since whatever power and knowledge there may be are, by definition, *its* power and knowledge; it is the ultimate substance, the "inner soul," of everything that exists. But the pantheistic God possesses no *individual mind* that would enable it either to *know* or to *act* as we understand these notions. According to Spinoza, "Neither intellect nor will pertain to God's nature," and if we were to attribute intellect and will to God, they "would have nothing in common with [human intellect and will] but the name; there would be about as much correspondence between the two as there is between the Dog, the heavenly constellation, and a dog, an animal that barks."[20] Perhaps the most striking point to be made, however, is that *the God of pantheism cannot distinguish between good and evil. All* actions performed in the universe are *equally* manifestations of the power of God; the notion that some of these actions are in an ultimate sense "good" and others "evil" must in the end be dismissed as an illusion. Pantheists may be, and often are, extremely upright and scrupulous in their personal ethics, but in the ultimate perspective good and evil—or, what we call good and evil—are transcended. And this contrasts the pantheistic God very sharply with the God of theism, who is a fighting God, unambiguously for good and against evil.

There is no reason why the God of process theism need be greatly different from the God of classical theism with respect to knowledge and goodness. The process theist's attitude toward divine power, on the other hand, is markedly different, as shown in the title of a recent book by Charles Hartshorne: *Omnip-*

otence and Other Theological Mistakes.[21] Why is omnipotence a mistake? Because classical theism depicts God as unilaterally imposing his will on things and persons in his creation, as exercising coercive power over them. Process theism, on the other hand, maintains that *God's power is always persuasive, never coercive.* God never unilaterally imposes his will on nature—thus, the process God performs no miracles. Furthermore, he is not able to compel human beings to do his will—rather, he "lures" them, as Whitehead said, by holding before their minds the highest and best possibilities to which they can attain by voluntarily complying with his intentions.

Classical theists typically see this as greatly diminishing the power and greatness of God—as making God distinctly less "worthy of worship" than if he were omnipotent. The reply to this is that, because of the inherent moral superiority of persuasive over coercive power, God's greatness is enhanced, not diminished, by his inability to use coercive power. However that may be, it is clear that this stance places process theism sharply in conflict with the theological traditions of all the theistic faiths, all of which clearly portray God as exercising *both* persuasive and coercive power.[22]

God and Human Freedom

The relationship between God's power or control and human free will has been a topic of intense dispute among those who believe in God. Quite a few believers have felt that it is important to attribute to God *absolute sovereignty*, meaning that *God completely controls and determines everything that happens.* As Augustine said, "The will of God is the necessity of things." It might appear that this immediately destroys any possibility of free will for human beings, but this need not be the case, if a certain definition of free will is accepted. One may say that a human action is "free" if the following requirements are met: (1) The immediate cause of the action is a desire, wish, or intention internal to the agent, (2) no external event or circumstances compels the action to be performed, and (3) the agent could have acted differently if she had chosen to. If these criteria are satisfied, the action comes, as we might say, "from within"; it cannot rightly be said that the agent is forced to perform it. Nevertheless, God in his sovereign management of affairs may have brought it about that the agent was in exactly that situation and, moreover, that the agent approached the situation in precisely the state of mind that would lead to the making of the very choice intended and decreed by God.[23]

The view of free will sketched above may be termed *compatibilist free will* (because it holds that free will is *compatible* with deterministic causation); as we have seen, it is entirely consistent with the view of total divine sovereignty, according to which God absolutely determines everything that comes to pass. But a good many philosophers and theologians are not satisfied with this way of understanding free will, because they do not think this sort of freedom is sufficient to make humans morally responsible for their actions. These philosophers and theologians insist, on the contrary, that in order for an action to be truly free it must have been *really possible*, with *all the antecedent conditions remaining exactly the same*, for the agent to have chosen differently. One philosopher has expressed this by saying that, when a person is free with respect to performing an action, she "has it in her power to choose to perform action A or choose not to perform action A. *Both A and not A could actually occur*; which *will* actually occur has *not yet been determined*."[24] And *this* understanding of free will (often termed *libertarian free will*) is *not* compatible with the view that God predetermines the outcome by controlling the circumstances; rather it holds that with all the circumstances exactly as they were, the outcome could have been quite different.

It is clear, then, that libertarian free will is logically incompatible with absolute divine sovereignty as defined above. Many theistic believers find this entirely acceptable; they see no need for such a strong doctrine of sovereignty. A widely held view is that God does not *determine* or *predestine* the outcome of human choices, but he nevertheless *knows beforehand*, with complete and detailed accuracy, how such choices will freely be made by human beings.

But is even *this* view truly compatible with genuine free will? The problem of divine foreknowledge and human freedom is one that has been discussed for two thousand years, and consensus on the matter remains quite elusive. This question, in fact, has received especially intensive scrutiny in the last twenty-five years or so. In order that the reader may begin to understand what is at issue here, we include the following sample of an argument for the *incompatibility* of foreknowledge and free will. The example concerns a certain Clarence, known to be addicted to cheese omelets. Will Clarence have a cheese omelet for breakfast tomorrow morning, or won't he? The argument proceeds as follows:

1. It is now true that Clarence will have a cheese omelet for breakfast tomorrow. (Premise)
2. It is impossible that God should at any time believe what is false, or fail to believe anything that is true. (Premise: divine omniscience)
3. God has always believed that Clarence will have a cheese omelet tomorrow. (From 1, 2)
4. If God has always believed a certain thing, it is not in anyone's power to bring it about that God has not always believed that thing. (Premise: the unalterability of the past)
5. Therefore, it is not in Clarence's power to bring it about that God has not always believed that he would have a cheese omelet for breakfast. (From 3, 4)
6. It is not possible for it to be true both that God has always believed that Clarence would have a cheese omelet for breakfast, and that he does not in fact have one. (From 2)
7. Therefore, it is not in Clarence's power to refrain from having a cheese omelet for breakfast tomorrow. (From 5, 6) So Clarence's eating the omelet tomorrow is not an act of free choice.[25]

It will be noted that step 2 consists of a definition of divine omniscience *without* the stipulation about what it is logically possible for God to know; thus, the conclusion is that Clarence does *not* have free choice about what to eat for breakfast. If we find the conclusion unacceptable (that is, if we believe that human beings do possess libertarian free will), then a reasonable response would be to adopt a definition of omniscience *including* the requirement of logical possibility, as given in the previous section; we could then conclude that the truth about Clarence's breakfast is one of the things it is logically impossible for God to know. Note, furthermore, that there is nothing in any way special about Clarence's decision with regard to the omelet. On the contrary, what is established here about this decision can be generalized to any decision made by anyone at any time. The conclusion will be, then, either that no created beings ever make any free choices at all, or that God is unable — *logically* unable — to know these decisions with certainty before they are made.

Is the argument given above correct? The matter is very much in dispute, and the arguments have become so complex that to pursue them here is impossible. By far the most common reply to arguments of this kind is to insist that, for instance, God's knowledge of Clarence's choice does not in any way *cause or compel* Clarence to make the choice he does. But while this may be true, it is hard to see how it constitutes an answer to the argument. The argument, after all, never claims that God's knowledge causes Clarence's action. The argument merely observes that it is impossible for it to be the case *both* that God believes that Clarence will eat the omelet, and that Clarence does not in fact eat one. And this is assuredly true. But as we have already observed, the discussions of this topic are far too complex to be pursued in detail here; the interested reader is urged to consult the appropriate literature.[26]

It should be clear, in any case, that concluding that comprehensive divine foreknowledge is inconsistent with human freedom does *not* require abandoning divine omniscience. Rather, this would simply be a striking instance of a group of truths that it is logically impossible for God to know. If it does not demean God's omnipotence that he cannot draw an "undrawable" figure such as a square circle, then neither does it detract from his omniscience that he cannot know "unknowable" truths about future free actions. As soon as these truths are available, God will be the first to know!

Nevertheless, this doctrine of *limited foreknowledge* (as we may call it) does imply that God's knowledge concerning the future is a good deal less complete than many theists have supposed it to be. Whether this constitutes a serious problem for theistic philosophy and theology is simply another aspect of the continuing dispute over freedom and foreknowledge.

God Eternal — Timeless or Everlasting

That God is eternal is a common conviction among theists. But how is this to be understood? The most straightforward and readily understandable way to interpret God's eternity is simply to say that God *always has existed and always will exist*. God, then, exists through time like other persons and things, but unlike the others, his existence has neither beginning nor end. In a word, God is *everlasting*.

Some philosophers and theologians, however, have found this to be an inadequate interpretation of God's eternity. They have said, rather, that God is *timeless, outside of time altogether*. God, on this view, does *not* experience the world moment by moment as we finite persons do; rather, he experiences the world's history all at once, in a total simultaneous present. For God, they say, there is neither past, nor present, nor future; God simply *is*. And all of time is present to God, all at once and changelessly, in his eternal present. Augustine put it like this:

> Nor dost Thou by time, precede time: else shouldest Thou not precede all times. But Thou precedest all things past, by the sublimity of an ever-present eternity; and surpassest all future because they are future, and when they come, they shall be past; but Thou art the Same, and Thy years fail not. Thy years neither come nor go; whereas ours both come and go, that they all may come. Thy years stand together, because they do stand; nor are departing thrust out by coming years, for they pass not away; but ours shall all be, when they shall no more be. Thy years are one day; and Thy day is not daily, but To-day, seeing Thy To-day gives not place unto to-morrow, for neither doth it replace yesterday. Thy To-day, is Eternity.[27]

One benefit often found in this view, is that it seems to resolve the problem of freedom and foreknowledge, discussed in the previous section. The argument for the incompatibility of freedom and foreknowledge, it will be recalled, relied heavily on the fact that God, in the past, already has known what each of us will do in the future. But if God is timelessly eternal, this is not true. It is not that God knew, in the past, what we would do; rather, God timelessly *knows* this, and he knows it as a present reality, for all times are present to him. As Thomas Aquinas said: "He who goes along the road does not see those who come after him; whereas he who sees the whole road from a height sees at once all those traveling on it."[28] The "height," of course, is God's eternity, from which he sees at once the whole "road" of time, which we temporal travelers come to know only bit by bit as we make our way along it.

But the fact that some action is known in the present, as it occurs, has no tendency to show that the action is not done freely — no more, then, should the fact that God in *his* present knows eternally what we do detract from the freedom of the action.

Whether this solution succeeds or not is itself, as one might expect, a disputed question. In any case, it is not the only reason, and perhaps not the most important reason, why the theory of divine timelessness has been accepted. The more fundamental reason seems to be the conviction, which has its roots in Greek philosophy and especially Neoplatonism, that the *changeability* that must characterize God if he exists through time is unacceptable as an attribute of the "most real being." A recent defense of divine timelessness puts it this way:

> Such radically evanescent existence [as that of temporal beings] cannot be the foundation of existence. Being, the persistent, permanent, utterly immutable actuality that seems required as the bedrock underlying the evanescence of

becoming, must be characterized by genuine [i.e., timeless] duration, of which temporal duration is only the flickering image.[29]

The doctrine of divine timelessness continues to be a topic of controversy among philosophers of religion. Probably the trend in recent years has been away from this view and toward accepting the view that God is everlasting, which is both easier to understand and apparently more in agreement with the scriptures, which depict God as acting in time and history. Yet timelessness continues to find able defenders and advocates. The earlier discussion of the various divine attributes employed the idea of God as everlasting, since this is the more familiar and easily understood concept. But the same attributes can, with appropriate modifications, be restated as attributes of a timeless God. The issue between these rival conceptions, then, remains very much in doubt.[30]

Here, then, we bring to a conclusion our exposition of the theistic concept of God. The concept seems to be logically consistent, though in view of its complexity it is difficult to be absolutely certain about that. And it is one that has fascinated and intrigued generation after generation of philosophers and theologians. But is it more than this? Is the concept one that applies to a *real being*, who in very truth is the creator and sustainer of all things other than himself, and who enters powerfully and intimately into the world process and especially into the lives of his worshippers? It is this question that must be addressed in the subsequent chapters.

STUDY QUESTIONS

1. Describe briefly the conception of God implied in the story of Shvetaketu and his father. How does this differ from the understanding of God you are familiar with?

2. How is the concept of God defined in the religious tradition with which you are most familiar? How (if at all) does this idea of God differ from that of classical theism, as explained in the text?

3. Does it seem correct to you to say that only a God who is absolutely perfect could be fully worthy of worship? Discuss.

4. Explain what is meant by saying that God is a "necessary being." Does it seem to you that an adequate conception of God should include this idea? Discuss.

5. Explain what it means to say that God is the creator. Why is the idea of creation an important part of the concept of God?

6. Do we have a more adequate idea of God if we think of God as wholly distinct from the universe (classical theism), or if we think of God as including the universe within himself (process theism)?

7. Does it lessen one's appreciation of divine power to say that God cannot do things that are logically impossible, such as changing the laws of arithmetic? Is it better to say that God is able to act in ways that are cruel and deceitful, or that he is unable to do these things?

8. Is God greater and more perfect if he exercises both persuasive and coercive power (as in classical theism), or if he exercises only persuasive power (as in process theism)?

9. In defining God's power and God's control over the world, is it important to preserve the possibility of free will for human beings? If so, how should free will be defined?

10. If it should turn out that it is logically impossible for there to be both comprehensive divine knowledge of the future and genuine free will for human beings, which is more important? Discuss.

NOTES

1. Quoted in Ninian Smart, *The Religious Experience of Mankind*, 3rd ed. (New York: Scribner's, 1984), p. 106.
2. For process theism, see John B. Cobb and David Ray Griffin, *Process Theology: An Introductory Exposition* (Philadelphia: Westminster Press, 1976). A good exposition of the conceptions of ultimate reality held by the various schools of vedanta is found in John M. Koller, *Oriental Philosophies*, 2nd ed. (New York: Scribner's, 1985), pp. 82–99.

   A note on terminology: Throughout this chapter, *theism* and *theistic*, when used without qualification, will refer primarily to classical theism; some but not all of what is said about theism will apply also to process theism.
3. This point is not uncontroversial. One philosopher suggested that we might feel no such regret were we to learn that God did not know some unimportant theorem of mathematics, especially if God *could* know the theorem if he wanted to. (Presumably, he just has not taken the time to work it out.)

   This may or may not be correct. But if it is correct, it seems likely that we would feel no regret because we do not, in the case described, really feel that God is significantly inferior, or lacking in excellence, as a result of not knowing that particular theorem. Suppose, on the other hand, that God is *unable* to know the theorem: "God is great at algebra, but he just can't seem to get the hang of solid geometry." Most likely this would indeed be disturbing to us, because in this case it would seem clear that God is less great than he might conceivably be.
4. *St. Anselm: Basic Writings*, tr. S. N. Deane (LaSalle, IL: Open Court, 1962), p. 7.
5. It could be pointed out, to be sure, that people have often worshiped gods that were very much inferior to this "perfect being" conception. But this is not a decisive objection, for two reasons: First, the religious attitudes in question may very well fall short of *worship*, in the strong sense that has been given to this word in our discussion. But second, insofar as it becomes generally recognized that a particular kind of god falls short of maximal excellence and perfection, gods of that kind tend to be *eliminated* as serious objects of worship—thus, for example, the decline in polytheistic worship that tends to occur in many advanced cultures.

6. A recent volume exploring this theme is Thomas V. Morris, *Anselmian Explorations: Essays in Philosophical Theology* (Notre Dame, IN: University of Notre Dame Press, 1987).

7. Process theists also think of God as the "absolutely perfect being," but their conclusions about what is implied by perfection are, as we shall see, somewhat different. Pantheists would probably say that God is *perfect*, but not *a perfect being*, since according to pantheism God is not *a being* at all.

8. Note that if there is no God and some sort of materialistic metaphysics is true, then *matter*, or matter-energy, will probably be necessary and self-existent in the senses defined. If theism is true, however, matter is radically dependent on God for its existence.

9. For Kant's arguments, see Immanuel Kant, "The Ideal of Pure Reason," in *Critique of Pure Reason*, tr. N. K. Smith (New York: St. Martin's Press, 1965), pp. 487–507.

10. See Robert Merrihew Adams, "Has It Been Proved That All Real Existence Is Contingent?" and "Divine Necessity," both in *The Virtue of Faith* (New York: Oxford University Press, 1987); also Alvin Plantinga, *The Nature of Necessity* (New York: Oxford University Press, 1974).

11. Note that we say God is "personal," not that God is *a person*. The latter assertion would be a controversial one, accepted by some theists but not by all. According to the Christian doctrine of the Trinity, there are *three* persons in one God, designated as Father, Son, and Holy Spirit; these persons are capable of personal relationships *between themselves* as well as with created persons. Jews and Moslems, on the other hand, emphatically reject the doctrine of the Trinity.

12. These comments refer primarily to the advaita school of Vedanta, which is the "purest" form of pantheism found in Hinduism. Hinduism taken as a whole permits an almost unlimited variety of conceptions of the divine; many Hindus worship personal deities such as Viṣṇu and Śiva, and these are sometimes said to be "aspects" of Brahman.

13. Alfred North Whitehead, in David Ray Griffin and Donald W. Sherburne, eds., *Process and Reality*, corrected ed. (New York: Free Press, 1978), p. 351.

14. Whitehead, p. 348.

15. It should be noted that our conception of omnipotence and other divine attributes will make an important difference to our understanding of the "problem of evil"; see Chapter 6 for more on this.

16. What seems the best solution comes from George Mavrodes ["Some Puzzles Concerning Omnipotence," *Philosophical Review* 72 (1963): 221–23], and may be stated as follows: The correct description of the task that the question sets for God is this: *to create a stone that God cannot lift*. Now since God is, by definition, a being of unlimited power, the idea of a stone that he cannot lift is *self-contradictory*. But if this is so, the creation of such a stone is a logically impossible task, and it in no way detracts from God's omnipotence that he cannot perform it.

17. Some philosophers have maintained that, while the *sentence* "Martha was married last Sunday" is tensed, the *proposition* expressed by that sentence is not tensed and does not change in truth-value over time. There seems at present, however, to be a majority view that this solution will not work and that we must accept the existence of tensed propositions.

18. It should be noted, however, that the philosopher of religion cannot well remain completely neutral concerning the nature of divine goodness; among other things, the view taken on this point will have an important effect on one's approach to the problem of evil.

19. On this point see Bruce Reichenbach, *Evil and a Good God* (New York: Fordham University Press, 1982), chap. 7.
20. *Chief Works of Benedictus de Spinoza*, Vol. II, trans. R. H. M. Elwes (New York: Dover, 1955), pp. 60–61.
21. (Albany: SUNY Press, 1984).
22. For a thorough critique of the process view of God's power, see David Basinger, *Divine Power in Process Theism: A Philosophical Critique* (Albany: SUNY Press, 1988).
23. For further discussion of this view, and the other views considered in this section, see David Basinger and Randall Basinger, eds., *Predestination and Free Will: Four Views of Divine Sovereignty and Human Freedom* (Downers Grove, IL: InterVarsity Press, 1986).
24. David Basinger, "Middle Knowledge and Classical Christian Thought," *Religious Studies* 22 (1986): 416.
25. William Hasker, *God, Time, and Knowledge* (Ithaca, NY: Cornell University Press, 1989), p. 69.
26. Two recent books on the topic are Jonathan L. Kvanvig, *The Possibility of an All-Knowing God* (New York: St. Martin's Press, 1986), and William Hasker, *God, Time, and Knowledge.*
27. *The Confessions of St. Augustine*, trans. Edward B. Pusey (New York: Random House, 1949), 11, pp. 252–53.
28. Thomas Aquinas, *Summa Theologiae*, trans. Fathers of the English Dominican Province, 2nd ed. (London: Burnes, Oates & Washbourne, 1920), I, 14, 13, reply obj. 3.
29. Eleonore Stump and Norman Kretzmann, "Eternity," *Journal of Philosophy* 79 (1981): 444–45.
30. The best recent exposition and defense is the article, "Eternity," by Stump and Kretzmann. For further discussion, see Kvanvig, pp. 150–71, and Hasker, pp. 144–85.

SUGGESTED READING

Basinger, David. *Divine Power in Process Theism: A Philosophical Critique*. Albany: SUNY Press, 1988.

Basinger, David, and Randall Basinger, eds. *Predestination and Free Will: Four Views of Divine Sovereignty and Human Freedom*. Downers Grove, IL: InterVarsity Press, 1986.

Cobb, John B., and David Ray Griffin. *Process Theology: An Introductory Exposition*. Philadelphia: Westminster Press, 1976.

Davis, Stephen T. *Logic and the Nature of God*. Grand Rapids, MI: Eerdmans, 1983.

Hartshorne, Charles. *Omnipotence and Other Theological Mistakes*. Albany: SUNY Press, 1984.

Hasker, William. *God, Time, and Knowledge*. Ithaca, NY: Cornell University Press, 1989.

Kenny, Anthony. *The God of the Philosophers*. Oxford: Oxford University Press, 1979.

Koller, John M. *Oriental Philosophies*, 2nd ed. New York: Scribner's, 1985.

Kvanvig, Jonathan L. *The Possibility of an All-Knowing God*. New York: St. Martin's Press, 1986.

Nash, Ronald H. *The Concept of God*. Grand Rapids, MI: Zondervan, 1983.

Stump, Eleonore, and Norman Kretzmann. "Eternity," *Journal of Philosophy* 79 (1981): 444–45.

Swinburne, Richard. *The Coherence of Theism*. Oxford: Oxford University Press, 1979.

Wierenga, Edward R. *The Nature of God: An Inquiry into Divine Attributes*. Ithaca, NY: Cornell University Press, 1989.

5

Theistic Arguments:
The Case for God's Existence

In 1961 Yuri Gagarin circled the earth in a spaceship and pronounced that God did not exist because he did not see him out of his tiny window. Although we would have been surprised if he had glimpsed God, we too might wonder whether there is any evidence to suggest that God exists. Many people believe that there is no evidence, and from this conclude either that it is unreasonable to believe in God or that evidence is not necessary for a rational belief in God. We shall pursue this last perspective in Chapter 7.

Other people have argued there is evidence for God's existence. The arguments produced are frequently referred to as theistic arguments or theistic proofs. Over the centuries, philosophers have sharpened and refined these arguments. In this chapter we will first examine the nature and function of proof, then evaluate several theistic arguments for their soundness, and finally make some suggestions about one perspective on the appropriate function of arguments in a theistic framework.

Theistic Arguments as Proofs

Before we consider particular theistic arguments, something must be said about what they purport to show or establish. In some quarters, the word *proof* is used to describe these arguments. But what constitutes a proof?

In Chapter 3 we noted the commonly held view, advocated by strong rationalists, that proofs are sound arguments that should be convincing to any reasonable person. Understood in this way, a theistic argument would be a proof of God's existence only if any rational person who seriously considered the argument would readily see the truth of the premises, recognize the validity of the reasoning, and affirm the truth of the conclusion about God's existence. But we rejected this strong definition of "proof," for rarely do we have this kind of conclusive and universally convincing argument about anything.

In its place we suggested a *person-relative view of proof*. A proof in this sense has three characteristics.[1] First, the argument must be *sound*; that is, the premises must be true and the conclusion must follow validly (without breaking certain formal rules of reasoning) from the premises. Second, proofs are events having to do with knowledge. But knowledge is always had *by* someone. Therefore, a proof is a sound argument that someone *knows* to be sound. The person for whom it is a proof must know that the premises are true and that the conclusions follow validly. Contrary to the assertion of the strong rationalist, however, not every rational being must know that it is sound. Consequently, it will be a proof only to the person who knows the argument to be sound. Third, the function of proofs is to *extend our knowledge*. This suggests two things: (a) The premises must be more readily knowable than the conclusion. This is important because in a proof we want to move from the more to the less readily knowable. (b) The person for whom it is a proof must know the truth of the premises without inferring them from the conclusion. This is important to avoid begging the question. In short, we hold that a proof is a sound argument that the person for whom it is a proof knows to be sound and whose premises that person knows as true apart from inferring them from the conclusion.

But if proofs are person-relative, why all the fuss over theistic arguments or proofs? In particular, is it essential that we have proofs of God's existence? On the one hand, we cannot require proofs for everything we know, otherwise either the conclusion we are supporting is a reason for one of the premises for that conclusion, or we have an infinite series of arguments, each supporting the premises in the logically subsequent argument. The former is unacceptable, for by inferring from the conclusion the premise that supports the conclusion, we argue in a circle. The latter is unacceptable because no finite person could ever construct the requisite infinite series of arguments.

On the other hand, it would seem that proofs play an important role in our intellectual life. Although we cannot demand proof of everything, it is inappropriate for reasonable persons not to demand any proofs. What, then, need we prove? One answer would be that at the very least we need to prove those statements that both are not obviously true and are really important or significant. But, first, how are we to know what is really important or significant? Perhaps what we are attempting to prove is trivial, while we have missed what is really significant. Second, we have no reason to think that the class of really important things belongs to the class of provable rather than nonprovable things. The fact that they are important (to us or to anyone else) fails to inform us whether they can be derived from premises less controversial than they are. They might belong to a class of basic truths for which there is no proof.

A second possibility would be to make the decision about what we need to prove relative to each person. Since proof is person-relative, it might be suggested that we need to prove those statements that *we* consider most important for our life and destiny. Their significance for others is irrelevant; what matters is that they function in a meaningful way in our own belief structures.

Do we then need a proof of God's existence? If proofs have a subjective dimension, then for some at least it is important that there be proofs for God's existence. In particular, it is important for those who reject the view that God's existence is a basic belief, and yet who deem it important to discern whether the proposition "God exists" is true. One way of doing this is to ask whether there is any evidence that is more known to us than God's existence and from which it follows that God exists. It is not that God does not exist if there are no proofs or if the proofs offered are not convincing to some people. Rather, it is our concern for truth that encourages us to turn to this purported avenue of establishing it.

Given this view of proofs, we can consider the theistic arguments as proofs so long as we have limited expectations of them. First, it is unreasonable to think that theists can discover an argument that will be convincing to all. It would be of first priority that they find an argument that they believe to be sound, convincing, and cogent, and only of second priority that it be this to others. On the other hand, since we think and work in a community, an argument that did not meet with at least some measure of acceptance by persons in the community, and that only one individual thought to be sound should raise some serious questions in that person's mind.

Second, the truth of the premises in the theistic arguments is frequently denied, or if not denied, is often viewed with as much skepticism as the conclusion they purportedly establish. But if the premises are no more certain than the conclusion, treating the arguments as proofs gets us nowhere, for the entire point of an argument is to move from what is more certain to what is less certain. However, this should not dismay the theist: If proofs are person-relative, then, though for the skeptic the argument might not be convincing, for others it might be successful. Here again the judgment of the community plays an important role, not so much as a corrective as to prevent us from being at the mercy of any one believer or skeptic.

Our conclusion, then, is that it is unrealistic and unnecessary to expect theistic arguments or proofs to be convincing to everyone. At the very least, they will function as proofs if they are sound arguments that are known to be sound by their proposers. However, their significance will increase if they play some role in providing within a larger community evidence for the belief that God exists.

The Ontological Argument

Without doubt the most intriguing and puzzling of the theistic arguments is the ontological argument. According to the Christian theologian Anselm (1033–1109), we can form the concept or idea of *a being than which none greater can be conceived*. That is, the idea of a being than which none greater can be conceived exists in some mind. But that than which none greater can be conceived cannot exist only in the mind or understanding. Suppose it were to exist only in the mind. Then it would not be what it is, the being than which none greater can be conceived, for existence in reality is greater than existence only in the mind. But the concept of a being than which none greater can be conceived is what we started with. Hence this being must exist in reality as well as in the mind. This being we name God.[2]

We might formalize the argument as follows.

1. A person can have the idea of a being than which none greater can be conceived.
2. Suppose this being exists only as an idea in the mind.
3. Existence in reality is greater than existence only in the mind.
4. Therefore, we can conceive of a being that is greater than a being than which none greater can be conceived — that is, a being that also exists in reality.
5. But there can be no being greater than that which none greater can be conceived.
6. Therefore, the being than which none greater can be conceived must also exist in reality.

Anselm does not deny that some persons can fail to see that God exists. However, for him this is because they have not properly understood the concept of God. Once one sees what God really is, his existence is undeniable.

There seems to be something seriously wrong with an argument that, like Anselm's, moves from a premise about *ideas* in our minds to establishing that something exists in *reality*. Yet despite these suspicions, it is difficult to discern precisely where it is vulnerable and to make a strong case that this is a vice rather than a virtue.

One who tried to discern the flaw was the monk Gaunilo, a contemporary of Anselm. Gaunilo suggested that the first premise of Anselm's argument is false, that one cannot conceive of a being than which none greater can be conceived.[3] This being (whom we call God) is unlike any other reality. When I conceive of "humans," I know what the term means because I have had experience with humans. But when I hear the words, "being than which none greater can be conceived," I can understand the meaning of the individual words, but I cannot understand the being that they signify. I can form concepts of things that are finite and familiar to me, but not of a transcendent God.

But Anselm's point is not that we can completely comprehend God's nature, that we can know God as God knows himself. Rather, he holds that we can know enough about God to know that, at the very least, he must be a being than which none greater can be conceived. And should the fool who denies God's existence reflect on what it is to be God, that fool cannot but understand that God exists.

Gaunilo also wondered whether one could use Anselm's argument form to prove the existence of all sorts of unreal things. Suppose, he argued, I conceive of an island more excellent than any other, an island that has inestimable wealth and delights. But that which exists in reality is more excellent than that which exists solely in the mind. Therefore this island exists. By this argument we could (absurdly) prove the existence of all manner of imaginary and nonexistent things.

Anselm never directly or adequately replied to the argument, but others have. One reply is that the argument Anselm developed applies only to things capable of having perfections. It does not apply to such things as islands because they are finite and hence incapable of perfection. The properties that would make an island perfect might include mineral wealth, smoothness of sand, number of palm trees, and abundance of fruits. But for any island one thinks of with these properties, one can think of an island with more of them. These properties have no intrinsic maximum. There is no limit to these characteristics, which one could designate as the perfect state. But the properties that apply to a being than which none greater can be conceived include properties for which there are maximums: knowledge, power, and moral perfection. Hence, the form of Anselm's argument cannot be used, as Gaunilo suggested, to establish the existence of all sorts of nonexistent, finite things.[4]

But might there not be some nonexistent things possessing properties with maximums that could then be plugged into Anselm's argument form? Consider the concept of a ten-thousand dollar bill a greater than which cannot be conceived. Would an argument similar to Anselm's show that this necessarily exists? Of course, there could be a greater bill — say a one million dollar bill — but that is not the point. The point is that there could not be a greater ten-thousand dollar bill, for any bill with this property is worth its maximum. One might question whether its other properties have intrinsic maxima — for example, being unwrinkled or of uniform color — but these are irrelevant to the essence of this bill — that is, of being a bill of a certain denomination. In this essential aspect there is a maximum, and hence, using Anselm's argument form, such a bill would have to exist.[5] Perhaps Gaunilo was correct in his thesis, but only chose the wrong example in the island.

A different criticism of Anselm's argument focuses on premise 3. For Anselm existence is a perfection. A perfection is something that makes whatever has it better or greater. For example, to say that health is a perfection is to say that being healthy is better, all else being equal, than being not-healthy. Similarly, to say that existence is a perfection is to say that something is better or greater because it exists, all else being equal. Or put another way, it is better for a thing to exist than to not exist. One has to be careful here. Anselm is not saying that it is better for *us* that things exist rather than not exist. This is obviously false, since there are many things — dust on my furniture, typing errors, mosquitoes, cancer — that I would be better without. Rather, Anselm's point is that it is better *for the thing itself* to exist in reality than merely as a concept in a mind.

But is existence a perfection? Norman Malcolm (1911-   ), for one, is dubious.

> The doctrine that existence is a perfection is remarkably queer. . . . A king
> might desire that his next chancellor should have knowledge, wit, and resolu-
> tion; but it is ludicrous to add that the king's desire is to have a chancellor who
> exists. Suppose that two royal counselors, A and B, were asked to draw up
> separately descriptions of the most perfect chancellor they could conceive, and
> that the descriptions they produced were identical except that A included

existence in his list of attributes of a perfect chancellor and B did not. One and the same person could satisfy both descriptions. More to the point, any person who satisfied A's description would *necessarily* satisfy B's description and vice versa![6]

But, contrary to Malcolm, one could argue that A and B do not produce the same description of the perfect chancellor, for a nonexistent chancellor could satisfy description B but not satisfy description A.[7] We could assume that all descriptions assume the existence of what is being described, but that begs the issue in question.

To ask whether existence is a perfection is to ask whether existence is a property, for every perfection is a property. When we say, "God is good," good is a perfection and property of God. The problem is that the word *exist* functions differently from other property words. For example, it makes sense to say, "Some libraries do not have good organization," but not to say, "Some libraries do not exist." Yet from an example like this it does not follow that "exist" is not a property, only that if it is one, it is an unusual one. But whether this unusualness is enough to vitiate Anselm's argument is unclear. Perhaps the problem has less to do with whether existence is a property than with the fact that there are different kinds of existences — in the understanding, in reality, in mythology — and that it is not clear how or on what grounds these are comparable.

Contemporary Versions of the Ontological Argument

Recent philosophers claim to have found a second, more persuasive argument in Anselm.[8] For example, Charles Hartshorne (1897–) notes that while great attention has been paid to the above Anselmian argument, a second, more persuasive argument in Anselm's *Proslogium* has been largely ignored. A major difference between the two arguments is how existence is to be treated. Hartshorne agrees with critics of Anselm that one cannot always treat existence as a property. However, it does not follow that existence is never a property. Although existence per se is not a property, *necessary existence* is. Consequently, for any two objects, if one exists necessarily and the other not (that is, exists contingently, such that it could either exist or not exist), the first is greater than the second.

It follows, then, that if God's existence were contingent, his existence would be by sheer chance or luck, or due to some cause, and he would not be the best conceivable being. But God, as the greatest possible being, possesses necessary existence.[9] Therefore, God's existence is either logically necessary or logically impossible. God's existence is not logically impossible. Hence, it is *logically necessary*.[10]

To make their argument succeed, Hartshorne and others interpret the necessity of God's existence as logically necessary existence (existence the denial of which is or entails a self-contradiction). But why should one think that God (or anything, for that matter) possesses logically necessary existence? Some have thought that Anselm, in his alleged second argument, held this view of

God, but there is textual evidence to the contrary. John Hick (1922–), for example, argues that Anselm did not mean the modern notion of logical necessity, but *ontological or factual necessity*. Such a necessary being is not dependent on any other being for its existence; it has its existence from itself.[11] It can neither come into nor pass out of existence. If it exists, it always has and always will exist. If it does not now exist, it never has and never will exist.

Modern Anselmians reply that logical necessity is indeed required for an adequate conception of God. God must be conceived as maximally perfect, as exemplifying "necessarily a maximally perfect set of compossible [mutually compatible] great-making properties."[12] And since necessary existence is a great-making property, God cannot not-exist. If a maximally perfect being (God) is possible, a maximally perfect being (God) exists. The debated issue concerns not only the status of necessary existence as an alleged great-making property, but the very conception of God himself.

It is not hard to see that for many, the jury on this argument is still out. For some, the ontological argument is obviously fallacious; one cannot argue from concepts to reality. For others, it is sound, but perhaps not a proof as delineated above, since one does not know the truth of the premises apart from the truth of the conclusion. Alvin Plantinga (1932–) writes,

> I think [the main premise—that maximal greatness is possibly instantiated] *is* true; hence I think this version of the ontological argument is sound. But here we must be careful; we must ask whether this argument is a successful piece of natural theology, whether it *proves* the existence of God. And the answer must be, I think, that it does not. . . . Not everyone who understands and reflects on its central premise . . . will accept it. Still, it is evident . . . that there is nothing *contrary to reason* or *irrational* in accepting this premise. What I claim for this argument, therefore, is that it establishes, not the *truth* of theism, but its rational acceptability.[13]

The Kalām Cosmological Argument

A second proof frequently given by theists is the cosmological argument. The cosmological argument is less a specific argument than an argument form. It begins by invoking an empirical fact about the world (contingent beings exist; there is something in motion; the universe began to exist). Then it seeks for the cause or explanation of this fact. It argues that an infinite series of causal conditions cannot provide an adequate explanation. Finally, it concludes to the existence of some necessary being, first cause, or personal agent. Two importantly different versions of this argument can be discerned. One, advanced by Thomas Aquinas (c. 1224–1274) and others,[14] considers the explanatory causal conditions in terms of their logical rather than their temporal relation to the effect, so that the first cause to which the argument concludes is not necessarily a first cause in time. The other, advanced by Arabic philosophers such as al-Kindi (c.870) and al-Ghazali (1058–1111) and more recently defended by

William Craig (1945–   ), argues for a first cause in time. Let us begin with the second version of the argument, referred to as the *kalām* argument.

The *kalām* argument can be formulated as follows:

1. Everything that begins to exist has a cause of its existence.
2. The universe began to exist.
3. Therefore, the universe has a cause of its existence.[15]

Premise 1 states a version of the causal principle that lies at the root of all cosmological arguments. Craig holds that this premise is intuitively obvious; no one, he claims, seriously denies it.

Perhaps the most serious objection to the principle comes from recent work in subatomic physics. Here it appears that electrons can pass out of existence at one point and then come back into existence elsewhere without any apparent cause. There is no way of tracing their intermediate existence. Further, the location of their reappearance is not precisely determinable, only statistically probable.

It is difficult to know what to say about this, given our present state of knowledge. Some argue that this phenomenon results from the limits of our investigative equipment. We simply are unable at this time to discern the intermediate states of the electron's existence. Others argue that the very introduction of the observer into the arena affects what is observed so much that it gives the appearance that there are effects without causes. But of course there is no way of knowing what is happening without introducing observers and the changes they bring. Still others maintain that though the causal principle operates at the supraatomic level, the principle is inapplicable at the subatomic, and hence is not universally true. The implications of this and other indeterminacy phenomena are unclear at this point. What can be said is that should indeterminacy be shown to be a real feature of the world, this would have significant implications for the more general causal principle. However, it might not affect the *kalām* argument in that quantum theory does not hold that electrons appear *de novo*; matter and energy are not continually being created out of nothing, which is what the first premise asserts.

Returning to the original *kalām* argument, what can be said about premise 2? Why should we think that the universe had a beginning in time? Craig provides four arguments, two *a priori* and two *a posteriori*, to support this premise. We have space to look only briefly at one of them. The argument relies upon recent developments in astrophysics. In 1965 two scientists at Bell Laboratories discovered background radiation in the universe. This radiation appears to be the remnants of some gigantic, early explosion, called the Big Bang. Two widely held but competing models of the origin of the universe are compatible with this.

According to the Oscillating Universe model, the universe goes through repetitive cycles of expansion and contraction. Following the big explosion, it expands to a certain point, where the gravitational force of matter takes over to slow and eventually end its expansion. This force pulls the universe back together, until it reaches a point of compact density (the Big Crunch), explodes, and begins to expand outward again. This process repeats indefinitely, though not necessarily in the same way. For this to be possible, our universe must not have passed the critical threshold beyond which the gravitational force can pull it back. The other model is called the Big Bang theory. According to it, the big bang occurred but once, and since then the universe has been expanding outward, until sometime in the future it will die a cold death.

Determining which model is true depends, in part, upon calculations of the total amount of matter in the universe. Some hold that the density of the matter is now insufficient to halt the expansion of the universe. Having passed the critical gravitational threshold, the universe will continue to expand forever. Should this be true, the universe at the point of the big bang had a beginning, which is the thesis of premise 2.

Evaluation of the argument depends upon our knowledge of the universe at any given time. If present calculations of the amount of matter in the universe are correct, then the argument stands a good chance of being sound. On the other hand, if, as some think, there is a great quantity of currently undetected, invisible or dark matter in the universe, scattered in dust clouds within or between the galaxies, then possibly we have not yet passed the critical threshold beyond which contraction of the universe is possible, and so we are unable to determine which is the correct model. Hence, acceptance of this argument for premise 2 depends upon the results of future investigations into the universe. The final verdict on this *a posteriori* version of the *kalām* argument must await further developments in astrophysics.

The Thomistic Cosmological Argument

The Thomistic type of cosmological argument does not attempt to prove the existence of a first cause in time. The universe might well have been eternal. Yet it is still contingent and hence dependent on something else for its continued existence. Thus, the cause to which the argument concludes might best be termed a sustaining cause rather than a first creative cause. It is that which is necessary for anything to exist.

Although the argument appears in various writers with different first premises, the fundamental structure and resulting issues are basically the same.

1. A contingent being exists.
2. This contingent being has a cause of its existence.
3. The cause of its existence is something other than itself.
4. What causes this contingent being to exist must be a set that contains either only contingent beings or at least one noncontingent (necessary) being.
5. A set that contains only contingent beings cannot cause this contingent being to exist.
6. Therefore, what causes this contingent being to exist must be a set that contains at least one noncontingent (necessary) being.
7. Therefore, a necessary being exists.

We introduced the terms *contingent being* and *necessary being* in Chapter 4. We noted that a *contingent being* is one that depends on something for its existence, so that even though it exists it might not have existed. For example, you are a contingent being. Although you exist now, it could be that you do not exist now (for example, if you had died last night); if you did not exist now, it is possible that you could have existed (for example, had your parents given birth to you a moment ago). So understood, premise 1 is true.

Premise 2 invokes a version of the *principle of causation*. According to this version, every contingent being has a cause of its existence.[16] This principle, it is contended, is a presupposition of reason that is held also to apply to reality.

One might object that though the causal principle applies to how we *know* the world, this does not mean that it describes what actually goes on in the real world. Principles of thought need not mirror the principles of reality. Two replies are possible. First, defenders of the causal principle argue that the success with which we have applied this principle refutes the thesis that reality operates differently in this respect from the way we think it does. If we consistently used this principle but it did not apply to reality, we should have bumped up against numerous contradictions by now. Second, if we begin at this fundamental point to drive a wedge between thought and reality, the outcome can only be skepticism about the real world.

Premise 3 makes the obvious claim that something cannot be a causal condition for its own existence; to do so it would have to exist already. The point here is not primarily about time, but rather a logical point: Something that is contingent cannot account for its own existence.

Some, such as Immanuel Kant (1724–1804), have objected to the conclusion (7) that a necessary being exists. If we use the cosmological argument to argue for the existence of a necessary being, he argues, the cosmological argument must presuppose the ontological argument. But the ontological argument is suspect. Thus, since the cosmological argument depends on it, it too must be suspect.[17]

However, the contention that the cosmological argument depends upon the ontological argument is based on a confusion. As we noted when we discussed the ontological argument, the term *necessary being* can be understood in different ways. Kant, like the modern defenders of the ontological argument, understands "necessary being" as having to do with logically necessary existence. But this is not the sense in which "necessary being" is understood in the cosmological argument. Necessity is understood in the sense of ontological or factual necessity described above. If it exists, a necessary being is self-sufficient and self-sustaining.

The critical premise is 5. In its defense it is argued, first, that if all the causal conditions are contingent, then each of them would require a cause of its existence. Hence, the set of conditions responsible for the effect must contain an infinite number of contingent beings. But, second, an infinite set of causal conditions cannot explain the existence of the contingent being. Two types of argument are given in defense of this.

The first argument (a) is that there cannot be an actually infinite set of anything in reality. Although in mathematics we can speak about actual infinites, mathematical actual infinites concern only the ideal world of mathematics. If they are applied to the real world, absurdities result. For example, if we had an infinite number of books, this would include all the books beginning with the letter A. Suppose that we also have an infinite number of books that begin with A. Then, though the first set contains the second set and more, both sets have the same number of books. But one would expect that if one set is the subset of the other, the subset would be less than the set.[18]

Now if the actual infinite cannot exist, then one cannot appeal to an actual infinite of present causal conditions to explain the existence of any given contingent being. Hence, the causal conditions must contain at least one noncontingent causal condition.

According to the second argument (b), even if an actually infinite set is possible, such a set of causal conditions cannot explain something's existence. Where each causal condition is contingent, each one itself needs an explanation for its existence. Since in an infinite series of contingent beings each needs a reason for its existence, an infinite series of contingent beings cannot explain the existence of any contingent being.

But why, it might be asked, do we need to explain the existence of something's every contingent causal condition in order to explain its existence? Richard Swinburne (1934–) terms this requirement the *completist fallacy*.[19] Cannot we circumvent both arguments (a) and (b) simply by providing those causal conditions that are necessary and sufficient for the thing to exist? An explanation is provided once we derive the existence of the contingent thing from some theory plus the existence of that which is necessary for its existence.[20]

Thomas Aquinas's response is that the very nature of the causal series requires this kind of explanation. The kind of causal series he has in mind is what is referred to as a *per se* series, in which each of the causes is an intermediate cause, transferring the causal activity from logically prior but temporally contemporaneous causes to the effect. These intermediate causes are like what is involved in swinging a bat: the arms that move the hands that move the bat are all contemporaneous, intermediate causes. They would not be causally efficacious unless they were caused to act at that very moment by something else. Furthermore, unless there is a first cause, neither the arms, hands, nor bat will be caused to move.

Applied to an infinite series, where there is no uncaused or self-explanatory causal condition, each contingent cause depends upon some other condition for its causal activity. But if the effect depends on something that itself depends on something else for its causal activity, we have not gotten a causal explanation of the effect. Consequently, an infinite series of contingent causal conditions cannot provide an adequate account of the causal activity that results in the existence of a contingent being.

A very critical problem remains, however. Do explanations ordinarily invoke this type of (*per se*) series, where the relevant causal conditions function as intermediates? In fact, there is a paucity of examples having to do with explaining the existence of something, where such series are structured with intermediate causes. They are more common in examples of movement (note Thomas's first way), but even here the Thomistic form of the argument invokes a problematic conception of causal relations.

The contemporary exponent of the argument probably should concede that this traditional defense of 5 is unsuccessful—that indeed each contingent thing exists because of the causal activity of other contingent things in the universe. However, even with this concession, the question still remains as to why there are contingent beings at all, when conceivably there could have been none. In particular, why is there a universe (as a collection of contingent things) rather than not?[21] "When the existence of each member of a collection is explained by reference to some other member *of that very same collection* then it does not follow that the collection itself has an explanation. For it is one thing for there to be an explanation of the existence of each dependent being and quite another thing for there to be an explanation of why there are dependent beings at all."[22] To say that there have always been dependent things fails to provide a sufficient reason for why there are any such things rather than not.

Bertrand Russell (1872–1970) argues that we cannot ask about the cause of the universe—that it is "just there, and that's all."[23] But there is good reason to think that the universe is contingent and hence requires an explanation for its existence. Since everything in the universe is contingent, the universe itself must be contingent. Now it is true that not in every case does the whole have the same characteristics as the parts. Russell is correct in noting that blanket arguments of this type commit the fallacy of composition. For example, the argument that all the bricks in the wall are small; therefore the wall is small, is fallacious. On the other hand, sometimes the totality has the same character as the parts on account of the parts—we built the wall out of bricks; therefore it is a brick wall. The universe's contingency is like the second case. If all the contingent parts of the universe, including matter and energy, ceased to exist simultaneously, then the universe itself, as the totality of these parts, would cease to exist. But if it can cease to exist, it is contingent and requires an explanation for its existence.

There is, then, good reason to think that this last version of the cosmological argument is sound. However, the question remains whether it constitutes a proof of God's existence. The answer to this, first, depends on whether one *knows* that the premises of the argument are true. In particular, it depends on whether one *knows* that the invoked principle of sufficient reason—that all contingent things must have an explanation of their existence—is true. Some question it; others hold it to be true.[24] In any case, attempts to argue for or against it appear to invoke it.

Second, it depends on whether the necessary being to which the argument concludes is *God*. Some suggest that the universe itself is the necessary being, but as we have seen this is not the case. Without there being any other reasonable candidate, it is likely that the necessary being is God. Of course, more will have to be said concerning its properties to establish this identification, for God understood religiously is a being who is personal, loving, good, all-knowing, and omnipotent, and who acts purposively. Perhaps other theistic arguments can help supply some of these characteristics.

The Analogical Teleological Argument

Undoubtedly, the most popular argument for God's existence is the teleological argument. Like the ontological and cosmological arguments, it too has a long history and reflects the prevailing scientific world view of the time. For lack of space we will leave aside the Thomistic argument constructed on an appeal to final causes, and instead focus on more modern conceptions of the argument.

One form, still found in popular religious literature, is the analogical teleological argument. This goes back at least to the end of the eighteenth century, when William Paley (1743-1805) argued that nature is analogous to a watch. On analyzing a watch, we are impressed with its intricate means-ends adaptation. All the wheels, gears, and springs are made and adjusted so that by their motion the watch keeps perfect time. Seeing this, we cannot help but conclude that the watch had an intelligent maker who fashioned it according to a design for a purpose. If we look at nature we quickly discover the same intricate means-ends adaptation. "Every indication of contrivance, every manifestation of design, which existed in the watch, exists in the world of nature; with the difference, on the side of nature, of being greater and more, and that in degree which exceeds all computation."[25] Just consider, for example, the astounding means-ends ordering between all the parts of the eye and the end of seeing; each part is well suited to contribute to the whole, so that if just one part functions poorly, sight is affected. Since the effects in nature and the watch are analogous, it is reasonable to conclude that the causes are analogous. Nature too has an intelligent, purposeful maker.

But will the analogy work? David Hume (1711-1776), anticipating Paley's argument, advanced three criticisms of an analogical teleological argument. First, the strength of the argument depends upon the similarity between the things held to be analogous (the analogs). The greater the similarity, the stronger the argument; the weaker the similarity, the weaker the argument. But, argued Hume, the two analogs are greatly disparate.[26] Our world is not similar at all to watches and other humanly contrived things. Indeed, composed as it is of vegetables and animals, it is as much organic as mechanical.

Second, it is unreasonable to think that the principle governing our creation of machines—that reason is the cause of means-ends adaptation—governs all of nature. There are many natural principles besides reason: generation, vegetation, gravity. Indeed, the number of principles is infinite. Why do we choose reason or mind as the ultimate governing principle? Why not choose vegetation as the dominant principle? Then, should the teleological argument work, what we really have is a proof for Linus's Great Pumpkin. Further, each principle rules over its own natural domain: vegetation in plants, generation in animals. We cannot project from one limited area to another part or to the whole of nature.

Third, suppose we grant that there is a mind that accounts for the order in the universe. Does not the principle of causation hold for mind and its ideas just as much as for the material world?[27] If so, this mind must have a cause for its own order. Hence we have an infinite regress of causes for any event, since we cannot invoke either the mental or the material to be the ultimate cause or explanation. But an infinite regress of causes yields no satisfactory explanation for the resulting order. Hence, either we deny the principle of causation (and do not require a cause for the means-ends adaptation in the material world) or we affirm the principle of causation and allow evidence showing that each area, material as well as mental, can organize itself.

It is the latter tack which nineteenth- and twentieth-century naturalists took. The order in the universe is not the product of conscious activity, but the result of natural selection, the prime mechanism of evolution. Individual examples of apparent purpose result when modifications produced by random mutations either are preserved when they benefit the individual, or are discarded when they are less successful. But survival of the fittest and natural selection are strictly natural principles of explanation; they do not require a divine mind. Chance and successful propagation govern nature, not purpose. Evolutionary naturalism, it is held, provides a reasonable alternative for explaining particular instances of means-end order in nature.

The Inductive Teleological Argument

Many contemporary proponents of the teleological argument grant that individual examples of means-ends ordering can be understood in terms of evolutionary principles. In this respect the theory of natural selection provides a *description* of the gradual development that characterizes various forms of life. More problematic, however, is the treatment of natural selection as a theory whose function is to *explain* the development of life. By using science's hypothetical-deductive method, it is argued,[28] we should be able to deduce specific outcomes from the theory and then test whether they occur. But this is what we cannot do with the theory of natural selection. By definition the survivors are the most fit. Hence, any organism brought as a counterexample to the theory can be included in the rubric because, whether or not we know what gives it its survival potential or could have predicted which changes would enable it better to survive, because it has survived, it was best fitted to its environment. Thus the theory can *describe* how some primates left the trees and roamed erect on the African savannas, but it cannot *explain* why some did and survived, and some did not and survived. It can describe how some reptiles gradually developed wings and survived; yet nonflying reptiles also abound.

Since it is consistent with most any event, the theory becomes nonpredictive and nonfalsifiable. It then is difficult to see how the principle of natural selection, understood as an explanation, is not trivial or circular. Since the fit are those that survive, are better fitted to survive, or leave the most offspring, natural selection as the survival of the fittest means the survival of those that survive or leave the most offspring. It is like saying, "May the best team win," and defining the best team as the team that scores the most points. Consequently, as an interpretative paradigm, natural selection can be made consistent with the biological data. After the fact we can describe the adaptive mechanisms. But consistency does not give it predictive explanatory power, and it is for this power that we adopt a theory.

An evolutionary naturalist might reply that this argument makes too much of prediction, that though we can expect specific predictions in sciences like physics, such is not appropriate in other sciences like biology. Perhaps having natural selection as an interpretative paradigm is sufficient.

Rather than being fatal to the theist's case, this reply accords with the thrust of the contemporary form of the teleological argument. All that is required by the inductive form of the teleological argument is that the door be left ajar for discovering the *best* interpretation of the data and that a theistic interpretative paradigm initially not be excluded. Defenders of the teleological argument then present the following sorts of cumulative evidence to show that the most reasonable explanatory hypothesis is theistic in character.

First, there are aspects of the universe that natural selection does not so easily explain. For example, natural selection has difficulty doing more than describing how living things came to be from the nonliving. If one analyzes the elemental chemical-physical components of the universe one can see that life is possible. But what natural selection cannot explain is why these components should give rise to *life* rather than to the nonliving. There are many possibilities; what makes these components move toward life-engendering combinations?

The inorganic contains a vast complex of seemingly unrelated conditions — the physical-chemical composition of the universe, the expansion rate of the universe, the size of the electric charge of the electron, the ratio of the masses of the proton and the electron, the distance of the earth from the sun, the composition of the atmosphere and the earth, the presence of water, oxygen, and carbon, the rotational speed of the earth — all of which are necessary for sustaining the life of those who observe the universe. Many of these conditions (for example, that the strong and weak nuclear forces have a specific value) have a very low, *a priori* probability, given what we know about the prior natural causes. However, looked at from the perspective of our contemporary situation, we see that such conditions are necessary for there to be intelligent human beings. We could not be what we are — living, knowing, valuing, aesthetic beings — without the universe having these specific conditions.

For example, had "the Big Bang expanded at a different rate, life would not have evolved. *A reduction by one part in a million million* at an initial stage would have led to recollapse before temperatures could fall below ten thousand degrees. An early *increase* by one part in a million would have prevented the growth of galaxies, stars and planets."[29] Or if the gravitational force were slightly greater, all the stars would be blue giants whose life span is too short to allow the evolution of intelligent life. But if it were slightly less, the universe would be devoid of many elements essential to life. Further, "if the electric charge of the electron had been only slightly different, stars either would have been unable to burn hydrogen and helium, or else they would not have exploded,"[30] giving us the heavier chemical elements. Or again, the universe must be so big to be so old, and it must be so old to create the chemicals necessary for the evolution of life. In particular, the basic element of life – carbon – could be formed only after the universe had cooled down from the Big Bang. But the time required for the evolution of the only possible basis for spontaneous generation of life requires a universe so big. In short, the inorganic fits into the narrow window of life-making possibilities. Hence, what is *a priori* unlikely is necessary not only for what exists now, but for the very possibility of seeing its purposefulness.

On a nonteleological schema, the *a priori* probability of the particular scenario occurring that resulted in carbonous life is extremely remote. However, on a teleological schema, viewed from our *a posteriori* perspective, the features of the scenario become probable as necessary for the present state of affairs (specifically, human observers); there is a purpose to the events. Thus, though we can describe the development of the prior, causally unrelated physical events naturally, that they occurred at all and in the pattern and narrow range necessary for life that they did points to the existence of a conscious designer. Hence, it is reasonable to claim that the best explanation for the particular concatenation of the universe will appeal to more than mere natural causes and laws.

It might be objected that the fact that an event is *a priori* unlikely does not entail that it cannot be adequately explained naturally. That it has a probability at all indicates that natural explanations can be given. Hence, to evaluate its necessity from our present perspective is misleading; it is looking for an explanation after the fact. The effect, as it were, is already there in the causes, and nothing need be added to those causes to account for it.

However, the possibility that these facts about the universe have a natural explanation does not affect the argument, for the point of the argument is that inductively what is sought is the best possible explanation not only of the conditions themselves, but also of the fact that among all the possibilities only those that make intelligent life possible exist. What requires explanation is not so much that those conditions exist, as that they are what they must be for life to be possible at all. The appeal to a conscious, purposive designer better explains the life-anticipating conjunction of these extremely narrowly ranged physical conditions and natural laws.

Second, natural selection, as a scientific theory concerning the processes of change in organic life, is directionless; it says only that the fit survive, but it places no requirements or direction on the fit. This means that though natural selection can account for individual cases of organic adaptation, it cannot account for the fact that species do not merely sustain their existence but show evidence of development toward higher and more complex organisms. Indeed, that there is direction and progression to the evolutionary process is one of the more striking features of nature. Many organisms have become increasingly more complex, even to the point of having psychical components. Yet survival is not necessarily related to complexity; among the fit survivors are both complex and extremely simple organisms.

Might one better suggest, then, that there is some creative mind behind this process, anticipating the process from the very beginning, creating the elements that make possible progress to higher, more complex life forms, and directing it toward the end of living, sentient creatures? The teleological argument here appeals no longer to individual cases of adaptedness, but to the apparent direction and hence directedness of the entire evolutionary sequence.

Third, on the micro level the entire process of organic development invokes information processing. Especially here, there are hints that something more than natural selection is required to explain the ordered phenomena. In particular, how does one get the information-chains found in DNA out of the basic physical elements of protons, neutrons, electrons, and so on? Once there are DNA sequences we can understand how they combine and recombine. But prior to there being sequences, what could order the *information-neutral* physical-chemical elements into *information-bearing* paired nucleotides linked on a spiral double helix? That is, what impels the nonvital physical elements to become informative; what creates information where there was none?

Further, information is meaningless unless it is read, but prior to there being living things there was nothing to read the information. Both the information and the reading of it must arise simultaneously in order for either aspect to be beneficial and hence worthy of being preserved. The problem is a version of the old chicken and egg dilemma, except that here the question is not which arose first, but what led to their arising together. There is, it seems, a kind of directedness that moves the basic physical elements toward the possibility of simultaneously being information carriers and readers.

Finally, the teleologist draws attention to the structure of the entire developmental process. What is striking is the way in which the various parts of nature and the individual scientific laws result in an all-pervasive order that conforms to mathematical formulas that we can not only understand but also use to predict future events. The Darwinian schema employs natural laws to explain how life in its particular and diverse forms developed from complex molecules, but what it cannot explain is those very laws themselves. "Science thus explains particular phenomena and low-level laws in terms partly of high-level laws. But from the very nature of science it cannot explain the highest-level laws of all; for they are that by which it explains all other phenomena." Not a scientific, but a personal explanation of "the vast uniformity in the powers and liabilities possessed by material objects,"[31] in terms of a conscious, purposive being, is indicated.

In sum, the inductive teleological argument asks not who made the amoeba or the elephant, but how one accounts for the entire system that, developing from the simple to the complex, from the nonliving to the living, portends conscious life. The more one reflects on the narrow window that makes sentient life possible, the more this question becomes very significant. Law-governed, life-anticipating order appears in a number of areas not directly linked, yet at the same time it is *a priori* unlikely. If teleology made sense only in one area, there would not be much of a case. But the fact that appealing to purposive ordering best explains this factor common to a number of important areas lends credence to the contention that any explanation of the universe must take into account the activity of a purposeful being. In other words, the argument is both cumulative and probabilistic.

Furthermore, this explanation gains additional credence when the teleological argument is viewed not as an independent argument, but as one that follows upon or adds to the cosmological argument. If the cosmological argument is sound in concluding to the existence of a necessary being — that is, if a necessary being exists — it then becomes reasonable to suggest that the teleological argument supplies a further important characteristic of this being — namely, that the necessary being has conscious intelligence. That is, if the necessary being is the sustaining cause of things, and if what is sustained manifests purposive design, it is reasonable to infer that this sustaining cause is a conscious being that acts in the world in purposeful fashion.

The Moral Argument

The final argument at which we will look is the moral argument. This argument was espoused in the context of a postulational metaphysic by Immanuel Kant[32] and more recently in the popular writings of C. S. Lewis (1898–1963). Although a version of Kant's argument has found some recent qualified support,[33] we will focus on Lewis's treatment.

For Lewis and other defenders of the moral argument, our moral discussions and moral behavior presuppose that there is an *objective moral law*. Moral acts can be determined rationally to be truly right or truly wrong. They reject moral relativism, according to which what a group or person thinks is right is right for them. For one thing, unless there is an objective moral law, there is no standpoint from which we can critique the moral behavior or ideologies of others. If what each person thinks is right is right for him, the only possible grounds for criticism would be our failure to act on what we thought or believed was right. But then the moral beliefs of Adolph Hitler and the Khymer Rouge would be morally equivalent to those of Jesus and the Buddha. Second, if moral relativism were true, there could be no moral progress. In order to get persons to progress in their moral beliefs, it must be possible for them to be mistaken about moral beliefs and for one set of moral beliefs to be better than another. But this is impossible when whatever a person or group thinks is right, is right for them. Further, those who advocate ethical relativism often do so on the grounds that moral relativism promotes tolerance, advances the good of the community, or preserves the species. But this only reintroduces objective moral values, for unless some values are better than others — tolerance better than intolerance, preservation of the species better than its demise — there is no ground for praising these virtues, other than that we approve them. Finally, Lewis argues that those who argue from belief relativism, which is the view that different persons or societies have different moral beliefs, to ethical relativism have failed to notice that there is a substantial agreement among various cultures about what is morally acceptable and

what is forbidden. The differences between cultures are less matters of value
than of fact. For example, what constituted murder in Aztec society, which
practiced ritual killing, is different from what constitutes murder in our society,
which does not practice ritual killing.

This objective moral law — if it is to be justified and not merely opinion —
must be grounded in or based on something. Lewis suggests two possible
grounds: the factual reality of human experience (what he calls "matter") and
mind. It cannot be grounded in the factual reality observed by science, for the
laws of nature tell us only what things actually do. But the moral law deals with
what *ought* to occur. Put another way, we ultimately cannot help but obey the
laws of nature, but we have a choice about obeying the moral law. Even though
we are commanded to obey it, we can refuse. The moral law must be grounded
in mind, for only mind can give instructions regarding doing the right. This
mind cannot be a human mind, for the moral law continues to hold despite the
births and deaths of individual human persons. Hence there must be a power
or mind behind the universe, "urging me to do the right and making me feel
responsible and uncomfortable when I do wrong. I think we have to assume it
is more like a mind than it is like anything else we know — because after all the
only other thing we know is matter and you can hardly imagine a bit of matter
giving instructions."[34]

Is Lewis correct that a naturalist account of ethics cannot suffice? There are
traditions of naturalistic ethics that are neither subjectivistic not emotivist, and
that give a rational though material basis for moral obligations. For example,
Aristotle (384–322 B.C.) argued that we can ground moral judgments in the
final causes of the universe. By seeing how things necessarily are, we can
discern how we ought to act. The *ought* is not grounded in the *is*, but in what
necessarily is the case, in the ideal structure that must be realized in order to
maximize the self-fulfillment of the organism. But this is still to ground obligations in nature, and not in any absolute or transcendent Mind. This Aristotelian natural law theory is compatible with theism, but does not entail it.

It might be replied that contemporary philosophers can no longer appeal to
Aristotelian natural law theory because they have long abandoned the notion
of final causation. This is true, but the point of the objection is simply to
affirm that the moral argument cannot conclude directly that the ground of the
moral law *must* be mind. Of course, this means that it is incumbent on the
naturalist to show that it can be adequately grounded in something else. At this
point, the discussion must turn to evaluate recent attempts to develop sophisticated naturalistic or perhaps intuitionist, nonnaturalistic ethics — a subject beyond our present scope.[35]

What, then, can be said about the moral argument? Some might doubt
whether it can function soundly as an independent theistic proof. Even if this is
so, it still might be useful for the theist as a supplement to the cosmological and
teleological arguments. Theists will argue that it provides another piece to the
puzzle, for at the very least it makes possible the justification of our moral
beliefs.

If there is a necessary being who is involved intelligently and purposively in the world, there is also reason to think that this being is related in some way to the moral law. Obviously it would seem related to the moral law in that its actions should be subject to evaluation by the moral law. That is, if it is an all-good being, all its acts should be morally right. But the theist wants to hold to more than this. If a necessary being is responsible for the existence of the universe, it is reasonable to think that God has embodied the moral law in the universe in some way, either in terms of the natural law (which in turn provides a way of understanding some of what we ought to do) or in terms of divine commands. In the former a naturalistic ethic is compatible with the stronger theistic claim that God through creation is the ground of the moral law; the latter theory itself entails the existence of God. In either case, moral obligation is grounded in the personal character of God. We will have more to say on the relation of God to the moral law in Chapter 13.

Cumulative Case Arguments and God

What one thinks the arguments for God's existence show depends in part on how one perceives their function in the first place. If people are looking for a knock-down, drag-out proof for God's existence—a definitive argument, convincing to all, having universal acceptance—they will be sorely disappointed. None is without its detractors. We rejected the "definitive" approach from the outset, for there are few significant theses which go uncontested. Where there is near-universal agreement on a matter, it is generally a trivial one. In place of this view, we advocated a person-relative notion of proof, in which each person must decide concerning the soundness of the proofs and what she knows about the truth of the premises.

Suppose we accept the soundness of one or more of these proofs and affirm that we know the premises to be true; how can they best fit into the theistic conceptual schema? It is a mistake to ground theism on any single argument or to treat the arguments independently. If the theistic arguments are to have any import, they must be seen as part of a *cumulative case for theism*, where the pieces support each other in a way that enables us to make sense of the entire picture. Together they indicate that there is good reason to believe in the existence of some sort of ultimate object. The cosmological argument strongly suggests that there exists a necessary being, a being that if it exists is not dependent upon other beings for its existence. The teleological argument indicates that such a being, as responsible for the conscious-life–anticipating dimension of the universe, acts purposively and so has conscious intelligence and will. The moral argument suggests that this being has some relation to the moral law, and that it is reasonable to conceive of the moral law as somehow grounded in it and manifested in the order of its creation.

But is this necessary, purposive being to be identified with the god of religion? If we are looking for the god of the Bible or the Koran to emerge from the proofs, again we will be disappointed. The arguments at best yield the concept of a being that has distinctively *philosophical* rather than specifically *religious* properties. The god of the proofs is not personal, loving, worthy of worship, concerned for our salvation. Can, then, the god of the philosophers be identified with the god of religious believers?

One way of exploring this is by what might be termed the *method of correlation*. This involves correlating the properties of the philosophical necessary being with those of the god of a particular religious tradition. Three steps are required. First, the characteristics of this necessary being must be determined. We have suggested that it is reasonable to see the being as an eternal, conscious intelligence, creatively and purposively involved in the world. Some hold that other properties, like omnipotence, omniscience, and goodness, follow from these properties. The second step is to choose a particular religious tradition and see how its god is described. What properties are appropriate to it? Is it held to be causally related to a contingent world separate from itself, to be a conscious, purposive being? Third, what properties in the two lists are consistent, inconsistent, or not duplicated? Where the lists are consistent, there is good reason to think that they are describing the same being. Where the lists are inconsistent (for example, the theistic arguments support a dualist tradition, in which God is separate from the world, rather than a monistic or pantheistic tradition), further thinking on the part of both scholar and believer is required. Where the lists have unrelated properties (for example, the arguments do not speak of a personal, loving, trinitarian being who cares about the creation), one might explore whether these properties might be derivable from the theistic arguments or at least might be consistent with the properties that do follow.

Whatever one concludes about the relation between the Ultimate Being of the theistic arguments and the god of religion, it is important to note that what is at stake is not a conflict or correlation between two gods, but between two concepts of god. When seen from this perspective, the work of philosophers and that of theologians complement each other. The cumulative case of natural theology provides grounds for thinking that belief in God is reasonable, whereas the theologian puts this belief in a larger, salvational, revelational context.

STUDY QUESTIONS

1. If you believe in God, to what evidence do you appeal to support your belief? If you do not believe in God, what argument would you give against his existence? Carefully evaluate the strength of the arguments you give.

2. Compare and contrast the strong rationalist's view of proof with that of the critical rationalist. Does the critical rationalist's view of proof weaken it too much? Why or why not?

3. What is the ontological argument? What argument would you give to defend its central thesis that existence is a perfection?

4. What are the similarities and differences between the two versions of the cosmological argument? Take one of the versions and note its critical premises, giving arguments either in support or in criticism of those premises.

5. What are the differences between the analogical and modern inductive versions of the teleological argument? Does the teleological argument beg the question in assuming that there is order in the universe?

6. Thomas Aquinas developed a version of the teleological argument from final causation (his fourth way). Find the argument in a book that contains his writings and analyze it for its strengths and weaknesses.

7. Attempt to lay out formally the moral argument for God's existence (as we did for the ontological argument). Then proceed to evaluate each of the premises for its truth.

NOTES

1. Our discussion here follows that of George Mavrodes, *Belief in God* (New York: Random House, 1970), chap. 2.

2. Anselm, *Proslogium*, in Sidney N. Deane, ed., *St. Anselm: Basic Writings* (LaSalle, IL: Open Court, 1903), chaps. 2–4.

3. Gaunilo, "On Behalf of the Fool," in Anselm, pp. 148–49.

4. Alvin Plantinga, *God, Freedom and Evil* (New York: Harper & Row, 1974), p. 91; see also Charles Hartshorne, "What Did Anselm Discover?" in John Hick and Arthur C. McGill, eds., *The Many Faced Argument* (New York: Macmillan, 1967), pp. 330–31.

5. William J. Abraham, *An Introduction to the Philosophy of Religion* (Englewood Cliffs, NJ: Prentice-Hall, 1985), p. 27.

6. Norman Malcolm, "Anselm's Ontological Arguments," in Hick and McGill, pp. 304–5.

7. Jerome Shaffer, "Existence, Predication and the Ontological Argument," *Mind* 71, no. 283 (1962); reprinted in Hick and McGill, p. 230.

8. Malcolm, pp. 301–20; Hartshorne, pp. 321–33; Plantinga, pp. 85–112.

9. Plantinga notes that one can dispense with the supposition that necessary existence is a perfection by arguing for the possibility that there exists a being with maximal greatness. A being has maximal greatness in any given world only if it has maximal excellence—which entails omniscience, omnipotence, and moral perfection—in every world. Hence, if God's existence is possible (or if maximal greatness can be instantiated), then God exists necessarily. Plantinga, pp. 108–12.

10. Hartshorne is careful to insist that though this argument establishes God's necessary existence, it does not establish his *actuality* or concreteness. For Hartshorne, God in his actuality has contingent properties; he is not necessarily unsurpassable, immutable, and independent. The ontological argument, then, establishes that God exists, but it does not tell us *how*; it does not give us his content.

11. John Hick, "A Critique of the 'Second Argument,'" in Hick and McGill, pp. 345–46.

12. Thomas V. Morris, *Anselmian Reflections: Essays in Philosophical Theology* (Notre Dame, IN: University of Notre Dame Press, 1987), p. 12.

13. Plantinga, p. 112. It should be noted that his use of "proof" smacks of the strong rationalism we rejected above.

14. Thomas Aquinas, *Summa Theologica*, trans. Fathers of the English Dominican Province (Westminster, MD: Christian Classics, 1981), Part I, Q. 2, A. 3; *On the Truth of the Catholic Faith* I (Notre Dame, IN: University of Notre Dame Press, 1975) chap. 13; Duns Scotus, *Opus oxoniense*, I, Dist. II, Q. 1, in A. Wolter, trans., *Duns Scotus: Philosophical Writings* (Indianapolis: Bobbs-Merrill, 1962), pp. 43–51; Bertrand Russell and F. C. Copleston, "A Debate on the Existence of God," in John Hick, ed., *The Existence of God* (New York: Macmillan, 1964), pp. 167–91.

15. William Craig, *The Kalām Cosmological Argument* (New York: Barnes & Noble, 1979), p. 63.

16. It is important to be clear about this principle. Some have mistakenly interpreted the principle to mean that *everything* has a cause of its existence. But then even the first cause, necessary being, or God must have a cause of its existence, and an infinite regress of causes is inevitable. But by definition necessary beings are self-sufficient and self-sustaining; hence, it makes no sense to ask whether they have a cause of their existence. Hence, the causal principle invoked is more restricted; it claims only that *contingent* beings must have a cause of their existence.

17. Immanuel Kant, *Critique of Pure Reason*, trans. Norman Kemp Smith (New York: St. Martin's Press, 1969), A606.

18. For the detailed argument, see Craig, pp. 66–95.

19. Richard Swinburne, *The Existence of God* (Oxford: Clarendon Press, 1979), p. 73.

20. Keith Yandell, *Christianity and Philosophy* (Grand Rapids, MI: Eerdmans, 1984), pp. 59–60.

21. This argument still differs from the *kalām* argument, for whereas the *kalām* argument asks for an explanation of the universe's *coming into existence*, this argument asks for an explanation of the contingent universe's *existence*, and thus is compatible with its eternal existence.

22. William Rowe, *The Cosmological Argument* (Princeton, NJ: Princeton University Press, 1975), p. 264.

23. Russell and Copleston, p. 175.

24. For discussions of the principle of sufficient reason, see Rowe, chap. 2, and Richard Taylor, *Metaphysics* (Englewood Cliffs, NJ: Prentice-Hall, 1983), chap. 7.

25. William Paley, *Natural Theology* (Charlottesville, VA: Ibis Pub., 1986), chaps. 1 and 3.

26. David Hume, *Dialogues Concerning Natural Religion* (Indianapolis: Hackett, 1980), p. 16.

27. Hume, Book IV.

28. Holmes Rolston III, *Science and Religion: A Critical Examination* (Philadelphia: Temple University Press, 1986), chap. 2.

29. John Leslie, "The Anthropic Principle, World Ensemble, Design," *American Philosophical Quarterly* 19 (April 1982); 141. For a nontheistic version, see John D. Barrow and Frank J. Tipler, *The Anthropic Cosmological Principle* (Oxford: Clarendon Press, 1986).

30. Stephen W. Hawking, *A Brief History of Time* (New York: Bantam, 1988), p. 125. Hawking accepts the weak but not the strong version of the anthropic principle invoked by the teleological argument.
31. Swinburne, pp. 139, 144.
32. Immanuel Kant, *Critique of Practical Reason*, trans. Lewis W. Beck (Indianapolis: Bobbs-Merrill, 1956), pp. 128–36.
33. Robert M. Adams, *The Virtue of Faith* (New York: Oxford University Press, 1987), chap. 10.
34. C. S. Lewis, *Mere Christianity* (New York: Macmillan, 1943), p. 34.
35. For Lewis's argument that no naturalistic account can provide a justification of a moral belief, see C. S. Lewis, *Miracles* (New York: Macmillan, 1960), chaps. 3 and 5.

SUGGESTED READING

Craig, William L. *The Kalām Cosmological Argument*. New York: Barnes & Noble, 1979.

_____. *The Cosmological Argument from Plato to Leibniz*. New York: Barnes & Noble, 1980.

Davis, Stephen T. "What Good are Theistic Proofs?" Louis P. Pojman, ed., *Philosophy of Religion*. Belmont, CA: Wadsworth, 1987, pp. 80–88.

Dore, Clement. *Theism*. Dordrecht, Netherlands: D. Reidel, 1984.

Flew, Antony. *God and Philosophy*. London: Hutchinson, 1966, chaps. 3–5.

Hick, John, and Arthur C. McGill, eds. *The Many Faced Argument*. New York: Macmillan, 1967.

Hume, David. *Dialogues Concerning Natural Religion*. Indianapolis: Hackett, 1980.

Kenny, Anthony. *The Five Ways*. New York: Schocken Books, 1969.

Lewis, C. S. *Mere Christianity*. New York: Macmillan, 1943.

Owen, H. P. *The Moral Argument for Christian Theism*. London: Allen & Unwin, 1965.

Plantinga, Alvin. *God, Freedom and Evil*. New York: Harper & Row, 1974, Part II.

Reichenbach, Bruce R. *The Cosmological Argument: A Reassessment*. Springfield, IL: Charles Thomas, 1972.

Rowe, William R. *The Cosmological Argument*. Princeton, NJ: Princeton University Press, 1975.

Swinburne, Richard. *The Existence of God*. Oxford: Clarendon Press, 1979.

Taylor, Richard. *Metaphysics*. Englewood Cliffs, NJ: Prentice-Hall, 1983, chap. 7.

Tennant, F. R. *Philosophical Theology* II. Cambridge: Cambridge University Press, 1930.

Yandell, Keith. *Christianity and Philosophy*. Grand Rapids, MI: Eerdmans, 1984, chap. 2.

6

The Problem of Evil:
The Case Against
God's Existence

Fyodor Dostoevsky's (1821–1881) classic novel, *The Brothers Karamazov*, portrays the reunion of Ivan and Alyosha Karamazov, long separated by the odysseys of their different lives. Ivan, a university-educated and worldly wise man turned atheist, seeks to elicit an answer to one of life's most profound problems from Alyosha, who has become a faithful monk:

> By the way, a Bulgarian I met lately in Moscow . . . told me about the crimes committed by the Turks and Circassians in all parts of Bulgaria through fear of a general rising of the Slavs. They burn villages, murder, rape women and children, they nail their prisoners to the fences by the ears, leave them till morning, and in the morning they hang them—all sorts of things you can't imagine. People talk sometimes of bestial cruelty, but that's a great injustice and insult to the beast; a beast can never be so cruel as a man, so artistically cruel. The tiger only tears and gnaws, that's all he can do.[1]

Ivan reveals that he collects stories of such evils, particularly those of the suffering of innocent children. His point is that God—Alyosha's God—is supposed to be mighty and just, but that the world is full of absurdity and injustice, pain and suffering. Ivan insists he cannot embrace a system of religious beliefs that fails so utterly to make sense of life.

Examples abound of thoughtful people who reject religious belief because of the world's evil. Theologian Eugene Borowitz (1924–) writes of the Holocaust:

> Any God who could permit the Holocaust, who could remain silent during it, who could "hide His face" while it dragged on, was not worth believing in. There might well be a limit to how much we could understand about Him, but Auschwitz demanded an unreasonable suspension of understanding. In the face of such great evil, God, the good and the powerful, was too inexplicable, so men said "God is dead."[2]

Whether encountered in the indescribable horror of the Holocaust, unrelenting hunger in underdeveloped countries, violent crime in large cities, political corruption, or the desperate suffering of terminal cancer patients—the presence of evil in our world cannot be ignored. Evil in one form or another touches all of us. Some think that theists have no intellectual right to believe in God unless they can somehow square that belief with the existence of evil.

While every major world view, whether religious or secular, addresses the phenomenon of evil, the problem of evil for Christian theism is very acute. Naturalism, Hinduism, Marxism, and other philosophies of life have their own distinctive explanations of what we commonly call evil. But Christian theism involves such high and lofty claims about the character and purposes of God that the abundance of evil becomes a particularly perplexing issue. For centuries, philosophers and theologians have recognized that evil constitutes a serious difficulty for religious faith. In fact, many thinkers hold that the problem of evil is the most potent rational objection to theistic belief, what German theologian Hans Küng (1923–   ) has called "the rock of atheism."[3] Just as the preceding chapter explored the major arguments for the existence of God, the present chapter considers the problem of evil as forming a major case against the existence of God.

It might seem desirable to start with a precise definition of *evil*. Some conceive of evil under the theological category of "sin," others define evil as "finitude," and so on. However, these definitions already assume a certain theory of evil to be correct and thus bias the discussion from the outset. It is advisable, therefore, to leave open the question of definition and proceed with a broad, common-sense notion of evil.[4]

Regardless of the divergence among the many definitions of evil, most people would agree on what sorts of situations really count as being evil. In philosophical parlance, they more or less agree on the *extension* of the term evil (i.e., the set of instances to which it applies); but they may disagree vigorously on the *intension* of the term (i.e., its meaning). The class of situations to which the term applies includes, at the very least, extreme pain, the suffering of innocents, physical deformities, psychological abnormalities, character defects, injustice, and natural catastrophes. We may legitimately characterize such phenomena as "negative" or "destructive," since such characterizations are minimal and do not bias the further examination of the problem. Although we must be wary of importing some theory-laden definition into the discussion, we may readily classify evils into two broad categories: *moral* evil and *natural* evil.[5] The category of moral evil contains the wrongful acts and bad character traits of free human beings. Actions such as murdering, lying, stealing, and traits such as dishonesty, greed, and cowardice merely begin the list of moral evils. Persons can be held morally accountable for all of these things. The category of natural evil covers the physical pain and suffering resulting from either impersonal forces or human actions. Included here are the terrible pain and death caused by events like flood, fire, famine and pain and death caused by diseases like cancer, tetanus, and AIDS; defects and deformities like blindness, deafness, and insanity must also be listed among natural evils.

Obviously, when physical suffering occurs by intentional human action, we have a complex evil—the physical pain or suffering involved and the moral wrong that brought it about.

The Logical Problem of Evil

Thoughtful nontheists have made evil the basis of a strong objection to theistic belief. Actually, the objection from evil has been formulated in two distinct ways, the logical problem and the evidential problem. Critics who advance the *logical version* of the problem allege that there is an inconsistency between certain theistic claims about God and evil. John Mackie (1917–1981) writes that "here it can be shown, not that religious beliefs lack rational support, but that they are positively irrational, that the several parts of the essential theological doctrine are inconsistent with one another."[6] On the one hand, the theist affirms that an omnipotent, omniscient, perfectly good God exists; on the other hand, he affirms that evil exists in the world. The critic who advances the logical version of the problem of evil claims that these two statements are inconsistent with each other, that they both cannot be true. Since no person is rationally entitled to believe an inconsistent set of statements, the critic charges that it is not rational to believe both. If the critic is correct, then the theist has made a serious logical mistake and must relinquish at least one of the statements in the inconsistent pair.

Of course, it is not immediately obvious that a statement asserting the existence of God is inconsistent with a statement asserting the existence of evil. If there is a contradiction between them it must be *implicit* rather than *explicit*, putting the burden on the critic to show exactly how the contradiction arises. Most critics say that some additional statements—or "quasi-logical rules," as Mackie calls them—are needed to make the contradiction explicit. Some additional statements that have been suggested include the following: that an omniscient being knows how to eliminate evil; that an omnipotent being has the power to eliminate evil; that a perfectly good being will want to or have an obligation to eliminate evil; that evil is not logically necessary; and so forth. These statements give fuller content to the meaning of key terms. The critic reasons that if God has the knowledge, power, and desire to eliminate evil, and if evil is not necessary, then evil should not exist. Yet the theist claims that evil does exist. This brings to the surface the alleged inconsistency.

The exact statement about evil that a critic selects gives shape to her particular rendition of the logical problem. For example, some critics have thought that the sheer existence of evil is perhaps not inconsistent with the existence of the theistic deity, but that the *vast amounts* of evil in the world might well be. This variation on the problem depends on conceiving of God as allowing the existence of *some* evil, but not a great amount. Other critics have thought that natural evil is most clearly inconsistent with the existence of God. This variation depends on conceiving of God as allowing moral evil (due to human free will) but not seemingly blind, natural evil. In fact, the contemporary philosophical literature contains many different formulations of the logical problem, each one employing slightly different statements about evil. What all such formulations have in common is the accusation that theism involves an inconsistent set of statements regarding God and evil, and that the theist is thereby irrational. All formulations of the logical problem focus exclusively on the logical relations holding among the statements that are essential to theism and does not depend on whether these statements are true or false. Clearly, then, each formulation reflects a certain way of construing theistic claims about God and evil.

No contemporary theistic philosopher has been more energetic than Alvin Plantinga (1932–) in trying to rebut the charge of inconsistency. His rebuttal, known as the Free Will Defense, offers a way of showing the consistency of the relevant theistic claims. Since the critic alleges that it is logically impossible that both God and evil exist, the theistic defender must show that it is logically possible. In other words, the defender must show that both claims *can* be true, though he need not show that they *are* in fact true. As Plantinga indicates, the general strategy for proving consistency between any two statements involves finding a third statement that is possibly true, consistent with the first statement, and in conjunction with the first implies the second statement. The third statement, of course, need not be true or known to be true; it need not even be plausible. The statement only needs to be possible, because the matter of determining consistency between or among propositions has to do with whether they can all be true together, not with whether any one or all of them are in fact true. What the Free Will Defender must do, therefore, is find a statement that will meet these conditions.[7]

Plantinga thinks that the ideas of contemporary logicians about possible worlds provide a method for discovering the needed statement. A possible world is simply a total possible state of affairs, a total possible way things could have been. Plantinga's search for the third key statement begins with a description of a possible world, a brief scenario of human freedom in relation to divine omnipotence.

> A world containing creatures who are sometimes significantly free (and freely perform more good than evil actions) is more valuable, all else being equal, than a world containing no free creatures at all. Now God can create free creatures, but he cannot *cause* or *determine* them to do only what is right. For if he does so, then they are not significantly free after all; they do not do what is right *freely*. To create creatures capable of *moral good*, therefore, he must create creatures capable of moral evil; and he cannot leave these creatures *free* to perform evil and at the same time prevent them from doing so. God did in fact create significantly free creatures; but some of them went wrong in the exercise of their freedom: this is the source of moral evil. The fact that these free creatures sometimes go wrong, however, counts neither against God's omnipotence nor against his goodness; for he could have forestalled the occurrence of moral evil only by excising the possibility of moral good.[8]

Plantinga extracts the requisite third statement from the heart of this story: God is omnipotent and it was not within his power to create a world containing moral good but no moral evil. The claim here is that it is possible (or possibly true) that God would create a world of free creatures who choose to do evil. In other words, for any world God might create, populated by whatever free creatures, it is not within God's power to bring it about that those significantly free creatures never go wrong.[9] And this new statement, together with one asserting the existence of God, implies that evil exists. It can now be seen to be possible for God to exist and for evil to exist. Thus, the critic's charge—that it is not possible for God and evil to exist—is refuted.

J. L. Mackie, Antony Flew (1923–   ), and other critics raise a formidable objection to Plantinga's ploy. Arguing that it is logically possible that there be a world containing significantly free creatures who always do what is right and that God's omnipotence is the power to bring about any logically possible state of affairs, they conclude that God could have created a world containing free creatures who always do what is right. There is surely no contradiction in the description of such a situation. But if the critics are right about this, then the Free Will Defense is mistaken. As Mackie queries, "Why could [God] not have made men such that they always freely choose the good?"[10] After all, God is all-powerful.

Plantinga's reply to Mackie's objection involves sophisticated reasoning about the logic of omnipotence and freedom that is reminiscent of certain points discussed in Chapter 4 of this book, and exhibits more clearly the force of the Free Will Defense. Many thinkers, both theists and their critics, accept the standard definition of omnipotence: that there are no *nonlogical* limits to what an omnipotent being can do. These theologians and philosophers hold that God has the ability to bring about any intrinsically possible state of affairs (i.e., a state of affairs the description of which is not logically inconsistent). God could bring about, for example, white polar bears and triangles, because they are intrinsically possible; but he could not bring about married bachelors and square circles, because they are intrinsically impossible.[11]

However, Plantinga revises the concept of omnipotence to allow for the fact that there are states of affairs that are possible in themselves (i.e., intrinsically), but that are not possible *for God* to bring about. This point depends on a proper understanding of the logic of free will. If a person is free with respect to an action, then whether she performs or refrains from performing that action is up to her, not God. Although a world in which all persons always freely do what is right is certainly possible, it is not a state of affairs that was within God's power to create; all of the free creatures in that world would have to help bring it about by their own choices. The Free Will Defender insists that God cannot determine the actions of free persons.

However, Mackie and Flew counter that such insistence is based on an *incompatibilist* view of freedom (free will and determinism are logically incompatible), whereas their view is *compatibilist* (free will and determinism, either physical or divine, are logically compatible).[12] The compatibilist typically holds that a person is free in that, if she had chosen to do otherwise than she did, she would have done otherwise; but that nonetheless the person was determined to choose in precisely the way she did. According to compatibilists

Mackie and Flew, then, God could indeed have created a world containing moral good but no moral evil. In such a world, persons could have chosen, say, to perform only right actions, although all of their choices were determined.

Plantinga responds that free will is not compatible with any form of determinism, and thus that God could not create just any world he pleased. He explains that God thought it good to create a world containing significantly free creatures, beings who, like himself, are centers of creative activity. Plantinga defines very precisely the concept of significant freedom that functions in the Free Will Defense: "A person is free with respect to an action A at a time t only if no causal laws and antecedent conditions determine either that he performs A at t or that he refrains from so doing."[13] If this is an acceptable definition of freedom, then the Free Will Defense stands. Morally significant freedom is not compatible with any form of determinism. So, while it is possible that there might be a world containing only moral good and no moral evil, whether such a world exists is actually up to the free creatures inhabiting that world and not up to God. Further exchanges between compatibilists and incompatibilists are certainly possible; but many contemporary philosophers believe that the Free Will Defense, with its implicit incompatibilism, is a strong and effective response to the logical problem of evil.

The Evidential Problem of Evil

Although Alvin Plantinga, Keith Yandell (1938–), and other theistic philosophers have cast serious doubt on the viability of all formulations of the logical problem of evil, some critics have framed a different sort of objection from evil. For some critics, the *evidential* version of the problem arises because the claims of theism do not seem to square with the facts of evil in the world. The challenge here is not that theism is inconsistent, but that it is *implausible*; the argument does not rest on a matter of logic, but on the issue of whether theistic beliefs provide a reasonable explanation of what appear to be the facts of evil. In their own ways, a number of nontheistic philosophers — such as Edward Madden (1925–), Peter Hare (1935–), Michael Martin (1932–), William Rowe (1931–), and Wesley Salmon (1925–) — have issued this kind of challenge to the theist.[14] Studying the various renditions of the evidential problem is enlightening, since they differ a great deal in quality and import.

It is instructive to review one form of the evidential argument which was advanced by Wesley Salmon. Employing a frequentist interpretation of probability to certain claims about the divine creation and design of the world, Salmon argues that the existence of God is *improbable*. That is, given the existence of evil, it is improbable or unlikely that God exists. Given the large number of things in our ordinary experience that arise through mechanical production rather than through divine creation, Salmon concludes that the likelihood of this universe being caused by mechanical production is high, whereas the likelihood of its being designed by an intelligent, benevolent creator is very low.[15]

Both Nancy Cartwright (1944–   ) and Alvin Plantinga replied to Salmon's probabilistic argument. Cartwright accuses Salmon of begging the question by comparing our universe as a whole with things within the universe that all arose by mechanical production. Furthermore, she argues that statistical or frequentist techniques are wholly inappropriate to treating metaphysical issues, such as that of God's existence.[16]

Plantinga's response to Salmon was meant to show that no sort of probabilistic argument from evil is promising. He argued that there is no extant theory of probability — personalistic, logical, or frequentist — that can be used to formulate a formidable argument from evil.[17] Among the obstacles facing critics are the inherent troubles and inadequacies in modern probability studies in general (e.g., the lack of any clear criterion for assigning probability to one statement on the basis of another), as well as the temptation for critics to appeal to their own presuppositions in assessing the probability of the existence of God (e.g., the belief that the universe is a completely natural product without a divine creator). While Plantinga exposes numerous weaknesses in attempts to construct an argument from evil in probabilistic terms, he still leaves unsettled the question of whether there might be a more cogent argument from evil that is broadly inductive or evidential in character.

Edward Madden, Peter Hare, and Michael Martin insist that a formidable evidential argument is indeed possible and that it more closely reflects the traditional formulation of the argument than do contemporary statements of the logical or probabilistic renditions of argument from evil. They speak of evil as being *evidence* against the existence of God insofar as they believe it cannot be explained on a theistic account of the world. In their estimation, the evil with which we are all acquainted is not what one would expect if an omnipotent, omniscient, perfectly good God created and superintends the world. For most of these critics, it is not the sheer existence of evil that puts pressure on theistic belief, since *some* evil seems subject to reasonable theistic explanation. Instead instances of evil for which there seem to be no good theistic explanation — evils that thus appear utterly pointless or gratuitous — constitute *prima facie* evidence against the existence of God.

In this form of the evidential argument, theism is treated as a large-scale hypothesis or explanatory theory that implies specific consequences for the way the world should be. If theism is true, then we would legitimately expect the world to turn out a certain way. Of course, complex global hypotheses seldom directly imply definite consequences on which to base our expectations, unless they are augmented by additional assumptions. In the case of the theistic hypothesis (i.e., that a certain kind of deity exists), no clear consequences follow regarding the state of evil in the world if we do not supplement the hypothesis with some other statements. Such statements would have to specify God's disposition toward evil. A fundamental assumption that critics introduce here, and that theists often accept as well, is that God would prevent or eliminate the existence of any pointless or meaningless evil. William Rowe states that such a claim "seems to express a belief that accords with our basic moral principles, principles shared by both theists and nontheists."[18] Terence

Penelhum (1929–   ) writes: "It is logically inconsistent for a theist to admit the existence of a pointless evil."[19] On this basis, critics reason that, if God exists, we should expect no pointless or meaningless evil in the universe. Yet pointless or meaningless evil does appear to exist; the reasons are very compelling for believing that it does. They conclude, then, that the theistic position does not adequately explain the way things are, and that it is unlikely that God exists.

Both theists and their critics have traditionally thought that the key to the success or failure of the evidential argument from evil centers on its factual premise—the claim that pointless evil exists. Keith Yandell, a theist, writes that "the crucial question is whether it is certain, or at least more probable than not, that there is unjustified evil, whether natural or moral."[20] William Rowe, a critic, agrees that whether the theist can overturn the evidential argument depends on finding "some fault with its [factual] premise."[21] On one side, theists have typically argued that all evils are somehow justified or meaningful and thus that the factual premises must be rejected. They have developed sophisticated theories about what sorts of greater goods are connected to evils that might at first appear gratuitous (e.g., suffering builds character). And they remind critics that their judgment about some evil's being gratuitous is entirely fallible, and that they cannot prove conclusively that there is gratuitous evil, and so forth. On the other side, critics have supported the factual premise by pointing out that there are cases of evil in which all available theistic explanations seem to break down, and that the prospects are dim that any adequate explanation will be found. Perceptive critics have even pressed the point that some cases of evil are so extreme that we cannot even sensibly imagine what sorts of justification they could ever have.

It may seem that theists and critics have reached a deadlock on the truth of the factual premise, a kind of rational stalemate. However, a stalemate—if that is the net result—clearly works to the advantage of the critic. After all, it is the theist who advances certain claims about the existence and nature of God, and then encounters serious difficulties in showing how those claims make sense of some very serious evils. The critic is thereby warranted in urging that the evidential problem of evil certainly reduces the credibility of the theistic position. Of course, in seeking to make a totally rational assessment of theism, one would have to take into account other criticisms besides the problem of evil, as well as any positive support, such as the traditional theistic arguments. Since most critics think that the problem of evil is effective and that the traditional arguments are bankrupt or at least unconvincing, they claim to be justified in saying that one ought not to affirm the truth of theism.

Seeking a different way of rebutting the evidential argument from evil, some theists have advocated accepting rather than rejecting its factual premise.[22] They defend the factual premise on both philosophical and theological grounds. Along philosophical lines, they point out the legitimacy of presuming the general reliability of our ordinary moral judgments, and they indicate that we judge much evil in the world to be utterly pointless. Shifting to theological grounds, these theists also support the factual premise by indicating that the standard tenet of traditional Christian theism is that God created humankind

with basically trustworthy rational and moral faculties. From this they conclude that it may be unwittingly inconsistent for theists to claim that the human
experience of gratuitous evil is regularly and systematically mistaken. They do
not intend to suggest that every judgment about an evil is correct, but to admit
that the weight of human experience has a bearing on the question of gratuity.

This means, of course, that theists must find something wrong with the
generally unquestioned theological assumption that God would not allow gratuitous or pointless evil. Obviously, theists cannot remain theists and surrender
the standard divine attributes. But some theists are beginning to think that the
assumption that God allows no gratuity is very questionable. If theists can
convincingly argue that there is a place for pointless evils within a theistic
conception of the world, then they stop the evidential argument from going
through.

One line of argument for gratuitous evil within a theistic universe traces out
the ramifications of significant free will.[23] Plantinga argued that evil is possible
in a theistic universe that contains morally free creatures. Now, if the range of
free choices available to free creatures is to be really significant rather than
trivial, then creatures must be capable of the highest goods as well as the most
terrible evils. For God to limit the possibility of very serious evils is to limit the
range of free choice. Carrying this thinking further, it would seem that significant freedom involves the ability to bring about utterly meaningless evil, a risk
inherent in God's program for humanity. For God to narrow the scope of free
choice is necessarily for him to rob the moral enterprise of much of its importance. If this way of drawing out the implications of Christian theism is essentially correct, then the critics' assumption can be rejected. What appears to be
meaningless or pointless evil is evidence against theism only if it is assumed
that the theistic deity would not allow it. Thus it looks as though the theist is
able to deflect the evidential argument from evil.

Defense and Theodicy

Just as the distinction between different versions of the problem of evil has
become very sharp, so has the distinction between different avenues of theistic
response. A *defense* is designed to establish that a given formulation of the
problem of evil fails to show theism to be inconsistent or improbable. A *theodicy*, however, seeks to provide a true and reasonable theistic explanation of why
God allows evil. In order to respond to the challenge from evil, the theodicist
must try to supply a systematic account of how various theistic beliefs about
God and the moral venture shed light on evil in the world.

In contemporary philosophy, defense has clearly become the major preoccupation among theists. We have seen its effectiveness in rebutting the logical
argument of Mackie and the evidential argument of Salmon. Even antitheistic
critics seem content to keep formulating new variations of their objection from
evil, which call forth innovative permutations of theistic defense, while never
demanding from theists any attempts at a full-blown theodicy.

Besides the disproportionate emphasis on defense over theodicy among philosophers of religion, several important arguments have been advanced that, if sound, would preempt the enterprise of theodicy altogether. Alvin Plantinga has made several provocative statements about theodicy, from which two of the most important arguments can be constructed. To be sure, in some of his writings, Plantinga adopts a somewhat conciliatory tone toward the enterprise of theodicy, but, in others, he delivers sharp criticisms. Without our attempting to determine what his exact position is, it is still fruitful to examine the two arguments that find a basis in his work. If certain of Plantinga's remarks are interpreted very strictly, he could be seen as endorsing the twin theses that theodicy is *a priori* impossible and the position that it is in principle unnecessary. While other objections to theodicy likewise deserve attention (e.g., that all theodicies are inconclusive or incomplete, leaving certain evils unexplained; that all available theodicies fail, thus casting doubt on the promise of the enterprise itself), these two arguments arising from Plantinga's work will occupy us here.

The first contention, that theodicy is *a priori* impossible, rests on what some thinkers see as the great disparity between the divine mind and finite human minds. Plantinga makes the claim that we can almost never know the definitive reason for a particular evil (e.g., the death of a close friend or some major catastrophe), and on this he seems to be correct. But he also suggests that we cannot even sketch, in a broad and general way, a theistic understanding of evil. He writes: "Perhaps God has a good reason [for evil], but that reason is too complicated for us to understand."[24] Here Plantinga is suggesting the stronger claim that God's plan for the world may be so lofty and complex that it exceeds the grasp of puny human intellects. However, it is not clear that this stronger claim is correct.

There are many Christian thinkers, by contrast, who do not construe the teachings of their faith (its Scriptures, doctrines, creeds, and all that they imply) to preclude theodicy. These theists argue that the Bible and historic church teachings affirm that it is God's good pleasure to give believers, and perhaps humanity in general, glimpses of divine purposes for the world. The basic materials for theodicy, then, can be extracted from these glimpses of God's purposes, which come through the basic teachings of the faith as well as through careful reflection on the human condition. Of course, it is not simply the issue of theodicy into which Christian theists claim to have some insight; they routinely declare that the teachings of the faith provide adequate, though not exhaustive, information on such important subjects as God's general will, the divine attributes, the meaning of human life, the purpose of the incarnation and atonement, and so forth. Hence, it would be odd indeed for theistic believers to think that their central religious beliefs generate no implications whatsoever for the issue of evil. Thus, the possibility of theodicy cannot be ruled out.

The second contention, that theodicy is in principle unnecessary, is implicit in Plantinga's "Reformed objection to natural theology"[25] as well as in his "Reason and Belief in God."[26] Since traditional theodicy is closely associated with the same impulse that motivates natural theology, both Plantinga's criticism of natural theology (as a means of justifying religious belief) and his endorsement of Reformed epistemology (as a positive alternative to natural theology) apply equally to the enterprise of theodicy. Traditional natural theology and theodicy endeavor to show that belief in the existence of the theistic deity is entirely rational. In order to accomplish this task, traditional theists consider the alleged evidence for and against the existence of God, seeking to show that the positive evidence outweighs the negative.

Essentially, Plantinga's objection to natural theology and to theodicy is that they rest on a mistaken notion of what it means to be *rationally entitled* to accept theistic belief — the notion that we must be able to give *arguments* or *evidence* for our belief. He tries to show that rational persuasion depends upon both the theist and nontheist sharing enough beliefs such that these beliefs could function as premises in a viable theistic argument. After all, if the nontheist does not accept the premises the theist uses, then he need not accept the theist's conclusion. In providing an alternative to the whole enterprise of theistic argumentation, Plantinga tries to show that, in appropriate circumstances, the theist can be rationally justified in accepting religious beliefs as "basic." Just as one can take perceptual beliefs ("There is a tree") and memory beliefs ("I had breakfast this morning") as basic and needing no argument, one can also take religious belief ("God exists") as basic. Thus, according to Plantinga, the nontheistic critic has no grounds for demanding that the theist produce arguments and evidence to support belief in God, and the theist has no obligation to supply such support. The net result is that the twin enterprises of natural theology and theodicy are rendered unnecessary.[27]

Plantinga and other Reformed thinkers deserve credit for showing that there are some contexts in which it is appropriate for a person to adopt certain beliefs without giving discursive arguments for them, and Chapter 7 looks at their position in detail. For example, it would not be fitting to demand anything resembling a comprehensive natural theology or a systematic theodicy from an intellectually unsophisticated believer or from a believer engaged in religious worship. Yet there seem to be other contexts in which arguments either are very appropriate or are even required — contexts in which a believer might try to produce theistic arguments for the existence of God and perhaps a theodicy to account for why evil does not militate against the existence of God. Although Plantinga admits that there might be circumstances in which arguments are not inappropriate (e.g., to meet an objection to theistic belief), he maintains that such argumentation is best considered secondary to the more immediate and basic way of believing in God.

Yet one context in which the demand for theodicy seems completely justified is the dialectical one of rational debate and discussion in which the theist and critic find themselves. The theist advances not an isolated claim, such as "God exists," but rather a whole set of logically interrelated claims regarding God's nature and purposes. He maintains that the whole system of beliefs that constitute theism is a correct interpretation of many important features of human life and the world at large. The critic then alleges that this theological interpretation has difficulty accounting for evil. The theist responds by trying to elucidate and explain how her theological beliefs do make sense of evil. Here the critic is not being eccentric or unfair to request that the theist make sense of her own belief in God, to trace out the ramifications of her professed point of view for the very significant issue of evil.

Explicitly *Christian* theism, for example, encompasses numerous insights and commitments that provide the raw materials from which strategies for theodicy can be drawn. Hence, it already contains at least an implicit theodicy from which a more deliberate and self-conscious theodicy might be constructed. Of course, there is no guarantee that all theists will work out the implications of their position in exactly the same way or that they will find sufficient common ground to persuade all critics. But it is now clear that the argument that theodicy is inappropriate or unnecessary is not sound.

Another context in which theodicy certainly seems appropriate is that of the theist's own search for better understanding of his own theological beliefs. Even if we grant that he may be entitled to accept belief in God as basic under certain conditions, it is naive to think that life's experiences will never invite deeper reflection upon that belief, reflections that include questioning as well as reaffirmation. By engaging in this kind of reflection, thoughtful theists explore the implications of their unique theological perspective for a large number of important issues — moral crises, the worth of certain humanitarian projects, the hope of life after death, and, for our purposes, the presence of evil. Thus, it is quite legitimate for the theist to try to formulate some reasonable understanding of evil for himself, and whatever understanding he obtains provides a measure of theodicy.

In the final analysis, then, the enterprise of theodicy cannot be shown to be either impossible or inappropriate in all situations. Theodicy is indeed possible in principle and, in some important kinds of situations, theodicy is certainly appropriate, if not required. Thus, the historical tradition of theodicy certainly has a legitimate place in philosophy of religion.

A Range of Responses

The whole enterprise of theodicy, as we can now see, is not a misguided one at all. Historically, theists have offered a wide variety of theodicies in response to the problem of evil. Several of these theodicies deserve our consideration because they contain worthwhile insights, and others because they make instructive mistakes. The traditional strategy has been to reconcile the classical concept of God with the existence or extent of evil, although process theodicy, which we must also consider, modifies the classical concept of God in order to address the problem of evil. Let us now explore several of the most popular answers to be offered by traditional theists, some of which have served as comprehensive explanations for evil and others as elements in larger, more comprehensive explanations.

One popular approach contends that evil is a *necessary contrast* to the good. The argument typically runs as follows: just as we learn what the color yellow is by experiencing the contrast between it and other colors, experiencing evil allows us to understand and properly appreciate the nature of goodness. While this theistic response has a certain point, it encounters enormous difficulties as a comprehensive explanation for evil. It seems that a much smaller amount of evil than we actually have would suffice to help us understand the good. Surely, we humans could get the point without all of the terrible suffering and catastrophe that occurs in our world.

Another approach that has had some uptake among religious believers is that evil is *punishment* for wrongdoing. For example, in the Old Testament book of Job, the "comforters" insisted that Job was suffering because he had sinned. They held the principle that God rewards righteousness with health and wealth, but punishes those who sin with sickness and misfortune. Yet Job replied that he had not done anything to merit his suffering. In perceiving that the world is much more complex than the comforters' simple theory envisioned, Job realized that a person must have purer motivation for serving God than mere material rewards.[28] Besides, the punishment theory, presented as a comprehensive theodicy, flirts with sheer absurdity in cases such as the death of innocent infants or the tragic destruction of the population of an entire village.

A very interesting, but more complicated, response to evil is to maintain that this is the *best of all possible worlds*. In the eighteenth century, Leibniz (1646–1716) reasoned this way: a perfect God has the power to create any possible world; being perfect, God would create the very best possible world; no creaturely reality can be totally perfect but must contain some evil; so, God created a world possessing the optimum balance of good and evil.[29] Since some goods are made possible only by the presence of evil (e.g., compassion is made possible by witnessing suffering; fortitude is made possible by hardship), God had to weigh the total value of all possible worlds and create the one in which the evils contributed to that world's being the very best one.

Although best-of-all-possible-worlds theodicy invites long and sustained discussion, several problems immediately surface. First, the concept of a best possible world may well be logically incoherent, just as the concept of the highest possible integer is logically incoherent. There simply is no end to the system of integers. Similarly, why would we think that there is some best possible world? Second, the Leibnizian approach seems to imply that our world is not capable of improvement, an implication that runs counter to our ordinary moral judgments. The third, and perhaps most serious, problem is that it might be asked why God consented to create a world at all given that it had to have this much suffering. Put another way, why did God create this world at all, if he could not create a better one? Remember Ivan Karamazov's poignant question to Alyosha: "If you were God, would you have consented to create the present world if its creation depended upon the unexpiated tears of one tortured child crying in its stinking outhouse to 'dear, kind God'?"[30] The anticipated reply to this rhetorical question is that a morally good being would not create this world at all.

Yet another type of theistic response to the problem of evil is the *ultimate harmony* solution. Actually, this view is ambiguous and can be split into two distinct positions: that *all is well with the world from God's perspective*, or that *all will be well in the long run.* One way in which the all's-well-in-God's-sight position has been developed relies heavily on the concept of omniscience. Since God's knowledge of the world is complete whereas human knowledge is partial and fragmented, only divine judgment about the state of things is ultimately valid. After all, a chord heard in isolation may sound dissonant, but when heard in context it sounds harmonious. The analogy, then, is that only God can see how the totality of events constitute a favorable arrangement, while we puny humans cannot. Unfortunately, this approach seriously frustrates all human moral judgments, since they will always be made from a limited perspective. And this result does not comport well with the historic Christian teaching that finite persons are creatures who bear God's image and can thus make reasonably reliable moral judgments.

Another way in which the all's-well position is sometimes developed revolves around the notion that God's morality is higher than human morality. So, even if we could see the events of the world in total context, we would not apply the same perfect moral standard as God would in appraising them. In its strongest form, this position implies that God's ways are so much "higher than our ways"[31] as to render our attempts at moral evaluation useless. Obviously, this position once again undercuts human moral judgment, since every moral judgment we make must be systematically mistaken. Moreover, the concept of a higher divine morality becomes simply meaningless, since we would not know what such a morality would be, let alone how it could be legitimately used to the advantage of the theist trying to grapple with the problem of evil.

Ultimately, the very disturbing result of the higher-divine-morality approach is that it projects a picture of God as a moral monster, as one whose moral standards are completely contrary to our deepest moral convictions. J. S. Mill (1806–1873) renounced such a notion of God:

> In everyday life I know what to call right or wrong, because I can plainly see its rightness or wrongness. Now if a god requires that what I ordinarily call wrong in human behavior I must call right because he does it; or that what I ordinarily call wrong I must call right because he so calls it, even though I do not see the point of it; and if by refusing to do so, he can sentence me to hell, to hell I will gladly go.[32]

So, the intelligent theist can affirm the perfection of God's morality and the imperfection of human morality, but will not insist on complete discontinuity between divine and human moral standards. But if our ordinary moral judgments are allowed, then the problem of evil cannot be answered by claiming that all is well according to the divine perspective.

The second distinct approach, the all's-well-that-ends-well strategy, does not claim that every evil is currently connected with a context of greater goods, even though it may be that only God correctly perceives the connection. Instead this approach claims that all evils will eventually result in higher goods in the future, either in temporal life or in eternity. While many of the considerations relevant to an assessment of the all's-well-in-God's-sight position are also relevant to an appraisal of the all's-well-that-ends-well position, a few additional points must be made. First, while there may be (or may not be) greater future goods to which present evils are connected, it is far from clear how such future goods *justify* the present occurrence of those evils. How, for example, does the fact that an orphaned child develops strong humanitarian motives and becomes a great missionary surgeon in an underdeveloped part of the globe justify, morally speaking, the brutal death of his parents at the hands of murderers? Or, how could the promised bliss and beatitude of heaven justify the excruciating suffering of a cancer victim during earthly life? It is quite a conceptual jump from the notion of a good *outweighing* an evil to the notion of *compensating* for an evil, and a very large jump to the notion of a good *justifying* the existence of an evil. In light of such difficulties, many all-will-be-well advocates simply say that we humans, with our limited powers, do not know how future goods make up for present evils, but that God's inscrutable wisdom does.

The preceding solutions have been used to address the problem of evil generally. Nevertheless it would be helpful at this point to consider one theodicy that has been offered specifically for the problem of natural evil. Perhaps the most important solution to the problem of natural evil is known as the *natural law* explanation. This explanation relies on the notion that it is reasonable to think that, as part of his creative program, God would bring about a natural order — a world constituted by objects that operate according to physical laws. The operation of physical laws of all sorts, then, makes possible a host of natural benefits, such as physiological feelings of pleasure or even helpful warnings of pain and simple bodily movements as well as complex behaviors. Futhermore, a generally stable and predictable natural order supports a moral order in which rational deliberation can take place and in which free choices can be carried out in action. But the possibility of natural evil is inherent in a natural system. The same water that quenches our thirst can also drown us; the same neurons that transmit pleasure can also transmit intense and unbearable pain.

Critics of natural law theodicy, such as H. J. McCloskey (1925–   ), have argued that God could greatly reduce or eliminate natural evils, either by miraculously intervening in the present natural system or by creating an entirely different natural system altogether.[33] Some theists, such as Richard Swinburne (1934–   ), have countered that to expect frequent divine intervention contradicts both the "omni-" attributes of God and the concept of a natural system.[34] After all, if God is omnipotent and omniscient, he would create a natural system in which he does not have to intervene frequently, and if he is perfectly good, he would create a natural system that is good on the whole. Moreover, the very concept of a natural system implies that it is not frequently adjusted from outside the system, that it runs more or less of its own accord and would be abrogated by frequent divine intervention.

It is also helpful to consider a solution tailored specifically for the problem of moral evil — *free will* theodicy. The appeal to free will as a basis for theodicy must be distinguished from the appeal for the purposes of defense. As we have already seen, Plantinga's Free Will Defense merely claims that it is possible that

God created creatures with free will. Free Will Theodicy, by contrast, claims that it is true that God created significantly free beings. This truth-claim about the creation of free creatures, along with other relevant theistic claims, is used to explain evil in an allegedly theistic universe.

A generic rendition of Free Will Theodicy runs as follows: According to the divine wisdom and goodness, God decided to create morally free beings. God knew that they would sometimes willfully choose to do wrong, but God granted free will anyway because a world of free creatures is more valuable than a world of automatons. God cannot extensively interfere with creaturely free choice because doing so would jeopardize genuine free will.[35] This scenario certainly captures a very important element in the theistic vision of the grandeur and the peril of being human.

Critics have suggested a number of ways in which the free will maneuver needs further justification. For one thing, they ask for reasons to accept the incompatibilist assumptions that underlie the free will explanation of evil. After all, there are several compatibilist views of the nature of free will. Among those critics who concede the incompatibilist assumption (which underlies the free will solution), some simply argue that God could have created free human beings with stronger dispositions toward right conduct than they actually have. Doing this would surely reduce much of the evil brought about by the misuse of free will. Theists typically respond that God has created humans with an inclination toward the good that is as strong as it can possibly be and still remain consistent with freedom of choice. And so the debate goes on.

There are many other responses to the problem of evil, but most of them have either marginal or no importance to the classic theistic tradition in general or to historic Christian theism in particular: evil as an illusion, evil as caused by demonic spirits, and so on. Many of the responses explored here are sometimes used by theists either as independent theodicies or as elements of larger, more complete theodicies.

Some Important Global Theodicies

In the history of theodicy, answers to the problem of evil and general insights into the human condition have been woven together in particular ways to fashion comprehensive scenarios of God's ways with the world. Certain solutions to aspects of the overall problem of evil are incorporated into larger visions of the origin and destiny of humanity, visions we may refer to as *global theodicies*. We here select three theodicies from the centuries of debate for closer examination: *Augustinian theodicy, Irenaean theodicy*, and *process theodicy*.

The early Christian philosopher and theologian St. Augustine (354–430), offered a large-scale theodicy that brings together several strands of thought. One of Augustine's ideas was that the universe—that is, the whole of God's creation—is good. Evil, then, at least metaphysically speaking, is not a positive, substantial reality that exists independently of God; rather it is the lack of good, the privation of goodness.[36] Unlike God, who is absolute and unchangeable, the universe was created out of nothing (*ex nihilo*) and is thus mutable or changeable. For Augustine, this explains how its original goodness is corruptible and thus can manifest evil.[37] It is particularly the misuse of free will that allows the entry of sin or evil into human experience. Augustine understood the Christian doctrine of the Fall to specify that an originally perfect creation rebelled against God through Adam's transgression. Augustine goes on to explore how this original sin brought guilt and punishment upon the whole race, how believers will be redeemed by divine grace, and how history itself will climax in the establishment of God's kingdom.[38]

Clearly, the Augustinian-type theodicy has dominated the collective imagination of Western Christendom from the fifth century A.D. onward, and even provides background for many of the popular Christian answers concerning the problem of evil in contemporary times. It has been subject to a great deal of scrutiny. Critics have charged, for example, that Augustine failed to account for evil in light of his strong view of the majestic power and unquestionable sovereignty of God. Perhaps one of the most vexing questions is how, on Augustine's account, an originally good creature, possessing free will, can engage in sin. If human beings once enjoyed an ideal state or "golden age" in which there was no evil, then how is it that they would choose to do evil? It is well known that, in the end, Augustine recedes into the "mystery of finite freedom."[39]

One alternative approach to theodicy can be traced to Bishop Irenaeus (ca. 130–ca. 202) whose work reflects certain Greek influences and is distinct from that adopted by Augustine and the Latin fathers. John Hick (1922–   ), a modern-day proponent of Irenaean-type theodicy, points out that it involves a quite different scenario from the one pictured by Augustine. According to Irenaean theodicy, Adam and the original creation were innocent and immature, possessing the privilege of becoming good by loving God and fellow creatures. But it would be an error to think that original innocence can be equated with original perfection. Indeed, it is not clear that God can instantaneously create morally mature persons, since moral maturity almost certainly requires the experience of temptation and, according to some, the actual participation in evil. Hence, evil as we know it is not to be explained as a decline from a state of pristine purity and goodness, but rather as an inevitable stage in the gradual growth and struggle of the human race.

Hick calls this explanation "soul-making" theodicy because it paints a picture of God's grand scheme of helping human beings become morally and spiritually mature. On this view, a special kind of environment is critical to the whole soul-making process. An environment conducive to spiritual and moral growth must be one in which there are real challenges, real opportunities for the display of moral virtue, and real possibilities of expressing faith in God. A major component of this environment will be a community of moral agents interacting in special ways and even a natural order of impersonal objects that operate independently of our wills. Obviously, in such conditions there is the genuine risk of evil—of failure and ruin, suffering and injustice. Interestingly,

Hick even deems it important that the world appear as if there is no God, and evil certainly plays an important role in forming this appearance.

For Irenaean theodicy, God's ultimate plan is the universal salvation of all persons, a process that extends even beyond earthly existence and into the life after death. For those people who, for whatever reasons, depart mortal life without having achieved the proper degree of moral maturity (or soulhood, as we might say), God pursues his same objective for them in the life to come. God will continue his efforts in the afterlife, providing occasions for exercising love and trust, until all persons are brought into the heavenly kingdom. This affirmation of divine persistence completes the progressive, developmental, indeed eschatological orientation of Irenaean theodicy.[40]

Hick's very famous version of Irenaean theodicy contains elements reminiscent of free will theodicy, natural law theodicy, and character-building theodicy as well as some distinctive concepts of his own. Various criticisms have been leveled against the different aspects of his view. G. Stanley Kane, for instance, has argued that the "epistemic distance" Hick postulates between humanity and God in order to make room for faith can be maintained at much less cost.[41] Severe moral and physical evils do not seem necessary to give the appearance that God does not exist, since there surely are other ways in which God can conceal his presence.

Hick's view has also been criticized as lacking empirical support for its central claim: that the world is engaged in a program of soul-making. There are enough failures in temporal life alone to cast grave doubt on whether a program of soul-making is under way. Surely, there are so many people whose characters do not develop and mature but are stunted or ruined that severe critics rightly question the effectiveness or even the existence of some process of soul-making. Moreover, many critics wonder whether the goal of soul-making, even if it did succeed in an ample amount of cases, could ever justify the means used to achieve it (e.g., great hardship, suffering, catastrophe). After all, we have all heard of persons who became shining examples of humanitarian concern and action or of moral courage and determination — but many of these persons had to fight through senseless losses of family members or to endure severe, prolonged, and involuntary pain. Hick shows himself keenly aware of this second point and has responded that each person must ultimately decide whether she thinks the soul-making process is worth it.

Another approach to theodicy emerges from the "process philosophy" of Alfred North Whitehead (1861–1947) and Charles Hartshorne (1897–). Process thought modifies the classical attributes of the theistic God. Its unique concepts and claims give rise to a distinctively different type of theodicy that has gained much attention in the contemporary period. Process thought in general is based on a view of reality as *becoming* rather than *being*, which is a direct reversal of the traditional approach. It is not surprising, then, that the central theme in process theodicy is the concept of change, development, and evolution — both in God and in finite creatures. Creatures are conscious, ever-changing centers of activity and experience. God, for process thought, has two natures, his primordial nature and his consequent nature. His primordial nature contains all eternal possibilities for how the creaturely world can advance; his consequent nature contains the experiences and responses of creatures as they choose to actualize some of these possibilities in their lives. As God's consequent nature changes in response to events in the creaturely world, God may be said to change or to be in process.

One key point in process theodicy is the rejection of the classical concept of divine omnipotence, which process thinkers take to be inadequate and laden with fallacies. Process philosophers and theologians deny that God has a monopoly on power or is "infinite in power" as traditional theology affirms. Finite creatures are also centers of power and thus can bring about new states of affairs as well. Process thinkers typically speak of this creaturely power in terms of "freedom," and thus their terminology is, at points, somewhat reminiscent of other more traditional discussions. This freedom, as they call it, is rooted in the very structure of reality, with each creature having the inherent power of self-determination. Thus, we may say that God has all of the power that it is possible for a being to have, but not all of the power that there is. Creatures, too, have some power of their own, which allows them to choose good or evil possibilities for their lives. God's power, then, according to process thinkers, must be viewed as *persuasive* rather than *coercive*: God can try to lure creatures toward the good and away from evil, but he cannot force them to choose the good. As process exponent David Griffin (1939–   ) states, God cannot eliminate evil because "God cannot unilaterally effect any state of affairs."[42] Instead God offers persons possibilities for the realization of good, adjusting his plans appropriately when finite creatures fail to live up to the divine plan and trying to lure them into fulfilling the next set of ideal possibilities, with the ultimate aim of enhancing and enriching their experience.

One intriguing theme in process theodicy is that, ultimately, all positive and negative experiences are conserved and reconciled in God's own conscious life. Thus, all things can be said to work out all right insofar as God "include[s] in himself a synthesis of the total universe."[43] In the Kingdom of Heaven, God brings about a kind of synthesis of all earthly experiences, but does not unilaterally rectify all evils. "Personal immortality" or "life after death" is not conceived by process thinkers as a central pillar in the defense of God's goodness against the problem of evil, as it sometimes is, say, in traditional Christian theism. Furthermore, there is no final, eschatological culmination of all things involving the setting right of evils that have occurred. Thus, for process thinkers, the continual, ongoing synthesis of all things in God's own conscious life is the basic hope for the triumph of good and the redemption of the world.

Few answers to the problem of evil have received more attention in the contemporary period than process theodicy.[44] This theodicy has certainly forced classical theists to rethink and refine their fundamental concepts. But classical theists as well as some nontheists have raised a number of serious objections to process concepts as well. For example, the process concept of divine power has come under severe criticism. The attack on the classical concept of power leveled by some process theists has been said to be pure caricature, using such loaded terms as "totalitarian" and "monopolistic." This caricature sets up an oversimplified "either/or" distinction between coercive and persuasive power. Critics of process theodicy have suggested that there may even be a range of modes of divine power, such as "productive power" or "sustaining power" or "enabling power," many of which are compatible with moral persuasion.[45] Also, there may be within the process model of power a confusion over the possession or ownership of power. With respect to property or things, ownership is exclusive (e.g., if one person has all of the marbles, then others have none). But with respect to power or agency, ownership is not exclusive. So, one person may have the power to pick up the pencil on the desk, but other persons and God may also have that same power. Many classical theists have not intended a monopolistic view of divine power, but one compatible with the possession of some power on the part of finite creatures.

Another general criticism of process theodicy focuses on the concept of divine goodness, declaring that its orientation is essentially aesthetic rather than moral. If the aims of the process deity are to make creaturely experience richer and more complex, even at the cost of pain and discord, then he runs the risk of violating many ordinary moral principles in the process. According to classical theology, God would not be morally perfect if he caused or allowed suffering in order to attain merely aesthetic aims. Process theists have replied that aesthetic value is a larger, more inclusive category than moral value, a maneuver that appears to make God's goodness unlike anything we are capable of recognizing and approving. Of course, hanging on the issue of whether God is morally good is the related question of whether he is worthy of worship.

Theodicy and the Assessment of Theism

The complete list of specific solutions and comprehensive theodicies into which they have been woven is much longer than we can treat here. However, the sampling of approaches above suggests the wide spectrum of moves available to theists and a number of countermoves open to critics. Interestingly, we can detect one common thread running through virtually all theistic solutions: *evil is necessary to a greater good*. Theists have typically taken the greater-good theme as integral to their search for a morally sufficient explanation for why God allows evil. Under the standard theistic assumption that God is omnipotent and omniscient, it would seem that his moral perfection must be upheld by arguing that he has a morally sufficient reason for permitting evil to exist.

Since many theists and their critics have thought that a morally sufficient reason must relate evil to a good that outweighs it, they usually take for granted that no explanation of evil can be acceptable unless it plausibly argues that the evil in question is inseparably connected to a greater good. A range of theodicies, then, simply offer different ways of construing what that good is. In effect, they conclude that no existing evils are pointless or gratuitous, and thus that they do not count as evidence against the existence of God. Of course, the common thread running through most antitheistic rebuttals is that at least some evil or some kinds of evil do not seem necessary for a greater good—

either that they seem to serve no good purpose whatsoever or the purpose they supposedly serve is not worth the price.

In the history of debate over theodicy, several salient points have been made by both sides. In future debates, perhaps critics could probe more deeply into the notion that a greater-good justificatory scheme is viable. After all, attempting to justify evil by reference to some good essentially makes the moral weight of the evil depend on an extrinsic factor. It may well be, however, that a more promising line for the critic is to say that some actual evils are intrinsically so negative and destructive that no external good could outweigh them.

Theists, on the other hand, could more fully explore a distinction between two sorts of greater-good theodicy: one type claims that the *actuality* of evil is necessary to a greater good and another type claims that the *possibility* of evil is necessary to a greater good. Clearly, many of the unacceptable greater-good theodicies are of the first type. Following this first type of approach, theists have to defend each actual evil or kind of evil by linking it to some actual good—an effort that is surely doomed. Some theists avoid severe difficulties by denying that God is morally obligated to make each specific instance of evil turn out for the best and arguing instead that God is morally obligated to create or pursue a certain kind of world. A good kind of world, it could be maintained, would be structured according to certain general policies. Such policies would include the granting of significant freedom to human beings, the establishment of a stable natural order, and so forth. But these structural features of God's created order would then make many particular evils possible, evils that may or may not always be connected to particular goods within the world system, either now or in the future. According to this approach, the greater good would be the overall structure of the world order. Thus, as long as the theist describes a very valuable kind of world (structured so that free creatures can make significant choices, have the opportunity to develop moral character, and so on), then the existence of such a world might well be seen as worth it.

Ultimately, the dispute over evil is one of several considerations relevant to the rational acceptance or rejection of theistic belief. A reasoned judgment, therefore, must be made in light of all of the relevant arguments for and against the existence of the God of theism. What is more, a final judgment would have to consider how well the overall theistic position fares in comparison to other world-views, either religious or secular.

STUDY QUESTIONS

1. Why is the problem of evil so acute for Christian theism? Explore how other world views might encounter their own distinctive problems of evil.

2. Carefully distinguish between the two main versions of the problem of evil. What must be the strategy of the critic of theism in pressing each problem? What must be the strategy of the theist in answering?

3. Explain the difference between defense and theodicy. Rehearse some of the arguments explaining why theodicy is not viable and some of the arguments explaining why it is. What do you think?

4. Sensing that evil somehow counts as evidence against the existence of God, some philosophers formulated the argument from evil in probabilistic terms. Is this a promising attack on theism? Why or why not? Is there a more promising way to formulate an evidential problem of evil?

5. Explore some of the standard solutions and theodicies that have been offered by theists. Which ones do you think are most effective? Least effective? Investigate some of the standard rebuttals to these solutions and theodicies that critics have offered.

6. Do you think that any feasible theistic answer to the problem of evil must rely somehow on a greater-good line of reasoning? Why or why not?

NOTES

1. Fyodor Dostoevsky, *The Brothers Karamazov*, trans. Constance Garnett (New York: Norton, 1976), p. 219. This encounter of Ivan and Alyosha constitutes one of the high points of world literature and deserves careful reading (Book Five, "Pro and Contra," chaps. 3–5).
2. Eugene Borowitz, *The Mask Jews Wear* (New York: Simon & Schuster, 1973), p. 99.
3. Hans Küng, *On Being a Christian*, trans. E. Quinn (Garden City, NY: Doubleday, 1976), p. 432.
4. See this suggestion in Edward Madden and Peter Hare, *Evil and the Concept of God* (Springfield, IL: Charles C. Thomas, 1968), p. 5.
5. See John Hick, *Evil and the God of Love* (1968; reprint and rev. ed., San Francisco: Harper & Row, 1978), p. 12; also, Alvin Plantinga, *God, Freedom, and Evil* (1974; reprint ed., Grand Rapids, MI: Eerdmans, 1977), p. 30.
6. John Mackie, "Evil and Omnipotence," *Mind* 64 (1955): 200.
7. Alvin Plantinga, *The Nature of Necessity* (Oxford: Clarendon Press, 1974), p. 165.
8. Plantinga, *Necessity*, pp. 166–67.
9. Plantinga's own very detailed argument delves into such concepts as "Leibniz's Lapse" and "transworld depravity." It can be read in more detail in his *God, Freedom, and Evil* or in very analytical detail in his *Necessity*, Part IX.
10. Mackie, p. 209.
11. More technically, we would say: states of affairs consisting in polar bears' being white, states of affairs consisting in bachelors' being married, and so on.
12. John Mackie, "Theism and Utopia," *Philosophy* 38 (1962): 153–59; Antony Flew, "Compatibilism, Free Will and God," *Philosophy* 48 (1973): 231–44.
13. Plantinga, *Necessity*, pp. 170–71.
14. Madden and Hare; Michael Martin, "Is Evil Evidence against the Existence of God?" *Mind* (87) (1978): 133–35; William Rowe, *Philosophy of Religion: An Introduction* (Belmont, CA: Dickenson, 1978), pp. 86–89; Wesley Salmon, "Religion and Science: A New Look at Hume's *Dialogues*," *Philosophical Studies* 33 (1978): 143–76.

15. In order to bolster his frequentist or statistical argument, Salmon contends that a statement such as "An omnipotent, omniscient, perfectly good God exists" has a "very low" numerical probability (a value much lower than 0.5) in relation to some statement such as "Evil exists." Conversely, he seeks to show that, given a statement of the existence of evil, the probability of the statement "An omnipotent, omniscient, perfectly good God does not exist" is high (definitely above 0.5). See Salmon, pp. 143–76.

16. Cartwright points out that the probabilistic argument from evil immediately faces the difficulty of specifying the appropriate reference class. Obviously, no person is directly acquainted with a whole class of universes such that we can arrive at a statistical measure of how many of them contain evil relative to how many were divinely created. Therefore, Salmon resorted to comparing the universe with other entities whose origins can actually be observed. But Cartwright contends that this move begs the question in advance by deciding to include in the reference class entities that are all brought about by mechanical production. Furthermore, Cartwright argues that frequentist techniques are wholly inappropriate for treating metaphysical issues, such as that of God's existence. If any type of inductive approach is appropriate, she holds that it would be the employment of experimental methods. She suggests, for example, that we imagine an experimental situation in which a bunch of random parts are thrown into a box and shaken together until they come out as a set of gears finally tuned to some end. Surely the probability of the initial random collection coming out in a highly ordered configuration is as near zero as can be, a conclusion completely opposite the one generated by Salmon's approach. See Nancy Cartwright, "Comments on Wesley Salmon's 'Science and Religion'," *Philosophical Studies* 33 (Fall 1978): 177–83.

    It would be interesting to explore Richard Swinburne's claim that frequentist techniques are appropriate to issues such as the existence of God. See Swinburne, *The Existence of God* (Oxford: Clarendon Press, 1979), pp. 5–21.

17. Alvin Plantinga, "The Probabilistic Argument from Evil," *Philosophical Studies* 35 (1979): 1–53.

18. Rowe, p. 88.

19. Terence Penelhum, "Divine Goodness and the Problem of Evil," in Baruch Brody, ed., *Readings in the Philosophy of Religion: An Analytic Approach* (Englewood Cliffs, NJ: Prentice-Hall, 1974), p. 226.

20. Keith Yandell, *Basic Issues in the Philosophy of Religion* (Boston: Allyn and Bacon, 1971), pp. 62–63.

21. Rowe, p. 88.

22. See Michael Peterson, *Evil and the Christian God* (Grand Rapids, MI: Baker, 1982), chap. 4; also, William Hasker, "The Necessity of Gratuitous Evil," paper read at the American Philosophical Association meeting, Cincinnati, OH, April 1988.

23. See Peterson, pp. 104–7.

24. Plantinga, *God*, p. 10.

25. Alvin Plantinga, "The Reformed Objection to Natural Theology," *Christian Scholar's Review* 11, no. 3 (1982): 187–98.

26. Alvin Plantinga, "Reason and Belief in God," in A. Plantinga and N. Wolterstorff, eds., *Faith and Rationality: Reason and Belief in God* (Notre Dame, IN: University of Notre Dame Press, 1983), pp. 16–93.

27. One can readily see why a theist who accepts Reformed epistemology would think that defense against the problem of evil is all that is rationally required. The critic advances an argument from evil against belief in God, and the theist defends

against it. But the theist need not feel that he needs to have an argument for belief in God; instead he can simply take belief in God as basic.

28. Several major passages in the book of Job indicate his growing awareness that the benefits and burdens of life are not equitably distributed according to merit. For example, chapters 7 and 12 argue that sometimes the righteous suffer and the wicked prosper.

29. Gottfried Wilhelm von Leibniz, *Theodicy* (LaSalle, IL: Open Court, 1984).

30. Dostoevsky, p. 226.

31. Isa. 55 : 8–9 (KJV) reads: "For my thoughts are not your thoughts, neither are your ways my ways, saith the Lord. For as the heavens are higher than the earth, so are my ways higher than your ways, and my thoughts than your thoughts." However, this passage is not best interpreted as meaning that God's purposes are radically alien to anything we could understand, or that divine moral standards are completely discontinuous with human standards.

32. John Stuart Mill, selection from *An Examination of Sir William Hamilton's Philosophy* included as an appendix in Richard Taylor, ed., *Theism* (New York: Liberal Arts Press, 1957), pp. 89–96.

33. H. J. McCloskey, "God and Evil," *The Philosophical Quarterly* 10, no. 39 (1960): 97–114.

34. See Richard Swinburne, "Natural Evil," *American Philosophical Quarterly* 15, no. 4 (October 1978): 295–301. Also see Bruce Reichenbach, *Evil and a Good God* (New York: Fordham University Press, 1982), chap. 5.

35. See Reichenbach, chap. 4.

36. Augustine, *Enchiridion*, (Lake Bluff, IL: Regnery Gateway, 1961), i. 8, 7.

37. Augustine, *City of God*, D. Knowles, ed. (New York: Penguin, 1984), xii. 1 and 6.

38. Augustine, *Confessions*, (trans. Edward Pusey [New York: Macmillan, 1961]), *City of God, Enchiridion*.

39. Augustine, *On Free Will*, trans. A. S. Benjamin and L. H. Hackstaff (Indianapolis: Bobbs-Merrill, 1964), III. xvii. 49.

40. For the specific way in which John Hick works out this type of Irenaean theodicy, see his *Evil*, Parts 3 and 4.

41. G. Stanley Kane, "The Failure of Soul-Making Theodicy," *International Journal for Philosophy of Religion* 6 (1975): 1–22.

42. David Ray Griffin, *God, Power, and Evil* (Philadelphia: Westminster, 1976), p. 280.

43. Alfred North Whitehead, *Religion in the Making* (New York: Macmillan, 1926), p. 98; also see his *Process and Reality* (New York: Macmillan, 1929), pp. 524–25.

44. See the full-scale discussion of process theodicy in Michael Peterson, "God and Evil in Process Theodicy," in Ronald Nash, ed., *Process Theology* (Grand Rapids, MI: Baker Book House, 1987), pp. 121–39.

45. Nancy Frankenberry, "Some Problems in Process Theodicy," *Religious Studies* 17 (1981): 181–84.

SUGGESTED READING

Griffin, David Ray. *God, Power, and Evil: A Process Theodicy*. Philadelphia: Westminster, 1976.

Hick, John. *Evil and the God of Love*. 1968; reprint and rev. ed., San Francisco: Harper & Row, 1978.

Mackie, J. L. *The Miracle of Theism*. Oxford: Clarendon Press, 1982, chap. 9.

Madden, Edward, and Peter Hare. *Evil and the Concept of God*. Springfield, IL: Charles C. Thomas, 1968.

Peterson, Michael. *Evil and the Christian God*. Grand Rapids, MI: Baker Book House, 1982.

Plantinga, Alvin. *God, Freedom and Evil*. 1974; reprint ed., Grand Rapids, MI: Eerdmans, 1977.

Reichenbach, Bruce. *Evil and A Good God*. New York: Fordham University Press, 1982.

7

Knowing God without Arguments:
Does Theism Need a Basis?

The French mystic Simone Weil (1909–1943) describes her first experience of God thus:

> In a moment of intense physical suffering, when I was forcing myself to feel love, but without desiring to give a name to that love, I felt, without being in any way prepared for it (for I had never read the mystical writers) a presence more personal, more certain, more real than that of a human being, though inaccessible to the senses and the imagination.[1]

Simone Weil's experience is all the more striking because there was so little in her background to prepare her for it. She was raised as an agnostic in a secularized Jewish home, and (as she says) had read none of the mystical authors who might have led her to anticipate such an experience. Weil, who was trained in philosophy, had studied the arguments for and against the existence of God and found the question undecidable. After her experience, however, she wrote:

> When we are eating bread, and even when we have eaten it, we know that it is real. We can nevertheless raise doubts about the reality of the bread. Philosophers raise doubts about the reality of the world of the senses. Such doubts are however purely verbal, they leave the certainty intact and actually serve only to make it more obvious to a well-balanced mind. In the same way he to whom God has revealed his reality can raise doubts about this reality without any harm. They are purely verbal doubts, a form of exercise to keep his intelligence in good health.[2]

Simone Weil's claim here is both clear and striking. On the one hand, she points out, philosophers raise questions about the "reality of the external world"; we may deal with these doubts intellectually — examine them, seek to refute them, and so on — yet all this leaves completely unshaken our certainty of the reality of the bread we have eaten. On the other hand, philosophers doubt the existence of God, and engage in debate using theistic and antitheistic arguments. This is all well and good — fine exercise for the mind, in fact — but for the person "to whom God has revealed his reality" these doubts no more

117

disturb her certainty of his existence than do the philosopher's doubts about the reality of bread and trees and stones.

It is safe to say that most philosophers who have considered the question of God's existence would not agree with Weil about this. Such a certainty, based on experience, as she attests to would often be dismissed as "purely subjective"; such experiences, before we rely on them, need to be confirmed by *rational*, as opposed to purely emotional, considerations. We need, in other words, to look at the question of God's existence in the light of *evidence and arguments* — just such arguments, in fact, as have occupied us for the last two chapters. One very natural way of looking at the matter would seem to be this: We estimate, on the one hand, the combined strength of the various arguments for God's existence, and on the other hand the strength of the argument from evil as well as other arguments against theism. Then, taking these two bodies of evidence together, we weigh them against each other, and the resulting balance determines whether it is reasonable to believe in God. Thus, if the problem of evil seems to be a strong argument against theism while none of the favorable arguments has much force, then it would be rational to reject belief in God, while if the theistic arguments are powerful and the antitheistic arguments can be refuted, belief in God is reasonable and appropriate. Or, it might turn out that the evidence for and against God's existence is quite evenly balanced; in this case it would be appropriate to suspend judgment, and neither believe nor disbelieve.

Evidentialism

This way of looking at the matter has a name; it is called *evidentialism*. It is, as has been said, a rather natural way of viewing the subject — so natural, indeed, that many philosophers have taken it for granted without question. Of course, it must be admitted that most ordinary people, including ordinary religious people, do not think this way at all. Most religious believers have never given much thought to arguments for or against the existence of God, and they may not feel that they have missed very much. Even those who have learned something about the arguments — say, in an introductory philosophy course — seldom make a really serious effort to find out how strong the arguments are or to guide their own beliefs by these arguments. They just go on believing, or disbelieving, without troubling themselves much about arguments.

Evidentialist philosophers, however, are not greatly concerned about the fact that most people do not think about God in the way evidentialism considers proper. The sad fact is, the evidentialists tell us, that most people are very far from being rational in the way in which they decide on important beliefs, especially religious beliefs. People believe for a variety of psychological, social, and emotional reasons that have very little to do with whether a belief is supported by evidence or whether it is likely to be true. Fortunately, however, there are a few individuals who do care about reason and truth, who do not want to be guided merely by their emotions, and it is these people who can and should be guided by evidence and arguments in determining their religious beliefs.

One of the most important developments in the philosophy of religion in recent years is the appearance of a group of philosophers who sharply reject evidentialism. These philosophers are not fideists in the sense defined in Chapter 3; they do not think that one's ultimate beliefs are immune to rational evaluation. But they maintain that it is possible for religious beliefs to be entirely rational and fully justified *even if there is no evidence supporting these beliefs*. This view is often referred to as "Reformed epistemology," because of the similarity between it and certain ideas that have been prominent in the Reformed, or Calvinistic, branch of Protestantism.[3] But the view itself is not logically tied to this branch of Christian belief; one need not be a Calvinist, or even a Christian, to be a Reformed epistemologist. The three leading exponents of Reformed epistemology are Alvin Plantinga (1932–), Nicholas Wolterstorff (1932–), and William P. Alston (1921–); we shall draw upon each of them in setting out and analyzing the position in the subsequent pages.

Critique of Evidentialism

The first thing we must do is to understand more precisely what is meant by *evidentialism*, so we can then see why the Reformed epistemologists object to it. Nicholas Wolterstorff presents the "evidentialist challenge" as follows:

> It was insisted, in the first place, that it would be *wrong* for a person to accept Christianity, or any other form of theism, unless it was *rational* for him to do so. And it was insisted, secondly, that it is not rational for a person to do so unless he holds his religious convictions on the basis of other beliefs of his which give to those convictions adequate evidential support. No religion is acceptable unless rational, and no religion is rational unless supported by evidence. That is the evidentialist challenge.[4]

Now, what is so objectionable about this? Unless we are content to be irrational, the requirement that we accept only rational beliefs is hard to contest. And it certainly seems reasonable that in order for religious beliefs to be rational they must be supported by evidence. Yet there is a problem lurking here, as we shall see.

But we need to be more precise about what it means for a belief to be *supported by evidence*. Many different views about this are possible, but modern philosophers who are evidentialists have for the most part been committed to an epistemological perspective known as *strong foundationalism*.[5] In order to understand this perspective, we must first discuss *foundationalism*, and then go on to consider what is distinctive about *strong* foundationalism.

Foundationalists distinguish between two kinds of beliefs that we all have. There are, on the one hand, beliefs that we hold because they receive *evidential support* from other beliefs that we have; these we may term *derived beliefs*. But there are also, it seems, some beliefs that are accepted *without* being supported by still other beliefs; these are our *basic beliefs*, and they form the "basis" on which our entire structure of belief and knowledge ultimately rests.

Now of course, one may accept a belief in a basic way (that is, without accepting it on the basis of other beliefs that are taken as evidence for it) when it is quite unreasonable to do so. For instance, one might believe that someone is guilty of a crime simply because one dislikes that person. But there must also, it seems, be some situations in which it is *reasonable and proper* to accept certain beliefs without other beliefs as evidence; those beliefs that it is reasonable to accept without evidence are our *properly basic beliefs.*

Now, a very important question arises that must be answered by any foundationalist: *What kinds of beliefs can be properly basic?* The answer to this question determines what the "foundations" are on which one's beliefs must be built, and thus goes a long way toward deciding what the final structure of beliefs will be like.[6]

Now, we are ready for the explanation of *strong* foundationalism. What makes strong foundationalism *strong* is just its idea about the sorts of beliefs that can properly be accepted as basic. The guiding idea has been that the properly basic beliefs should be *beliefs concerning which it is impossible, or nearly impossible, to go wrong.* If the foundations are as solid as it is humanly possible to make them, then the belief-system erected on them can also be solid and secure. In order to achieve this, strong foundationalists usually require that properly basic beliefs should be of only two kinds: they must be either *self-evident* or *incorrigible.* *Self-evident* beliefs are seen to be true by anyone who understands them; simple truths of arithmetic, such as "$1+2=3$," would be examples. *Incorrigible* beliefs deal with one's own, immediate experience; examples would include "I am feeling pain," "I seem to be seeing something red," and the like. It may or may not be possible to go wrong over such beliefs (that has been debated), but they would seem to be about as immune from doubt as any we can imagine. And if all our other beliefs can be built on these foundations, the goal of attaining real, solid, unchallengeable knowledge seems within reach.[7] To sum up, then, we may define the strong foundationalist's position as follows: *A person is rational in accepting a given belief only if that belief is self-evident, or incorrigible, or is derived from self-evident or incorrigible beliefs using acceptable methods of logical inference.*

From Wolterstorff's talk about the "evidentialist challenge" to religious belief it might seem that evidentialists oppose religion, but this is not necessarily the case. Quite a few evidentialists—such as Descartes (1596–1650), Locke (1632–1704), and Leibniz (1646–1716)—have thought that belief in God's existence, and other typical religious beliefs, are fully capable of being defended in a way that meets the challenge. As time went on, however, more and more philosophers concluded that theism *cannot* be defended in a way that satisfies the requirements of evidentialism. And if that is true, then evidentialism and religion are indeed enemies.

But just what is wrong with evidentialism and strong foundationalism (aside from their possible conflict with theism)? Actually, the answer to this is surprisingly simple: When we apply strong foundationalism to itself it *defeats itself*—or, we may say, it *self-destructs.* (The favorite philosopher's term for this is that this view is *self-referentially incoherent.*) To see what this means, consider the statement of strong foundationalism given above: *A person is rational in accepting a given belief only if that belief is self-evident, or incorrigible, or is derived from self-evident or incorrigible beliefs using acceptable methods of logical inference.* Is this statement of strong foundationalism itself self-evident? Not likely! In fact, many people have understood it and considered it carefully without thinking that it is true. Furthermore, it is not an "incorrigible" report of one's immediate experience; it is not at all like "I seem to be seeing something red." Finally, there is no reasonable way in which this statement could be *derived* from self-evident or incorrigible propositions, so as to be justified in that way. So we get the following, extremely interesting result: *If strong foundationalism is true, then no one is rational in accepting strong foundationalism.* For a strong foundationalist, this situation is extremely embarrassing.

There is, however, another problem with strong foundationalism that is equally serious: *If strong foundationalism is true, then we are wrong about most of what we think we know.* This point needs some explanation. Earlier, in explaining foundationalism, we pointed out that the strong foundationalists wanted to have an *absolutely secure basis* on which the structure of our knowledge could be erected. The idea was that, by taking as foundations only beliefs that were immune to doubt, we could secure a foundation on the basis of which our other beliefs could be built up with a very high degree of confidence and certainty.

Unfortunately, this noble project has proved to be a failure again and again. Many of our ordinary beliefs — things, indeed, that we would readily say that we *know* to be true — turn out to be unsupported when tested by these standards. Consider, for instance, this question: How do you know that you have been living for longer than, say, 45 minutes? It is not *self-evident* that you have lived longer than that; after all, you might just have been cloned by a very speedy scientist! Nor is this something you can know by an *incorrigible* report of your own experience. You may say that you *remember* having lived for many years past — but how do we know that these are real memories of what actually happened rather than, for example, having been implanted directly in your brain by a scientist? Nor is this the only sort of ordinary belief that cannot be justified to satisfy the strong foundationalist's standards. If you are going to take this view seriously, you might have to give up your beliefs that trees, mountains, and other physical objects really exist separate from your perception of them, and also your beliefs that other people really have experiences and feelings of their own, as opposed to being preprogrammed robots. But this, surely, shows that there must be something badly wrong with strong foundationalism.

If strong foundationalism is rejected, does this mean that evidentialism must go too? Possibly not; the two views are not logically equivalent. Nevertheless, evidentialists have usually in fact been strong foundationalists, and there do not seem to be well-developed examples of evidentialist positions that are *not* instances of strong foundationalism. Plantinga has argued, furthermore, that if strong foundationalism is rejected it will be hard if not impossible to construct a form of evidentialism that will create serious difficulties for theism.[8] Nevertheless, it would be well to keep in mind the possibility that someone might develop a variety of evidentialism that does not depend on strong foundationalism, and that therefore would escape the criticisms given above.

So far, though, all this is merely negative. Does anything of *positive value* for religion emerge from the rejection of evidentialism? For consideration of this matter, we turn to Alvin Plantinga.

Plantinga on Properly Basic Beliefs

We must not suppose that, when the Reformed epistemologists criticize strong foundationalism, they are rejecting foundationalism as such. They still accept the foundationalist's distinction between basic and derived beliefs, as well as the assumption that there must be *properly* basic beliefs from which all of our other beliefs have to be derived if they are to be rationally justified. What they reject is merely the strong foundationalist's overly restrictive criterion for what can qualify as properly basic beliefs.

How, then, shall we decide what beliefs can be properly basic? Here Plantinga, following Roderick Chisholm, suggests that we should not begin by setting up in advance a general requirement, such as is done by strong foundationalism. Instead, we should begin from the structure of belief and knowledge that we already have, and we should assume provisionally that this structure of belief is pretty much in order—that, as Chisholm says, "we do know most, if not all, of those things that ordinary people think that they know."[9] And we should take our actual beliefs as examples: Taking some belief we think to be reasonable and justified, we should ask ourselves whether we hold this belief because it is evidentially supported by other beliefs of ours, or whether it is one that is or could be reasonably held even if it were not supported by any other beliefs as evidence. If the latter is the case, we put this belief down as a *basic* belief, and indeed as a *properly basic* belief. Examples of the kinds of beliefs that might turn out, through this procedure, to be properly basic might include the following: ordinary perceptual beliefs ("That is a tree over there"), memory beliefs ("I had scrambled eggs for breakfast"), beliefs about other people's thoughts and feelings ("Mary really got angry when you said that to her")—and there will be other kinds as well. And when we have carried out the procedure with a number of examples of different kinds, we can begin to get an overall picture of the kinds of beliefs that can be properly basic—that is, of the *foundations* of our structure of belief.

So far, so good. But at this point, Plantinga has a radical suggestion to make: Why should the belief that *God exists* not be part of the foundation? Why should *this* not be one of our properly basic beliefs? The theist, after all, will certainly think that this belief *is* one that she is rationally justified in holding. And if she finds (as Plantinga thinks most believers in God will find) that it is *not* a belief that she holds because it is justified inferentially from other beliefs, then the procedure just described will lead her to consider it a *basic*, and indeed a *properly basic*, belief. And why not? What is wrong with this possibility? Is there any reason why "God exists" *cannot* be a properly basic belief? And if it is properly basic, then there is *no need* for the theist to produce proofs or arguments for God's existence, in order to be justified in believing in God.

Many philosophers have found this proposal of Plantinga's to be bold and even startling. It raises a great many issues and questions, only a few of which can be taken up here. Note, first of all, that the fact that a belief is properly basic in no way guarantees the *truth* of that belief. One who *actually holds* a particular belief in a properly basic way will think that it is true, of course, but then anyone who holds *any* belief in any way whatsoever necessarily thinks that belief is true. But it is entirely possible for a properly basic belief to be false. For example: You walk into a friend's house and, because of what you are hearing, form the belief that someone is playing the saxophone in the next room. This is a basic belief, not inferred from other beliefs of yours. (You do not say to yourself, "I am hearing something that sounds like a saxophone; usually, when I hear something that sounds like a saxophone, there is a saxophone nearby; therefore, what I am hearing is probably a saxophone." Rather, you just hear the sounds and find yourself with the belief that there is a saxophone in the next room.) Furthermore, you are quite familiar with saxophones and perfectly capable of recognizing a saxophone when you hear one. This, then, is a *properly basic belief*. Nevertheless, your belief turns out to be false — your friend is testing out his new digital stereo system with a recording of solo saxophone music, and the reproduction is so good you could not tell it from the real thing.

In the same way, it *might* be true that "God exists" is a properly basic belief for some person even if God does *not* in fact exist. That a belief is properly basic for a person does not *guarantee* that the belief is true; this constitutes one of the important differences between the strong foundationalism criticized above and the more moderate foundationalism embraced by Chisholm and by the Reformed epistemologists. (The other important difference is that moderate foundationalism begins by assuming the general soundness of the structure of knowledge and beliefs we already have; it is not a procedure by which to *replace* or *radically reform* that structure.) But that a belief is properly basic for some person *does* guarantee that the person is *rationally justified* in holding that belief; so if "God exists" is properly basic for you, then it is rational for you to believe in God.

There is an objection to Plantinga's procedure here that has been stated forcefully by Gary Gutting (1942–   ):

> How can a believer just blithely claim that it's utterly obvious that he's entitled to believe without having any reasons for his belief? What of the fact that there are all sorts of honest and intelligent people who've thought a lot about religious belief and simply don't see belief in God as properly basic? . . . As philosophers, we surely have to take as clear cases only those that would be admitted as such by just about any rational person.[10]

Gutting has also said, "Isn't it just common sense to admit that, when there is widespread disagreement about a claim, with apparently competent judges on both sides, those who assert or deny the claim need to justify their positions?"[11]

Plantinga is well aware of this objection, and his response to it is illuminating:

> Criteria for proper basicality . . . should be . . . argued to and tested by a relevant set of examples. But there is no reason to assume, in advance, that everyone will agree on the examples. The Christian will of course suppose that belief in God is entirely proper and rational; if he does not accept this belief on the basis of other propositions, he will conclude that it is basic for him and quite properly so. Followers of Bertrand Russell and Madalyn Murray O'Hair may disagree; but how is that relevant? Must my criteria, or those of the Christian community, conform to their examples? Surely not. The Christian community is responsible to *its* set of examples, not to theirs.[12]

Plantinga is saying, then, that a theistic philosopher is fully justified in taking "God exists" to be a properly basic belief, *even if others do not agree*. And in saying this, he is in effect giving up something that has often been thought of as an important goal of the philosophical enterprise. Philosophers have often assumed that if they hit upon the right *method* for approaching philosophical problems, and applied that method carefully and correctly, then agreement on *substantive conclusions* would be bound to result. Descartes's *Discourse on Method* is a striking illustration of this assumption, but it can be found in many other philosophers, going back at least as far as Plato (427–347 B.C.). To be sure, philosophers have for the most part been unsuccessful in actually *bringing about* this agreement they have sought. Plantinga is saying that it was unreasonable to expect this in the first place—that philosophers come to their task bringing with them deeply rooted *prephilosophical commitments*, and those commitments may prevent them from reaching agreement even if both sides in a dispute conduct themselves correctly in terms of the standards for philosophical reasoning and argument.[13] And on the other hand, if the theist makes the mistake of allowing the atheist to set the rules for the discussion by determining what beliefs can be properly basic, then we should not be surprised if the theist comes out second best. It is clear, then, that Plantinga is thoughtful and deliberate in his rejection of a "universal rationality" that can be relied on to bring philosophers to agreement despite differences in initial beliefs. But the student of Reformed epistemology likewise needs to be aware of this, and to realize that giving up this ideal of rationality is part of the price for being a Reformed epistemologist. (In considering this point, the reader may want to review the discussion of "critical rationalism" in Chapter 3, as well as the discussion of proofs as "person-relative," in Chapter 5.)

This line of thought may lead to a further objection, which may be stated as follows: Does not this mean that just anything goes? If the theist can take "God exists" as properly basic, then why cannot anyone else who holds a belief, no matter how bizarre, specify that this belief is properly basic and thus make himself immune to criticism? So that, for instance, Linus in the *Peanuts* comic strip, who believes that the Great Pumpkin comes every Halloween to those who believe and who wait for him in a "sincere" pumpkin patch, may believe this in a properly basic way and be perfectly rational and justified in his belief. (This has become known to philosophers as the "Great Pumpkin Objection.")

Plantinga's answer to this has two parts, depending on just how the objection is taken. On the one hand, if the objector is saying that the Reformed epistemologist is bound to accept that the belief that the Great Pumpkin returns every Halloween is properly basic, then this is just wrong. Belief in the Great Pumpkin will not, of course, be among the Reformed epistemologist's "set of examples," and there is no reason whatever to suppose that the Reformed epistemologist will or should come to the conclusion that this is a properly basic belief. Plantinga admits, to be sure, that the Reformed epistemologist "is committed to supposing that there is a relevant *difference* between belief in God and belief in the Great Pumpkin if he holds that the former but not the latter is properly basic."[14] But Plantinga thinks that differences of the right sort will not be hard to find.

The objection, however, might be taken in another way, as claiming that *the Great Pumpkinite himself*, following Plantinga's procedure for determining which beliefs are properly basic, might reasonably and properly conclude that his belief in the Great Pumpkin falls into this category. Philip Quinn (1940–   ) writes: "The difficulty is . . . that this is a game any number can play. Followers of Muhammed, followers of Buddha, and even followers of the Reverend Moon can join in the fun."[15]

Plantinga's reply to this is, in effect, "Sure, but what's the problem?" He says, "Different philosophers employing this method may arrive at different conclusions: true enough, but do we know of some reasonably viable philosophical method (for reaching epistemic criteria) of which this is not true? That's just life in philosophy."[16]

This answer brings us back to the point already made: Philosophers, like other people, bring with them deeply held prior commitments, and these commitments may sometimes make reaching substantive agreement on important philosophical questions (such as the criteria for properly basic belief) impossible. No doubt this is in some way regrettable, but (say the Reformed epistemologists) it is the way things are and there is no point in denying it.

It is possible that by this time the reader is experiencing a certain degree of frustration. Perhaps he or she is wondering just *how it is* that the belief that God exists acquires its status as properly basic. Obviously, it is not just the fact that this *is believed* that makes it properly basic, or even that it is believed *strongly*, with commitment and emotional intensity. So what is it that gives the belief this status? It would seem we are in need of an answer to this question, unless we are supposed just to take the Reformed epistemologist's word for it that this belief is properly basic.

In order to answer this question fully, the Reformed epistemologist would need to set out his own criteria for properly basic beliefs — his replacement, as it were, for the discredited standard of strong foundationalism. Plantinga, however, has so far been unwilling to do this; probably he thinks more spade-work is needed, more detailed consideration of examples, before we settle on a general formula. But failing this, there are still things that can helpfully be said. One important point, not stressed until now, is that generally if not always the status of a belief as properly basic is dependent on the *conditions in which that belief is held*. In the example discussed above you were rational to believe, in a basic way, that someone was playing the saxophone in the next room. But if on entering the house you had heard nothing at all, or only the sound of a child crying, you would *not* have been rational to believe there was someone playing the saxophone. The justification of your belief depends crucially on the *experiential conditions* under which you believe.

Now, how might this be applied to belief in God? In answering this, it is helpful to consider some examples Plantinga gives of properly basic beliefs about God. He writes,

> There is in us a disposition to believe propositions of the sort *this flower was created by God* or *this vast and intricate universe was created by God* when we contemplate the flower or behold the starry heavens or think about the vast reaches of the universe. . . . Upon reading the Bible, one may be impressed with a deep sense that God is speaking to him. Upon having done what I know is cheap, or wrong, or wicked, I may feel guilty in God's sight and form the belief *God disapproves of what I have done*. Upon confession and repentance I may feel forgiven, forming the belief *God forgives me for what I have done*.[17]

There are more examples, but these suffice to make the point. What Plantinga is saying, clearly, is that under certain conditions one may have an *experience* of God's majestic wisdom in creation, or of God's speaking to one through the Bible, or of God's disapproval of one's sins and his subsequent forgiveness. And when one does have such an experience, it may be entirely appropriate and rational to believe, in a basic way, the kinds of propositions cited in the examples above. There are, furthermore, a few points that should be noted about these examples: First, in the examples it is not, strictly speaking, the belief that *God exists* that is properly basic but rather certain other beliefs, about what God does or has done, and says or has said. But of course, none of those other beliefs could be true if God did *not* exist, so the difference is relatively minor. Second, it is important to be clear that the beliefs in the examples are all held in a *basic* way. I do not, for example, first examine the flower, then form certain beliefs about its structure and functioning, and then go through a process of reasoning (no doubt some version of the Teleological Argument) and reach the conclusion, on the basis of all this, that something with the design and function of that flower must have been created by a divine being. I might do that on some other occasion, of course, but in Plantinga's example I simply look at the flower and *see* it as God's creature — or, what amounts to the same thing, I see that God created it. And finally, note that the experiences cited in the examples are not rare and dramatic occurrences — the sorts of thing that might happen to Moses, Mohammed, the apostle Paul, or St. Francis of Assisi but not to ordinary men or women. Rather, they are the kinds of experience that are had by many, perhaps by most, religious believers at some time or other, and by some rather frequently.[18]

The point we have come to, then, is this: The belief that God exists, and other beliefs about God, are rightly and reasonably held in a basic way by one who finds that she *experiences* God's presence and activities. (Remember

Simone Weil's description of her experience at the beginning of this chapter!)
This conclusion, if correct, is an important one, and requires the revision of a
great deal of thinking in the philosophy of religion. It seems clear, furthermore, that the conclusion is one that calls for further discussion and investigation. For this, we turn to William P. Alston.

Alston on Perceiving God

Already in Chapter 2 we have considered Alston's argument for the similarity
of religious experience to sense perception. His basic thesis about the role of
religious experience in religious knowledge is that "the experience, or, as I shall
say, the *perception* of God plays an epistemic role with respect to beliefs about
God importantly analogous to that played by sense perception with respect to
beliefs about the physical world."[19] Evidently this is a strong claim, one with
sweeping implications. To be sure, Alston does not want to claim that religious
experience is our *only* way of knowing about God, any more than sense perception is our only way of knowing about the physical world. (Scientific reasoning,
for example, carries us to conclusions about the world that go far beyond those
justified by sense perception alone.) But sense perception is the *essential basis*
for our knowledge about the physical world, and in a somewhat similar way
religious experience is the essential basis for our knowledge of God. In each
case, certain "basic" beliefs are justified directly by the experience in question,
and then various reasoning processes are used in order to justify other beliefs,
which go beyond what is "perceived." The kinds of religious beliefs that are
justified by religious experience Alston calls *M-beliefs* (for "manifestation");
they are beliefs about "What God is doing, or how God is 'situated,' vis-à-vis
that subject at that moment. Thus by experiencing the presence and activity of
God *S* can come to know (justifiably believe) that God is sustaining her in
being, filling her with His love, strengthening her, or communicating a certain
message to her."[20]

Now it is evident that very many religious believers do in fact have experiences that indicate to them that God is relating to them in some or all of the
ways mentioned. Among philosophers, however, there has been a strong inclination to think that these experiences cannot be taken at face value. At the very
least, one would need to have *independent reason* to believe that God exists and
that he might be doing some of these things, before it would be reasonable to
believe that the experiences are what they seem to be. The experiences by
themselves cannot bear the weight of justifying our beliefs.

Alston thinks this is wrong—that it shows arbitrariness and prejudice
against religious experience to say that it cannot stand on its own in justifying
religious beliefs. And much of his discussion is directed to defending this point,
and to showing that if we accept sense perception as the basic justification for
our beliefs about the physical world, then as a matter of fairness and reasonableness we ought to accept religious experience as the justification for beliefs
about God.

Why might one think that religious experience is *not* on a par with sense experience as a means of justification? One such reason is given in the assertion that "one doesn't really *experience* God, one is aware of some intense subjective feeling of elation, rapture, or whatever, which one *interprets* as due to the presence of God. One has to have independent support for that interpretation if one is to be justified in supposing God to be present to one."[21] This objection is saying, in effect, that beliefs about God's presence and activity must be considered as *derived* beliefs; the *basic* beliefs, which alone are directly justi-fied by the experience, are beliefs about one's own psychological states.

But of course, exactly the same thing can be said about sense experience. When you seem to see a tree, that fact by itself (according to this view) does not justify your claiming to know anything about a *tree*; all you can claim on the basis of that experience is that you do have that sort of experience. In order to know that there is a real tree, a physical object, before you, you need an argument to justify your "interpretation" of your experience.

This, as we have noted, is exactly what was said about sense experience by the adherents of strong foundationalism — with disastrous results. If it takes an *argument* to justify reasoning from my "tree-experience" to the existence of a real tree, then it seems pretty clear that no such argument can be found and our belief in the existence of trees is merely a superstition. Of course this is absurd, which is one reason why strong foundationalism must be given up. But — and this is the important point in the present context — it will not do to give up strong foundationalism for trees but keep it for God! M-beliefs are not *inferred from* our religious experiences, they are *directly justified* by those experiences. At least, this is the view we ought to take unless some strong argument *disquali-fies* religious experience as a way of knowing, and Alston does not think there is any successful argument of this kind.

It needs to be kept in mind that in saying that M-beliefs are *directly justified* by religious experience (that, in Plantinga's terminology, they are "properly basic" beliefs), Alston is not asserting that all such beliefs are *true*. For M-beliefs as for ordinary perceptual beliefs, there can be good reasons to conclude that "things are not as they seem." In certain circumstances it may look to me as though water is running uphill, but other things I know about the world keep me from accepting that as the truth. And if I tell you that (for example) God has ordered me to kill all Presbyterians, you will rightly disbe-lieve my "revelation" on the ground that God would not give me any such command as that. This situation is best described by saying that experience provides a *prima facie* justification for our beliefs,[22] which is to say that such beliefs should be accepted *unless there is compelling reason to think they are false*. And this is true both for perceptual beliefs and for M-beliefs.

It may seem, however, that we have good reason to think that sense percep-tion is more likely to be reliable than religious experience. What we perceive with our senses shows a great deal of consistency between different observers, so long as they are not impaired in some way. Also, sense experience gives us a precise and detailed knowledge of physical things in the world, and enables us to make predictions about them with considerable accuracy. None of this is true of religious experience. Many people fail to have any such experiences.

Among those who do have them, different people—especially people in different cultures and religions—experience God as having contradictory characteristics, and there is no readily available way to resolve these conflicts. In particular, there is no way to make predictions that are precise enough to serve as confirmations of religious beliefs.

Alston acknowledges the truth in these complaints, yet he maintains they do not undermine religious experience as a source of justification for M-beliefs. Rather, he argues, the differences point to ways in which our situation over against God is different from our situation with regard to physical objects. We could not expect to have the kind of thorough, detailed, knowledge of God that we have of ordinary physical things; God is too great and mysterious, too far beyond us, for that to be possible. In the same way it is out of the question to suppose we should be able to predict God's actions—or to run a "controlled experiment" on God. As to the fact that many people seem not to have such experiences, it is in keeping with the teachings of the major religions that "God has decreed that a human being will be aware of His presence in any clear and unmistakable fashion only when certain special and difficult conditions are satisfied."[23] These conditions, of course, pertain to the religious life, and those who make no effort to satisfy them have no reason to complain if they do not have such experiences.

Of all these objections, it would seem that the most difficult ones for Alston (and also Plantinga, though he has so far shown less interest in this aspect of the problem) to deal with are those based on the fact that persons in different cultures and different religious traditions conceive of God—and, apparently, experience God—in quite different ways. One of the most striking differences, though by no means the only one, is the difference between theistic religions, in which God is experienced as a personal being with whom one can enter into a personal relationship, and religions, such as the advaita form of Hinduism, that conceive of God as an impersonal unity and maintain that the ultimate form of religious enlightenment is to experience the fact that there simply *is no difference* between oneself and God: "That *you* are, Shvetaketu."

Now, suppose that what Alston has argued so far is correct, and that religious experience does provide *prima facie* justification for M-beliefs. Then of course the question must be asked, *whose* experience and *whose* M-beliefs? It may be, of course, that both the theist's M-belief that she is in loving communion with a personal God and the advaitist's M-belief that he is indistinguishable from Brahman are *prima facie* justified. But these beliefs cannot both be *true*, and one's whole religious way of life will be dramatically different depending on which one is accepted. On what basis should the choice be made?

This whole matter will come up for discussion in Chapter 12 on "Religious Pluralism." Here we must limit ourselves to mentioning a few of the ways in which the Reformed epistemologist might respond to this question. One possibility would be to say that the differences between religions are not as significant as is generally thought, that they all "really" are saying the same thing. This, however, is not a very promising line to take, in view of the magnitude of the differences that exist. It seems necessary, then, to give some reason why the understanding of God in one's own tradition is more likely to be correct than its rivals. Perhaps this can be done by showing that the rival view is ultimately incoherent — this is often said, for example, of the monistic-pantheistic scheme of advaita. Another possibility is suggested by Alston when he says, "It may be that some religious ways of life fulfill their own promises more fully than others."[24] Or, one might argue for the superiority of one's own faith-tradition on the basis of what is claimed to be divine action in history — Christians, for instance, have often argued in this way based on the resurrection of Jesus. There are many possibilities, too many even to list all of them here, let alone evaluate each one. But whatever route is taken, it seems likely that we will be involved in some kind of an appeal to evidence and will not be able to remain content with "basic beliefs" resting directly on religious experience.[25] It seems, in fact, that Alston now accepts this; he has written:

> The knowledgeable and reflective Christian should be concerned . . . [and] should do whatever seems feasible to search for common ground on which to adjudicate the crucial differences between the world religions, seeking a way to show in a non-circular way which of the contenders is correct. What success will attend these efforts I do not presume to predict. Perhaps it is only in God's good time that a more thorough insight into the truth behind these divergent perspectives will be revealed to us.[26]

Observations

At this point it may be helpful to make a few observations summarizing the significance of what has been presented, and connecting Reformed epistemology with other themes in the philosophy of religion. It would seem that the central and most important claim of Reformed epistemology is that religious experience plays an *independent role* in the justification of religious beliefs; it does not require a prior *argument* showing that such experience is reliable. Furthermore, the beliefs grounded in religious experience are *basic* beliefs, just as the beliefs grounded in sense experience are basic beliefs. These claims are summed up in Plantinga's assertion that beliefs about God can be "properly basic" and Alston's claim that in our religious experience we are "perceiving God." Whether these claims are correct the reader must decide for herself. It does seem that in deciding this question, an important role is played by one's willingness (or unwillingness, as the case may be) to give up the goal of a "universal method" for reaching philosophical agreement, and to accept that the different starting points and belief-commitments of philosophers may give rise to disagreements that cannot be decided by means of a common philosophical rationality.

Even if the Reformed epistemologist's basic claim is accepted, and religious experiences are viewed as playing a crucial role in the justification of religious beliefs, there remains the important problem created by differences of religious experiences, and the interpretations of those experiences, in different religious traditions. As we have seen, Alston now concedes that, faced with this situation, the believer may be forced to appeal to evidence and arguments that lie outside the sphere of what is directly experienced.

The abandonment of "neutral rationality" has often been associated with fideism, and Reformed epistemology is sometimes considered to be a form of fideism.[27] But this does not seem correct, at least when "fideism" is defined as in the present text. The Reformed epistemologist does not consider his fundamental beliefs as being exempted from rational evaluation; rather, he welcomes such evaluation. He is, however, concerned not to allow the rules for the discussion to be set in ways that prejudice the result against theism — as, for example, by strong foundationalism.

Is Reformed epistemology indifferent to evidence? Again, clearly not. Reformed epistemologists are very concerned to consider, and answer, evidence and arguments *against* the existence of God — for example, the problem of evil. Indeed, their position requires them to do so, because the justification conferred by religious experience is only *prima facie* justification; it could be overridden if there were compelling reasons, drawn from some other source, showing that the theistic God does *not* exist. So, Reformed epistemologists need to show that there are no such compelling reasons.

But how do Reformed epistemologists view arguments *for* the existence of God, such as the ones presented in this book? What is clear is that they hold such arguments to be *unnecessary* — one can be fully rational and justified in believing in God entirely apart from such arguments. But does this mean that there are not, in fact, good theistic arguments? Different Reformed epistemologists may hold different views about this; their basic position does not require them to answer the question one way or the other.[28] And they need not deny that such arguments might be quite useful; Plantinga, for instance, has said that "If there were some clearly valid arguments for the existence of God . . . these arguments could obviously serve as *confirmations* of the existence of God — for at least some believers. Further, such arguments could be useful in preparing the way for faith and in leading some people closer to it."[29] It is characteristic of Reformed epistemology, however, to hold that it is somehow *better* to believe in God in a basic way that does not depend on arguments. Plantinga has said that "the mature believer, the mature theist, does not typically accept belief in God tentatively, or hypothetically, or until something better comes along. Nor, I think, does he accept it as a conclusion from other things he believes; he . . . *commits* himself to belief in God; this means that he accepts belief in God as basic."[30] Probably we should not understand Plantinga here as saying that theists who believe in God in a nonbasic way are personally, emotionally, or intellectually immature. But they may in a sense be immature *as theists, as believers*, in that they have not yet come to believe in God in the way that is religiously most adequate and satisfying. Nevertheless, if one finds oneself unable, at a given juncture, to believe in God in a basic way, clearly the right thing to do would be to avail oneself of good arguments, if there are any, in order, as Plantinga says, to "prepare the way for faith."

Perhaps more than any other topic in this book, Reformed epistemology is a recent arrival on the scene of philosophy of religion. It is too early for philosophical thought on this topic to have reached any stable resolution; what can confidently be said is that the topic will continue to be debated vigorously for many years to come.

STUDY QUESTIONS

1. What is your reaction to Simone Weil's experience, and her comments on it? After reading her account, are you inclined to agree that she was able to know with certainty that God exists?

2. What is evidentialism, and why does evidentialism tend to be opposed to religious belief?

3. What is foundationalism? What is a basic belief? What is a properly basic belief?

4. Explain what strong foundationalism is, and discuss the reasons that have led philosophers to embrace strong foundationalism.

5. Discuss the objections to strong foundationalism as given in the text. Do these objections strike you as convincing?

6. Explain the Reformed epistemologists' reasons for saying it can be reasonable to believe in God even if there are no good arguments for God's existence.

7. Is it reasonable to say that, just as in sensory experience we perceive physical objects, in religious experience we perceive God? Why, or why not?

8. How can Reformed epistemology deal with the objection that, whereas everyone has sensory experience of physical objects, many people do not have religious experiences in which they perceive God? Does the answer to this objection strike you as satisfactory? Discuss.

9. How can Reformed epistemologists deal with the problem of the conflicting ideas of God in different religions? Is their solution to this problem satisfactory? Discuss.

10. Is the belief that God exists a properly basic belief?

NOTES

1. Simone Weil, *Waiting for God*, trans. Emma Craufurd (New York: Harper & Row, 1973), p. 24.
2. Weil, p. 212.
3. This connection is brought out in Alvin Plantinga, "The Reformed Objection to Natural Theology," *Christian Scholar's Review* 11 (1982): 187–98; reprinted in Hen-

drik Hart, Johan Van Der Hoeven, and Nicholas Wolterstorff, eds., *Rationality in the Calvinian Tradition* (Lanham, MD: University Press of America, 1983), pp. 363–83.

4. From the Introduction to Alvin Plantinga and Nicholas Wolterstorff, eds., *Faith and Rationality: Reason and Belief in God* (Notre Dame, IN: University of Notre Dame Press, 1983), p. 6.

5. There is some variety in the terminology used at this point; Wolterstorff and Plantinga speak of "classical foundationalism" and "modern foundationalism." Sometimes, indeed, this view is simply referred to as "foundationalism" without a qualifier, but this tends to be confusing; as we shall see, the Reformed epistemologists are themselves foundationalists of a certain kind.

6. There is also, to be sure, the question about *how* one belief may support another — what sorts of arguments are used to show this, and so on. This is an important topic, but it is also quite complex and will not be discussed further here.

7. The reader may notice a similarity between strong foundationalism and *strong rationalism*, as discussed in Chapter 3; strong foundationalism is, in fact, the leading variety of strong rationalism.

8. See Alvin Plantinga, "Coherentism and the Evidentialist Objection to Belief in God," in Robert Audi and William J. Wainwright, eds., *Rationality, Religious Belief, and Moral Commitment* (Ithaca, NY: Cornell University Press, 1986), pp. 109–38; also, Plantinga's "Replies," in James E. Tomberlin and Peter Van Inwagen, eds., *Alvin Plantinga*, Profiles Volume 5 (Dordrecht, Netherlands: D. Riedel, 1985), pp. 390–93.

9. Roderick Chisholm, *Theory of Knowledge* (Englewood Cliffs, NJ: Prentice-Hall, 1966), p. 57.

10. Gary Gutting, "The Catholic and the Calvinist: A Dialogue on Faith and Reason," *Faith and Philosophy* 2 (1985): 241. It should be noted that, because this article is in dialogue form, one cannot automatically assume that what is said by the participants reflects the author's own view. We believe, however, that this speech of "Catholic" does reflect Gutting's view on this point. (For confirmation, see the following quotation.)

11. Gary Gutting, *Religious Belief and Religious Skepticism* (Notre Dame, IN: University of Notre Dame Press, 1982), p. 83. (*Note:* We have emended the text of this quotation, with the author's agreement; the printed version actually reads, "widespread agreement.")

12. Alvin Plantinga, "Reason and Belief in God," in Plantinga and Wolterstorff, eds., p. 77.

13. The idea that philosophical and other scholarly work is deeply shaped by prior world-view commitments is one of the important ideas which "Reformed epistemology" takes from the Reformed tradition of Christian theology. This idea, of course, fits well with the approach of "critical rationalism" as discussed in Chapter Three.

14. Plantinga, "Reason and Belief in God," p. 78.

15. Philip Quinn, "On Finding the Foundations of Theism," *Faith and Philosophy* 2 (1985): 473.

16. Plantinga, "The Foundations of Theism: A Reply," *Faith and Philosophy* 3 (1986): 303.

17. Plantinga, "Reason and Belief in God," p. 80.

18. This point has led to yet another objection, which, because of its somewhat technical nature, is relegated to a note. In Plantinga's view it would be correct to say that the basic belief that (for example) "God has created this flower" is *grounded in* the experience of seeing the flower in that particular way, even though there is no

evidence for the belief (because, as Plantinga is using "evidence," evidence must consist of *another belief* that is the basis of the belief in question).

Now, this has led Philip Quinn (among others) to make the following point: Whenever I *do in fact* hold such a belief as "God has created this flower" in a basic way, it would also be *equally possible* for me to *infer* this belief, using as one of my premises "It seems to me that God has created this flower." And my belief in God as creator of the flower would be *equally justified* whether it is basic or inferred (derived). And this, it seems, tends to undercut the importance of the question, whether such beliefs are basic or nonbasic. As Quinn says:

> Although such propositions [as "God has created this flower"] would not need to be based on the evidence of other propositions, they always could be so based. So the cautious philosopher who did so base them would be every bit as justified in believing in the existence of God as the reckless mystic who did not. (Quinn, p. 479).

Plantinga's reply ("The Foundations of Theism: A Reply," *Faith and Philosophy* 3 [1986]: 303–6) centers on the following point: In general, it simply *is not true* that experientially grounded basic beliefs could also be held in a nonbasic way without loss of justification. All of us, under certain circumstances, will believe in a basic way such propositions as "There is a tree here before me." Now, could one with equal justification *infer* this belief from "There seems to be a tree before me"? The answer, drawn from the history of philosophical reflection on this topic, seems to be, definitely not! For in order to do this, one would have to *justify* the inference from the "seems" statement to the "is" statement—and this amounts to solving the problem of the "proof of the external world," surely one of the hoariest and most resistant to solution of all philosophical problems. Yet there is no reasonable doubt (skeptics aside) that our *basic* beliefs about trees and the like are fully justified. And in the same way, basic beliefs about God may be fully justified even if *arguments* designed to show God's existence are uniformly unsuccessful.

19. William P. Alston, "Perceiving God," *Journal of Philosophy* 83 (1986): 655.
20. Alston.
21. This quotation is taken from a longer version of the paper "Perceiving God"; it is not included in the version published in the *Journal of Philosophy*. Used by permission of William P. Alston.
22. *Prima facie* means "at first view"; *prima facie* evidence is evidence that is sufficient to establish a conclusion, unless it is rebutted by stronger contrary evidence.
23. William P. Alston, "Christian Experience and Christian Belief," in Plantinga and Wolterstorff, eds., p. 129.
24. Alston, "Christian Experience," p. 129.
25. For further discussion of the need for evidence at this point, see William Hasker, "On Justifying the Christian Practice," *The New Scholasticism* 60 (Spring, 1986): 129–144; also David Basinger, "Plantinga on Justified Religious Belief: Some Misgivings," *Faith and Philosophy*, forthcoming.
26. William P. Alston, "Religious Diversity and Perceptual Knowledge of God," *Faith and Philosophy* 5 (1988): 446.
27. For instance, by William J. Abraham, *An Introduction to the Philosophy of Religion* (Englewood Cliffs, NJ: Prentice-Hall, 1985), pp. 88–97.
28. Plantinga's views on this point seem to be softening. He has always maintained that none of the theistic arguments are successful when judged by the standards of strong foundationalism or of classical natural theology—but then, there are no successful arguments for *any* interesting philosophical conclusions that meet those excessively high standards. But if we are willing to lower our sights a little, and

accept arguments whose premises are acceptable to many sensible people if not to all, then some very interesting arguments are available. Plantinga himself has on several occasions delivered a lecture entitled "Two Dozen (Or So) Theistic Arguments"! (For the publication of this material we must await the volume containing Plantinga's Gifford Lectures, delivered at the University of Aberdeen in 1987 and 1988.)

29. Alvin Plantinga, "The Reformed Objection Revisited," *Christian Scholar's Review* 12 (1983): 58.
30. Alvin Plantinga, "Is Belief in God Rational?" in C. F. Delaney, ed., *Rationality and Religious Belief* (Notre Dame, IN: University of Notre Dame Press, 1979), p. 27.

SUGGESTED READING

Alston, William P. "Christian Experience and Christian Belief." Alvin Plantinga and Nicholas Wolterstorff, eds., *Faith and Rationality: Reason and Belief in God.* Notre Dame, IN: University of Notre Dame Press, 1983, pp. 103–34.

———. "Perceiving God," *Journal of Philosophy* 83 (1986): 655–65.

———. "Religious Diversity and Perceptual Knowledge of God," *Faith and Philosophy* 5 (1988): 433–48.

Boyle, Joseph, J. Hubbard, and Thomas Sullivan. "The Reformed Objection to Natural Theology: A Catholic Perspective," *Christian Scholar's Review* 11 (1982): 199–211.

Gutting, Gary. *Religious Belief and Religious Skepticism.* Notre Dame, IN: University of Notre Dame Press, 1982.

———. "The Catholic and the Calvinist: A Dialogue on Faith and Reason," *Faith and Philosophy* 2 (1985): 236–56.

Hasker, William. "On Justifying the Christian Practice," *The New Scholasticism* 60 (Spring, 1986): 129–44.

Plantinga, Alvin. "Is Belief in God Rational?" C. F. Delaney, ed., *Rationality and Religious Belief.* Notre Dame, IN: University of Notre Dame Press, 1979, pp. 7–27.

———. "The Reformed Objection to Natural Theology," *Christian Scholar's Review* 11 (1982): 187–98.

———. "The Reformed Objection Revisited," *Christian Scholar's Review* 12 (1983): 57–61.

———. "Reason and Belief in God." Alvin Plantinga and Nicholas Wolterstorff, eds., *Faith and Rationality: Reason and Belief in God.* Notre Dame, IN: University of Notre Dame Press, 1983, pp. 16–93.

———. "Replies." James E. Tomberlin and Peter Van Inwagen, eds., *Alvin Plantinga,* Profiles Volume 5. Dordrecht, Netherlands: D. Reidel, 1985, pp. 390–93.

———. "The Foundations of Theism: A Reply," *Faith and Philosophy* 3 (1986): 298–313.

———. "Coherentism and the Evidentialist Objection to Belief in God." Robert Audi and William J. Wainwright, eds., *Rationality, Religious Belief, and Moral Commitment.* Ithaca, NY: Cornell University Press, 1986, pp. 109–38.

Quinn, Philip. "On Finding the Foundations of Theism," *Faith and Philosophy* 2 (1985): 469–86.

Wolterstorff, Nicholas. "Can Belief in God Be Rational If It Has No Foundations?" Alvin Plantinga and Nicholas Wolterstorff, eds., *Faith and Rationality: Reason and Belief in God.* Notre Dame, IN: University of Notre Dame Press, 1983, pp. 135–86.

8

Religious Language:
How Can We Speak
Meaningfully of God?

A fascinating science fiction story portrays a high lama purchasing a Mark V Automatic Sequence Computer to install in his monastery in Tibet. However, the lama requested that the computer be modified to print out letters and not numbers. The curious purpose of all this, as he expressed it, was to accelerate the completion of a list of all of the names of God that his monks were compiling. A task that would originally have taken another fifteen centuries would now take only one hundred days. When sequences of letters were systematically combined in a special alphabet, all of the real names of God would eventually be listed. It was not long until the computer had been installed in the lamasery in the mountains of Tibet. George and Chuck, the two engineers sent to oversee its operation, were about to go stir-crazy watching the monks tirelessly pasting long strips of names into books.

When Chuck was finally able to inform the high lama that the machine was on its last cycle, he received such an enthusiastic response that he inquired further into the religious significance of the computer's activity. "Well," said the lama, "they believe that when they have listed all His names — and they reckon that there are about nine billion of them — God's purpose will be achieved. The human race will have finished what it was created to do, and there won't be any point in carrying on." Chuck later relayed this incredible story to George, "when the list's completed, God steps in and simply winds things up . . . bingo!" At the thought that the end of the project would be the end of the world, George gave a nervous little laugh. Thinking the matter over, the two Americans realized if the world did not end when the project was finished, it could mean trouble for them at the hands of hundreds of angry monks whose lifework would have been spoiled by a computer. They made plans to leave "Project Shangri-La," as they called it, before the computer finished its last long series of names. On the evening of the last day, Chuck and George said good-by to the monks and rode the tough mountain ponies down the winding road from the lamasery toward the old DC3 that was waiting for them at the end of the runway. They descended the mountain in the cold, perfectly clear Himalayan night, ablaze with the now familiar stars:

> George glanced at his watch.
>
> "Should be there in an hour," he called back over his shoulder to Chuck. Then he added, in an afterthought: "Wonder if the computer's finished its run. It was due about now."
>
> Chuck didn't reply, so George swung round in his saddle. He could just see Chuck's face, a white oval turned toward the sky.
>
> "Look," whispered Chuck, and George lifted his eyes to heaven. (There is always a last time for everything.)
>
> Overhead, without any fuss, the stars were going out.[1]

Human Language and the Infinite

The story reminds us of the universal preoccupation with language about God — from the primitive who thinks that naming the divine gives magical power, to the intellectual who ponders how human words can appropriately apply to deity. In the twentieth century, philosophers have become particularly concerned with the nature and role of language in general, and have developed a number of different theories about religious language in particular.

There are two major reasons that philosophers pay close attention to religious language. One is that they are interested in questions of *meaning*, and thus in how words about God derive their meaning. For example, the language the Judeo-Christian tradition employs to talk about God is drawn from ordinary discourse, from the language we use daily to speak of common and familiar things. Expressions such as "God is my rock and my salvation" and "David did what was right in the eyes of the Lord" are plentiful in religious discourse. Philosophers naturally seek an account of how it is that words used to speak of creaturely phenomena make sense when applied to God. Does not the Judeo-Christian tradition teach that the Creator is not the creature, that he is "high and lifted up" — indeed that God is "transcendent"? How can language about the finite realm refer to God? We know what we mean when we speak, for instance, of ordinary rocks and ordinary eyes, but what can it mean to speak of God as being a "rock," or as having "eyes," since rocks and eyes are mere creaturely realities.

Another reason for the intense interest philosophers have shown in religious language is that they seek to analyze and evaluate *beliefs*. Beliefs, of course, are expressed in the form of *statements* or *propositions*. Understanding the language in which various religious beliefs are couched is crucial to a complete understanding of the beliefs themselves and a prelude to further philosophical scrutiny. Of course, much religious language is not used to make direct assertions of belief, but is instead used for a variety of distinctively religious purposes, such as prayer, liturgy, and admonition. Yet philosophers know that other religious uses of language rest upon or assume certain prior beliefs. Worshiping God, for instance, assumes that there is such a being as God and that he is worthy of our adoration and devotion, petitioning God presupposes that God actually hears and responds to prayer, and so forth. When the precise beliefs behind these and other religious activities are made explicit, we have a set of *theological statements*—truth-claims about God and his relationship to the world. So, once we grasp the meaning of theological terms and, in turn, of the theological statements in which they appear, we can ask questions about what rational grounds one could have for accepting or rejecting those statements. While other chapters in this book concentrate on such matters as whether there is rational justification for certain theological claims—such as "God exists" or "God is perfectly good"—here we examine the meaning of theological discourse itself.

The Theory of Analogy

The great medieval thinkers were well aware of the problem of using creaturely language to speak of God. They did not question whether religious language has any meaning, but realized the difficult problem of accounting for its meaning. Thomas Aquinas (c. 1224–1274) developed the famous, and now classic, theory of "analogy" or "analogical predication" as a solution to the problem—a theory that has received fresh attention by some modern thinkers.

A predicate term in a sentence attaches some property, relation, or activity to the subject term. Thus, predicates define or characterize the subject in particular ways. Typical examples of the sorts of statements employed in both academic theology and popular religion are not difficult to find:

> God created the heavens and the earth.
> The Lord is my Shepherd.
> God brought the Israelites out of Egypt.
> Yahweh spoke to the prophets.
> God is just.

Aquinas held that when a word—say, the word *just*—is applied both to a created being and to God, it is not being used *univocally* (i.e., with the exact same meaning) in the two instances. Yet, neither is the word being used *equivocally* (i.e., with two completely different meanings), as when "hot" is used to apply to peppercorns and race cars. There is a connection between divine justice and human justice, a similarity between a certain quality in God and a certain quality in persons. Because of this similarity, the predicate term *just* is not used equivocally, but because of the differences between God and finite human beings, it is not used univocally either. As Aquinas indicates, the word is used *analogically*.[2] It is the similarity within difference and difference within similarity that allow the analogical use of the same term in two different contexts.

James Ross (1927–) believes that the traditional analogy theory provides, as intended, a helpful middle way between the univocal and equivocal uses of terms when speaking of God, and thus avoids *anthropomorphism* and *agnosticism*, respectively. Used here, anthropomorphism is the view that God differs from creatures merely in degree and thus that no alteration of meaning in our terms is necessary to speak of him; agnosticism is the view that God is so different from us that we cannot say anything intelligible about him at all. So, the promise of the analogy theory is that we can actually express truths about God in human language while never having to suppose that he has anything precisely in common with creatures.

Ross admits, however, that the theory of analogy is a very complicated matter that has already received volumes of commentary and still deserves careful discussion. Drawing from various passages in Aquinas, we can discern a sophisticated theory of analogy, which Ross attempts to augment and systematically present in terms of modern semantic analysis. As does Aquinas, Ross takes it to be obvious that ordinary terms already have meaning when used appropriately in religious contexts, and hence offers the theory of analogy as a positive account of how meaning is transferred from ordinary contexts to religious ones. Such transfers of meaning plainly occur in a multitude of common situations where we are already familiar with the objects and qualities involved, making analogy part of the structure of ordinary discourse in general that must be explained by an overall theory of language. Consider the multitude of ordinary cases in which we say such things as "Susan's anger is volcanic" or "the fox is very clever." The peculiarity of a theory of religious language is that it must describe the transfer of meaning from contexts in which terms are used to speak of the familiar, observable realities of the creaturely realm to contexts in which those terms speak of God and spiritual realities.

In neither ordinary contexts nor religious contexts can we simply employ any alleged analogy we choose. There are constraints built into our language for how a term can be used analogously. Aquinas and other Scholastic philosophers stated these constraints in terms of rules for analogy, with the rule called the *analogy of proper proportionality* considered to be the basis of the meaning of religious language.

The assumption underlying this form of analogy is that there are similarities between God's attributes and activities and human attributes and activities. In the two statements "Socrates is wise" and "God is wise," Socrates is said to stand in a certain relationship to some activity called *being wise* in a way similar to that in which God stands to his activity called *being wise*. The term "being wise" is employed with respect to God because we recognize the similarity of his activity we call *being wise* to that of a creature's activity of *being wise*. Yet the reason the term "being wise" is not univocal in the two statements rests on the difference between the two modes of being that are exemplified by a human and God. Socrates is wise in the manner in which a human person is wise, in a way appropriate to his distinct creaturely mode of being, which is finite; God, too, is wise in a way appropriate to his mode of being, which is infinite. Thus God and creatures have qualities or engage in activities in proportion, so to speak, to their respective modes of being.

This sort of shift in meaning occurs in many contexts. The statements "Fido is faithful" and "John is faithful," for example, exhibit a shift in the type of faithfulness. Although there is a similar relationship here, it is not the same relationship, because the mode of faithfulness possessed by Fido is different from that possessed by John. But there is a perceivable likeness in patterns of behavior that allows us to use the same term for both animal and human. The same rule of proper proportionality holds in myriad other contexts.

Frederick Ferré as well as other critics of the analogy of proper proportionality maintain that the theory is completely unable to provide any substantive knowledge of God. In our example, it is given that God's nature, as we shall say, is "infinite" and that one of his attributes is "wisdom." Then the formula of the analogy becomes something like the following:

$$\frac{\text{God's wisdom}}{\text{God's infinite nature}} = \frac{\text{Socrates' wisdom}}{\text{Socrates' finite nature}}$$

However, as Ferré asserts, the theory "cannot move a step toward explaining the 'givens' of its own formulation, nor can it explain the possibility of the independent, nonanalogical knowledge on which they depend."[3] In other words, this kind of analogy has not one but two unknowns—God's wisdom and God's infinite nature. And Ferré thinks that we just cannot have any positive knowledge of these matters.

Ross points out that this criticism distorts the theory by interpreting it on a simply mathematical model that is presented in pseudo-mathematical terms. The very purpose of Aquinas was to make the meaningfulness of religious language obvious and clear by pointing out its similarity to everyday language, with all of its nuances and degrees of connotation—not by stipulating some exact mathematical relationship. Besides, as Ross observes, such mathematical modeling of the theory results in confusing Aquinas's use of analogy as a *theory of meaning* with a *theory of inference* in which analogy is used to lead to some knowledge about God, a pattern of argument that Aquinas never used. Aquinas simply did not intend this theory of meaning to be an avenue of arriving at information about God.[4]

Ross thus defends the doctrine of analogy not as purporting to spell out the concrete character of God's perfections or attributes, but only as explaining how predicates applied to God have meaning. Equipped with this theory of meaning, we can understand what assertions about God mean and thereby avoid fatal equivocation when we do construct arguments about God.

The theory of analogy merits much further discussion.[5] Questions must be faced, say, about whether the notion of "similarity" can be given any clear definition or about how the important medieval doctrine of divine simplicity affects the way analogy is construed. But the fact remains that religious language has historically been believed to be meaningful and that the theory of analogy has been a widely accepted account of its meaning. It is only in the contemporary period that wholesale challenges to the meaningfulness of religious language have been waged.

Problems of Meaning and Verification

Although traditional philosophers of religion had never seriously doubted that it is possible to speak meaningfully of God, early in this century, a group of philosophers known as *logical positivists* strongly questioned this confidence. They developed a theory that ties the meaning of language to empirical observation. Taking science to be the best representation of careful, testable language, the logical positivists constructed a standard or criterion by which we could judge those statements that are cognitively meaningful and those that are not. A. J. Ayer (1910–1989) expressed it in this way:

> The criterion which we use to test the genuineness of apparent statements of fact is the criterion of verifiability. We say that a sentence is factually significant to any given person, if, and only if, he knows how to verify the proposition which it purports to express — that is, if he knows what observations would lead him, under certain conditions, to accept the proposition as being true, or reject it as being false.[6]

Restating what came to be called the "verifiability principle" in a slightly different manner, we get: *a statement is a genuine factual assertion if, and only if, there could be empirically observable states of affairs that would show it to be either true or false.*[7] As the positivists would say, statements that are not empirically verifiable are simply not cognitively meaningful. For them, language has *cognitive* meaning only if it speaks of matters for which it is in principle possible to give empirical evidence, matters about which questions of truth and falsity make sense. Such language, then, has *factual* or *informative* status or significance, and thus can be properly understood.

Positivists and their intellectual followers thought that the verifiability principle handled scientific language as well as much of our ordinary talk. But they thought that theological language failed to meet the empirical standard of verifiability and thus is pure nonsense.[8] If this is correct, then attempts to defend theism — and indeed any ordinary religious utterances — are totally improper, because the language in which they are couched is nonsense. Likewise, traditional attacks on theism, using the same language, of course, are just as meaningless.

Antony Flew (1923–   ) expressed the positivist challenge in the form of a "falsifiability principle," which grew out of continued attempts to refine and articulate the basic point of the positivists' view of cognitive meaning. He develops his colorful challenge from a tale entitled "Gods" by John Wisdom (1904–   ):

> Once upon a time two explorers came upon a clearing in the jungle. In the clearing were growing many flowers and many weeds. One explorer says, "Some gardener must tend this plot." The other disagrees, "There is no gardener." So they pitch their tents and set a watch. No gardener is ever seen. "But perhaps he is an invisible gardener." So they set up a barbed-wire fence. They electrify it. They patrol with bloodhounds. (For they remember how H. G. Wells's *The Invisible Man* could be both smelt and touched though he could

not be seen.) But no shrieks ever suggest that some intruder has received a shock. No movements of the wire ever betray an invisible climber. The bloodhounds never give cry. Yet still the Believer is not convinced. "But there is a gardener, invisible, intangible, insensible to electric shocks, a gardener who has no scent and makes no sound, a gardener who comes secretly to look after the garden which he loves." At last the Skeptic despairs, "But what remains of your original assertion? Just how does what you call an invisible, intangible, eternally elusive gardener differ from an imaginary gardener or even from no gardener at all?"[9]

Flew contends that religious believers allow nothing to count against their claims, continually modifying and qualifying in order to prevent them from being falsified.

Flew's reasoning is straightforward. When the believer states that "God loves us as a father loves his children," we would expect divine help in times of serious trouble or disease. Yet God seems silent. So, the believer makes some qualification — "God's love is not like human love" or "it is an inscrutable love" — making misfortune and suffering compatible with the original theological pronouncement. In response to this maneuvering, Flew puts forth the central question: "What would have to occur or to have occurred to constitute for you a disproof of the love of, or of the existence of, God?"[10] The point is that if there is no state of affairs that would count against the original theological statement, then it is not really a genuine assertion at all. It says nothing, neither affirming nor denying that anything is actually the case. Flew contends that religious believers kill their own claims by a thousand qualifications.

The positivist critique prompted spirited discussion and debate. At stake is the question of the cognitive status of theological statements — in other words, whether they say anything meaningful. Most philosophers who agreed that the verification or falsification principle defines the issue essentially divided into two camps: those who thought that the theological language is meaningless, and those who thought that it could be shown meaningful on the basis of the principle.

Granting that religious language is cognitively meaningless, R. M. Hare (1919–   ) endorsed the view that religious utterances reveal a "blik," a term that he coined to denote a deeply rooted interpretation of the world that cannot be overturned by empirical observation.[11] He even devised a parable of his own about a lunatic who thought that all Oxford professors were out to kill him and who could not be dissuaded from his belief by appeal to numerous inoffensive and even friendly encounters with professors. Hare indicates that all persons have "bliks" that are not held at the level of factual claims and thus cannot be overturned by contrary facts. Bliks are ways of interpreting the facts.

According to Hare, the religious believer has a "blik" that God exists and that a certain religious way of life is correct, and nothing can change that confidence, not even seemingly contradictory evidence. Of course, Hare's position seems to be naive about the way facts and interpretations of the facts interact, for normal persons would almost certainly change their minds about the homicidal tendencies of Oxford professors or about the love of God in the face of certain circumstances in which their former interpretation clearly breaks down. So, for them, the theory of precritical bliks does not shed much light on the nature of religious language or explain adequately the features of religious utterance and belief that Flew identified as problematic.

Basil Mitchell (1917–) was among the philosophers who were convinced that religious utterances are cognitively meaningful according to the positivists' requirements. Also embedding his philosophical point within a parable, he tells a story about a member of a resistance movement meeting a stranger who impressed him very deeply: "The Stranger tells the partisan that he himself is on the side of the resistance—indeed that he is in command of it, and urges the partisan to have faith in him no matter what happens. The partisan is utterly convinced at the meeting of the Stranger's sincerity and constancy and undertakes to trust him."[12]

The two never met intimately again. Sometimes the Stranger is seen helping members of the resistance, and the partisan says to his friends, "He is on our side." But sometimes he is seen in the uniform of the police taking patriots into the custody of the occupying power. On these occasions the partisan's friends complain, but the partisan still says, "He is on our side." The partisan retains he confidence that, despite appearances, the Stranger did not deceive him. Sometimes his friends ask in exasperation, "What *would* he have to do for you to withdraw your confidence?" As Mitchell says,

> The partisan of the parable does not allow anything to count decisively against the proposition "The Stranger is on our side." This is because he has committed himself to trust the Stranger. But he of course recognizes that the Stranger's ambiguous behaviour *does* count against what he believes about him. It is precisely this situation which constitutes the trial of his faith.[13]

Mitchell's strategy is to show that certain facts, such as suffering, do count against theological claims, and thus that the claims are indeed factually significant.

For Mitchell, theological claims simply resemble other factually significant, nontheological claims (e.g., historical claims) in not being conclusively falsifiable. He emphasizes that there is no determinable point at which a given believer will relinquish his religious claims in light of contrary evidence. He rejects the notion that religious beliefs are merely tentative hypotheses that can be discarded or modified as events change, such as those that the physical scientists entertain. Instead he insists that religious beliefs are articles of faith that are not easily shaken. Mitchell's view appears to be much more realistic than Hare's about the characteristics of religious language. But while he indicates that believers recognize the pressure of negative evidence on their beliefs, it is questionable whether he explains exactly how a believer's degree of religious confidence is related to his assessment of the facts.

John Hick (1922–) attempted to go further than Mitchell by providing specific verification conditions for showing the factual significance of religious claims. Expounding what he calls "eschatological verification," Hick too tells a parable, of two travelers walking along a road, one who believes that the road leads to a Celestial City and one who believes that it leads nowhere. During the journey together, both men encounter moments of refreshment and delight as well as periods of hardship and danger. One interprets the good times as previews of heavenly bliss and the bad times as obstacles to make him worthy; the other considers the journey to be aimless rambling. During the journey, the issue between the two travelers is not an experimental one; it cannot be decided by empirical observation. "And yet when they do turn the last corner it will be apparent that one of them has been right all of the time and the other wrong. Thus, although the issue between them has not been experimental, it has nevertheless from the start been a real issue."[14] Since Hick takes the essence of verification to be "the exclusion of rational doubt," the afterlife, if it should be a reality, could contain experiences that would suffice to eliminate doubt. He is even prepared to specify what such experiences might be—social existence in the Kingdom of God and perhaps a strong sense of the presence of God.

The strength of Hick's approach lies in its taking verificational analysis to demand that the cognitive significance of statements derives from their being connected to relevant actual or possible observational experiences. He clearly provides a scenario in which religious statements are meaningful not by virtue of experiences available in temporal life, but by virtue of possible experiences in the afterlife. Of course, if there is no afterlife, then there will be no verification of religious claims. Technically, Hick may have satisfied the pure logic of a verification/falsification type of challenge, but one wonders what benefit it is to us at present to suppose that actual verification or falsification is located in the afterlife, which is something we cannot now experience.

For a number of reasons, the verification/falsification issue has receded into the background while other issues occupy the current attention of philosophers of religion. One reason is that all attempted formulations of principles of cognitive meaningfulness were not meaningful according to the very empirical standards they were supposed to express.[15] After all, no observational experiences could possibly verify this statement of the verification principle: *A statement is a genuine factual assertion if, and only if, there could be empirically observable states of affairs that would show it to be either true or false.* (Here, the verification principle of meaning encounters the problem of self-reference just as the criterion for foundational propositions becomes self-referentially incoherent, as shown in Chapter 7's discussion of strong foundationalism.) Another, somewhat ironic, reason for the demise of positivism was that its own principles of meaning did not make completely good sense of science. The history and practice of science is replete with cases in which scientists advanced and pondered claims—claims they took to be perfectly meaningful—for which they were at the time unable to specify exact verification or falsification conditions. The debate between the wave and corpuscular theories of light just begins the list of such cases. Positivism failed to describe correctly the ground of meaning not only for scientific statements, but also for numerous other kinds of statements that we ordinarily use and find meaningful (e.g., ethical statements).

While no longer a major position, the verification/falsification view presents us with a number of valuable lessons. For one, the whole concept of a fact needs serious review, particularly with respect to religion. Many religious believers rightly understand that there is a factual dimension to religious language for which positivism cannot account. Indeed key theological statements entail definite cosmological assertions that, while more complicated and less accessible than assertions about the physical realm, nonetheless purport to be large-scale facts about the way things are. The statement "God is always with his children," for example, when interpreted in context, entails the factual claim that "An invisible, eternal, omnipresent, omniscient spirit exists and somehow communes with and guides those who place their trust in him." After we have rejected positivism, it remains to be seen how we can best account for the factual significance of such statements. Another lesson is that religious language, regardless of how we account for its factual aspects, should not be interpreted exclusively as "fact-talk." Certain important uses of religious language, for example, closely resemble the kind of discourse we employ in talking of persons and interpersonal relationships (e.g., "I trust John").[16] One more lesson to be learned is that we must not confuse questions of *meaning* with questions of *truth*, as the positivists did. Settling the problem of how our statements have meaning cannot be made to depend on solving the quite different problem of how we can come to know their truth.

The Functions of Religious Discourse

Some thinkers thought that allowing positivism to set the framework for discussing religious language was simply wrong-headed, holding that questions of factual significance are either peripheral or irrelevant. For them, "God-talk" has other, more primary dimensions of significance. Refusing to engage in the verification/falsification debate, many of these philosophers turned their attention to what Frederick Ferré calls "functional analysis."[17] Following Ludwig Wittgenstein's (1889–1951) admonition to "look and see" the multifaceted aspects of language, they identified several important functions: *imperative* ("Bring me the glass"), *performative* ("I now pronounce you husband and wife"), and *interrogative* ("What time is it?"). It is inappropriate to apply the verification principle to such statements and yet they function perfectly well in our human linguistic commerce.

New and intriguing theories about the various functions of religious language or, better, of ordinary language used in religious contexts were pioneered. Rather than stipulate conditions of meaning that relate language to an external reality (as the positivists had tried to connect statements to observable states of affairs), functional analysts tried to understand the functioning of religious language. They sought to learn what kinds of tasks it performs. They came to see language as a complex social phenomenon that is adaptable to the ever-changing purposes of human beings. And religious language was seen, therefore, as serving certain unique human purposes. Although functional analysts who studied religious language differed among themselves on *the* basic function of religious language, a brief inspection of a few noteworthy studies is enlightening.

An early leader in this approach, R. B. Braithwaite (1900–   ), declared that religious utterances function essentially as *moral* statements. One distinctive feature of religious language is that it involves stories that picture and reinforce a moral way of life, such as the tale of the Good Samaritan or the various narratives of Jesus's compassion for people. While these religious stories may appear to be direct assertions of fact, they actually serve to express the intentions of the one uttering them to live morally. For Braithwaite, it is not necessary that the stories be true or that they even be believed to be true for them to fulfill their primary purpose. He takes the connection between the stories and a moral way of life to be "a psychological and causal one," based on the fact that most people find it naturally easier to act in a certain way if they associate their actions with certain stories.[18]

Braithwaite's analysis accents one important use of religious language: to express moral intentions and reinforce moral behavior. However, his attempt at functionally analyzing the language of religion simply transforms it into the language of morality embellished by stories—an error comparable to the positivistic mistake of trying to reduce religious statements to empirical facts.[19] Donald Hudson (1940–   ) has called this kind of mistake a violation of the "depth grammar" of religion, arguing that religious discourse has its own unique character and function.[20] The philosopher's task, then, is to clarify how religious language works, to expose its role.

Paul van Buren (1924–   ) developed an interpretation placing the language of Christianity "at the edges of language."[21] Following Wittgenstein, van Buren explains that human language is a complex phenomenon, consisting of many "language-games." The language-games metaphor points to identifiable linguistic behaviors employed by human beings in order to accomplish certain purposes: "Giving orders . . . Describing the appearance of an object . . . Speculating about an event . . . Forming and testing a hypothesis . . . Presenting the results of an experiment in tables and diagrams . . . Making up a story; and reading it . . . Play-acting . . . Singing catches . . . Guessing riddles . . . Making a joke; telling it . . . Solving a problem in practical arithmetic . . . Asking, thanking, cursing, greeting, praying."[22] Followers of Wittgenstein began to speak of the language of science, the language of romance and love, the language of ethics, the language of religion, and so forth. Each of these different linguistic activities occupies a definite region on the overall map of human language. Each language-game has rules or social understandings for how words function within its sphere. The word *solid*, for example, means one thing when speaking of solid bodies in physics, and something related to but distinct from this when speaking of a person's having a solid character in ethics. These rules for language-games, of course, are not written in any book, but are followed somewhat unconsciously by members of the linguistic communities involved. The rules, then, are there for philosophers to uncover.

In locating the language of Christianity on the linguistic map, van Buren writes of those areas of human speaking that are far from the "clear, rule-governed center" where misunderstandings seldom occur. He identifies *puns, poetry*, and *paradox* as linguistic activities which have a strong kinship with the language of Christianity. That bond is their common attempt to say more than we can normally say with our language, to stretch the use of words beyond their usual employment, almost to the point of lapsing into nonsense. Consider how a pun stretches language ("A door is not a door when it is ajar") or how poetic speech attempts to go beyond our normal linguistic frontiers ("Your eyes outshine the stars in heaven").

Our modern, materialistic Western culture, according to van Buren, pressures us to live linguistically within the safe, central parts of our language — science, economics, history, and common sense. But to live in the central regions of language is to forfeit a certain richness of experience, to forego a certain way of being in the world. For van Buren, then, the vital role played by religious language is that of expressing a certain aspect of our humanity. Christians, as he indicates, refuse to be confined to the mundane center of language and seek to say more about ourselves and our world than can be said in ordinary or scientific talk. An example of Christian "edge-talk" is the utterance "God raised Jesus from the dead," which is misunderstood if taken as a statement of historical fact. It is actually a statement of faith that tries to press language to its limits in talking about Jesus and his ongoing influence; it performs an entirely different function for believers than it does for historians.[23] Talk of a God who is "personal, but not a person" and of a "spiritual body" just begins the list of examples of Christian edge-talk.

Those who engage in functional analysis have helped reveal a host of different employments of religious language. In a list that proceeds much as Wittgenstein's does, they have shown us that language in religion is used in a variety of ways: to pray and petition, to sing praises, to comfort, to exhort, to affirm commitment, and so forth. Yet van Buren, along with all functional analysts, runs the risk of falling into a certain form of fideism, the view (discussed in Chapter 3) that faith is immune to external critique.[24] Since religious language has its own unique character and function, it is not subject to the sorts of questions and linguistic procedures that occur in other linguistic territories. For example, it would be inappropriate, according to van Buren, to ask whether the word *God* names someone or some thing — to ask whether some object bears that name, or whether it refers to something real. Such questions are appropriate, say, to the physical sciences or to other factually oriented linguistic activities that involve the technique of naming objects. But religion cannot ask whether its most fundamental term — the term *God*, which constitutes and governs its whole field of discourse — can play by the rules of other fields in which naming and referring are key techniques.[25] Focusing exclusively on the *function* of religious language within a religious community neglects its informative dimension. It is as though functional analysts have surrendered to the positivist charge that religious language is cognitively meaningless and have looked elsewhere to find some other way in which it can be meaningful — *functionally* meaningful.

Van Buren and other Wittgensteinian thinkers have rightly called our attention to the intimate connection of language with all areas of human life; they have forced us to recognize that much of our humanity is indeed bound up with being linguistic creatures. However, only by assuming that science and ordinary talk are central linguistic practices — a capitulation to the positivists — can van Buren justify placing religion at the "edges" of language. A more adequate interpretation may well perceive that religious language has its own inherent standards of precision and meaning, just as science does, without assigning preeminence to the standards of science.

Moreover, it appears that van Buren fails to see the complex fabric of religious language as involving metaphysical, ethical, and historical statements that are intended by religious believers to be just that — metaphysical or ethical or historical assertions. By reducing religious language to the activity of expressing a distinct perspective on the world, van Buren still leaves unresolved the more fundamental question of whether our language can be used to say anything about that Ultimate Reality that believers take to be God. Traditional thinkers such as Aquinas would say that van Buren's approach (like that of Braithwaite and other functional analysts) fails to take seriously what ordinary religious believers understand themselves to be saying. Believers regularly understand themselves to be asserting the factual truth of certain theological teachings and narratives, or at least to be engaging in liturgies and other religious behaviors that assume such factual truths.

Literal or Symbolic Talk of God?

Neither verificational nor functional analysis give an adequate account of the nature of religious language. Verificational analysis denied cognitive meaning to religious discourse, and functional analysis sought to find uses for it that were basically noncognitive. Most contemporary philosophers now admit that religious language has legitimate cognitive meaning, but a number of them deny that its meaning can be *literal*. They rightly wish to avoid the anthropomorphism involved in talking about God as we would talk about creatures. A plethora of nonliteral interpretations has emerged: Some authors speak of theological "models," some of "stories," others of "metaphor," and still others of "parable" as the essential mode of religious discourse.[26] In essence, these different views endorse a *symbolic* interpretation of God-talk. In contrast to noncognitive interpretations, which hold that it is impossible to say anything meaningful about God at all, and functional interpretations, which transform God-talk into a special expression of our humanity, the symbolic interpretation attempts to explain how it is that religious language has *bona fide* cognitive status.

That it is impossible to speak literally of God has virtually become the prevailing assumption of twentieth-century theology. Statements such as "Yahweh spoke to the prophets" and "The Lord is my Shepherd" are not commonly considered to be capable of literal interpretation. Since these sentences are predications, attaching properties, relationships, and behaviors to a subject, the present issue pertains to how theological predicates have meaning. According to many modern theologians, when God is the subject of predication, all properties, relationships, and activities ascribed to him are symbolic. After all, God does not really "speak" by expelling air across physical vocal cords, nor is he a "shepherd" as we typically understand the term.

Of course, there are many cases of broadly symbolic speech in ordinary language. We speak of the "mouth of a river" or of an "electric wire's being alive." In ordinary discourse, such symbolic or metaphorical talk can be translated literally. We can show, for instance, that what is meant by saying that the river has a "mouth" is simply that it has an opening out of which things flow, or that a wire is "alive" in that it has electric current flowing through it. However, a widespread view among contemporary theologians is that talk of God is fundamentally symbolic or irreducibly metaphorical and cannot therefore be translated into literal assertions.[27]

A deep ontological problem lies behind the notion that all language about God must be symbolic or metaphorical. The problem arises from a certain way of thinking about God as "transcendent" or "wholly other."[28] One line of reasoning goes as follows: how can human speech, which is suited to talk about the familiar objects and events of human life, be employed to say anything about God, who is radically unlike anything else we know? Paul Tillich (1886–1965) represents this position, maintaining that God is not *a* being at all, but is rather "the Ground of Being."[29] According to him, God is infinite, not limited by the structure of finite existence. Obviously, on Tillich's view, literal talk of God must be banned, for it treats God as a particular, discrete being among other beings. That is, such talk incorrectly supposes that God is a being of a certain kind, has certain properties, and performs certain actions – a supposition that would violate God's ultimacy. For Tillich, God is "beyond" all of that. Thus, it is utterly impossible to specify literally *what* it is that symbolic statements are asserting about God.

In contrast to the contemporary symbolic interpretation, one traditional view holds that in general, theological language may be either symbolic or literal, and that a literal translation of any symbolic God-talk is entirely possible. Also, this traditional view does not reflect a crude and simplistic notion that the divine being is just one being among others or that words apply to God in exactly the same way they apply to other things. Aquinas, like Tillich, wanted to maintain that God is radically different from any creature.[30] In their own ways, they both affirm that God is Being-Itself, not one being among many others, and thus is not subject to the categories and distinctions that apply to finite beings. Of course, Tillich's conception of Being-Itself, unlike Thomas's, is as near to pantheism as makes no difference. By contrast, Aquinas conceived of Being-Itself as one whose essence is pure existence and in whom there is no internal differentiation. It is not surprising, therefore, that Aquinas and Tillich draw quite different conclusions about the nature and interpretation on talk about God.

On what we might call Tillich's pan-symbolic view, nothing can ever be asserted of God in the strict sense, since God cannot be described in terms of the predicates in our language. Thus, we are never claiming with respect to some property or attribute that God possesses it, and that our claim is true if, and only if, God actually possesses it. Questions of literal truth and falsity are quite beside the point. But while Tillich does not think that the symbol can be translated literally, he thinks it can be an avenue of revelation, a means of focusing on one's ultimate concern, or an occasion for encountering God. However, in Aquinas's view, believers have beliefs about what God is like and what God does—beliefs that, when expressed linguistically, make theological claims or assertions. Such assertions are thought to be true if, and only if, those attributes or activities actually attach to God. Thus, for Aquinas, when symbolic statements are spelled out in literal terms, they can be evaluated in terms of truth and falsity.

How is it that Aquinas can partially agree with Tillich on the identification of God with Being-Itself and yet not derive a pan-symbolic interpretation of talk about God? How is it that he can endorse a literal interpretation of God-talk without falling into hopeless anthropomorphism? We have already seen that Aquinas's theory of analogical predication allows us to speak of God as "like" creaturely realities in certain respects. This is essentially a theory of language designed to explain two or more occurrences of a term within different sentential contexts. But it remains to be seen how the radical otherness of God—his not being *a* being that falls under our usual categories—can permit the application of literal language. This way of approaching the problem brings the ontological difficulty to the forefront and forces us to ponder the linkage between language and Ultimate Reality.

William Alston (1921–   ) develops a view of how we can speak literally of God that is reminiscent of Aquinas's position. Alston suggests that Aquinas's distinction between the "mode of signification" (the form of our language) and the "perfection signified" (the reality about which we speak) is a key to solving such problems.[31] (Here "perfection" is synonymous with the "property" or "attribute" to which a predicate can refer.) Alston admits that our language is defective for speaking about God. Its very structure (i.e., "subject–predicate" form) assumes a distinction between an object and its properties—that a subject is one kind of being rather than another. But God is Being-Itself; the divine essence has no distinctions and is not an instance of any kind of being. God *is* Being; creatures merely *have* being. Thus human language is somewhat inappropriate for speaking of Being-Itself. To predicate love of God, for example, is to speak as if there is a distinction between God and the attribute of love as there is between creatures and their love. Yet the distinction is not a real distinction in God, but only a feature of our language.

However, as Alston argues, the possibility remains that our human terms are not defective with respect to their specific content. That is, there can be a genuine reality that is the intended target of our terms. There is nothing about the concepts of love, knowledge, and power that makes them inherently unattributable to God. Alston reminds us that the "mode of signification" may be defective, but may still be used to signify a certain "perfection." It is possible to purify our concepts of love, knowledge, power, and so forth, by eliminating all features pertaining to temporality, embodiment, and other creaturely conditions, leaving a core of meaning that can be attributed to God. Thus purged, these terms can be literally applied to God and used to make statements that are true of God.

So, we can speak literally of God in that there is no barrier to using purified concepts to apply to the divine being. We can know that the reality apprehended by these concepts is *somehow* involved in the divine being. It is not that we cannot know *that* God loves, but we cannot fully comprehend *how* he loves. This is not to say that God is not loving, or that he exhibits some contrasting characteristic, such as hate or animosity. It is simply to recognize that our creaturely forms of speech and thought do not adequately capture the reality about which we speak. Hence, the fact that makes our statement true is not suitably mirrored by the statement itself.

It should now be apparent that the problem of speaking literally about God divides into two subordinate and related issues, one *ontological* and the other *linguistic*. The ontological issue pertains to the structure of the divine being — of what God is like in contrast to creatures. The linguistic issue pertains to the form of our language and the extent to which it may be used to speak of the divine being. Tillich and his intellectual followers land in the position of pan-symbolism because he does not negotiate these tandem issues in the same way as Aquinas and Alston do.

For Tillich, God is so radically unlike creatures, and language is so inept for speaking of God, that literal predication is impossible. At best, certain terms can be used as symbols. The symbols, of course, serve the purpose of helping us encounter God in our experience, but do not in any way denote a reality in God. Interestingly, it follows from this position that "symbolic statements" do not stand in normal, logical relations to one another, such as contradiction, negation, and implication, and thus defy reasoning about their literal truth and falsity. Thus, to say symbolically "God is love" is not to contradict "God is hate" or "God is cruel," because relations such as contradiction just do not apply. Even quite opposing statements could all be symbolically efficacious or "true" as long as they enable one to encounter the holy, or open up new avenues of experience. For instance, a given statement may function as a symbol for one person and a very different statement may perform the same symbolic function for another person. In the strict sense, then, religious language never asserts anything of God (say, that he has a certain attribute or performs a certain activity), but at most says something about how God can be encountered in experience.

Alston, like Aquinas, agrees that there are important respects in which the divine is unlike creatures, but does not conclude that human language is hopeless for speaking about God. His approach to the linguistics of the situation is quite different from Tillich's. For Alston, we simply have to refine our concepts as much as possible in order to speak of God and to try to avoid being misled by the forms of our language. Thus, Alston does not need to draw a pan-symbolic interpretation of religious language from the view that God is Being-Itself. His approach certainly comports better with the way ordinary religious believers as well as classical theistic thinkers have understood their position. They understand themselves as having certain beliefs about God that are not obviously false, absurd, or extraneous, and accept that they can think about and reason about those beliefs. Likewise, the way is open for nontheists to reason about such beliefs and make meaningful denials.

STUDY QUESTIONS

1. Discuss various reasons for philosophical interest in religious language. Must one have a philosophical theory of religious language before using it?

2. Explain how the theory of analogy approaches the problem of meaning. Explore the ways, if there are any, in which shifts of meaning between ordinary and religious contexts differ from shifts of meaning between one ordinary context and another.

3. Consider the ramifications of the verifiability principle for ordinary language, ethical language, and metaphysical language.

4. What could it mean to criticize the verifiability principle by saying that it confuses issues of meaning and truth?

5. Is verification or falsification a totally logical and impersonal process — in which case it is the same for all people? Or does it have a psychological aspect that takes into account the mental states of individual people — in which case it can differ from person to person?

6. What exactly is the difference between saying that a religious statement is meaningless and saying that it is false?

7. How is it that the functional analysis of religious language generally ignores matters of truth and falsity?

8. Explore the various functions that language in general seems to fulfill. Explore the functions that religious language seems to perform. Can any one function be identified as "basic"?

9. To what extent must philosophers of language take seriously the way in which religious believers themselves understand their religious discourse? Might the believers be mistaken and thus stand in need of correction by philosophers of religious language?

10. Make a case, as Tillich would, for all talk of God being symbolic. How does Alston, after the fashion of Aquinas, take a different approach to the issue?

NOTES

1. From Arthur Clarke, "The Nine Billion Names of God," in his collection of short stories entitled *The Nine Billion Names of God* (New York: Harcourt, Brace, and World, 1967).

2. Thomas Aquinas, *Summa Theologica*, trans. Fathers of the English Dominican Province, (Westminster, MD: Christian Classics, 1981), Part I, 13, A. 5; also see *Summa Contra Gentiles*, trans. Anton C. Pegis (Notre Dame, IN: University of Notre Dame Press, 1975), Book 1, chaps. 28–34.

3. Frederick Ferré, "Analogy in Theology," *The Encyclopedia of Philosophy* (New York: Macmillan Pub. Co., 1967), vol. 1, pp. 94–95.

4. Accepting the rebuttal that analogy theory is distorted if it is mathematically modeled, a counter might still be made: that while the analogy theory is, admittedly, a theory of meaning, there are *two* unknowns, not one, on the God-side of the equation. Suffice it here to say that a sophisticated version of analogy theory seeks to account for the fact that the mode of God's being (which we here call "infinite") as well as the intrinsic character of his attributes are not really objects of full conceptual knowledge. As Ross says, the infinity of God is only approximated "when we say that God is infinitely wise, infinitely good, infinitely intelligent, etc." We can say *that* God is wise, for instance, but we do not understand *how* he is wise. Such matters slip through our finite, conceptual net, so to speak. See James F. Ross, *Philosophical Theology* (Indianapolis: Bobbs-Merrill 1969), p. 56. Obviously, this topic deserves further discussion along other lines as well.

5. An excellent treatment is James F. Ross, "Analogy as a Rule of Meaning for Religious Language," *International Philosophical Quarterly* 1, no. 30 (1961): 468–502.

6. A. J. Ayer, *Language, Truth, and Logic* (New York: Dover Books, 1952), p. 35.

7. Most formulations of the verifiability principle include the condition that the statements in question are not analytic, that is, that their truth or falsity is not simply a function of their logical structure.

8. As it also turned out, neither metaphysics nor ethics fared well under the positivist criterion of meaning.

9. Antony Flew, "Theology and Falsification," in Antony Flew and Alasdair MacIntyre, eds., *New Essays in Philosophical Theology* (New York: Macmillan, 1955), p. 96.

10. Flew, p. 99.

11. R. M. Hare, "Theology and Falsification," in Flew and MacIntyre, eds., pp. 99–103.

12. Basil Mitchell, "Theology and Falsification" in Flew and MacIntyre, eds., pp. 103.

13. Mitchell, p. 104.

14. John Hick, "Theology and Verification," *Theology Today* 17 (1960): 260–61. Hick develops his case further in his *Faith and Knowledge*, 2nd ed. (New York: Macmillan, 1964), chap. 8.

15. Actually, this point leads to an interesting debate over first-order statements and second-order rules for meaning. Defenders of the verifiability criterion held that it is just *that*, a *criterion*, and therefore that it did not have to meet its own standard of meaning. In other words, it was a second-order rule that was to be applied to first-order language. Critics, of course, held that it should have to meet its own standard of meaning, and since it is not meaningful according to its own standard, it is self-defeating.

16. This kind of point is made by Dallas High, *Language, Persons, and Belief* (New York: Oxford University Press, 1967); also see James Kellenberger, *Religious Dis-*

covery, Faith, and Knowledge (Englewood-Cliffs, NJ: Prentice-Hall, 1972), especially chaps. 1–2.

17. Frederick Ferré, *Language, Logic and God* (New York: Harper Torchbooks, 1961), p. 58.

18. R. B. Braithwaite, "An Empiricist's view of the Nature of Religious Belief" in John Hick, ed., *The Existence of God* (New York: Macmillan, 1964), pp. 229–52.

19. Other mistakes: First, it initially assumes an inadequate theory of moral language in which statements of objective norms ("Murder is wrong") translate into expressions of subjective intentions ("I never intend to murder anyone"). Hence, whatever course of action one intends to follow becomes *moral* — a result that blatantly conflicts with our common moral experience! Second, Braithwaite mixes religious stories of quite diverse logical types — some intended as historical statements about the life of Jesus, others as parabolic, and so forth. Thus, Braithwaite overlooks numerous subtle differences in the uses of Christian stories. And, third, he totally ignores what religious believers themselves understand as the function and meaning of their various assertions and stories.

20. W. Donald Hudson, *Ludwig Wittgenstein* (Richmond, VA: John Knox Press, 1968), p. 62.

21. Paul van Buren, *The Edges of Language* (New York: Macmillan, 1972).

22. Ludwig Wittgenstein, *Philosophical Investigations*, trans. G. E. M. Anscombe (New York: Macmillan, 1953), §23 (p. 11ᵉ).

23. Van Buren, p. 157.

24. See Chapter 3 of this book for a fuller discussion of fideism.

25. Van Buren, p. 134, also p. 137. "The word 'God' marks the point at which the religious man has come up against the final limit of what he can say about the object of his concern" (p. 135).

26. On models, see Ian T. Ramsey, "Talking about God," in F. W. Dillistone, ed., *Myth and Symbol* (London: SPCK, 1966), pp. 76–97, and Kellenberger, chap. 3; on story, Alasdair MacIntyre, "The Logical Status of Religious Belief," in *Metaphysical Beliefs* (1957; 2nd ed. London: SCM Press, 1970) pp. 158–201; and Ian Crombie, "The Possibility of Theological Statements," in B. Mitchell, ed., *Faith and Logic* (London: George Allen and Unwin, 1957), p. 60; on metaphor, see Paul Ricoeur, "Biblical Hermeneutics," in J. D. Crossan, ed., *Semeia* 4 (Missoula, MT: Scholars Press, 1975): 29–148; on parable, Ronald Hepburn, *Christianity and Paradox* (London: C. A. Watts & Co. Ltd, 1958), pp. 192–204.

27. A small selection from the range of symbolic, nonliteral interpretations is as follows: George Santayana, "Reason in Religion," in *The Life of Reason* (New York: Scribner's, 1905–1906); W. M. Urban, *Language and Reality* (New York: Macmillan, 1939); Philip Wheelwright, *The Burning Fountain* (Bloomington: Indiana University Press, 1954).

28. Among the thinkers who take this kind of approach are Paul Tillich, Karl Barth, John Macquarrie, Emile Bruner, and Rudolph Otto.

29. This theme runs through Tillich, *Systematic Theology* (Chicago: University of Chicago Press, 1951–63) and *The Dynamics of Faith* (New York: Harper & Row, 1957).

30. Thomas Aquinas, *Summa Theologica*, Part I, Q. 3, A. 4; Q. 13, A. 11; Part I, Q. 4, A. 2; also see his *Summa Contra Gentiles*, Part I, chaps. 28–29.

31. William Alston, "Being-Itself and Talk about God," *Center Journal* 3, no. 3 (1984): 21.

SUGGESTED READING

Ayer, A. J. *Language, Truth, and Logic*. New York: Dover, 1952.

Ferré, Frederick. *Language, Logic and God*. New York: Harper & Row, 1969.

Gilkey, Langdon. *Naming the Whirlwind*. Indianapolis: Bobbs-Merrill, 1969.

Gilson, Etienne. *Linguistics and Philosophy*. Notre Dame, IN: University of Notre Dame Press, 1988.

High, Dallas, ed. *New Essays in Religion Language*. New York: Oxford University Press, 1969.

Mascall, E. L. *Words and Images*. New York: Ronald Press, 1957.

Ramsey, Ian. *Religious Language*. London: SCM Press, 1957.

_____, ed. *Words about God: The Philosophy of Religion*. New York: Harper & Row, 1971.

9

Miracles: Does God Intervene
in Earthly Affairs?

> Blinded and paralyzed on one side of his body, a retired French accountant refused to believe that nothing would help him just because his doctors couldn't find a cure. . . . [So he] decided to journey to the famous "Our Lady of Lourdes" shrine and beg the Lord for a miracle. . . . Within hours of bathing in the spring, he regained his sight and could walk without crutches.[1]

Dramatic healings such as those linked to the spring at Lourdes form only a small portion of the class of events alleged to be miraculous. A person being spared in a devastating earthquake that killed everyone else involved, water being turned into wine, a baby being born of a virgin—all these events and more have been called miracles. And, of course, miracles are typically invested with religious significance. Thus, the concept of miracle is inevitably linked with concepts of God and his relation to the world. It is no surprise, then, that philosophers of religion have long been interested in this intriguing subject.

Miracles Defined

The term *miracle* is used in ordinary discussions to refer to a wide variety of occurrences. Some individuals use it to describe any *unexpected event*—from the unanticipated passing of a difficult exam, to the rediscovery of a hopelessly lost heirloom, to a rapid, welcomed change in a person's behavior. Others use the term in a more restricted sense, applying it only to those very unusual events that apparently conflict with known scientific laws—events such as the survival of a 10,000-foot fall by a flight attendant or the total recovery of a person dying of cancer.

However, "miracle" is most frequently defined in a distinctively religious sense. That is, for most individuals, a miracle is not only an unusual event, but also the *result of some sort of divine activity*. For example, the contention in the opening story is not simply that the retired accountant regained his sight

156

and the use of his legs, but that God brought these things about. It is this sense of the term that has generated the greatest volume and intensity of philosophical discussion.

What exactly does it mean to say that God has caused a certain event? Most believers hold that many events are acts of God in the broad, fundamental sense that God has created the universe, established the "laws" upon which causal interaction within this universe is based, and continues to sustain such interaction by divine power.[2] In this sense, the birth of a baby or a summer thunderstorm can be said to be acts of God. Most believers, however, also maintain that there are some events — for example, answers to prayer or healings — that would not have occurred in the exact manner in which they did if God had not *directly* intervened — that is, if God had not at some point and in some manner directly circumvented or modified the general cause-effect patterns already in operation. Miraculous occurrences, not surprisingly, are normally considered to fall within this category of "direct acts of God."

But just how unusual or extraordinary must a direct act of God be before it can be labeled miraculous? Since the time of David Hume (1711–1776), it has been very popular in philosophical circles to define miracles as direct acts of God that "violate" natural laws. But what exactly does it mean to say that a natural law has been violated? This question stands at the threshold of a very complex and debatable issue. However, it is possible to state what most individuals seem to have in mind when they speak of miracles as violations.

Natural laws are, at least in part, statements that describe what will (or probably will) happen or not happen under specifiable conditions.[3] They describe the inherent tendencies or dispositions of things in the world to act and react in certain ways. Our knowledge of well-established scientific laws leads us to believe, for example, that water does not turn instantly into wine and that those who have genuinely died do not (at least in a physical sense) come back to life. But let us assume that someone actually were to turn water instantly into wine or rise from the dead. We would then be forced to acknowledge the occurrence of an event that our knowledge of scientific laws gives us good reason to believe will not occur. Moreover, it is very difficult to see how such an event could ever be explained naturally. To be forced to acknowledge the occurrence of an event of this sort is what most individuals appear to have in mind when they talk about what it would mean to acknowledge that a natural law has been violated.

However, some individuals deny that a miraculous direct act of God must be an event for which no plausible natural explanation is available. Consider, for example, the following story related by R. F. Holland (1932–). A child riding his toy motor-car strays on to an unguarded railway crossing near his house when a wheel of his car gets stuck down the side of one of the rails. At that exact moment, an express train is approaching with the signals in its favor, and a curve in the track will make it impossible for the driver to stop his train in time to avoid any obstruction he might encounter on the crossing. Moreover, the child is so engrossed in freeing his wheel that he hears neither the train whistle nor his mother, who has just come out of the house and is trying to get his attention. The child appears to be doomed. But just before the train rounds the curve, its brakes are applied and it comes to rest a few feet from the child. The mother thanks God for the miracle, although she learns in due course that there was not necessarily anything supernatural about the manner in which the brakes of the train came to be applied. The driver had fainted, for a reason that had nothing to do with the presence of the child on the line, and the brakes were applied automatically as his hand ceased to exert pressure on the control lever.[4]

The event sequence described in this situation includes no component for which a natural explanation is not available. Boys sometimes play on train tracks, engineers sometimes faint, and the brakes of trains have been constructed to become operative when the driver's hand releases the control lever. But the fact that the driver fainted at precisely the moment necessary to save the child's life is quite extraordinary. And in the minds of some individuals, events such as this — assuming that they are also direct acts of God — can also be labeled miraculous. The sequence of events in such cases is so extraordinary, they argue, that these events are just as awe-producing as those direct acts of God for which no natural explanation can be found and, thus, have just as much right to be considered miracles.

When we consider the miraculous in either of these senses, various philosophical questions can arise. One set of questions is concerned with what is possible: Can miracles occur? More specifically, can God intervene in earthly affairs and (for violation miracles) can natural laws be violated? Let us turn first to the question of whether a violation of a natural law is possible. Alistair McKinnon (1925–) offers us a popular negative response. Natural laws, he tells us, are simply "shorthand descriptions of how things do, in fact, happen" — that is, shorthand descriptions of the "actual course of events." Accordingly, to claim that an occurrence is a violation of a natural law is to claim that the event in question is a "suspension of the actual course of events" and this, of course, is an impossibility. Events may well occur, he acknowledges, that seem at present to be incompatible with how we believe things normally happen. But a true counterinstance to what we now believe to be a natural law only shows the law to be inadequate. Since natural laws, by definition, describe "the actual course of events," we must in principle always be willing to expand our laws to accommodate any occurrence, no matter how unusual. We can, by definition, never have both the exception and the rule.[5]

But this line of reasoning is questionable. Of course, *if* we assume that all events have solely natural causes, then any occurrence incompatible with the relevant natural laws does throw the adequacy of these laws into doubt. Let us imagine, for instance, that a glass of water has turned instantaneously into wine. *If* we assume that this is the result of some undetected (and possibly undetectable) natural causal force that has acted upon the known properties of water, then our scientific laws leading us to believe that water does not naturally turn into wine must indeed be considered inadequate.

However, *if* we assume that the water has been turned into wine as the result of direct divine activity, then those scientific laws leading us to believe that water does not turn into wine under any set of natural conditions have not been rendered inadequate. What has been rendered inadequate, rather, is the belief that all events can be explained adequately in terms of natural laws. And if this is so, then *unless* it can be demonstrated that supernatural causal activity is an impossibility, we can — contrary to McKinnon's contention — claim to have both the exception and the rule. The law remains as adequate as ever within the natural realm, and yet we can acknowledge that the counterinstance occurred.[6]

But can it be demonstrated that supernatural causal activity is impossible? Specifically, can it be established that divine intervention is impossible? It is true, of course, that many people believe there actually is no supernatural being. And even some who affirm the existence of such a being — for example, process theists — deny that God can unilaterally intervene in earthly affairs in the sense necessary to produce "miraculous events." However, few philosophers today believe that God's existence or ability to intervene directly can be shown to be impossible. And, accordingly, few philosophers today claim that miracles are impossible.

Most philosophers are at present concerned instead with another type of question related to the miraculous: What can be known or reasonably believed? Specifically, they are interested in three related but distinct questions: Under what conditions can a person reasonably maintain that certain unusual events have actually occurred as reported? Under what conditions can a person reasonably maintain that an event could have no natural explanation? And under what conditions can a person reasonably maintain that God was directly involved in bringing about a given occurrence? Each will be considered in some detail.

Miracles as Historical Events

Many believers do not claim only that certain types of events *could* justifiably be considered miracles *if* they were to occur. They claim that certain events meriting the label of miraculous *have* actually occurred. Now, of course, if these events have natural explanations available, as is the case in Holland's story about the boy and the train, the accuracy of such claims can be assessed in the same way we assess any historical report. We can, for example, try to determine whether the original source was trustworthy and whether what was originally reported has been faithfully transmitted.

But what of those allegedly miraculous events for which no natural explanation is available? What, for instance, of the Christian belief that Jesus came back to life after he had been dead for three days, or that Jesus turned water into wine? Are there conditions under which a believer can (or at least could) justifiably claim that seemingly unexplainable events of this sort have actually occurred as reported?

Antony Flew (1923–) is the most influential of those philosophers who are skeptical about such accounts. It is clearly possible that events that are incompatible with our current natural laws have occurred, he tells us. However, as Hume has rightly pointed out, the wise person proportions his or her belief to the evidence. And when we consider the evidence rationally, it is not difficult to see the problem at hand. We have well-known natural laws that justifiably lead us to believe, for instance, that dead people remain dead and that water does not turn into wine. Such laws are not the product of inaccessible scientific studies or outmoded historical hearsay. Such laws can be, and are, tested and reconfirmed daily. The dead stay dead, and untreated water persists as water.

On the other hand, the reported "violations" of natural laws are supported only by *personal testimony* from the past, and such testimonial evidence will by its very nature always be weaker than the evidence for the laws they contradict. For one thing, while many people have found the laws in question to hold, only a few, possibly biased individuals claim that the law was "violated." But, more importantly, we face the problem of *repeatability*. Scientific law, as just stated, can be tested by anyone at any time. But the occurrence of a past historical event cannot be tested in this objective, public fashion; we have only the subjective testimonial reports of those who claim to have witnessed it.

Accordingly, Flew concludes, the historian can never have better reasons for believing that an alleged violation of natural law has actually occurred — for example, that Jesus rose from the dead — than for believing it did not. If such events could be produced by anyone in a systematic fashion, then the scientist and historian would need to take them seriously. The relevant natural laws might even need to be modified or discarded. But otherwise "no matter how impressive the testimony might appear, the most favorable verdict history could ever return must be the agnostic and appropriately Scottish 'not proven'."[7]

Is Flew correct? Some have argued that Flew's line of reasoning demonstrates an arbitrary and dogmatic naturalistic prejudice. What right, they maintain, does Flew have to assume that the laws of science have the ultimate or final voice in relation to history? How can other, nonnatural factors be ruled out automatically? For example, many theists believe that certain specific "miraculous" events have occurred because they are recorded in "holy writings" such as the Bible, sources whose accuracy is thought to be guaranteed by their divine origin. Moreover, the types of miracles recorded in such revelations are often thought to furnish believers with clues as to how God still works in the world today. For example, many Christians believe the Bible to teach that God sometimes intervenes in response to prayer. Thus, when such believers are told of alleged occurrences that fit these divine patterns, such reports are often initially granted a reasonable degree of reliability. In short, many believers do in fact believe nonnaturalistic evidence to be quite relevant to the question at hand. And how can Flew be justified in dismissing such evidence completely?

This criticism, however, is misguided. Flew repeatedly emphasizes that he is, in this context, only discussing what the historian can conclude on the basis of the historical (natural) evidence alone. He is not attempting to rule out the possibility that the historicity of certain events could, for some people, be settled on the basis of nonnatural criteria — for example, a revelation from God. Moreover, it is not clear that Flew's decision to consider only "natural" historical criteria can in this context be considered arbitrary.[8] He makes this decision because he is assuming that believers generally wish to use miracles to help establish or support religious belief. And he rightly sees that an alleged miracle can have this apologetic value only if, among other things, the occurrence in question can be established objectively on "natural" grounds.

Now, of course, some religious believers today do not desire or even believe it is possible to certify in some objective, public sense that particular allegedly miraculous events have actually occurred as reported. Instead they want to hold only that they are justified in believing this for themselves. Historically, however, theists have often wanted to use miracles to support belief in God's existence, or establish that Jesus is God, or support the claim that the Bible is an authentic divine revelation. Thus, to the extent that this is still the case, Flew's line of reasoning cannot be accused of involving arbitrary, dogmatic naturalism. In this context, the question of how the actual occurrence of reported events can be authenticated in a public, objective sense remains paramount.

But even granting all this, it is still not clear that Flew's line of reasoning is sound. Let us assume, for example, that a large group of internationally renowned physicians report that they have all observed a severely deformed and withered leg instantaneously return to its normal size and shape. Such an occurrence would obviously be inconsistent with currently accepted natural laws. Thus, given Flew's line of reasoning, those of us who heard this claim would not have a justifiable basis for believing that this event had actually occurred as reported until events of the same type could be produced. In fact, given Flew's perspective, even the doctors themselves would be forced to withhold affirmation until repeatability was demonstrated.

But it is questionable whether this would necessarily be the proper response. Flew is clearly correct in arguing that natural laws are continuously open to confirmation or disconfirmation. Thus, we are indeed justified in using such laws to predict in general what will or will not occur under appropriate conditions. We do, for example, have well-established laws that justifiably lead us to believe that a withered leg does not instantly return to its normal condition, and, thus, we should not expect such an occurrence. Moreover, it is of course true that no past occurrence can itself be repeated or any longer observed directly. However, Flew's contention that this reflects negatively on the trustworthiness of our apparent memories of the past and the trustworthiness of the reports of others about their memories of the past is in need of further analysis.

Human beings appear to be naturally endowed with a considerable number of belief-forming faculties. As a result, many of us simply find ourselves believing we are "seeing" a tree, that we ate eggs for breakfast yesterday, that we have a headache, or that it is wrong to torture children. Now, in general, we cannot prove that such immediate beliefs are true and, on this basis, that our faculties are reliable. Some of the greatest philosophical minds — for example, Descartes and Hume — have tried, but with notable lack of success. However, the onus is not on us to furnish such proof. We all rely on these faculties daily, and in general they serve us quite well. In fact, the reliability of such faculties must be assumed to be true by anyone who wishes to formulate natural laws in the first place. As Flew himself acknowledges, natural laws are, at least in part, descriptive generalizations that summarize the *reported observations* of individuals (or groups of individuals).[9]

Now, of course, seemingly trustworthy observational reports can be mistaken. We all at times perceive wrongly or fail to communicate effectively what we accurately perceive. It is possible, for example, that the physicians in our scenario have been victims of an elaborate hoax or that they have intended to deceive us for some unknown reason or that their observational report has been misinterpreted or communicated inaccurately. Moreover, the fact that an alleged occurrence is incompatible with known natural laws is, of course, a good reason to suspect misperception or miscommunication. Accordingly, those of us hearing the physicians' claim would have to convince ourselves that we have not been deceived or that the report has not been miscommunicated or misunderstood. Even the physicians would have to convince themselves they have not been deceived in some manner.

However, Flew admits that natural laws are not immune from change. Some natural laws have been revised or discarded, and will continue to be revised or discarded. And as Flew also admits, some reported occurrences that were, at the time they were initially reported, incompatible with highly confirmed natural laws are now believed by all to have occurred. Therefore, there appears to be no strong basis for refusing automatically to acknowledge the accuracy of an occurrence report that challenges our current natural laws. We do in all such cases have the evidence of the general, testable natural laws that count against the reliability (accuracy) of the report in question. But we may in some such cases have no other reason to doubt that the visual belief-forming faculties of those making the initial report were functioning properly. And Flew has given us no objective grounds for maintaining that preference *always* ought to be given to the admittedly well-entrenched natural laws in question.

Moreover, as Richard Swinburne (1934–   ) rightly points out, we do not have merely the assumed reliability of our belief-forming faculties and the evidence of the relevant natural laws to consider; we must also consider any relevant physical traces.[10] In the scenario under discussion, such relevant traces might be X-rays (or photographs) of the leg taken just before and just after the alleged "healing." An even more compelling physical trace would be a videotape of the incident. Now, of course, X-rays, photographs, and videotapes can be altered. Thus, such physical traces could not conclusively verify that the event had actually occurred as reported. And since the traces would in this case be incompatible with well-established natural laws, caution in drawing a conclusion would indeed be justified. But we have generally accepted methods for assessing (analyzing, testing) the authenticity of X-rays, photographs, and videotapes, and if it proved highly likely that they were reliable, such data would obviously stand as very strong evidence for the accuracy of the report in question.

But at exactly what point can it be justifiably said that the presumed reliability of our belief-forming faculties and/or the "physical traces" that support counterinstances outweigh the relevant natural laws that oppose such anomalies? This is not an easy question to answer. To some extent, of course, a person's response will be related to her noetic commitments. If an individual — for religious or nonreligious reasons — believes unusual events of this type may well occur, then she will be more favorably impressed by the evidence in this case. On the other hand, if a person is predisposed to doubt the occurrence of events of this type, the evidence will quite naturally appear less convincing.

But even given this fact, several points are important to remember. It seems reasonable, for example, to maintain that if we only read reports of alleged counterinstances in the newspaper or history books, if none of the individuals directly involved is still alive, or if the report is given to support some system to which the "witness" is strongly committed, we ought initially to be suspicious and then require more information before giving credence to what has been reported. Some might even go so far as to say that apart from those cases in which the persons claiming to have observed counterinstances can be directly interviewed and investigated, or in which there are widely accepted, compelling physical traces, we ought at best to suspend judgment with respect to the accuracy of their reports.

However, let us assume that we ourselves directly observe a counterinstance under normal conditions and have no reason to doubt the reliability of our belief-forming faculties or to believe we are the victims of some elaborate hoax. Or let us assume that we have very good reasons to believe that knowledgeable, reputable individuals have claimed to have observed a counterinstance, and we have no reason to believe such individuals have a vested interest in making such a claim or have been the victim of a hoax or have faulty visual faculties. Or let us assume that we have very reliable physical traces related to a seeming counterinstance — for example, reliable videotapes of the event. Under such conditions, it would appear quite reasonable to assume at least tentatively that the event has indeed occurred as reported.

It might be argued in response that we have missed the essential point. Particular types of evidence might *hypothetically* make it most reasonable for a scientist or historian to accept the occurrence of a nonrepeatable counterinstance. However, as Hume pointed out, our minds have a natural propensity to give credence to "surprises and wonders," especially when such occurrences bolster some cherished belief. Moreover, as Hume adds, miraculous claims have abounded predominantly among ignorant people. There has never been a miraculous event attested to by a sufficient number of witnesses whose "unquestioned good sense, education and learning" ensured that they had not deluded themselves or were not fakes. In short, it might be argued that there has never been a compelling basis for accepting the actual occurrence of nonrepeatable events.[11] Thus, Flew's "occurrence criterion" remains a useful historical tool for assessing actual cases.

Such reasoning can be challenged on two counts. First, it is not clear that individuals have never in fact had a sufficient basis for believing that such counterinstances have occurred. But, even more importantly in this context, to argue in this fashion misses the point of Flew's argument. Flew is not simply claiming that there has never in fact been a compelling basis for accepting the occurrence of a nonrepeatable counterinstance. His claim is that there could *in fact* never be such a basis. Thus, even if it were true that the occurrence of no counterinstance has been established to date, this would not mean that no counterinstance could be established in the future.

We must conclude, then, that the historian cannot in a categorical manner rule that all reports of nonrepeatable counterinstances should be considered inaccurate. The fact that a reported occurrence is incompatible with well-established natural laws does count strongly against the report. And it is not easy to say exactly when the assumed reliability of our faculties and/or the physical evidence can justifiably be held to counterbalance or even outweigh the long-standing scientific evidence. But a decision concerning such occurrence reports must be made on a case-by-case basis. Miracles cannot be ruled out so easily.

Miracles as Unexplainable Events

As we saw earlier, not all individuals believe that a miracle must be an event for which no plausible natural explanation is available. However, since the time of Hume, the majority of philosophers have conceived of miracles as "violations" of natural laws. That is, they have assumed for the sake of discussion that miracles are events for which no totally natural explanation could be forthcoming. And for such philosophers, a second important question quite naturally arises. Could we ever be in the position to claim justifiably that an event is permanently unexplainable in this sense? If, for instance, someone were raised from the dead after three days, would we be in a position to claim justifiably that this occurrence could never be explained naturally?

It might appear that a promising response is inherent in the very definition of miracle. As was stated earlier, most individuals hold that miracles should be defined as direct acts of God in the sense that they are events that would not have occurred in the exact manner they did if God had not directly circumvented or modified the relevant natural cause/effect patterns. But this is simply another way of saying that such events do not have totally natural causal explanations. Accordingly, it might appear that any direct act of God is automatically an event that is permanently unexplainable naturally. That is, to be more specific, it might appear that the question of whether we can justifiably claim that an alleged miracle could have no adequate natural explanation actually collapses into the question of whether we can justifiably claim that an event is a direct act of God.

However, this line of reasoning is seen by some philosophers to be based on a confusion. It is true, they grant, that if an event is a direct act of God, this occurrence itself can have no totally natural causal explanation. But natural science, they maintain, is not *primarily* interested in identifying the actual causal conditions for any specific occurrence (for any event-token). Its main objective, rather, is to map regularity patterns between certain types of occurrences and certain sets of causal conditions, and then use these patterns to formulate general explanatory (and thus predictive) laws. For instance, as these philosophers see it, the primary purpose of natural science is not to determine what actually caused the birth of any specific baby; its primary purpose is to identify the natural conditions under which we can expect babies to be produced with regularity — that is, *its purpose is* to consider birth as an *event-type*.

Accordingly, they conclude that an alleged miracle cannot necessarily be considered permanently unexplainable naturally even if we can justifiably claim that it is a direct act of God and, hence, is not, as an *event-token*, solely the product of natural causation. To label an occurrence permanently unexplainable in the relevant sense, we must be in a position to claim justifiably that science could never stipulate solely natural conditions under which events of the same *type* as the one in question could be produced with regularity.[12]

If we accept this reading of the issue, what ought we to conclude? Could we ever be in a position to label an event permanently unexplainable in this sense? The most common argument denying this possibility is stated succinctly by Flew. It might now appear, he grants, that some type of event could never be explained. But it is always possible that new information (generated by further scientific investigation) will force us to revise our current set of natural laws related to any given type of occurrence. Therefore, we can never decisively state that any given type of event could never be given a natural explanation.[13]

Not all philosophers, however, agree. Such philosophers are not assuming that they have complete and incontrovertible knowledge of the natural order, nor do they even assume that any specific law can ever justifiably be considered immune from revision. Their claim is weaker: Even granting that we might gather significant new scientific data and greatly revise our current set of laws accordingly, if some events were to occur, we could justifiably rule that events of this type could never be given a natural explanation.

But what are the criteria by which such events are to be identified? The key, according to Swinburne, lies in our ability (or inability) to devise new scientific laws to accommodate seemingly unexplainable events. We have to some extent good evidence about the "laws of nature," and some of these laws are so highly confirmed that any modification we would suggest to account for the odd counterinstance would be so clumsy and *ad hoc* that it would upset the whole structure of science. For example, let us imagine that we experience the "resurrection of . . . a man whose heart has not been beating and who was dead by other currently used criteria." Or let us assume we see "water turning into wine without the assistance of special apparatus or chemical catalysts." The relevant laws in such cases are well entrenched; they cannot be modified or given up easily. Accordingly, Swinburne concludes, if events of this type were to occur, they could justifiably be considered violations of the laws of nature — that is, permanently unexplainable events.[14]

Margaret Boden (1936–) argues in an analogous manner. She grants that observable phenomena cannot normally be dismissed as lying forever outside the range of science, but she is not convinced this would always have to be the case. She invites us to consider the logically possible case of a leper whose missing fingers reappear instantly under the most stringent, fraud-detecting conditions—for instance, in the presence of doctors or TV cameras. Such an event, she argues, would conflict with so many accepted scientific facts that any attempt to revise our present scientific laws to accommodate events of this type would so weaken the predictive power of such laws that they would no longer be of practical value. Accordingly, she concludes, if such an event were actually to occur, the scientist, of necessity, would be forced to identify it as a permanently unexplainable phenomenon.[15]

Such reasoning has a *prima facie* appeal, but an obvious question arises. Swinburne and Boden freely acknowledge that the scientific enterprise is continually discovering new, often startling and unexpected, information about the causal relationships that obtain in our universe. Also, they freely acknowledge that the annals of science record numerous instances in which supposed counterinstances to long-standing scientific laws were later demonstrated—sometimes only after significant conceptual shifts—to be consistent with such laws or revisions of them. Accordingly, is it not the height of scientific provincialism for anyone to maintain solely on the basis of the data now available that certain events could justifiably be labeled permanently unexplainable?

Swinburne and Boden obviously think not, and it is important to understand why. It is not, as mentioned before, because they believe they have some privileged understanding of the "true nature of reality." It is rather that when faced with an acknowledged counterinstance to very highly confirmed laws, they see only two basic options: either to modify the laws to accommodate the occurrence, or to affirm the adequacy of the laws and declare the event permanently unexplainable. And they feel that in some conceivable instances, the latter would be the more reasonable choice.

But is there not another opinion? Let us assume that after extensive testing, we cannot explain how water has turned into wine. Why should we assume that we must then either radically modify the relevant laws or declare the event permanently unexplainable? Why cannot we simply continue to run further tests or label the occurrence a "freak event" and await the occurrence of similar events before seriously investigating further?

According to Holland, such a noncommittal posture would place the relevant laws in a state of uncertainty and would therefore weaken the strength of the scientific method.[16] But not everyone has found such a response convincing. Only *repeatable* counterinstances, it is argued, falsify natural laws. As long as a counterinstance—no matter how unusual—is not repeatable, we are presented with no competing hypothesis to challenge the relevant laws. In other words, some believe that Swinburne and Boden have set up a false dilemma. If, when faced with acknowledged counterinstances to well-established laws, we were forced to either modify such laws or declare the counterinstances to be permanently unexplainable, the latter might well in some cases be the most reasonable choice. But there is, these critics maintain, another option open to us. As long as seeming counterinstances are not repeatable, both the "law" and the counterinstance can be acknowledged. We can (indeed should) continue to affirm the adequacy of the relevant laws while continuing to search for new or modified laws to accommodate the unusual events in question.[17]

Even if these critics are correct, however, little of religious significance *necessarily* follows. As stated before, although many philosophers are interested in determining whether certain types of events can justifiably be said to be violations of natural laws, it is doubtful that most religious believers share this concern. For most believers, what is of primary importance is whether, and only whether, the events in question would have occurred at the exact time and in the exact manner they did if God had not somehow acted.

Miracles as Acts of God

This brings us to our final and most important set of questions: those concerning our ability to establish that God has directly intervened in earthly affairs. For some philosophers, the crucial question continues to be the following: Are there imaginable conditions under which all rational individuals would be forced to admit that God has directly intervened — that is, are there imaginable conditions under which no rational individual could remain a strict naturalist?

Tan Tai Wei (1942–) is one of a number of philosophers who think so. Let us assume, Tan begins, not only that Jesus called upon God to raise Lazarus and that Lazarus arose, but that such feats were common in response to requests from Jesus for divine intervention. And let us further assume that such events have continued to occur frequently when divine intervention has been requested by other persons. Under these conditions, he continues, it would be unreasonable to continue indefinitely to seek for "an ordinary natural regularity that relates such exceptional events with the intentions and commands of this sort of religious personage." At some point, the acknowledgment of supernatural intervention would be the more rational posture "because here some of our ordinary criteria . . . governing the rational acceptability of purported coincidences as merely ordinary ones, would not be met."[18]

Grace Jantzen (1948–) argues in a similar manner. Let us assume that we have compelling evidence for believing that Jesus rose from the dead. In this case, she tells us, to attempt to revise the relevant natural law would hardly be the appropriate response — for what could be gained by making this law read, "All men are mortal except those who have an unknown quality, observed on only one occasion and hitherto accountable for only by divine intervention." "Where there is a single exception to a perfectly well-established and well-understood law, and one that is inexplicable unless one appeals to divine intervention . . . the skeptical response would be inadequate."[19]

Neither Jantzen or Tan, it must be emphasized, is arguing only that supernatural activity can justifiably be considered a plausible causal explanation when it cannot be shown that "nature left to her own devices could manage." Their claim is stronger: that if some conceivable events were to occur, it would be most reasonable for all rational individuals to assume that God has directly intervened.

It is not clear, however, that this line of reasoning is correct. Many people grant that there are conceivable situations that, when considered in isolation, make divine intervention a plausible causal hypothesis. But no actual event, and thus no causal hypothesis for it, can be considered in isolation from the rest of the relevant evidence. Let us assume, for example, that a remarkable healing occurs in the context of fervent petitions to God. To acknowledge divine intervention in this context would also be to acknowledge implicitly that God exists and that God's existence is compatible with other relevant experiential data. It would be to acknowledge, for example, that God's existence is compatible with the evil we experience.

Accordingly, if such a "healing" were to occur, the crucial question would not be, as Tan and Jantzen imply, whether divine causation is the most plausible causal explanation for this event alone. The crucial question would be whether divine causation is the most plausible explanation, given what this implies for all of the relevant data.

Now let us assume that in comparing the plausibility of believing that God has healed the individual in question (and, hence, that God's existence is compatible with the amount and types of evil in the world) with the plausibility of believing that God's existence is not compatible with all that we commonly experience (and, hence, that God did not heal the individual in question), someone decides that God's nonexistence is more compelling overall. In other words, let us assume that the *prima facie* evidence for God's existence that has been generated by the "healing" in question is not of sufficient weight in the mind of a given individual to make the supernatural perspective the most plausible explanation for all the relevant data. Could Tan or Jantzen justifiably accuse such an individual of being stubborn or intellectually dishonest or irrational? It is by no means obvious that they could, or even that most believers would want them to try. After all, the line of reasoning used against Tan and Jantzen is the same as that used by believers such as Alvin Plantinga (1932–   ) when they maintain that even if it is granted that a specific instance of evil appears to count strongly as evidence against God's existence, it is the totality of the relevant evidence (which Plantinga and other believers see as favoring theism) to which we must finally appeal.[20]

For many believers, though, the crucial question is not whether there are imaginable conditions under which all rational individuals would have to acknowledge divine intervention. The important issue, as they see it, is whether the *believer* can (could) justifiably claim that God is, at least in part, directly responsible for certain occurrences. That is, the important question is whether there are conditions under which the believer can reasonably claim that certain events are direct acts of God?

In response, a believer might assume a purely defensive posture. She might maintain that unless it can be shown that a given occurrence is not a direct act of God, she is justified in claiming that it is. And given our discussion of this approach to religious belief in Chapter 7, she might be successful.

However, many believers have positive reasons for maintaining that God does (or at least can) directly intervene in earthly affairs. Specifically, as has already been mentioned, many believers claim that they possess accurate information about God's general "patterns of action" in our world. And they believe that when they observe (or at least if they were to observe) some specific event fitting such a pattern, they can (or at least could) justifiably label it a direct act of God.

To accept a divine-pattern thesis of this sort, it must be stressed, is not to argue that God can act only in accordance with recognized patterns. Consider, for instance, the following situation. One day Jim notices a peculiar phenomenon in his garden: His vegetables continually grow from seed to full maturity in one hour and then quickly regress again to seed. Try as he will—for example, by discussing the occurrence with respected botanists—Jim can find no specific natural cause for this strange phenomenon. Moreover, although Jim is a proponent of the divine pattern thesis, he is not aware of any divine action pattern in which this unusual phenomenon fits. Accordingly, Jim will quite likely refrain from claiming that this is a direct act of God. He will not thereby be claiming that the occurrence is *in fact* not a direct act of God. He will be indicating only that he has at present no sufficient reason for thinking God is directly involved.

Also, theists who accept this divine-pattern thesis are not arguing that God must always intervene in a predictable manner. Consider, for example, the following situation. John, a believer, has grown up in a home in which the Bible is accepted as literally true. He has been taught, accordingly, that if one prays to God in time of trouble, God will directly answer. In other words, John believes he has acquired "knowledge" of a specific divine behavior pattern related to petitionary prayer. One day John finds himself in a serious personal crisis. His little girl is gravely ill, and there seems little hope for her recovery. John prays to God, beseeching that he save her life. Happily, the next day the girl is inexplicably improved and later goes on to make a full recovery. However, if John claims that this is a direct act of God because the "healing" fits an accepted pattern of how God interacts with the world, he would not thereby be saying that his prayer "forced" God to act. He would be claiming only that the fact that the healing fit an accepted divine action pattern was a sufficient reason to believe God had in this case chosen to intervene directly.

Moreover, even in such cases, theists are not professing absolute certainty. They are claiming only that they are justified in believing that it is more likely than not that a given occurrence is a direct act of God.

Of course, even in light of these clarifications, an important question arises. Are the believers in question justified in assuming that the sources from which the divine action patterns are derived—normally written revelation and tradition—yield accurate information? In some specific cases, such an assumption may not be justified. Perhaps it can be shown, for example, that specific patterns affirmed by some Christians cannot actually be supported by proper biblical interpretation or by correct knowledge of Christian tradition, or that a specific historical source trusted by some Muslims is unreliable. However, few philosophers today believe that God's existence can be conclusively disproved, and few philosophers would argue that the concept of divine communication with humans is self-contradictory. Thus, it is difficult to see how belief in the accuracy of divine action patterns could, in principle, be shown to be unjustified. And this in turn means that it is difficult to see how a believer who labeled an event a direct act of God because it fit such a pattern could, in principle, be shown to have made such a determination unjustifiably.

Practical Considerations

Have any miracles, though, actually occurred? More specifically, are theists justified in believing that any specific "miracle" — for example, the resurrection of Jesus or a healing at Lourdes — has actually occurred? This is, of course, an interesting and important question, one on which much has been written.[21] But philosophers, in their role as philosophers, have traditionally been more interested in discussing methodology than fact — that is, more interested in discussing the conditions under which we can justifiably believe something than that which is actually believed. Accordingly, since this is a philosophical discussion of the miraculous, no analysis of the alleged evidence for or against any specific "miracle" will be undertaken.

There is, though, one practical difficulty surrounding the miraculous that clearly merits attention in this context. Let us consider again our scenario concerning John and his daughter. John believes that God can and will occasionally intervene and, thus, when his daughter becomes gravely ill, he beseeches God for assistance. When she recovers, he attributes the recovery in part to God's direct activity and thanks God for this demonstration of divine compassion.

But, now, let us expand our story. Tom, a friend of John, is very happy about the seemingly miraculous healing of John's daughter. He too has always believed that God can intervene occasionally in earthly affairs and is pleased to think that God has actually done so in the case of John's daughter. Accordingly, when Tom encounters a number of starving children during a business trip to India, he beseeches God for help. After all, he reasons, if God can heal John's daughter, surely God can also help some of these children. Yet in spite of his fervent prayer, all the children die slow, painful deaths.

The *prima facie* moral tension here is obvious. Why did God intervene in one case but not in the other? When considering instances of seemingly unnecessary suffering, many believers, as we have seen in Chapter 6, emphasize the extent to which God is self-limited. God cares for everyone, it is argued. But God has created a moral context in which human freedom and the natural order that undergirds it are normally allowed to function uninhibited. And in such a universe undesired evils are unavoidable. However, why then has John's daughter been healed? If God's creative agenda keeps God from directly intervening in the case of starving children in India, how can God directly intervene in the case of John's daughter without violating the structure of our moral universe? How can we think that God intervenes on behalf of some and not for others?

The basic question here is not whether God can occasionally intervene, but why such interventions do not occur in a more understandable, orderly fashion. Or, as process theist David Griffin states this point, why would a God who can unilaterally intervene not do so more frequently "in order to prevent particularly horrendous evils?"[22]

Of course, many responses are available to believers. It can be argued that while situations may look analogous from our perspective, they may not be so from God's, or it can be argued that although situations may be analogous, God is under no moral obligation to act in ways *we think* are appropriate. God justifiably does what God wants for reasons beyond human understanding.

But for some believers the tension remains, and it is strong enough to cause them to question whether God does *in fact* intervene today. Moreover, even for those believers who have resolved this "tension" for themselves, a general point must be made. The acknowledged frequency of undesired but unavoidable evil and the expected frequency of beneficial, direct divine intervention stand in an inverse relationship. To the extent that a believer responds to specific instances of evil by claiming that God is barred from removing them because of the nature of our moral universe, such a believer has less reason to expect beneficial (miraculous) intervention in any specific situation. Moreover, to the extent that a believer resolves the tension in question by claiming that "God's ways are above our ways," the less able he is to predict when and where any such intervention might occur.

This type of tension, though, must be placed in perspective. It is true that the miraculous *is* a complex concept, and it is true that serious theoretical and practical questions concerning our ability to identify "miracles" *do* exist. But nothing argued in this chapter indicates that theists cannot in principle justifiably believe that miracles can possibly occur, or even that miracles have actually occurred.

STUDY QUESTIONS

1. What do you think most believers have in mind when they speak of miraculous divine intervention? Specifically, is it similar to what philosophers have traditionally had in mind?

2. How do you think "miracle" is best defined? Specifically, could an event be considered a miracle, as you see it, if a natural explanation were available?

3. Why does Flew believe we cannot acknowledge the occurrence of nonrepeatable counterinstances to well-established natural laws? Do you agree?

4. Are you sometimes skeptical when you hear reports of alleged miracles? Why? Under what conditions is such skepticism justified?

5. Swinburne and others believe that we can conceive of some events that could never be given natural explanations. Why? Do you agree?

6. Tan and Jantzen believe that, if some conceivable events were to occur, it would be most reasonable to acknowledge supernatural causation. Briefly

outline their line of reasoning and the types of criticism to which they must respond.

7. Those who believe God does miraculously intervene in earthly affairs face an obvious question: Given all the pain and suffering present in the world, why does God not intervene more frequently, or at least in a more systematic manner? How might a believer respond to this question?

8. What relationship do you see between miracles and a Free Will Universe — a universe in which God has chosen to given humans significant control over what occurs?

9. Do you believe that any miracles, as you define them, have actually occurred? Why or why not?

10. Do you think that someone who believes that miracles can occur will be less likely to search for a *natural* solution to personal and social problems?

NOTES

1. *Prayers God Has Answered* (West Palm Beach, FL: Globe Communications Corp., 1985), pp. 5–6.
2. Medieval philosophers distinguished God's "primary causation" from the "secondary causation" of creatures that the divine power upholds in existence.
3. David Hume, *Enquiries Concerning the Human Understanding and Concerning the Principles of Morals*, 2nd ed., L. A. Selby-Bigge, ed. (Oxford: Clarendon Press, 1972), pp. 109–31.
4. R. F. Holland, "The Miraculous," *American Philosophical Quarterly* 2 (1965): 43.
5. Alistair McKinnon, "'Miracle' and 'Paradox'," *American Philosophical Quarterly* 4 (October 1967): 309.
6. Another criticism of the view of natural law McKinnon affirms appears on pp. 165–67.
7. Antony Flew, "Parapsychology Revisited: Laws, Miracles and Repeatability," *The Humanist* 36 (May/June 1976): 28–30.
8. Antony Flew, "Miracles," *Encyclopedia of Philosophy*, Vol. 5 (New York: Macmillan, 1967), p. 351.
9. Chapter 7 furnishes a more comprehensive discussion of this point.
10. Richard Swinburne, *The Concept of Miracle* (London: Macmillan, 1970), pp. 33–50.
11. Hume, pp. 116–27.
12. This line of reasoning appears implicitly in Swinburne, pp. 23–32. A more explicit discussion occurs in David Basinger and Randall Basinger, *Philosophy and Miracle: The Contemporary Debate* (Lewiston, NY: Edwin Mellen Press, 1986), pp. 68–71.
13. Antony Flew, "Miracles," pp. 348–49.
14. Swinburne, pp. 29–32.
15. Margaret Boden, "Miracles and Scientific Explanation," *Ratio* 11 (December 1969): 137–41.
16. Holland, pp. 43–51.

17. Basinger and Basinger, pp. 59–71.
18. Tan Tai Wei, "Recent Discussions on Miracles," *Sophia* 11 (October 1972): 24.
19. Grace Jantzen, "Hume on Miracles, History and Politics," *Christian Scholar's Review* 8 (1979): 325.
20. Alvin Plantinga, "The Probabilistic Argument from Evil," *Philosophical Studies* (January 1979): 1–53.
21. See, for example, Gary Habermas and Antony Flew, *Did Jesus Rise From The Dead?* (San Francisco: Harper & Row, 1987).
22. David Griffin in John B. Cobb and W. Widick Schroeder, eds., *Process Philosophy and Social Thought* (Chicago: Center for the Scientific Study of Religion, 1981), p. 193.

SUGGESTED READING

Ahern, Dennis. "Miracles and Physical Impossibility," *Canadian Journal of Philosophy* 7 (1977): 71–79.

Basinger, David, and Randall Basinger. *Philosophy and Miracle: The Contemporary Debate*. Lewiston, NY: Edwin Mellen Press, 1986.

Brown, Colin. *Miracles and the Critical Mind*. Grand Rapids, MI: Eerdmans, 1983.

Hume, David. *Enquiries Concerning the Human Understanding and Concerning the Principles of Morals*, 2nd ed., L. A. Selby-Bigge, ed. Oxford: Clarendon Press, 1972.

Kellenberger, James. "Miracles," *International Journal for Philosophy of Religion* 10 (1979): 145–62.

Lewis, C. S. *Miracles*, rev. ed. London: Collins, Fontana Books, 1960.

McKinnon, Alistair. "'Miracles' and 'Paradox,'" *American Philosophical Quarterly* 4 (October 1967): 308–14.

Nowell-Smith, Patrick. "Miracles – The Philosophical Approach," *The Hibbert Journal* 48 (1950): 354–60.

Odegard, Douglas. "Miracles and Good Evidence," *Religious Studies* 18 (1982): 37–46.

Walker, Ian. "Miracles and Violations," *International Journal for Philosophy of Religion* 13 (1982): 103–8.

Young, Robert. "Miracles and Epistemology," *Religious Studies* 8 (1972): 115–26.

10

Life after Death:
Are There Reasons for Hope?

And the people from the margin,
Watched him floating, rising, sinking,
Till the birch-canoe seemed lifted
High into that sea of splendor,
Till it sank into the vapors
Like the new moon slowly, slowly
Sinking in the purple distance.
　　　And they said, "Farewell forever!"
Said, "Farewell, O Hiawatha!"
And the forests, dark and lonely,
Moved through all their depths of darkness,
Sighed, "Farewell, O Hiawatha!"
And the waves upon the margin
Rising, rippling on the pebbles,
Sobbed, "Farewell, O Hiawatha!"
And the heron, the Shuh-shuh-gah,
From her haunts among the fen-lands,
Screamed, "Farewell, O Hiawatha!"
　　　Thus departed Hiawatha,
Hiawatha the Beloved,
In the glory of the sunset,
In the purple mists of evening,
To the regions of the home-wind,
Of the Northwest-Wind Keewaydin,
To the Islands of the Blessed,
To the kingdom of Ponemah,
To the land of the Hereafter!

Henry W. Longfellow,
The Song of Hiawatha

The theme that death is not the end of human life sounds through all religions. The ancient Egyptians buried their mummified nobility with the food and valuables necessary for the journey to the next life, in elaborate tombs decorated with statues or paintings of Osiris, god of that world. Confucians and practitioners of traditional African religions remember and appease ancestors with special ceremonies on their graves or at sacred sites, while Hindus and

Buddhists speak of karma and reincarnation. The *Koran*, which uses the term "hereafter" (*al-'akhira*) 113 times, frequently discusses the resurrection and judgment. Many Christians worship by regularly reciting the Apostles' Creed: "I believe in . . . the resurrection of the body and the life everlasting." In fact, the belief in life after death is so central to religion that one author contends that it is more fundamental than the belief in God, so that if God did not exist, he would have to be created in order to "function as the benevolent purveyor of man's immortality."[1]

Yet since we all die, is it reasonable to believe that we will live again after our deaths? Polls indicate that many people believe we will. But statistics from opinion polls provide little help in determining the truth of the belief. Our task must be to assess the evidence.

Terminology

The first problem concerns the terminology we should use to discuss the subject. Though people frequently speak of *immortality*, we should use this term cautiously. Literally, it means "not-dying," and this appears to conflict with the fact that all persons die. If immortality, understood literally, is to be possible, there must be some part of us, with which we associate our personal identity, which can survive physical death and corruption. For many, such a thing is called a soul. When the body dies, the soul that we have (or better, are) lives on — in another sphere of existence, with or without a body of some sort.

An associated concept is reincarnation. Literally, it means that after death we again take up bodily existence. Typically, though not always,[2] this view invokes a belief in a soul or self that survives death and can exist independently while it transmigrates from one body to another. Those who believe in reincarnation generally hold that this transmigration occurs numerous times, until the person achieves final liberation.

Others use the term *resurrection*. According to one traditional interpretation, bodies are resurrected to be rejoined with a continuing soul. The Catholic tradition holds that unless the body that is reunited with the soul is the self-same body that died, the deceased and resurrected persons cannot be the same.[3]

Still others speak of the *re-creation* of individual persons sometime after their death.[4] There is no literal immortality, no persisting soul, but simply life after death. Human existence is gap-inclusive: we live, die and our bodies disintegrate, and in the future are re-created to live again. What is re-created is our entire psychophysical being, which, though it allows the re-created to be the same person as the deceased, might have many features (for example, appearance, physical composition, lack of certain diseases) different from those we have now.

It is obvious that there is no philosophically neutral way to address the topic. Language about immortality invokes the concept of a *soul* or *self* that is both the locus of personal identity and capable of persisting through physical death. One can witness one's own funeral. Language about life after death accords with the truism that we all die, but in doing so (if understood literally) rules out the identification of ourselves with a persisting soul-entity. Of course, one might take a more restricted view of death as applying solely to the body, and understand life after death as life after the death of the body. Then "life after death" is compatible with viewing persons as ensouled beings, but it leads to a different understanding of death (that is, death of the body versus death of the person).

In what follows we shall have to make a language choice. Since the term *life after death* seems the most neutral, we generally will speak of the problem of life after death, though in some contexts the term *immortality* will more accurately capture the thought.

Concepts of Life after Death

Just as the language about life after death is diverse, so are different people's concepts of life after death. Four bear noting.

First, according to one widely held view, we achieve our immortality in the living presence of ourselves in the things or persons that continue after our death.[5] We will term this view *immortality by remembrance*. Craftspersons, writers, and artists put something of themselves—their beliefs, hopes, fears, and views of the world—into their work. They hope that their creations will have lasting significance, so that their fame will long outlive them. Other persons gain immortality by painting on the canvas of history: holding political office, winning or losing battles, revolting against authority, committing outrageous crimes, or making great discoveries or inventions. Still others obtain their immortality by helping change the lives of others.

The philosopher George Santayana (1863–1952) suggested that the human desire for immortality and the frustration resulting from recognizing our own mortality find their outlet in human reproduction.[6] We seek to prolong our lives in the lives of our children. Consequently, many desire to have male children to continue the family name, give their children their own or their forebears' names, or put parental pressure on their children to espouse their beliefs, values, and ideals or take up their own occupations.

One problem with this view is that it is divorced from the moral and spiritual dimensions that usually are associated with immortality. In religious contexts, belief in immortality and preparation for it encourage and reinforce moral action. But immortality as remembrance only advises accomplishment of the noteworthy or memorable. This means that immoral and inhumane acts are equally if not more likely to bring remembrance than moral acts. A Lee Harvey Oswald is remembered as well as, if not better than, a William Wilberforce. A second problem is that this view fails to touch on the historical question of our own future existence. It is not insignificant that we want others to remember us, but we also want to know what will happen to *us* after we die. For example, will we be resurrected?

The philosophical absurdities that haunt the concept of a literal resurrection have led some to advocate a second view of life after death. For example, Rudolph Bultmann (1884–1976) concludes that "an historical fact which involves a resurrection from the dead is utterly inconceivable!"[7] Dead persons cannot be resuscitated. Resurrection, as a mythological event, must be demythologized to ascertain its *existential significance for our present life*. Resurrection language is language about power over sin and our freedom from guilt. Resurrected persons are those who live with renewed commitment to the full realization of their authentic selves.

Similarly, D. Z. Phillips (1934–   ) suggests that the immortality of the soul has nothing to do with a life that extends beyond or begins after death.[8] Death is not an event that a person experiences, like drinking coffee or getting chicken pox; rather, it is the end of all that person's possibilities. Accordingly, it is necessary to reinterpret immortality in terms of our present experience and life. Eternal life is not an extension of one's life, but the present reality of goodness. It is not more life, but quality of present life. Thus, when religion speaks about the eternal life of the soul, it indicates that what is important is overcoming death, not in the sense that we survive death, but that we die to ourselves by living unselfishly for others.

The emphasis on the quality of our present life helpfully corrects the previous view of immortality as remembrance. The doctrine of life after death should have implications for our moral living. But this view wrongly takes such implications as the doctrine's meaning, and in doing so has reduced its quantitative dimensions to the qualitative. That is, this view too leaves the historical question untouched. As we shall see, such questions as "Is death the end of our existence?" or "Should we prepare for a future life?" are not meaningless.

A third view, prevalent in Vedāntic Hinduism and Mahāyāna Buddhism, is that after death we experience *union with the One* or Non-dual. Reality ultimately is one, though it can be viewed either from the perspective of the reality that evolves itself as this world (*Brahman*), or the subject or self (*ātman*). The self that I am (*ātman*) transcends my senses, mind, intellect, feeling, and will; it is pure consciousness. But my consciousness is not independent of all other consciousness; rather, in my self cosmic or universal consciousness is manifested. Since *ātman* is *Brahman*, individual human consciousness manifests the One. We have forgotten our essential unity or identity with the One; we wrongly believe we are distinct from it. Thus we are caught in the cycle of suffering. At some future time our separation from the One will be recognized to be an illusion, and we will be liberated to (re)gain union with it.

Here the historical question about the individual's future existence is answered, but in a way that might seem to have little significance for the individual. Once union with the One occurs, the individual no longer is aware of any uniqueness or distinct existence. It is like putting a drop of water into the ocean; the drop adds to the whole, but its identity is not preserved. Indeed, desire to preserve our identity is the root of our problems. The acceptance of this view as true depends on one's larger view of reality and the human predicament—that is, on whether one believes that all is one and that the source of suffering and unhappiness is our alienation from the One.

A fourth view might be termed *personal life after death*. On this view, individual persons either continue to live subsequent to their bodily death, or begin to exist sometime after their own death. Two requirements must be met. First, that which makes for personal identity must be present in the person in the afterlife. Second, individuals must have sufficient reason to think they are the same person that they were prior to death. That is, there must be an awareness of self-identity. If this is not present, their immortality has no more significance for *them* than would the birth of someone in Tanzania after they die. This identification can be ensured, at least in part, by an awareness of who one is and the presence of true memories about the previous life.[9]

It is this last view—the actual or historical existence of the individual person—that we will discuss. What we want to know is whether individual, personal life after death really does or will occur. But to ask this question presupposes a prior one, for only if it is *possible* that persons can live subsequent to their death can it *actually* occur. In fact, almost without exception, the denial of life after death is grounded not on arguments against its actuality, but on the contention that it is impossible.

But what critical factors govern its possibility? Its possibility turns on the following considerations. The first concerns whether a powerful mediating agent exists to make life after death possible. If living on is a natural event, if the soul can survive and in some natural way acquire another body, as is held in Hinduism, the existence of a separate, powerful agent is unnecessary and not an issue. If living on is not a natural state, it requires the existence and action of a being who has the special power to bring it about that persons live subsequent to their death. That is, if it is true that we all die, not simply in body but in self, then unless an omnipotent or extremely powerful God exists, there is no ground for thinking that there can be any life after death. For our purposes, and following from earlier chapters in this book, we shall assume that it is reasonable to believe that a God with this power exists.

The second consideration concerns the nature of human persons. Objections to the possibility of life after death generally presuppose particular views of the human person. Hence, if life after death is to be possible, human persons must be the sort of being that can live subsequent to their death. If they are not, then whether life after death is actual is a moot issue. Thus, before discussing the question "What good reasons can be given for believing in life after death?" we must discuss the philosophically prior question: "What is the nature of human persons?"

Personal Identity and the Soul

"What is the nature of human persons?" is no easy question to answer. One approach argues that we cannot identify ourselves with our physical being. Although we believe that we have the same personal identity we had several years ago, our physical bodies and their components continually change. Our body is something that we have, in contrast to something that we are. Our posture, movement, appearance, and physical characteristics express the self that we are but do not constitute it.

Furthermore, the person cannot be identified with the mind — that is, with individual states of consciousness, categories of thought, memories, and the particular way we experience and understand the world. First, individual memories, categories, and states of consciousness can be altered or lost without loss of personal identity. We do not remember most of what occurred when we were 5 or 10, or even last year. And we think about things differently from the way we did a number of years ago.

Second, memory claims are not infallible. We might claim to remember certain things that never happened. Hence we must distinguish between memory claims and true memory claims. Only the latter would suffice as the criterion of personal identity. But what makes my memory claim a true memory claim? Two things, at least: For one, it must accurately report what in fact occurred; and for another, it must be *my* memory claim. But if only genuine memories can be used as criteria for personal identity, and if my genuine memories are memories only had by me, then it becomes impossible to hold that memory claims constitute personal identity without begging the question. In sum, our mental states might be used as evidence for establishing or assigning personal identity, but they do not constitute personal identity.

Perhaps we are a nonreducible, ultimate, unanalyzable self.[10] We do not say we have a self, but that we are a self. Although we recognize the personal identity of others through their distinctive physical characteristics and behavioral patterns, we know our own self either through some inner, intuitive self-awareness or through having experiences.[11] The self, the subject and center of our experiences, is the agent of thinking, remembering, feeling, and understanding.

Four kinds of evidence can be given in defense of this notion. First, one way in which we understand ourselves is as conscious beings who have self-awareness, beliefs, desires, intentions, and feelings. It is not that each of us uniquely has these, but rather that each has his own individualized set. Further, access to this set is private. I might infer from your behavior what you are thinking or feeling, but my access to you is never direct; it is always mediated. But in my own case it is immediate. I have a good idea about how I feel at this moment — and even if I am mistaken, I am not mistaken that I think that this is the way I feel.

The physical, however, is public. Our body and its processes are perceptible to others. Since the public and the private are contradictories, that which is about something private cannot at the same time be about something public. Consequently, introspective reports about our selves and our mental states cannot be about something public.[12]

A second line of argument begins with the observation that an essential feature of ourselves is that we are persons to whom can be ascribed moral responsibility. But if we are to be held morally accountable for our thoughts and actions, we must be free. But what is it to be free? One notion, the incompatibilist view of freedom, maintains that given the same causal conditions, a person can choose to perform either one action or another, or alternatively described, can choose to do or refrain from doing a certain action. But if we are identified with our physical components, if our psychological language refers to nothing over and above the physiological events that occur in the brain and central nervous system, then our choices are products of and explainable in terms of prior causal conditions, and these in terms of other causal conditions that extend beyond ourselves, even prior to our own existence.

If our choices and actions ultimately depend upon causal conditions outside ourselves, and if these in turn are placed in the larger deterministic causal chain, our actions are not free. But without freedom, the indeterminist holds, we cannot be held morally accountable for our deeds; neither can there be a true *ought*, which requires that we act one way rather than another. What this suggests is that for humans to be free, there must be something in us that is not part of any physical, deterministic causal chain, and that whatever this is, it is essential to our personhood, insofar as the capacity to make moral choices and moral accountability for our actions are essential features of our personhood.

A third argument is based on a strange but real phenomenon—that of one body housing, as it were, several different personalities or persons. Each has its own memories, its own behavioral patterns that affect even the appearance of the body, and even its own name. Some of these persons are known to the others housed in the same body and are in contact with them; others are unknown and isolated.[13] If one body can house several different persons, or if several different persons can share the same body, it would appear that the body cannot be the locus of personal identity.

What is not obvious is how best to describe this phenomenon. Should we say that there are several persons in one body (a case of multiple personalities), or should we say that there is one person manifesting several different aspects of one personality (a case of split personality)? The fact that each person has a distinct self-concept; personality; and set of character traits, ways of thinking and acting, and memories, and that each at times can know the other as a separate person (for example, Eve Black holds she is not married to Eve White's husband) argues that the former interpretation is correct. On the other hand, one might suggest that this is an abnormal case, that here is a person who is so fragmented that she cannot hold the various aspects of herself together—something most of us are able to do. It is true that we show different sides of ourselves in different contexts, but these different perspectives do not leave us fragmented. However, in a pathological condition, what holds these perspectives together is lost, so that what results is a kaleidoscope rather than a whole person. The fact that the persons have different memories or experiences does not argue for their plurality, but rather is caused by a repression of some states, which under proper conditions reappear despite the repression. Which of these options is correct even psychiatrists who treat such cases have difficulty deciding.[14]

A fourth argument is developed from the alleged existence of human paranormal powers. Minds purportedly have the power to communicate with other minds where no normal communication (in terms of a physical causal chain) would be possible (telepathy), to discern physical states of affairs without being able to perceive them (clairvoyance), and to move physical objects without using physical means (psychokinesis). For example, experiments have been conducted showing that persons can communicate telepathically with others at a distance, even when the subject is enclosed in chambers walled with lead or iron.[15] But paranormal phenomena are incompatible with a materialistic conception of the mind, for they presuppose that the mind is capable of receiving information about the world and other minds or producing physical effects without requiring, as brains do, intermediate physical agencies.[16]

For some, extrasensory experiences such as these are an undisputed fact.[17] Others are more dubious, grounding their worries on the possibility that the experiments either are not carefully enough constructed to exclude fraud or else are subject to serious allegations of irregularity. So whereas some treat such experiences as established fact, others affirm that "it is fair to claim that so far, no paranormal results have been satisfactorily repeatable."[18]

For many, these four strains of evidence suggest that humans are some sort of nonphysical self (which might be termed a soul) that currently exists in a body. The functions of this self include self-awareness, memory, conceiving, and emoting. Although currently occurring in conjunction with the body, these functions might occur apart from it.

The implications of this view for life after death are obvious. If the self is identified with a nonphysical entity, then since dying is a physical process, there is no reason to think that the soul's existence would terminate at physical death. Of course, death might significantly affect the quality of soul-life. The corruption of the body would end those functions, such as sensation, that require mutual involvement of both the physical and nonphysical. However, what is not dependent upon the physical could survive and continue. Furthermore, since the soul is the self, there are sufficient grounds for holding that life after death is personal. We would survive physical death with our self-identity and self-awareness essentially intact.

Criticism of the Soul-Concept

This view of human persons is not without difficulty. Perhaps the most substantial problem is that after death, this immaterial self would have to sustain such functions as conceptualization and memory recall, which implies that the physical brain is not a necessary condition for these and other sorts of cognitive processes. But this runs counter to the latest psychological and physiological research. For one thing, there is good evidence that certain mental abilities and the degree to which they function successfully are in part inherited. For example, researchers have compared the intelligence of members of natural families. The highest correlation exists between identical twins, and progressively diminishes, though remains significant, for fraternal twins, siblings, parents and children, and grandparents and grandchildren. The farther removed the genetic relation, the lower is the correlation. Moreover, diseases affecting the mind, such as Down's syndrome, or susceptibility to diseases such as Alzheimer's are genetically based. This indicates that the physical process of heredity plays a major role in determining mental ability and function.

Second, damage to the brain directly affects awareness, consciousness, memory, and conceptual ability. For example, a person whose brain hemispheres have been severed (a split brain person), when presented with an object on the left that is sensed only by the right hemisphere of the brain, cannot tell what he saw, though he can point to it with his left hand. The right brain, which controls the left hand, knows the object, but the left brain, which is the main area for speech and communication, does not know of the object because no information passes through the severed corpus callosum.

Third, certain mental abilities, such as memory, seem to be locatable in the brain. It is true that individual thought processes cannot yet be correlated with particular energy transfers in the brain, and probably never will be. Yet we can discern patterns of energy events. This makes possible brain research into mental functions. Finally, intelligence of certain kinds, though not specifically localized, is associated with specific cerebral hemispheres. Analytic, conceptual, verbal intelligence is located in the left hemisphere of the brain, while the right hemisphere controls the artistic and intuitive mental processes.

This means that a dilemma confronts defenders of the soul thesis. Either they deny that the soul continues to be conscious and to perform cognitive activities after death, or else they deny the mass of psychological and physiological evidence indicating that the brain is necessary for the existence and functioning of the mind. The latter is unacceptable in light of contemporary brain research. The former is impossible for believers in the immortality of the soul, since removal of its ability to perform mental activities effectively deprives it of any significant function.

To escape this dilemma, believers in the soul might maintain that though in our present life something physical, such as a brain, is necessary for consciousness and thinking, this can be supplied in the afterlife by something else, perhaps something quasiphysical. For example, there might be an ethereal body appended to the soul immediately at the death of the physical body.

This suggestion raises one final question — namely, what kind of existence after death does the believer in the soul envision? There are two major schemas, though each has many permutations. In the one, the soul at death immediately unites with a body of some sort. Some religions, which hold to reincarnation, believe this to be another physical body. Others hold that it is a spiritual body. In both cases verification is difficult. It is problematic in the latter case because presumably the spiritual body exists on a different spatiotemporal plane. It is problematic in the former case since with the exception of yogis who have achieved the higher meditative states, the reincarnate generally lacks any awareness of previous existence, so that for the individual person there is no meaningful experiential difference between being reborn and being born new.

In the other schema, the soul continues to exist disembodied, either temporarily until united with a body or permanently. During its disembodied state its activities would be of a paranormal sort. Perception would require the addition of new and different powers or the extension of currently little-used perceptual powers such as clairvoyance and telepathy. Its agency would be described in terms of thoughts and desires alone causing certain events, as in psychokinesis. H. H. Price (1899–1984) suggested that the next world is composed of souls having mental images, about which they have beliefs and desires. "There might be a set of visual images related to each other perspectively, with front views and side views and back views all fitting neatly together in the way that ordinary visual appearances do now."[19] Such a group of images might also contain tactile, taste, auditory and olfactory images, so that a nexus of interrelated images would constitute an object. One might even have a visual image of the body one had in the prior life. This body image might form the center of one's image world, much as our body now does. The entire environment of the disembodied individual would be composed of such families of mental images and would serve as the immortal's world. Development of some such scenario would be necessary to avoid solipsism (the view that the individual self is the whole of reality).

The Self as a Psychophysical Unity

Because of the problems of understanding the self as a soul, many contemporary philosophers have sought personal identity in our psychophysical unity. One contemporary view, called the Identity Theory or Central State Materialism, holds that human beings are nothing more than physical organisms. This should not be taken to imply that mental or psychical states such as perceiving, conceptualizing, or remembering are not real. What it does mean is that insofar as a statement about a mental state is a report of something, that something is a brain process, brain state, or a process within the central nervous system.[20] That is, the event that the mental language reports is ultimately the same as or identical to the event that would be reported by the neurologist. The mind is what the brain does. Thus what those who hold these views deny is not that we can speak about minds or mental states, but that states of consciousness are irreducibly psychical.

Other instances of identity between things in different categories illustrate this relationship.[21] Lightning can be reported by using either the physicist's language about an electrical discharge occurring at a particular place and time, or the language of the ordinary observer who reports a bright flash of light, jaggedly etched across the stormy sky. Although the two people use noninterchangeable language systems, both genuinely report one and the same event.

The major problem facing the Identity Theory concerns the nature of this cross-category identity. Defenders of the view claim that mental and brain states are neither merely related causally nor simply constantly correlated. They opt for strict identity between the two. But according to a traditional principle (called Leibniz's principle of the identity of indiscernibles), two things are identical only if every property of one is also a property of the other. But the properties of mental states and brain states differ, not the least in that the former are nonspatial and private, whereas the latter are spatial and public. One might respond that Leibniz's principle does not apply to cross-category identities. In particular, one cannot expect total identity of properties where the application of the property to one category would be meaningless (as would be the case in applying spatial predicates to mental states). But then what criteria do two things with different category-sets of properties have to meet to be identical? In the case of the mind and body, we have mental events and brain events occurring at the same time. But what shows that they are not causally related rather than identical?

Recent reductionists such as Douglas Hofstadter (1945-   ) have taken the materialist perspective a step farther: I am not my body; I have a body. The physical body can be artificially replaced. What is significant is the brain, for were I to undergo a body transplant, I would stay with the brain, not go with the body. But I do not seem to be simply my brain either. Were I to commit a crime and then be separated from my brain, which continues unabated in a vat of nutrients, the authorities would not rest content with incarcerating my brain (as me) while letting my body roam free.

What then are we? The self is the locus of meaning, understood on the symbolic level as a representational system, that is, "an active, self-updating collection of structures organized to 'mirror' the world as it evolves."[22] These high-level structures are composed of lower-level active patterns, and these of still lower patterns, until we reach the lowest level, which consists of nothing more than neural firings. Taken individually, these neural firings are random and meaningless, but statistical regularity reveals patterns that encode the information necessary for the organism to respond interactively to other patterns of symbols in its environment. When the patterns of firings are interpreted at the highest levels, we give them meaning, and these meaning-assigned patterns become alternative ways of explaining who we are.

Hofstadter gives the analogy of an ant colony. A colony has different levels: the colony itself, groups of different ants such as workers, teams of ants, and the individual ants themselves. We assign meanings to the higher levels (for example, that a group of worker ants is removing the carcass of a fly) and hold that these higher levels encode information for the colony. But these higher-level patterns of behavior are ultimately the mere products of the random motions of individual, unintelligent ants.

We thus exist as programmable machines, replicable by sophisticated (though yet undeveloped) computers. But computer hardware is interchangeable. One kind of hardware can be made to emulate a different kind if it is fed the proper software. Thus, ultimately, it is the patterns—the software—that matter. The precise nature of the hardware is insignificant except as it is able to cause or recognize these patterns.

But are these higher-level patterns, described in language about meanings, intentions, and ends (teleological language), real? Hofstadter suggests that this is ultimately not the case. These higher-level patterns only emerge from the fundamental, nonintelligent actions of the neurons, just as the ant colony emerges from the actions of individual ants. And just as there is no colony over and above individual ants, there is no person over and above neural firings. Hence, we need not appeal ultimately to meaning to account for reality. Of course, we *can* do so, but only because it is easier to explain things this way, because of our penchant to use language ascribing purpose. We even speak of (unconscious) ant colonies as having the goal to reproduce. Thus, language about persons simply becomes one way of speaking about the higher-level patterns that carry coded information. Does this then mean that the concept of person is dispensable? Ultimately we must say yes, for "with some effort I can always remember the other point of view if necessary, and drain all these systems of meaning, too."[23] Since there cannot be any top-down causation, there seems little role for the concept of person in this model, except to cater to our need for easier explanations. Indeed, even freedom or volition is nothing more than a complicated, internal, causal configuration that enables the object to react to its environment as a representational system.

Should we accept such a view? First, there is no doubt that computer simulations of brain processes have contributed enormously to our understanding of brain functions. But the relation between computer and brain seems to be simulation, not replication. Second, this strong view of artificial intelligence damages our humanistic conception of persons. This view, in denying the fundamental reality of persons considered as teleological, meaning-bestowing, free agents; in arguing that the concept of person ultimately can be reduced to the level of causally determined neural activity; and in contending that the higher patterns of meaning have no causal influence on the lower levels leaves us mechanistic shipwrecks, reacting to events in ways that can be described as having meaning, but really do not.

Critical evaluation aside, what are the implications of these materialistic views of the person for the possibility of life after death? Clearly, life after death is not guaranteed by any continuing thing, as in the soul doctrine. If there is to be life after death, the activity of an omnipotent and omniscient God is necessary. In what way? Since on the Identity Theory we are identical with our physiological organism, and since at base that organism is composed of coded matter, it is possible that we could be physically re-created and programmed to possess all the physical and psychical characteristics we had before we died. Specifically, since consciousness is a brain process, our brain could be re-created and programmed to have neural components and structures identical to those of the deceased, so that we would have substantially the same memories, ideas, perspectives, and personality traits as we had before we died.

The radical reductionistic view of persons makes re-creation even more feasible. If we are nothing but programs that are, to some extent, hardware independent, then an omnipotent, omniscient God could re-create us simply by re-creating our program. We would have to be programmed into hardware of some sort, but the specific hardware is insignificant, so long as it is capable of booting up and running the relevant programs.

But would the re-created person be the same as the deceased? In particular, the re-created is neither spatially nor temporally continuous with the deceased. And is not spatiotemporal continuity a necessary condition for all cases of personal identity? It is true that we frequently use spatiotemporal continuity as a criterion to recognize identity; if my painting by Van Gogh were destroyed by fire and then re-created by a skilled copyist, I would hesitate to say that it is an authentic Van Gogh. But why should we think that this criterion specifies what constitutes personal identity? Care must be taken not to confuse the criteria by which we discern identity with those that constitute identity. Furthermore, the fact that all our experience invokes spatiotemporal continuity would not prove that it is necessary to *all* cases of personal identity. Re-creation of persons could very well be the exceptional case.

An interesting exception to our use of the criterion of spatiotemporal continuity occurs in magic. Magicians by their actions encourage us to believe that the object they make reappear is identical with the object they made disappear, despite our — and perhaps anyone's — inability to trace its interim existence. This does not prove that it happens, but the fact that magicians bring their audience to believe this suggests that at least we believe it is possible. Similar things might be said concerning the way we treat characters in television serials. We experience no logical difficulty treating them as gap-inclusive people — as persons who continue to exist after commercials or on weekly installments. How else can one explain the fact that people constantly write letters to these characters?

But are the deceased and the re-created identical? The answer depends, of course, upon the criteria we use for constituting personal identity. If they include internal states of consciousness (including conceptual categories and memories) and personality traits or patterns, then it is possible that these can be repeated in the re-created person, and if repeated, then there are grounds for suggesting that the same person lives again.

But, it is objected, making memory claims about being the person who did such and such at some previous time does not compel us to assert the identity of the individual who makes the claim with the deceased. It is logically possible that there be two persons who make identical memory claims and have identical personalities. Where we have two claimants, James and John, both claiming to be re-creations of Peter, these criteria would provide no grounds for deciding which is really Peter.[24] However, though it is true that there is no way of deducing identity from the above features, two people cannot have the same memories (true memory claims) about experiences had only by one person and still not be the same. Identity appears to be deducible from true memories. Hence, though we might not be able to discern whether it was James or John who was identical with the deceased Peter, both cannot be identical, for only one can make true memory claims (assuming that the same person cannot be in two different places at the same time).

Of course, we could create all kinds of scenarios. For example, we might envision a case whereby one person had half of the deceased's true memories, and the other person the other half. Or we could have persons dividing like amoebas into two identical beings, in which case both could be making true memory claims. But these speculative possibilities would create difficulties only if there were two claimants. It does not follow that, where there is only one claimant, he cannot be the same as the deceased.[25] The theistic re-creationist could cogently suppose that God would re-create only one person who would make the relevant memory claims concerning the experiences of the deceased. Consequently, where there is only one claimant, it would be reasonable to hold that true memory claims, in conjunction with similarity of personality characteristics and perspectives of understanding, would provide good grounds for identifying the re-created with the deceased.[26]

The conclusion of all this is that both perspectives on the human person — that we are souled beings or that we are psychophysical unities or even mere programs — allow for the possibility of life after death. One cannot reject the doctrine on the grounds that it is contradictory or absurd.

A Posteriori *Arguments for Life after Death*

Granted, then, that life after death is possible, is there any reason to think that it actually occurs? Two sorts of arguments can be suggested: *a priori* philosophical arguments and *a posteriori* arguments from certain sorts of experience. We will look at the *a posteriori* first, and then turn to the *a priori*.

Three types of *a posteriori* arguments hold attraction. The first appeals to claims about near-death or life-after-life experiences of persons who either have almost died or have died but were resuscitated (depending on one's definition of death). As the persons lie dying they hear themselves pronounced either dying or dead. They then find themselves leaving or out of their body, witnessing from a different perspective (often from above) their body, immediate surroundings, and the people working to resuscitate their body. They now possess a new body, variously described as an amorphous cloud or a spiritual body shaped as the physical body was, which is incapable of interacting with the physical environment of their original body. After this they experience passing through a dark place, often described as a tunnel, until they come to a different realm. Here they encounter other persons, not physically embodied though often recognizable, with whom they communicate in some telepathic way. They also encounter a being of light, exuding love and compassion, who helps them to recall (as if by an instantaneous videotape) and evaluate their past. Despite their strong desire to stay and enjoy this peaceful and happy experience, they either want to or are told to return to their physical bodies.[27]

There is no doubt that people have such experiences. The problem is how to understand or explain them. Some have argued that these are products of hallucination. Physiological conditions in the body can cause a person to have unusual experiences, similar in part to those described. "A change in blood pressure in the inner ear can evoke a sense of rising, hovering, floating in space." Such a change can occur when the bloodflow through the body is checked, as with cardiac arrest. Likewise, the experience of visualizing one's body "as if from the outside itself becomes more common when a person is subject to serious emotional stress," as happens in near-death experiences, or is taking powerful drugs, as is sometimes the case with dying persons.[28] Yet descriptions given by these persons of the immediate circumstances surrounding their body have an amazing accuracy, not characterized by what one would expect in a drug-induced account. Sometimes they even describe what is going on in the room or in nearby rooms that they could not observe from their patient-bed. Paul Badham (1942–   ) cites a case of a patient accurately reporting two coins on the top of a high cupboard in the room. However, experiments — for example, when secret numbers have been placed near the ceiling in a position that could be viewed only from above — have failed to yield consistently positive results.

Perhaps these after-death experiences can be explained as religious phenomena. Christians, for example, have a penchant for interpreting the being of light as Jesus, Hindus as the death god Yama or other Hindu deities. This suggests that these experiences may be individual projections or mystical or religious visions, colored by the persons' religious backgrounds and beliefs, and occasioned by the traumatic experience through which they are going.

Yet the descriptions vary significantly from standard religious expectations. Raymond Moody (1944–   ) writes, "I have not heard a single reference to a heaven or a hell anything like the customary picture to which we are exposed in this society. Indeed, many persons have stressed how unlike their experiences were to what they had been led to expect in the course of their religious training."[29]

In addition to the being of light, they also report seeing relatives. This would not be striking, except for the fact that sometimes they encounter people whom they had not met before but later recognize in a picture or people who (unknown to them) have just died. Badham gives the case of a "child met by her grandfather's mother of whom she had no previous knowledge, but whose photograph she recognized with great enthusiasm when first visiting an uncle's home some time after her recovery. Apparently she had never seen that photo before, nor did any other member of the family possess a photograph of this long departed relative."[30]

Part of the puzzle of these cases is the difficulty experienced in recounting the kind of body possessed. It is invisible, able to move through physical objects, and weightless (floating), yet it has powers of perception and can hear (though more so in terms of thought-transfer than having auditory experiences). This suggests that this world and the people in it are "embodied" in a way that makes them recognizable and locatable from a particular perspective, yet possessing only a partial, one-way relationship to our present world. That is, they are briefly aware of the physical environment, yet cannot influence it at all. However one interprets this new body, two of the elements we deemed necessary for personal immortality are present: awareness of their own identity and recollection of their past.

The second *a posteriori* argument comes from psychical research into mediumistic communication with deceased persons. If mediums really do communicate with deceased persons, this would provide evidence that people survive death.

Appeal to mediums working through séances is often discounted, not only because of the possible and proven cases of fraud, but because what they recount of the deceased can be accounted for more easily by appealing either to role-playing by various parts of the medium's conscious or unconscious personality, or to telepathic communication from those present and seeking information about the deceased. It is the sitters' expectations that are met, expectations that perhaps in some way can be communicated to the alleged medium.[31]

However, some cases are more difficult to explain in this fashion. There are instances wherein deceased persons have appeared to the living and conveyed to them information that was verifiable but previously unknown. C. D. Broad (1887–1971) recounts the case of a North Carolina farmer who appeared four years after his death to inform a surviving son about the location of his lost last will.[32] There are also the attempts by people involved in the Society for Psychical Research to communicate after their death with the living. One deceased person allegedly dictated thousands of pages through the automatic writing of mediums in Great Britain, Australia, and the United States. These writings were like a jig-saw puzzle that, individually interpreted, made little sense, but when fitted together contained alleged evidence that they were produced by one person.[33]

Yet even here reasonable suspicions can be entertained. Why must the communications from these individuals be so cryptic, complex, and filled only with allusions? How these diverse messages can be correlated is itself subject to differing speculative interpretations, suggesting that the finished product is more the work of the collator than of a communicating, deceased person. Further, the communicants give no indication that their life has continued on in any meaningful way in the afterlife.[34] They give no detailed indication of their new surroundings, occupations, or interests, and what is said often contains vague generalizations easily ascribable to the medium's beliefs about the afterlife.

A third *a posteriori* argument commences from the claim that certain persons actually have come back to life. In Christianity, the belief that Jesus was resurrected from the dead is coupled with the theological assertion that this event both foretokens and makes possible our resurrection. The Apostle Paul's argument is this: If Christ was raised from the dead, we will be raised from the dead. Christ was raised. Therefore we will be raised.[35]

The soundness of this argument depends on the truth of both premises. The first premise is theological. Thus, knowledge of its truth depends on accepting a number of other claims, including that God exists, that he can reveal his promises and purposes, that he is trustworthy to keep and powerful enough to implement them, and that he actually revealed this to Paul. The orthodox Christian theist presumably would have little problem with any of these presuppositions. The truth of the second premise depends on whether the claim that Jesus was resurrected is historically true. Christians often introduce claims about witnesses to the living Jesus, the empty tomb, and the rise and success of the Christian Church as evidence that it really occurred.[36]

Each of these *a posteriori* arguments depends upon claims persons make about experiences they have had. To evaluate the claims means that we must consider the criteria that we ordinarily invoke to evaluate the testimony or report made by other persons. The difficulty, generally, is not that people have had the experiences they claim to have had, but how to understand and interpret those experiences. And this brings us back to the larger world-view each of us brings to our experience. It is to the shaping of this world-view that this book is addressed.

A Priori *Arguments for Life after Death*

In addition to these *a posteriori* arguments, there are numerous *a priori* arguments. Let us note three of them.

The first argument was developed by Thomas Aquinas (c. 1224–1274).[37] He argued that we are made for an ultimate end, which is happiness. But happiness cannot be achieved in this life, for our individual fortune is fickle, our body and will weak, and our knowledge imperfect. But since God cannot have made us in vain, we must be able to achieve the end for which we were made, and this requires that we continue to live after death.

But why should one think that we cannot achieve happiness in this life? Aristotle[38] (384–322 B.C.) suggests that happiness is not a momentary feeling of pleasure, but a state in which the person manifests virtues throughout his lifetime. If we engage in the activity of reason or contemplation, we can attain it. We need not lose happiness simply because of momentary adversity.

Thomas, however, understands happiness differently. Human happiness must relate to the ultimate end for which we were made, which is God. Since our knowledge of God by faith is an act of the will, not the intellect, our present knowledge of God by natural reason can be erroneous and uncertain. Hence, knowledge or contemplation of God, in which lies our ultimate happiness, is not (except momentarily) attainable in this life. To fully experience this beatific vision, we must live subsequent to our death.

Thomas's argument rests on the very interesting (and debatable) thesis that we would have been made in vain if we cannot achieve our ultimate end. But is God's creation of us compromised if we fail to achieve our ultimate end, no matter what other ends we realize? If we achieve limited fulfillment of human potential or a partially realized life of happiness, or if we come to know God in our own limited way and actualize our intellectual capacity through contemplation of what truth can be known, and live a virtuous life, participating in the grace of God, there would seem to be no grounds for the claim that we have lived in vain. On the other hand, if part of our end is fulfilled in contemplative communion with God, it would seem reasonable to think that God would not let us fail to achieve this highest end for which we are made. Clearly this argument comes laden with theological as well as philosophical presuppositions.

A second *a priori* proof, using basically the same argumentative structure, commences from moral premises. In general, the moral argument asserts that since finite human existence is insufficient either to achieve the moral ideal or to provide an adequate basis on which to recommend the performance of good rather than evil, humans must be immortal. The former contention is advanced by Immanuel Kant (1724–1804).[39] The moral law tells us that we must strive to achieve the highest good. But unless we can realize this highest good, we cannot be commanded to attain it. But this highest good—the perfect alignment of our individual wills with the moral law, so that we act solely out of respect for the moral law (what Kant calls holiness) and not out of inclination—is not achievable in this life. Hence, if the moral law is to have any bite, if we are to be obligated to live under it, we must be able to live past death, at least to the point at which we can become holy. Life after death is a postulate of the moral law.

But why, one might ponder, must we be able to realize completely the highest good in order to be commanded rationally to pursue it? Often goals are ideals toward which a person strives, which may, at best, be only partially realizable. I have the ideal to be truthful, and am commanded morally to speak the truth, though I have no illusions about attaining perfect truthfulness. In Kant's defense, however, it might be argued that there is a difference between commanding that we *strive* to attain a goal and commanding that we *attain* it. The moral law commands the latter, not the former.

A third argument was advanced by Plato (428–347 B.C.), and applies to the dualist conception of the human person. Plato argued that the soul is immortal because it is imperishable, it is imperishable because it is indestructible, and it is indestructible because it is simple (not divisible into parts).[40] But why cannot the soul perish in other ways—for example, by simply being annihilated? There seems to be no reason why what is simple cannot be annihilated. On the other hand, since annihilation would require the activity of some outside agent, Plato's argument does suggest that it is reasonable to believe that, in itself, the soul does live on and does not die with the disintegration of the physical body.

Prospects

What conclusions can be drawn from our discussion? First, we have seen that there is considerable debate over how best to understand the human person. Perhaps the conclusion the investigator draws depends less upon the particular evidence marshalled than upon how it fits into one's larger philosophical schema. In any case, we have argued that life after death is possible no matter what the perspective on the human person. If one adopts the view that the soul is the real person, then there is reason to think that immortality is possible, since physical death does not necessarily mean the end of the soul. It is possible that the soul persists through death. If one adopts a materialistic view of the person, then the possibility of life after death depends upon the existence of a powerful, omniscient God who is capable of re-creating persons to be essentially the same as the deceased. If one denies the existence of God or refuses to ascribe to him the relevant powers, then life after death for the anthropological materialist seems impossible. If, however, God exists, then at least the possibility of re-creation exists.

But what about its actuality? Here the evidence is far from clear. The *a posteriori* arguments depend upon claims that might have other plausible explanations. The *a priori* arguments rest on claims concerning, for example, the appropriate goal of human action or what the moral law requires. In both cases the reader must evaluate the claims for herself, judiciously deciding which explanation best accounts for the data.

Often those who find arguments for immortality convincing have already adopted a particular theistic world-view in which these claims not only make sense, but contribute in an intrinsic way to a present, meaningful existence in which encounter with God and the desire to realize their end in him play an essential role, and in which the afterlife simply provides for a higher realization of these possibilities. This is not a defect, but a recognition that any view of the world should have a coherence of structure and meaning.

STUDY QUESTIONS

1. Do you believe in life after death? To what evidence or arguments do you appeal to support the response you give.

2. What presuppositions about the nature of human persons are made by those who talk literally about human immortality? How might these presuppositions differ from those held by someone who speaks simply about life after death? Why do you think that language matters when we speak about important topics?

3. We noted four different views of life after death. In what ways are they similar and different? Present an argument that might be given in support of each view, and another that is critical of each.

4. What is personal identity? What do you consider to be the most significant evidence to show that our personal identity is to be found in a nonreducible, ultimate self? Note a strength and weakness of this evidence.

5. Give a description of the materialist conception of human persons. What problems face this view? What are the implications of the view for the possibility of life after death?

6. In what ways would the characteristics of the afterlife differ for the believer in a soul from those described by the materialist? What problems (for example, population, human fulfillment, time consciousness) might result from humans living after their death?

7. Which of the arguments presented in this chapter for the actuality of life after death do you think is the strongest? Why do you think so? Note the critical premise of that argument and evaluate its truth.

NOTES

1. Corliss Lamont, *The Illusion of Immortality* (New York: The Philosophical Library, 1965), p. 7.
2. According to the Theravāda Buddhist doctrine of *anātta*, there is no persisting self substance. See David Kalupahana, *Buddhist Philosophy* (Honolulu: University of Hawaii, 1976), pp. 38–42.
3. Thomas Aquinas, *Summa Theologica*, trans, Fathers of the English Dominican Province (Westminster, MD: Christian Classics, 1981), Part III supplement, Q. 79, A. 2. Paul Badham quotes a 1976 Catholic catechism for adults approved in Ireland and the United States, which states that each person will one day rise again "as the same person he was, in the same flesh made living by the same spirit." Paul Badham and Linda Badham, *Immortality or Extinction?* (New York: Barnes & Noble, 1982), p. 5.
4. John Hick, *Death and Eternal Life* (New York: Harper & Row, 1976), chap. 15; Bruce R. Reichenbach, *Is Man the Phoenix? A Study of Immortality* (Grand Rapids: William B. Eerdmans, 1978), chap. 5.
5. "After his death his words remain established. This is what the ancient saying means. I have heard that the best course is to establish virtue, the next best is to establish achievement, and still the next best is to establish words. When these are not abandoned with time, it may be called immortality." *Tso chuan*, in Wing-Tsit Chan, *A Source Book in Chinese Philosophy* (Princeton, NJ: Princeton University Press, 1963), p. 13. For its place in African religions, see J. S. Mbiti, *African Religions and Philosophy* (New York: Doubleday, 1970), pp. 32–33.
6. George Santayana, *Reason in Religion* (New York: Collier, 1962), pp. 174f.
7. Rudolph Bultmann, in Hans Werner Bartsch, ed., *Kerygma and Myth* (New York: Harper & Row, 1953), p. 39.
8. D. Z. Phillips, *Death and Immortality* (London: Macmillan, 1970), pp. 41–55.
9. A problem relating to the second of these conditions dogs those who advocate reincarnation. Alleged reincarnates are born with their unique genetic code inherited from their parents and go on to develop their own physical characteristics, personality, memories, and categories of understanding. They begin life as infants who have no recollection of former lives, and few ever remember it. Thus, apart from the philosophical theory that they are reincarnated persons, there is no empirical way to distinguish them from new persons. In such cases there might be continuity of a spiritual soul, but where there are no memories, awareness of self-identity, and consciousness of continuity or consistency of experience with the past, we cannot discern whether the person is a reincarnated person or a new individual.
10. Richard Swinburne, *The Coherence of Theism* (Oxford: Oxford University Press, 1977), p. 119.
11. H. D. Lewis, *The Self and Immortality* (New York: Seabury, 1973), p. 45.
12. Kurt Baier, "Smart on Sensation," *The Australasian Journal of Philosophy* 40 (1962); reprinted in C. V. Borst, ed., *The Mind/Brain Identity Theory* (New York: Macmillan, 1970), chap. 8.

13. Corbett H. Thigpen and Harvey M. Cleckley, *The Three Faces of Eve* (New York: McGraw-Hill, 1957), pp. 50–51. See also Flora Rheta Schreiber, *Sybil* (Chicago: Henry Regnery, 1973).

14. Thigpen and Cleckley, p. 38.

15. L. L. Vasiliev, *Experiments in Mental Suggestion* (Church Crookham: Institute for the Study of Mental Images, 1963).

16. Keith Campbell acknowledges that "parapsychology could in principle refute Central-State Materialism," though paradoxically he goes on to suggest that "if some paranormal results were established as genuine, they might . . . be accommodated in a new, expanded, physical science." *Body and Mind* (New York: Doubleday, 1970), pp. 96–97.

17. Hick, p. 121; Badham and Badham, pp. 90–92.

18. Campbell, p. 96. It is puzzling that just a page earlier Campbell apparently does grant credence to Vasiliev's work.

19. H. H. Price, "Survival and the Idea of 'Another World,'" *Proceedings of the Society for Psychical Research* 50, Part 182 (Jan. 1953); reprinted in Terence Penelhum, *Immortality* (Belmont, CA: Wadsworth, 1973), pp. 25–26.

20. J. J. C. Smart, "Sensations and Brain Processes," *The Philosophical Review* 68 (1959); reprinted in Borst, ed., p. 56.

21. U. T. Place, "Is Consciousness a Brain Process?" *The British Journal of Psychology* 47 (1956); reprinted in Borst, ed., p. 47.

22. Douglas R. Hofstadter and Daniel C. Dennett, *The Mind's I* (New York: Basic Books, 1981), p. 192.

23. Hofstadter and Dennett, p. 174.

24. B. A. O. Williams, "Personal Identity and Individuation," *Proceedings of the Aristotelian Society* 57 (1956–57): 239.

25. Hick, p. 292.

26. This stipulation is unsatisfactory if one takes these characteristics as constituting personal identity, for then whether a person's identity continues depends not on empirical factors about the person, but on extraneous factors, such as whether God decided to create two beings rather than one, or whether both entities of the amoeba-like split survived.

27. See Raymond A. Moody, Jr., *Life After Life* (New York: Bantam, 1976).

28. Badham and Badham, p. 73.

29. Moody, p. 140.

30. Badham and Badham, p. 80.

31. Hick (pp. 131–38), with others, terms this *unconscious fraud*.

32. C. D. Broad, *Lectures on Psychical Research* (London: Routledge & Kegan Paul, 1962), pp. 137–39.

33. See Badham and Badham, pp. 95–98, for more details and references.

34. "The spirits do not seem to speak out of the context of a continuing life; they seem to lack a credible environment of their own, a community of which they are a part, real next-world tasks, interests and purposes. They seem instead to be still very much what they were in this world." Hick, p. 140.

35. 1 Cor. 15:12–23 (NIV).

36. For an extended argument to this effect, see Frank Morison, *Who Moved the Stone?* (London: Faber & Faber, 1930).

37. Aquinas, *Summa Theologica*.

38. Aristotle, *Nicomachean Ethics* (Indianapolis: Bobbs-Merrill, 1962), Bk. I, chaps. 7–10.

39. Immanuel Kant, *Critique of Practical Reason*, trans. Lewis W. Beck (Indianapolis: Bobbs-Merrill, 1956), Bk. II, chap. 2.
40. Plato, *Phaedo*, trans. G. M. Grube (Indianapolis: Hackett, 1977), 100b–107a.

SUGGESTED READING

Badham, Paul, and Linda Badham. *Immortality and Extinction?* New York: Barnes and Noble, 1982.

Hick, John. *Death and Eternal Life*. New York: Harper & Row, 1976.

Lewis, H. D. *The Self and Immortality*. New York: Seabury, 1973.

Moody, Raymond A., Jr. *Life After Life*. New York: Bantam Books, 1976.

Penelhum, Terence. *Immortality*. Belmont, CA: Wadsworth, 1973.

_____. *Survival and Disembodied Existence*. London: Routledge & Kegan Paul, 1970.

Perry, John. *Personal Identity and Immortality*. Indianapolis: Hackett, 1979.

Phillips, D. Z. *Death and Immortality*. New York: Macmillan, 1970.

Reichenbach, Bruce R. *Is Man the Phoenix? A Study of Immortality*. Grand Rapids, MI: William B. Eerdmans, 1978.

Shoemaker, Sidney, and Richard Swinburne. *Personal Identity*. Oxford: Oxford University Press, 1984.

Swinburne, Richard. *The Evolution of the Soul*. Oxford: Oxford University Press, 1986.

11

Religion and Science:
Compatible
or Incompatible?

In 1616, the Holy Office of the Roman Catholic Church condemned the view that the earth moves around the sun as false science and contrary to biblical teaching:

> It has . . . come to the knowledge of the said Congregation that the Pythago-rean doctrine—which is false and altogether opposed to the Holy Scripture—of the motion of the Earth, and the immobility of the Sun, which is also taught by Nicolaus Copernicus in *The Revolutions of the Planets* . . . is now being spread abroad and accepted by many.[1]

Copernicus's (1473–1543) work was placed on the list of forbidden books.

At same time, the Church instructed Galileo (1564–1642) to abandon the Copernican position, which he had been advocating in both written and public discussions. But Galileo, courageous as he was brilliant, continued to defend the Copernican position. His writings on planetary motion, sunspots, ocean tides, comets and other natural phenomena clearly supported the heliocentric theory. In 1633, at the age of sixty-nine and in poor health, Galileo was summoned to appear before the Grand Inquisitor in Florence. He was found guilty of teaching falsehood, forced to recant, and placed under house arrest for the remaining eight years of his life.[2]

The Galileo affair bristles with issues—from the abuses of authority by institutionalized religion and the unfair lobbying activities of Ptolemaic scientists to the curious method used by theologians to derive scientific facts from Holy Scripture. Yet the most pervasive, most significant issue regards the relationship between science and religion. This whole event made painfully clear the need to understand the purposes and methods of these two powerful and important human activities. Adopting a thoughtful position on the relationship between science and religion is a prelude to approaching a multitude of specific problems that arise at the interface of science and religion.

From one perspective, then, the controversy between Galileo and the Church can be seen as one more stage in the gradual differentiation of the enterprises of science and religion. Historians of science know that the Church was actually willing to allow Galileo to advance the heliocentric theory, but it did not want him to claim that the theory truly depicted the behavior of the sun and planets. Wanting to protect its unique right to make pronouncements about reality, the Church offered Galileo and other progressive scientists the opportunity to say that the heliocentric theory is a mathematical fiction—just one of several possible calculational schemes that could account for observed heavenly phenomena.

When he wrote the preface to Copernicus's *Revolutions*, Andreas Osiander (1498–1552) tried to make that work more palatable to the scientific community and to church theologians. He maintained that the heliocentric hypothesis is simply a convenient device for predicting planetary motion and not a true account of the causes of planetary motion. Osiander thought that he could defuse the controversy by sharply separating the domains of science and theology: Science formulates mathematical fictions, but theology describes reality. Osiander was right that the enterprises of science and theology must be differentiated. The key, however, lies in precisely how the difference is defined. Galileo did not accept Osiander's option of denying to science the task of describing reality and discovering the hidden causes of observable events. Galileo believed that the heliocentric theory genuinely described reality, and thus he remained in direct conflict with the Church's geocentric view.

Over the centuries that followed, many of the controversies between religion and science that took place can be seen as boundary disputes, disagreements over their proper domains. For example, debate over creation and evolution has been one of the most heated controversies in this area for more than a hundred years.[3] But other issues abound. Freudian psychoanalytic theory calls into question the legitimacy of a religious way of life by suggesting that it has roots in repression and wish fulfillment.[4] Einsteinian relativity theory drastically reinterprets our concepts of space, time, and causality, and thus challenges us to rethink how God relates to the world.[5] Technological advances in computers and artificial intelligence seem to endanger the unique status of *homo sapiens*.[6] And the discovery of the DNA molecule threatens to put "the secret of life" into the hands of scientists.[7] Adequate resolution of such controversies, then—both now and in the future—depends on an adequate understanding of the relationship between the activities of science and those of religion.

Serious thinkers can approach the relationship between science and religion quite differently. In order to gain appreciation for the different approaches, we will proceed in several stages. Since most discussions revolve around the relationship of *natural* science to religion, we will first evaluate three distinct views of that relationship. Some maintain that there is outright *conflict* between science and religion—that the two enterprises are essentially in competition. Others believe that there is not conflict but *compartmentalization*, because the two enterprises are so very different that a clash is impossible. Still others seek a type of middle way, a *complementary* relation between science and religion.

They hold that science and religion have some contact but without vicious border disputes. After considering these three options, it is interesting to see how the discussion is affected when the focus becomes the relationship of *social* science and religion. Then, in the end, we must look at what religion might have to say about the broad metaphysical structure of the kind of world in which science as we know it can work.

Do Religion and Science Conflict?

Early in the history of Western civilization, almost all intellectual investigation—into the motions of the planets, the nature of music, the forms of government, the composition of ultimate reality, and much more—came under the general canopy of *philosophy*, the "love of wisdom." Gradually, as the precise objects and specific methods of each inquiry became more clearly defined, new disciplines were born, fields of study capable of conducting their business independently of philosophy. The constellation of different disciplines that now exists—the natural sciences, the social sciences, mathematics, theology, and so forth—has emerged through a slow process of differentiation.

To attempt to define and distinguish any of the various branches of intellectual activity from one another is a *philosophical* undertaking. So, trying to draw conceptual distinctions between science and theology is a distinctively philosophical exercise. Mapping out their respective territories depends on one's philosophical view of science as well as one's philosophical view of religion. All intellectual disciplines can be distinguished according to certain general features: their *objects, aims*, and *methods*.

Competition and even *conflict* between science and religion becomes possible when they are conceived in ways that closely equate their objects or aims or methods. When the proper objects of theology include the same natural and physical phenomena that science studies, the stage is set for competition. Likewise, when the aims of theology include providing for natural objects and events an explanation that would stand on the same footing as any proposed scientific explanation, then competition is certainly possible. And, when the method of theology is put on a par with that of science, or at least when it is not sufficiently distinguished, then the path is open for competition between the two disciplines.

A noteworthy example in which many of these factors operated is the debate over the biological theory of evolution, which continues from the middle of the nineteenth century into the present. Traditional theology, wanting to protect the biblical concept of creation, came under increasing pressure from the theory of evolution and the widespread success of modern science. The dynamics of this debate reveal that the disputants take religion and science to be competitive in such a way that if a theory in one discipline were correct, a contrary theory in the other discipline would have to be incorrect. First of all, most disputants envisaged both science and religion as providing *explanations*. Second, the nature of their explanatory missions were understood in ways that brought them into direct confrontation. For example, many took science and religion as capable of explaining the same *objects* (i.e., geological and biological phenomena) and having the same *aims* in view for such explanations (i.e., ascertaining "how" they came about). These conceptions of the respective roles of science and religion have been present, if mostly implicitly, in the ongoing evolution-creation debate.

On the one hand, science offered explanations of the origin and development of biological species in terms of the conditions and mechanisms of evolution, such as the great antiquity of the earth, natural selection, and survival of the fittest. On the other hand, religion—in the form of Protestant biblical literalism—offered explanations of the same phenomena in terms of creation by God, such as his bringing the world into being in six 24-hour days, with all species fixed in their present form and the special creation of humanity.

Of course, most disputants agreed that the actual *methods* employed by religion and science did differ. Protestant literalism, perhaps best known in this century as *fundamentalism*, derived its explanatory concepts from a certain interpretation of the Genesis creation account. In other words, religionists made factual pronouncements of a scientific nature based on their reading of the Bible. Modern scientists, by contrast, derived their explanatory concepts from an empirical hypothesis that became increasingly confirmed by further research. Recognizing the clear conflict between their creationist claims and the claims of evolutionary scientists, fundamentalists decided that no compromises could be made with science. The famous Scopes "monkey trial" in 1925 was the best known of many battles between those who became known as "creationists" and those who embraced the theory of evolution.[8] In recent decades, certain educated fundamentalists have tried to validate their creationist position by scientific means. Calling evolutionary theory "false science," they have sought to show that "true science" agrees with the literally interpreted biblical account of creation.[9] In this case, religion almost reverts to the *method* of science or, more accurately, tries to corroborate its views by delving into science.

When the objects, aims, and perhaps even the methods of science and religion are so closely identified, the clear result is competition, often developing into a dynamic of conflict and the attempted resolution of conflict. Obviously, the reaction of the fundamentalist Christians to the apparent clash between science and religion was to give priority to claims derived from the Bible or at least from their interpretation of the Bible. In the words of Nicholas Wolterstorff (1932–), the fundamentalists used their theological claims as "control beliefs."[10] That is, certain beliefs viewed as connected to Christian commitment were allowed to function as basic and unquestioned—as "givens"—for purposes of judging scientific beliefs (i.e., theories). At the very least, these religious beliefs influenced what *sort* of theories were taken as acceptable or what *sort* as unacceptable. Thus, the theory of evolution—insofar as it was taken to involve the nonexistence of God, the lack of purpose in the universe, the loss of special dignity for humanity, and the relativity of ethics—was one sort of theory that Christian fundamentalists would reject. At the very most, certain Christian beliefs were taken as including fairly specific scientific theories (e.g., young earth theory and fixity of species) that clearly contradicted various elements of evolutionary theory. However, the fundamentalist way of negotiating the conflict between religion and science was not the only one.

Other movements reacted differently to the perceived conflict between religion and science. A notable instance is *evolutionary naturalism*, which simply rejected Christianity along with all forms of theism. Charles Darwin (1809–1882) himself moved from a vague belief in a Supreme Power to a pronounced agnosticism. Motivated by what he understood to be the implications of evolution for religion, Julian Huxley (1887–1985) aggressively attacked notions of biblical authority and all attempts at natural theology.[11] It is significant that this genre of evolutionary thinkers adopted the perspective of *philosophical naturalism* as the ally of their evolutionary science. Philosophical naturalism holds that physical nature alone is real; all phenomena are simply configurations of matter. It maintains that there is no Supreme Being who exists apart from the physical world, governing nature and overseeing human affairs. Supplemented by these philosophical commitments, the biological theory of evolution was erected to the status of a world-view: *evolutionary naturalism*. This view holds that humanity stands alone in an essentially hostile universe, having to make the best of an existence that has no underlying purpose. Thinkers committed to this kind of philosophical evolution rejected religion altogether and embraced science as the only hope for the progress of humanity. Indeed they looked to science for a universal explanation of human existence and destiny, an interpretation of life that had traditionally been drawn from theology and metaphysics.

One clear moral emerges from the prolonged debate over evolution and creation: When the objects, aims, and methods of religion and science are not sufficiently differentiated, the way is open for competition and conflict. We might make a few generalizations over the history of the issue. When a blurring of disciplinary or intellectual boundaries prevails, we find some theologians meddling in the affairs of science, even wanting to overturn its findings for theological rather than scientific reasons. On the other side, we find some scientists and other scientifically informed thinkers taking the results of modern science to discredit religion altogether. Obviously, what is really needed is a better understanding of the nature of religion and science.

Are Religion and Science Compartmentalized?

In contrast to treating religion and science as competitive and thus susceptible to conflict, these disciplines can be treated as functioning in entirely separate spheres. This basic view can be supported by arguing, in one way or another, that religion and science differ markedly in terms of their objects, methods, and aims. Thus, any possibility of conflict is eliminated. Compartmentalization has been endorsed from a number of different perspectives that have gained prominence in the twentieth century: *neo-orthodoxy, existentialism, positivism*, and *ordinary language philosophy*. A brief inspection of these positions reveals quite different ways of making a case for much the same conclusion.

The theological position known as *neo-orthodoxy* and the philosophical position of *existentialism* are very similar in holding that there is sharp contrast between religion and science. Protestant theologian Karl Barth (1886–1968), the celebrated exponent of neo-orthodoxy, maintained that theology and science deal with radically different objects—the former with God's self-revelation in Christ and the latter with the natural world. Likewise, he held that the methods of the theology and science are utterly distinct: the mysterious and transcendent God can be known only through his own self-revelation to us, whereas the realm of nature can be known through the exercise of human reason. Since, according to Barth, sin has blinded human reason from the knowledge of God, it is absolutely necessary for God to bridge the gap and reveal himself to us.[12] Furthermore, the aim of religion is to effect personal encounter with God, whereas scientific knowledge seeks to understand the patterns of the empirical world. Given the drastic differences in the objects, methods, and aims of science and theology, as seen by neo-orthodoxy, there can be no intersection between them and hence no possibility of conflict.

Existentialism also stresses the divergence of science and theology. Although there are two distinct strands of existentialist thought—theistic and atheistic—the theistic strand is of particular interest here. Since its nineteenth-century origin in the work of Søren Kierkegaard (1813–1855), existentialism has always maintained that scientific knowledge is impersonal and objective while stressing that religious knowledge is deeply personal and subjective. The objects of science are material things and their functions, but the objects of religion are personal and moral realities. Noted Jewish theologian Martin Buber (1878–1965) poignantly makes this distinction, stating that the relation between a person and a material object is an *I-It* relationship, but that the religious believer's relation to God is an *I-Thou* relationship.[13] Buber stresses, as do other theistic existentialists, that the aim of religious knowledge is actually the concerned reciprocity between two selves—the believer and God. Religion simply cannot be understood in the neutral categories of dispassionate science. And because their objects and aims are distinct, their methods must be also be distinct: the detached, rationalistic posture of the empirical scientist is very different from the stance of the religious believer, which is that of intense personal involvement. Both the neo-orthodox and existentialist positions here express versions of *fideism*, the position (discussed more fully in Chapter 3) that faith is not subject to rational scrutiny; religion and science are simply viewed as inhabiting sealed compartments that can never interrelate.

Twentieth-century *positivism*, which developed mainly as a philosophy of the sciences, also insisted on the separation of the domains of science and theology, but for reasons quite different from those of the neo-orthodox theologians and existentialist philosophers. Because of the empirical and publicly testable character of its theories, positivists considered science to be the only rational and objective method for gaining knowledge. As discussed earlier, in Chapter 8, positivists believed that theological claims, by contrast, fail to conform to the methods of science and thus do not deliver any kind of legitimate knowledge at all. For the positivists, only empirical objects provide the points of reference for meaningful language. Since the language of religion refers largely to nonempirical objects (e.g., God, soul, immortality), most positivists dismissed it as cognitively meaningless. Actually, many modern intellectuals, who did not concur with the wholesale rejection of religion, adopted the prevailing positivistic interpretation of science alongside a neo-orthodox or existentialist version of theology, thus enforcing the compartmentalization from both sides.[14]

Still another philosophical position that separates science and theology is *ordinary language philosophy*. In contrast to the positivists, who saw the only legitimate function of human language to be that of reporting empirical facts, ordinary language philosophers were fascinated by the variety of functions language performs. Taking their cue particularly from the later work of Wittgenstein, ordinary language analysts of many stripes have tended to say that science and religion are two distinct but equally legitimate "language-games," each with its own categories and logic. Other domains of human language include the moral, the aesthetic, and so forth. The strong proclivity among analysts has not been to ask whether the respective statements of science and theology are "true" in some independent sense, but rather to study their function—how they are used by human beings seeking to accomplish certain ends. Whereas the aims of scientific language are typically prediction and control, theology uses language for such purposes as worship and comfort. Here again science and theology are treated as vastly different activities—having different methods, objects, and aims—with essentially no possibility of interaction or conflict.[15]

The Question of Complementarity

By now it is evident that there is a great diversity of views on the relation of religion and science. Some views see science and religion as competitive and in frequent conflict; others see them as compartmentalized. In an effort to find some viable connection between the two, other views treat theological claims as though they are scientific hypotheses or actually transform or assimilate them into large-scale hypotheses.

George Schlesinger (1946–   ), for example, advocates trying to derive the factual implications of theological claims and then subjecting them to evaluation by observation, with the same standards of evidence and logic by which we scrutinize scientific theories.[16] He readily admits that the objects, methods, and aims of the two disciplines *per se* are completely different, but he seeks to determine the results of investigating those of theology according to the method of science. Of course, thinkers are divided on the outcome of this strategy, some insisting that religion is confirmed and others that it is disconfirmed by a scientific approach. Actually, it appears that we end up raising many traditional issues (already discussed in Chapters 5 and 6) in new guise. And we may begin to wonder whether the more traditional manner of argument for or against theological claims is both broader and more facile than the scientific approach.

Another example of looking for a viable connection between religion and science is *process philosophy*. Process thought does not merely treat religion as if it is a scientific hypotheses, but rather stresses an organic unity of science and religion, proclaiming a close, harmonious relationship between the two. Following Alfred North Whitehead (1861–1947), process thinkers propose an all-inclusive interpretation of reality drawing data from both religious and scientific experience. The process alternative was a comprehensive world-view that relied heavily on modern scientific concepts of nature, such as the primacy of change and the intimate interdependence of all events.[17]

Another intriguing proposal aimed at displaying the harmonious relation of science and theology comes from Donald MacKay (1922–1987), a British philosopher and scientist. MacKay attempts to improve upon other views, which lead either to conflict or compartmentalization. *Conflict* arises when one thinks, say, as fundamentalists did, that science and theology try to provide the same sorts of explanation for the same sorts of phenomena. *Compartmentalization* results when one thinks instead, that they try to provide different sorts of explanations about quite different sorts of things.

MacKay, however, suggests that we understand science and theology as attempting to give different kinds of explanations – with different methods and aims – about the same objects. MacKay, then, envisages the relation between science and theology as one of *complementarity*. The roots of this type of position can be traced back at least as far as the work of Charles Coulson (1910–1974) and Karl Heim (1874–1958).[18] Complementarity here means that both scientific and theological explanations of the same event can be true and complete at their own levels. But the methods and aims of the two enterprises differ markedly. The job of science is to construct – using its own approach and standards – an accurate and correct explanation of empirical phenomena; it seeks the *causes* of events. The job of theology is to construct – using its distinctive concepts – a complete explanation of certain important subjects. Thus, it aims to deliver the *meaning* of events. Although neither type of explanation, strictly speaking, needs the other, we might say that we need both the scientific and the theological accounts for the fullest possible understanding.

The term *complementarity* is somewhat ambiguous and must be understood exactly as MacKay intends it. He emphasizes that he is not talking about two or more *supplementary* descriptions or explanations of the same thing, with each description or explanation filling in information lacking in the others but each being the same sort of explanation as the others. An example of this would be the way an architect (or even different architects) might draw different plans for the same building. Some drawings would show what the floor space would look like to an imaginary observer overhead; others would show the outside of the building from different angles and elevations; still others would show the details of electrical wiring and plumbing. Here each perspective is blind to the other; a blueprint of floor space does not show outside perspectives, and so on. The complementary descriptions are developed at the same level using concepts of the same kind but in different patterns of relationship.

However, MacKay is talking about complementarity as a very distinct type of relationship. For him, complementarity is a relationship among descriptions or explanations that involve differences in *viewpoint*. In this case, the same evidence is available, but the description and explanation of it varies with the system of concepts that is adopted. Suppose, for example, that a person wanted an explanation for a large lighted sign which reads DRINK COCA-COLA. Using the set of concepts peculiar to physics, we could explain to him how the strength and stress factors in the steel posts that hold the sign are adequate to support its weight. We could also explain how the movement of electricity through neon gas in the lights causes them to glow. Or we could adopt a wholly different set of concepts—those of human motivation and intention—and say that a certain manufacturer intends for the sign to advertise its product. Complementarity thus means not that a person cannot entertain both explanations, but that the schemes of explanation are mutually exclusive. Complementarity in this sense characterizes the different ways an artist, a poet, or an astronomer might view a sunset from their respective conceptual frameworks, creating different levels of understanding.

It is in precisely this sense that MacKay thinks a relation of complementarity exists between science and theology: These two activities involve two different sets of concepts and proceed from two very distinct viewpoints:

> In the context of science and theology, it (complementarity) offers an alternative both to the view that makes all divine activity supplementary to the (presumed incomplete) chain mesh of scientifically describable cause and effect ("God in the gaps"), and to the "watertight compartment" theory that religious and scientific statements are logically independent.[19]

Complementarity opens the possibility of two exclusive and exhaustive—and yet logically compatible—explanations of the same thing, so, a "scientific" explanation and a "theological" explanation might be given of the same event.

MacKay believes that his "principle of complementarity" sheds light on a number of unfortunate disputes. For instance, MacKay would say that there is no incompatibility in claiming that "the formation of the universe as we know it is the result of natural processes" and that "the cosmos is God's creation." The first general type of explanation is scientific, the second theological. Each type of explanation offers an account of origins from within a particular conceptual framework. For the religious believer, then, nothing is really at stake theologically, say, in the debate between "big bang" and "steady state" cosmologies in science. Likewise, the scientist *per se* has no resources for drawing conclusions about whether the universe was divinely created; such subjects cannot be addressed by the method of that discipline.

As a general view of science and religion, MacKay's position provides valuable insights into the distinctive features of two genuinely different disciplines.

Understanding the matter in terms of complementarity has the clear benefit of eliminating the indiscriminate application of scientific methods to religious subjects, as well as dismissing the inappropriate extension of theology to scientific issues. Many unnecessary disputes would be eliminated if the parties involved were more enlightened about the quite different natures of science and religion. There simply are questions that can be posed and answered in strictly scientific terms (e.g., regarding the structure of the solar system or whether biological evolution is the case). Thus, the Catholic Church's declaration that the earth is the center of the solar system can be seen as theology's mistaken attempt to deduce a purely scientific fact from a theological teaching—that is, the geocentric theory from the belief that the human situation must be the center of divine concern. Conversely, there are other questions that can, and perhaps must, be raised and answered in theological terms—for instance, whether miracles are possible or whether there is life after death. In this light, Carl Sagan's statement that "the Cosmos is all that is or ever was or ever will be"[20] becomes the ill-advised attempt of a scientist to deal with topics appropriate to theology and metaphysics.

Although MacKay's proposal promises to shed light on numerous controversies between science and religion, fascinating problems arise from MacKay's own application of the principle of complementarity. These problems seem to be generated by the fact that, after the complementary relationship of science and theology is affirmed, several options remain open on the precise nature and assumptions of these two enterprises. Is it possible, for example, to adopt certain assumptions for scientific inquiry that yield implications that are incongruous (if not outright contradictory) either with theological teachings or with the assumptions on which those teachings rest? To what extent would such incongruity or paradox be an acceptable consequence of the complementarity principle? A concrete case in which these questions come quickly to the fore is found in MacKay's interaction with his critics.

Some critics think that MacKay himself has unwittingly generated a difficult paradox of his own: the problem of reconciling what science assumes about human personhood and what theology typically teaches about it. In *The Clockwork Image*, MacKay writes: "My own research department at Keele is concerned with the mechanisms of the brain, and . . . our working hypothesis is that the brain is capable of being studied as a mechanistic system."[21] Here he affirms the legitimacy of assuming that the operation of the human brain is determined, much as the movements of a "rare clock" are determined. Critics question whether a deterministic assumption in science can be squared with the typical assumption in Christian theology (MacKay's own theological heritage) that a human being is a free and responsible moral agent. The problem, put simply, is that the concept of human freedom seems to be undermined by proceeding from a deterministic assumption in science.[22] One reply MacKay has made is that science uses the mechanistic hypothesis as a *working assumption* (i.e., as a way of studying the brain "as if" it were a mechanistic system) whereas theology's position on freedom and responsibility purports to express a truth about *moral and spiritual reality*. At this point, MacKay risks being interpreted as saying that the working hypothesis for generating fruitful and interesting results should never be elevated to a claim about the way things actually are. However, this strategy is not faithful to the historic conception of science as providing some insight into reality. And, really, this interpretation does not make full sense of the larger bearing of MacKay's work, which clearly does take science as providing insight into *reality*. Hence, the pressure is surely present for the mechanistic hypothesis to be considered as more than merely a useful way of viewing the brain. And once the working assumption of mechanism is taken as a truth about reality, then the path is open for competition and conflict between theology and science.

The issue of freedom and determinism, arising in the present instance from the tension between assumptions of moral accountability in theology and mechanistic assumptions in science, is just one case among many that must be worked out in order to discover how the principle of complementarity applies. If complementarity portrays theology and science as using logically distinct sets of concepts to explain the same phenomena, then can just any two explanations be compatible? While complementarity rightly cautions us about the generically different approaches of theology and science, it may be that the blanket statement that there is no possibility of conflict cannot be made *a priori*. Although the basic approaches of theology and science may clearly differ, who is to say in advance that none of their claims will ever conflict? Might the two admittedly different methodologies generate claims that at least appear to be contradictory? In this light, the complementarity principle seems too strong, guaranteeing not only the integrity of theology and science as independent disciplines, but also that none of their specific claims will clash. The very fact that the separate methodologies are allowed to explain the *same* objects seems to cast doubt on any such guarantee.

At this juncture, it looks as though there is no easy answer to the question of what to do when certain claims of religion and science seem to clash. Resolution of such conflicts may have to proceed on a case-by-case basis, forcing the thinkers involved to decide how much weight to assign to the respective claims in any given clash. They will have to consider questions such as the degree and kind of support for each belief as well as the possibility of error in interpretation. They will also have to decide the place or role of the beliefs under review: Is a certain belief central to one's theological vision or more peripheral? How central is a given belief to a scientific understanding of reality? To what extent could varying interpretations influence the way the conflict is viewed? Is this a matter on which a legitimate range of opinion should be allowed?

Furthermore, what may be a deeper and more interesting question does not concern the weight assigned to conflicting beliefs, but the status or significance given to religion and science as knowledge-seeking or belief-forming practices.[23] What does one do if two acceptable or justified belief-forming practices generate conflicting beliefs in specific situations? Can one practice take precedence over another? A strict complementarity thesis simply does not go far enough in explaining just how it is that the practices of religion and science are indeed complementary, and what to do in the face of apparent conflict. Are there any constraints as to how much incongruity there can be between explanations? And if religion and science are conceived in ways that generate paradoxical conclusions, how is it that complementary perspectives provide insight into one, unified reality?

A number of thinkers claim that the complementarity thesis divorces science and religion in such a way that no conceptual interaction is possible. But the very fact that one can sense an incongruity or inconsistency between certain scientific and theological beliefs suggests that perhaps the complementarity thesis makes an artificial distinction and that these two spheres of intellectual activity cannot be quite so easily drawn. Historians of science are familiar with numerous examples in which scientists derive hunches and expectations for research, and metaphors for their explanations, from their general cultural environment, which is rich with political, religious, and other ideas. For instance, Chinese cosmology, which allows for change, made it possible for Chinese astronomy to detect movement in the heavens long before Western astronomers, who embraced a static cosmology, could detect it.[24] Conversely, church historians know of the tendency of theologians throughout the centuries to borrow elements from their contemporary culture when formulating their theological systems. And popular culture is always replete with the current scientific, as well as other, beliefs. For example, the Einsteinian revolution in physics has ushered in drastically new concepts of space and time that in turn will influence how theologians come to articulate the relation of God to the world.[25]

A fruitful study lies ahead for those who will trace the interplay of scientific and theological ideas. Of course, those who advocate complementarity could simply say that hunches, metaphors, intuitions and the like are indeed available for borrowing and cross-fertilization, but that complementarity, strictly speaking, is meant to pertain to the respective explanatory missions science and theology. Following this line of thought, one could say that once an idea— regardless of its field of origin—gains uptake in a given discipline, it must ultimately gain credibility by conforming to the methodology of that discipline.[26] Staying with our earlier example, although Chinese astronomy borrowed from Chinese cosmology the notion of change, whether the concept was a fruitful and acceptable one for astronomy had to be established in the terms of that science.

Theology and the Social Sciences

Up to this point, we have probed some of the problems of defining and distinguishing the disciplines of theology and science. One of the serious issues that arose in the work of MacKay was that of how to handle our own humanity within those frameworks. But no topology of knowledge, purporting to show the relation of theology and science, would be accurate if it proceeded as though all of the "sciences" could simply be grouped together as a rather homogeneous collection, on the one hand, to be distinguished from theology, on the other. There is a long-standing debate in the philosophy of science as to whether the "social" sciences (e.g., psychology and sociology) possess unique characteristics that sharply distinguish them from the "natural" sciences (e.g., physics, chemistry, and biology).

Most advocates of the distinction assert that the proper objects of the social sciences (sometimes called "human sciences") are human beings, considered either individually or collectively. They typically try to expose the shortcomings in the classic scientific method for studying human beings and to articulate the special methods suited for that purpose. These thinkers often attack cause-effect analysis, generalization to universal laws, and the presumption of objectivity, which are features of the natural sciences not appropriate to the social sciences. They argue that the study of human beings demands quite different approaches from those employed in the natural sciences.[27] Wilhelm Dilthey (1833–1911), for example, claims that cause-effect generalization to universal laws has little place in analyzing human behavior, and argues for a special kind of "sympathetic understanding" that human inquirers can have of other humans (an operation often labeled by the German word *Verstehen*).[28] His point is that the subjects of social inquiry are rational agents, who are free to operate according to reasons and intentions that can be empathetically understood in a manner not available to the natural sciences. Others who, for various reasons, hold that the social sciences are unique include R. G. Collingwood (1889–1943)[29] and Peter Winch (1926–   ).[30]

Opponents of the split between the natural and social sciences usually contend that all of the sciences are unified methodologically in principle, although the relatively young social sciences have not yet refined and perfected the application of scientific method to their declared objects of study. The modern movement known as *positivism* supplied many of the influential arguments for such a position, emphasizing such points as the empirical nature of all science and the necessity of causal analysis. B. F. Skinner (1904–   ) is one thinker who follows this basic line of thought and supports the unity of the sciences by attempting to show how extensively causes operate in the human realm, making human behavior amenable to the same mode of inquiry used for lower animals.[31] Perhaps the most persuasive arguments for the unity of the sciences revolve around the thesis that they share the very same *logic* of justification (for the validation of theories).[32] Consider Carl Hempel's (1905–   ) well-known paper "The Function of General Laws in History," in which he makes a case for the identification of general regularities and the articulation of "laws" as conditions for explanation in social science.[33]

We cannot pursue here a detailed examination of the dispute between those who contend for the special character of the social sciences and those who embrace the ideal of a unified science, yet we can note some fascinating questions relating to the general theme of this chapter. For instance, if the uniqueness of the social sciences could be established, what differences would it make in how the relationship of theology to science is conceived? While the natural sciences could be distinguished from theology, say, in virtue of their causal study of impersonal objects, how would the social sciences be distinguished from theology? Obviously, we might say that the social sciences, while distinct in certain ways from the natural sciences, still study mundane, creaturely realities just as the natural sciences do, while theology studies divine reality or at least its relation to creaturely realities. We could proceed to differentiate further between the theology and the social sciences. Nonetheless, if we grant for the sake of discussion the likely success of those who argue for the uniqueness of the social sciences, we may discover some interesting analogies between the social sciences and theology. These analogies revolve around the notion of what it means to try to describe or explain the actions of rational agents in terms of reasons and intentions.

Richard Swinburne (1934–   ), for instance, seeks in his own way to distinguish between science and theology according to their particular modes of explanation. He advances the distinction between "scientific explanation" and "personal explanation" (which is reminiscent of one way in which MacKay tries to illustrate complementarity). An explanation of any phenomenon, for Swinburne, relates both *what* and *why*—that is, it tells both what particular object brought about the phenomenon and why the phenomenon occurred. In scientific explanation, the objects and their circumstances are the causes, while their inherent powers and liabilities supply the reason for the efficacy of those causes. In personal explanation, however, the objects that bring about the events under investigation are personal agents, and the reasons for their activity are their rational intentions. For Swinburne, therefore, neither kind of explanation can be reduced to the other; they are logically distinct. Scientific explanation focuses on the powers and liabilities inherent in impersonal physical objects, while personal explanation focuses on the intentions of rational, personal agents.

According to Swinburne, science explains how various physical objects bring about their effects, but religion explains certain events as having been brought about by the action of God conceived as a rational agent.[34] A physicist might explain the origin of the universe as "a concatenation of atoms," whereas a theologian might explain it as "the free and purposive creation of God." Obviously, Swinburne's emphasis is not on the possible distinction between the natural and social sciences, but the distinction he proposes parallels exactly the distinction many make between the two broad domains in science. We may wonder whether this parallel could be fruitfully explored in greater detail, since many religions posit some kind of kinship between humans and the divine. Judaism and Christianity, for example, teach that persons are created "in the image of God" (*in imago Dei*), thus lending some support to the notion that the explanation of human action may be similar in important respects to the explanation of divine action. Certainly, the concept of personhood, nourished by the Christian tradition, for example, often serves as a rallying point for thinkers who wish to prevent the various forms of dehumanization that can occur at the hands of modern science.[35]

Of course, Swinburne's attempt, like all attempts, to distinguish science and religion assumes that they have explanatory missions in the first place, or at least that providing explanation is a major characteristic of both science and religion. However, there is a small minority of thinkers in the philosophy of science, such as the instrumentalists, who deny that the task of science is explanation. These thinkers typically reject the notion that science can or should seek knowledge of the way things really are and of why events happen as they do; instead they emphasize the capacities of science for prediction and control. Likewise, in the philosophy of religion, some thinkers, forming not so small a minority, deny that the main task of religion is one of explanation, claiming instead that religion has other functions, such as the regulation of individual and corporate living. But reviewing the debates over the precise degree to which these two human enterprises differ lies beyond the scope of this book.

In What Kind of World Does Science Work?

Up to this point, we have been concerned with the relationship between science and theology as disciplines that have identifiable and distinctive objects, methods, and aims. But now we need to consider the question of their relationship along other lines. Let us pose the question as follows: In what kind of world does science work? Or, what sorts of broad structural features must characterize a world in which the scientific endeavor is possible? It is common among philosophers of science to say that science rests on certain *presuppositions*, beliefs that science cannot establish but that shape the whole enterprise. These presuppositions, taken together, provide a sketch of the essential characteristics of the world in which science takes itself to operate. We need to examine some of the more typical assumptions that philosophers of science have identified and then ask whether a religious perspective has any impact on them.

A basic presupposition of science, for instance, is that physical nature is real—that it is an objective reality apart from ourselves. Another important presupposition is that nature is intelligible. Obviously, unless we think that the world is understandable, there would be no reason to study it. Still another assumption is that nature is uniform, that the regularities and processes discovered on a limited scale hold throughout the universe. Clearly, if we did not think this were so, then we would consider useless all of the hard work spent trying to discover patterns in nature. We would have no confidence that causal connections discovered today will hold tomorrow or that present scientific knowledge is a basis for predicting future events in our world.

These and associated presuppositions lie at the philosophical foundations of science. Such presuppositions are often discussed as though they are simply a rather unremarkable collection of general beliefs that no sane person would want to dispute. However, these beliefs have not always been so widely accepted. Indeed their acceptance in modern times has a long and interesting history. In the development of Western thought, various philosophical perspectives have questioned these beliefs which we now strongly embrace. Investigating the development of our concepts of nature and our knowledge of nature actually promises important insight into the relationship between science and theology.

When speaking of the roots of modern science, it is customary to express our indebtedness to classical Greek thought, to say that its confidence in a rational structure in nature provides one of our modern philosophical presuppositions for science. However, a deeper look into the Greek world-view raises enormous doubts about whether it could have evolved in the direction of modern science. For one thing, both Plato (428–347 B.C.) and Aristotle (384–322 B.C.) held that the true nature of things is found in their "form," not in their matter. Convinced that the world is a rational order and that form is accessible to rational thought, Greek thinkers conducted science by attempting to *define* the essences of things. In fact, Aristotelian science—the brand of science that held sway even at the time of Galileo—was based on the belief that nature was a necessary emanation from God's reason. Every phenomenon in the world is necessarily determined by God's purposes and cannot be otherwise. Thus, Aristotelian science sought to discover the ultimate rational causes of things in the divine mind through a process of reasoning apart from empirical investigation.

The ancients believed that if a natural object can be defined, its properties can be deduced from its essence, without the need for empirical investigation that is a hallmark of modern science. A classic example is Aristotle's nonexperimental statement that all unsupported objects fall to the earth at a rate proportionate to their weight. Thus, a grapefruit should fall faster than a grape. But Galileo's experiments established that all objects fall at the same rate of acceleration. Galileo did not just try to deduce from the essential idea of a thing what properties and powers it has, but instead used hypothesis and experimentation in order to discover them.

Some argue that Galileo and other thinkers, struggling to give birth to modern science, approached the knowledge of physical reality differently from the ancients because they held a fundamentally different picture of the world, derived from a distinctive view of God and his ways. In contrast to the Greek view, the Judeo-Christian doctrine of creation teaches that God freely chose to bring the world into existence, not that it is a necessary emanation from the divine reason. Michael Foster (1905–1959) argues that this doctrine of creation provides the only philosophy of nature that could have overthrown the Greek perspective and given solid support to modern science:

> A world which is created by the Christian God will be both contingent and orderly. It will embody regularities and patterns, since its Maker is rational, but the particular regularities and patterns which it will embody cannot be predicted *a priori*, since he is free; they can be discovered only by examination. The world, as Christian theism conceives, it is thus an ideal field for the application of scientific method, with its twin techniques of observation and experiment.[36]

These and other implications of the doctrine were not all seen at once, but came to be understood after centuries of reflection by Christian thinkers. As further implications were drawn, Christian philosophers realized that they were committed to the affirmations that matter is real and intelligible *per se*, and that appropriate methods had to be developed for studying it. Thus, the conceptual seeds for modern science were planted.

Of course, some thinkers who recognize the important link between the Judeo-Christian world-view and the scientific enterprise do not take the very strong line Foster does. They argue, more modestly, that the presuppositions about nature and the knowledge of nature found in this unique world-view are *more conducive* to the conceptualization of what the enterprise of science is than are conceptualizations found in competing religious world-views. However, they would be unwilling to argue that this particular religious conception is either a necessary or sufficient condition for science. To claim that the Judeo-Christian view is a necessary condition for science is to maintain that science is not possible without it. To claim that the view is a sufficient condition for science is to assert that its presence alone was capable of bringing about the rise of science. To argue along either or both of these lines, according to some thinkers, would be to exaggerate their case.

However, it seems clear that the fully amplified Judeo-Christian view of creation was, historically, a very significant factor in the rise of science, and it was an important factor because of the distinctive logic of its concepts of God and the world. Furthermore, it appears that no other historic views had the same fruitful logic and suggestiveness that could give science momentum. A survey of the prevailing conceptions of nature in other religious traditions provides considerable support for this measured interpretation of the importance of the Judeo-Christian contribution to science. The kinds of worlds envisioned by other religious traditions are simply not those in which modern science works. As we have seen, Greek views of deity and the necessitation of things by divine reason generated a nonexperimental orientation toward science. But a world created by the Judeo-Christian God, populated by things with definite natures of their own, is a natural order to be investigated empirically.

It would also be interesting to explore the assumptions for science that nonreligious traditions might offer and see how the argument for the Judeo-Christian world-view might go. Although the naturalist tradition did not, as a matter of historical *fact*, give birth to science, we still might ponder whether, as a matter of *logic*, it could have done so. The various materialist and naturalist traditions at least initially seem to envision a world of orderly things determined by laws and the like — thus seeming to offer many of the presuppositions needed by science. However, a complete and careful analysis of the history of naturalism reveals much diversity of opinion. There are disagreements, for instance, over the inherent intelligibility of the universe and over the degree of optimism about our interaction with nature. Also, there are disagreements about whether the world is worth our investigative efforts, with some thinkers claiming that an atheistic scenario makes life hopeless and others coming close to the deification of the natural sphere. Further dissention can be found over what motive or impulse, if any, should drive us in our scientific encounter with nature. While sorting out the implications of all these differences for the scientific enterprise would be an exciting task, it is too extensive a matter to be settled within the scope of this chapter.

While such thinkers as Pierre LaPlace (1594–1679) insisted that we "have no need of that hypothesis," Isaac Newton (1642–1727) countered that we must conceive of the universe theistically. So the conceptual task, which remains to be completed, is that of deciding whether the view that the physical world, assumed to be a self-sufficient, deterministic system (perhaps after the fashion of LaPlace), is indeed an environment in which natural science can exist. Adding the consideration of the philosophical foundations of social science — and of what assumptions the Judeo-Christian view would offer in contrast to a naturalistic view — complicates the task even further.

Some thinkers link the Judeo-Christian doctrine of creation not only to the method of science, but also to its driving impulse. Contrary to the Greek view, the physical realm is not brutish or unimportant. In historic Christian thought, the world is good, the product of a loving God. Understanding the intelligible forms behind nature is no longer the primary goal, but direct involvement in material life is also a worthy human activity. The hidden causes operative in the natural realm are knowable on their own terms and not through church decree. That this unique theological orientation is viable has already been proved by the centuries of invention and discovery it has made possible. The radically new view of the kind of world we inhabit spawned a dramatically new direction for science. Without a doubt, other conditions also had to be in place for modern science to grow and flourish: Ample human imagination and genius, adequate leisure and peace to sustain careful study, and certain developments in mathematics barely begin the list. But in light of the retarding influence of Greek natural philosophy, one of the most decisive conditions was the rise of the new philosophy of nature.

Similar evaluations can be made of the relatively underdeveloped state of science in other ancient and premodern cultures. For example, modern science, which advances through commerce with the empirical realm, could not take root in Hindu culture, where this realm is conceived to be either illusory or unreal, and where the chief goal is release from this world, trapped as it is in an endless cycle of birth-death-rebirth. Neither could an empirical science of nature grow in Chinese culture, where the pantheistic naturalism of Taoism teaches that the real causes of natural patterns are spiritual and hidden. Enlightening comparisons could be continued.

Now that science has suitably organized its methods and aims as a knowledge-seeking enterprise, it more or less proceeds without continually questioning the assumptions upon which it is based. Indeed, practitioners of science often recite the list of foundational presuppositions as though such beliefs can virtually be plucked out of thin air in order to make the method work. This means that the many practitioners of science can use its method without embracing the distinctive view of nature that gave it birth. In other words, they can maintain the assumptions of orderliness and intelligibility and the like, but not the other religious concepts that historically accompanied these assumptions — that the world and its general features are to be viewed as created by the God defined within the Judeo-Christian religious tradition.

None of this changes the fact that science makes sense only in a certain kind of world — the kind that was in fact first envisioned by Christian theism. It appears that other religious world-views did not yield implications that could support modern science. And, given the basic metaphysical and epistemological commitments of many of these other religious world-views, convincing arguments can be made that these views probably could not yield the requisite implications to form a conceptual foundation for science.

Obviously, the Church's reaction to Galileo betrayed its own misunderstanding of the ramifications of important Christian concepts for science. Thus, there is a sense in which the rise of modern science can be characterized as being possible only after it, as an activity of human reason, broke from established religious ideas. We might say that the Galileo affair is one striking event in the long process through which science gained autonomy from religion. But the prevailing religious ideas from which scientific reason has had to separate can be shown to be distortions or misunderstandings of the philosophical implications of the historic Christian world-view. For example, science had to break from certain notions about religious authority — either the infallibility of a religious leader or sacred scripture. As an enterprise of reason, science helped show the exaggeration and distortion in such claims to infallibility: all we really ever have are our own *fallible* human ideas in science or our own *fallible* human ideas in religion. Hence, we can now see that to declare that, in case of conflict, theological claims take priority over scientific claims is simplistic and naive — a response that fails to take stock of the very sensible and yet quite profound ramifications of the Christian world-view.

What all of this comes to is that there is an important relationship between science and religion. While some modified version of complementarity may correctly depict the independent explanatory missions of the two enterprises, the dependence of science on certain important assumptions must be acknowledged. The origin of these assumptions in the Judeo-Christian doctrine of creation is a matter of historical record, and the logic generated by these assumptions has special application to the scientific enterprise. This is not to say that all scientists are Christian believers or that they will be better scientists if they are believers, but it is to indicate that the presuppositional level of science cannot be ignored. Theological doctrines and themes have a demonstrable bearing on the conception of the kind of world in which science operates and the kind of rational methods by which it can be known.

STUDY QUESTIONS

1. Try to classify some of the different views of the relationship of religion and science. Explore the reasons given for each view.

2. The relation of religion and science is very complex. On one level it is a philosophical relation; on another level it is a political and institutional one. Discuss what this means.

3. For centuries, theological inquiry has been conducted with an awareness of the contribution of Newton to our scientific understanding of the world. Do your own reading and thinking about how the contribution of Einstein might affect the way theology is done in our time.

4. Are there significant differences between the natural and social sciences? Discuss in light of the distinguishing features of *methods, aims*, and *objects*.

5. Does the relation theology has to natural science differ in important ways from the relation it has to the social sciences?

6. Explore the idea that science as we know it necessitates that we make certain assumptions about the structure of reality. What do you think of the suggestion that the assumptions found within the Judeo-Christian world-view are more conducive to science than those found in other major religious world-views?

7. Explore the ramifications of the Judeo-Christian concept of humanity for social science.

8. If Judeo-Christian theism envisions a world order run by natural laws, could some specific natural laws be those that define the theory of biological evolution? Explain.

9. Explore further the question of whether the naturalistic world-view provides assumptions for science that preclude the need for assumptions drawn from the Judeo-Christian world-view.

NOTES

1. *Opere*, XIX, 323. Quoted in Jerome Langford, *Galileo, Science and the Church* (New York: Desclee Company, 1966), pp. 97–98.
2. Langford, chap. 6.
3. Although there were evolutionary-type works in geology and some other sciences that predated Darwin's work, it is fair to say that the heated debate as we know it started with Darwin's work. See Charles Darwin, *The Descent of Man, and Selection in Relation to Sex* (New York: A. L. Burtt, 1874); and *The Origin of Species by Means of Natural Selection* (Chicago: Encyclopedia Britannica, 1955).
4. Sigmund Freud, *Totem and Taboo*, trans. A. A. Brill (New York: Dodd Mead, 1919); *The Future of an Illusion*, trans. W. D. Robson-Scott (New York: Liveright, 1928); *Moses and Monotheism*, trans. K. Jones (New York: Knopf, 1939). These

psychoanalytic themes run through this general writings; see *The Complete Psychological Works of Sigmund Freud: Standard Edition*, J. Strachey, ed. and trans. (New York: Norton, 1976).

5. Albert Einstein, *Relativity, the Special and the General Theory: A Popular Exposition*, trans. R. W. Lawson (London: Methuen, 1954, 15th edition). Also see Hans Reichenbach, *The Philosophy of Space and Time*, trans. M. Reichenbach and J. Freund (New York: Dover, 1957).

6. A seminal work in this area was A. M. Turing, "Computing Machinery and Intelligence," *Mind*, 59, no. 236 (1960), reprinted in Alan R. Anderson, ed., *Minds and Machines* (Englewood Cliffs, NJ: Prentice-Hall, 1964), pp. 4–30. Among recent treatments of the issues, see D. Hofstadter and D. Dennet, *The Mind's I* (New York: Basic Books, 1981).

7. A seminal work in this area is J. D. Watson and F. H. C. Crick, "A Structure for Deoxyribose Nucleic Acid," *Nature* 171 (1953): 737.

8. See Roland Frye, *Is God a Creationist? The Religious Case against Creation-Science* (New York: Scribner, 1983) for a set of articles discussing the ensuing controversy and making a case against creationism. Also see David B. Wilson, ed., *Did the Devil Make Darwin Do It? Modern Perspectives on the Creation-Evolution Controversy* (Ames: Iowa State University Press, 1983).

9. See, for example, Henry Morris, *The Twilight of Evolution* (Grand Rapids, MI: Baker Book House, 1963) and Morris, ed., *Scientific Creationism* (San Diego, CA: Creation Life Publishers, 1974). Also see the many publications produced by the Institute for Creation Research in San Diego, CA.

10. Nicholas Wolterstorff, *Reason within the Bounds of Religion* (Grand Rapids, MI: Eerdmans, 1976), pp. 65–66.

11. Julian Huxley, *Evolution in Action* (New York: Harper & Brothers, 1953); also, *Religion without Revelation* (New York: Harper & Brothers, 1927).

12. Barth provides a manageable introduction to his thought in *Dogmatics in Outline* (London: SCM Press, 1949).

13. Martin Buber, *I and Thou*, trans. R. G. Smith (Edinburgh: T. & T. Clark, 1937).

14. See, for example, Paul Holmer, *Theology and the Scientific Study of Religion* (Minneapolis: Denison, 1961).

15. A helpful summary is given in Frederick Ferré, *Language, Logic and God* (New York: Harper & Brothers, 1961).

16. George Schlesinger, *Religion and Scientific Method* (Dordrecht, Netherlands: D. Reidel, 1977), pp. 1–6. Numerous issues arise, of course, with Schlesinger's approach, including how to satisfy the ideal requirement of total evidence and how even a positive confirmation of theism is relevant to genuine religious faith.

17. Alfred North Whitehead, *Religion in the Making* (New York: Macmillan, 1926), pp. 31, 57.

18. Charles Coulson, *Science and Christian Belief* (Chapel Hill: University of North Carolina Press, 1955), pp. 66ff; Karl Heim, *Christian Faith and Natural Science* (New York: Harper & Row, 1953), pp. 44ff.

19. D. M. MacKay, "Complementarity in Scientific and Theological Thinking," *Zygon: Journal of Religion and Science*, 9, no. 3 (1974): 226.

20. Carl Sagan, *Cosmos* (New York: Random House, 1980), p. 4.

21. Donald MacKay, *The Clockwork Image* (Downers Grove, IL: InterVarsity Press, 1974), p. 12.

22. See William Hasker, "MacKay on Being a Responsible Mechanism: Freedom in a Clockwork Universe," *Christian Scholar's Review* 8, no. 2 (1978): 130–40.

23. See the highly suggestive discussion of belief-forming practices in William Alston, "Christian Experience and Christian Belief," in A. Plantinga and N. Wolterstorff, eds., *Faith and Rationality: Reason and Belief in God* (Notre Dame, IN: University of Notre Dame Press, 1983), pp. 103–34.

24. See Thomas Kuhn, *The Structure of Scientific Revolutions* (Chicago: University of Chicago Press, 1962, 1970), p. 116.

25. See G. D. Yarnold, *The Moving Image* (London: Allen & Unwin, 1966).

26. A case can be made for an even stronger connection between science and theology. Nicholas Wolterstorff has introduced the concept of *control beliefs*, arguing that in complex networks of beliefs, various beliefs have distinct functions. Control beliefs would play the role of guiding or limiting what other beliefs one accepts. Wolterstorff says, for example, that one's religious beliefs might function as *control beliefs* as he devises and weighs scientific theories. Control beliefs are simply beliefs that one employs within a given context to evaluate and judge other beliefs. Perhaps, then, the theological belief that human beings are responsible agents would put pressure against accepting the working hypothesis that treats them mechanistically. Of course, it might also turn out that a given person would allow certain scientific or other factual beliefs to function as control beliefs in some of his theological speculation. See Wolterstorff, *Reason Within the Bounds of Religion* (Grand Rapids, MI: Eerdmans, 1976).

27. See C. Stephen Evans, *Preserving the Person: A Look at the Human Sciences* (Grand Rapids: Baker, 1982); see also Edward Madden, ed., *The Structure of Scientific Thought* (Boston: Houghton Mifflin, 1960), especially the essays in part 3.

28. Wilhelm Dilthey, *Gesammelte Schriften*, Vol. 7. For an exposition in English, see Herbert Hodges, *The Philosophy of Wilhelm Dilthey* (1952; reprint ed. Westport, CT: Greenwood Press, 1974), chap. 5.

29. R. G. Collingwood, *The Idea of History* (New York: Oxford University Press, 1956), part 5, sections 1 and 4.

30. Peter Winch, *The Idea of Social Science and Its Relation to Philosophy* (London: Routledge & Kegan Paul, 1958).

31. B. F. Skinner, *Science and Human Behavior* (New York: Macmillan, 1953). Also see Skinner, *Beyond Freedom and Dignity* (New York: Vintage/Bantam, 1972).

32. For further discussions of the matter, see Quentin Gibson, *The Logic of Social Enquiry* (London: Routledge & Kegan Paul, 1960) and Richard Rudner, *Philosophy of Social Science* (Englewood Cliffs, NJ: Prentice Hall, 1966).

33. Carl Hempel, "The Function of General Laws in History," in his *Aspects of Scientific Explanation and Other Essays in the Philosophy of Science* (New York: Free Press, 1965), pp. 231–43.

34. Richard Swinburne, *The Existence of God* (Oxford: Clarendon Press, 1979), chap. 2, especially pp. 44–48.

35. C. Stephen Evans, *Preserving the Person: A Look at the Human Sciences* (Grand Rapids, MI: Baker, 1982).

36. E. L. Mascall, *Christian Theology and Natural Science* (New York: Ronald Press, 1956), p. 132.

SUGGESTED READING

Barbour, Ian G., ed. *Science and Religion: New Perspectives on the Dialogue.* New York: Harper & Row, 1968.

Davies, Paul. *God and the New Physics*. New York: Simon & Schuster, 1983.

Dillenberger, John. *Protestant Thought and Natural Science*. New York: Doubleday, 1960.

Hawking, Steven. *A Brief History of Time: From Big Bang to Black Holes*. New York: Bantam, 1988.

Nebelsick, Harold. *Theology and Science in Mutual Modification*. New York: Oxford University Press, 1981.

O'Connor, Daniel, and Francis Oakley, eds. *Creation: The Impact of an Idea*. New York: Scribners, 1969.

Mascall, E. L. *Christian Theology and Natural Science*. London: Oxford University Press, 1979.

Polkinghorne, John. *One World*. Princeton, NJ: Princeton University Press, 1987.

_____. *The Way the World Is: The Christian Perspective of a Scientist*. London: Triangle, 1983.

Ratzsch, Del. *Philosophy of Science: The Natural Sciences in Christian Perspective*. Downers Grove, IL: InterVarsity Press, 1986.

Rolston III, Holmes. *Science and Religion: A Critical Examination*. Philadelphia: Temple University Press, 1986.

Schlesinger, George. *Religion and Scientific Method*. Dordrecht, Netherlands: D. Reidel, 1977.

12

Religious Pluralism: How Can We Understand Religious Diversity?

A Zen Buddhist gave the following description of his religious experience and beliefs:

> Reached a white heat today . . . Monitors whacked me time and again . . . their energetic stick wielding is no longer an annoyance but a spur . . .
>
> At next dokusan [the roshi or Zen master] asked for Mu.[1] Quickly raised my hand as though to smack him. Didn't intend to really hit him, but roshi, taking no chances, ducked . . . How exhilarating these unpremeditated movements — clean and free . . .
>
> . . . Didn't intend to tell roshi of my insight, but as soon as I came before him he demanded: "What happened last night?" . . . [H]e began quizzing me: "Where do you see Mu? . . . How do you see Mu? . . . What do you see Mu? . . . How old is Mu? . . . "
>
> Threw myself into Mu for another nine hours with such utter absorption that *I* completely vanished . . . *I* didn't eat breakfast, *Mu* did. *I* didn't sweep and wash the floors after breakfast, *Mu* did. *I* didn't eat lunch, *Mu* ate . . .
>
> Hawklike, the roshi scrutinized me as I entered his room, walked toward him, prostrated myself, and sat before him with my mind alert and exhilarated . . .
>
> "The universe is One," he began, each word tearing into my mind like a bullet. "The moon of Truth—" All at once the roshi, the room, every single thing disappeared in a dazzling stream of illumination and I felt myself bathed in a delicious, unspeakable delight. . . . For a fleeting eternity I was alone—I alone was. . . .
>
> "I have it! I know! There is nothing, absolutely nothing. I am everything and everything is nothing!" I exclaimed more to myself than to the roshi, and got up and walked out. . . . [2]

The kinds of beliefs and practices expressed in this description of a Zen Buddhist's religious experience seem worlds apart from those most of us experience. Yet, for him, they embody both a set of religious beliefs and a way of religious life that he takes as true and fulfilling. How do these beliefs relate to our religious beliefs? Can they both be true? If not, how do we decide which are true and which not? In short, how can we understand religious diversity?

Religious Diversity

In our complex world, we cannot affirm one particular religious perspective and merely ignore others. Much more than missionary proselytizing could ever do, modern communications, tourism, educational exchange, immigration, and international business now force adherents of the various religions to notice each other. This new cultural integration is hailed as a hallmark of the last half of the twentieth century. Yet it is probably true that there never was a time when any of the major religions existed in complete isolation; their origins and development intertwined with those of other religions.

Judaism developed its unique particularism amid numerous Semitic religions; Christianity was an outgrowth of Judaism; Islam developed later in contact with both. Buddhism arose in reaction to Hindu ascetic culture, while Hinduism itself was an amalgam of Aryan thought and the Dravidic religious ideas and practices indigenous to India. And what is true of the major religions applies even more to the sects and now-independent religions that grew out of them: Bahai out of Islam; Mormonism, Jehovah's Witness, and Christian Science from Christianity; Unificationism out of Protestantism, Neo-Confucianism, and Buddhism; Sikhism out of Hinduism and Islam.

From a purely historical point of view, then, it is difficult to think of religion in isolationist terms. One could construct not only an integrated history of the individual religions, but perhaps also a history of religious faith and practice in a generic sense.[3] Such an account would look very different from standard religion texts, wherein distinct chapters are devoted to particular religions and their beliefs and history. It would be a history that elicits the actual influences in belief and practice one religion had on another—containing, for example, a tale about a wealthy prince who renounces his worldly power and goes off to live in ascetic poverty, which originates in Hinduism or Jainism, is passed down through Buddhism, Manicheism, and Islam, and finally is Christianized to play a role in the Christian religious experience of Tolstoy; or tracing such religious practices as the use of prayer beads from Buddhism to Islam to Catholicism.[4]

Even if we could not trace direct historical influences of one religion on another, we cannot ignore the similarities between religions. People in different religions often perform similar rituals. Many religious ceremonies use candles and incense; Hindus and Christians eat a divine meal; Muslims, Hindus, and Sikhs remove footwear before entering places of worship. Not only do practices resemble each other, but so do many religious beliefs as well: for instance, monotheism in Judaism, Christianity and Islam; the presence and activity of avatars (physical incarnations of deity) in Christianity and Hinduism; and the centrality of the Golden Rule in Confucianism and Christianity.

But there are also notable differences. Theravāda Buddhism is nontheistic; Vedāntic Hindus believe that Ultimate Reality (termed *Brahman* or *nondual Absolute*) lacks any distinctions; orthodox Christianity is trinitarian and Hinduism polytheistic, whereas Islam and Judaism are neither. We could go on, but a detailed study of comparative religions is beyond the scope of our book. Our point is simply that different religions make both similar and different truth-claims—and this raises the fundamental question of this chapter: How should an advocate of one religion approach another religion?

Our question is often misunderstood. We are not asking how an advocate of one religion should approach an advocate of another religion, but how one should approach *what* another person advocates. On the one hand, to ask how we should approach other religions is an epistemological question about what beliefs it is rational to hold and an ontological question about the referents of those beliefs. Answers to these questions require that we consider the truth-claims of the various religions. The questioner seeks to understand sympathetically the religious claims of other persons, to interpret what they mean and what significance they have for believers' lives, and to evaluate critically the alleged truth of those claims. On the other hand, to ask how we should approach other persons is a moral question. Advocates of other religions should be treated, at the very least, as the ethics of our religion demand persons should be treated.

It is often forgotten that evaluating persons' truth-claims and relating to persons are separate issues. Thus some suggest that unless we adopt the relativist claim that whatever persons think is correct is correct for them and renounce any belief that there are religious truths that can be evaluated intersubjectively, we will be intolerant of the persons themselves. From this vantage point, the blemishes of the exclusivistic religions—jihads, crusades, inquisitions, and pogroms—are trotted out to demonstrate what happens when we attempt to evaluate critically other religions and their claims. We should not ignore the wrongs that believers have done in the name of their religion; they were and are deplorable, whether committed in Amritsar, Beirut, Belfast, or Jerusalem. But we should not make the faulty inference that statements regarding how we should treat those with whom we disagree follow directly from epistemological claims about the truths or falsehoods they hold. That people hold a false belief does not allow us to mistreat them, nor should we give them special treatment if they make true claims.

Exclusivism

John Hick (1922–   ) has classified three types of approaches to the diversity of religions.[5] For the first—*exclusivism*—salvation, liberation, human fulfillment, or whatever else one considers to be the ultimate goal of the religion is found solely in or through one particular religion. There are truths in other religions, but one religion is exclusively true; it alone provides the way of salvation or liberation. This means that adherents of other religions, though sincere in their piety and upright in their moral conduct, cannot attain salvation through their religions. To be saved, they must be told about the unique way. Beliefs of this sort help explain religious evangelistic fervor and missionary zeal.

The fundamental argument for exclusivism is theological. Many exclusivists hold that salvation can be accomplished only by a divine act of grace. Since attempts to save ourselves are doomed to failure, it is critical that we discover the locus of the divine salvific initiative. Once we discover where God has truly revealed his unique purposes, it would be folly to go elsewhere for salvation.

For example, the Protestant theologian Karl Barth (1886–1968) contrasts religion with revelation. Religion stands opposed to faith as the defiant, arrogant, human endeavor pitted against the revelation of God. Religion is our impossible and sinful attempt to understand God from our viewpoint and overcome our estrangement from him by our own efforts. It is impossible because reconciliation can be accomplished only by God; it is sinful because it replaces God with something we have made and hence is idolatry:

> We cannot, therefore, interpret the attempt as a harmonious co-operating of man with the revelation of God, as though religion were a kind of out-stretched hand which is filled by God in His revelation. . . . In religion man bolts and bars himself against revelation by providing a substitute, by taking away in advance the very thing which has to be given by God.[6]

Salvation comes only through the true revelation of God, in which he shows and gives himself to us. "There is only one revelation. That revelation is the revelation of the covenant, of the original and basic will of God. . . . Apart from and without Jesus Christ we can say nothing at all about God and man and their relationship one with another."[7]

Barth does not deny that other religions contain truths, high moral ideals, and aesthetic values, or that their adherents are moral or sincere. Indeed, Barth denies that Christianity is the true religion in the sense that it is the climax or fulfillment of all human religion. Christianity in itself is not a superior religion. However, because of the uniqueness of Jesus Christ, Christianity is the *locus* of true religion. In the event of Jesus Christ, God uniquely reveals the truth and provides the means by which we can be reconciled with God. Revelation not only destroys religion, it creates true religion. Thus, even Christians must realize the inadequacy of their own religion when viewed outside of grace and revelation.

Exclusivism is not a distinctly Christian phenomenon. For example, many Muslims hold that polytheists are infidels and Christians heretics. Exclusivists often hold that the prophet, teacher, or founder of their religion is a unique locus of divine activity. This may be a distinct individual (as Christians believe with Jesus or Muslims with Mohammed) or a whole series of individuals (the bodhisattvas of Mahāyāna Buddhism). Through their revelation God uniquely has spoken or is present, so that only through believing in that divine mediator and his or her teachings, or by practicing the particular conduct prescribed can salvation or liberation be achieved.

But why should one think that the infinite God reveals himself in only one way, person, series of persons, or community? Just as advertisers can tailor their message to different audiences, so God could speak in diverse ways to different cultures. But to communicate effectively he would have to adapt his message to the motifs of that culture. Hence, if there are many revelations, they would have different characteristics and contents because they are expressed in diverse cultural dresses. Thus, religion need not be pitting human creative reason against divine revelation, but might embody diverse perceptions of the divine revelation or salvific truth. Barth presupposes that there is only one revelation; hence he can contrast all religion with that revelation. But this presupposition can be questioned, given both an infinite God capable of communicating in different forms and different people claiming either to have received diverse divine revelations or to be that revelation.

Many find it difficult to believe that persons in other religions are doomed because they have not heard the gospel of a given religion and sought salvation in the prescribed manner. Men and women who live morally upright or profoundly righteous lives devoted to God and to others — saints — abound in all religions. They are living evidence that their religion delivers on its promise to transform humans. Can they be thought to have failed on the ground that they do not acknowledge a particular religious mediator, follow that person's teachings, or conceive of God or Reality in a particular manner? Further, if God truly desires that all persons come to know, love, and worship him, one would think that he would not narrowly bind his revelation solely to a particular time or culture.

Finally, given that there are many exclusivist claims — not simply Christian or Muslim — to which ought we adhere? We cannot decide on the basis of the moral lives prescribed or lived, for the virtues and acts encouraged often are not that different, while adherents of all faiths seem capable of living morally praiseworthy lives. One could suggest that we evaluate the truth-claims made; we shall return to this issue later.

Pluralism

Perhaps we should simply abandon exclusivist claims and acknowledge that though different religions manifest different responses to the divine Reality, each can successfully facilitate salvation, liberation, or self-fulfillment. As Hinduism affirms, there are many coequal routes to liberation or salvation.[8] Of course there could be some checks and balances regarding religious claims, but these are met when the religious tradition has produced through the centuries profound scriptures, impressive intellectual systems, new visions of human existence, and saintly lives. This second position, adopted by Hick himself, he terms *pluralism*.

Several questions arise. First, how can all the diverse religious conceptions of God or Reality be true? Hick admits that some religions have fundamentally differing views of Reality. For some, Reality is nondual, apersonal, beyond everything and nothing, transcending the illusory world in which we live and think. For others, Reality is personal—the creator God who is immanently involved in human affairs. These conceptions of Reality seem to be irreconcilable. To explain this, Hick distinguishes between Reality as it is in itself (the noumena) and Reality as it is humanly and culturally perceived and experienced (the phenomena). When religious persons try to speak about the noumenal Ultimate, all they can describe is how it appears to them. Their characterization depends upon the interpretative concepts they use to understand and structure their world and give meaning to their existence. Thus, those who hold that Reality is nondual and indescribable employ one set of interpretative concepts, metaphors, and images; those who see God as personal use another set. In fact, since Reality is infinite, both are probably partly correct, though we cannot know since neither has delineated the noumena.

Hick employs the familiar story of the blind men and the elephant:

> An elephant was brought to a group of blind men who had never encountered such an animal before. One felt a leg and reported that an elephant is a great living pillar. Another felt the trunk and reported that an elephant is a great snake. Another felt a tusk and reported than an elephant is like a sharp plough-share. And so on. . . . Of course they were all true, but each referring only to one aspect of the total reality and all expressed in very imperfect analogies.[9]

We cannot tell which perspective is correct, because there is no ultimate perspective from which we can view the blind men feeling the elephant. The moral is that we are all blind, trapped by our individual and cultural concepts.

Hick believes that those who hold that religious concepts are projections of human characteristics on the divine are partially correct. However, the presence of anthropomorphic projections should not be used to debunk religion. They register our conscious attempts to relate our conceptual framework to the Ultimate and to respond to the activity of the Ultimate in our lives. It is not that one set of concepts or structures is true and another false. According to Hick, statements about the Ultimate are metaphors that are validated in terms of their efficacy in bringing about salvation or transformation, and are preserved in religious traditions because they are continually meaningful to many persons.

Second, what can pluralists say to exclusivists? For example, what can they reply to Barth, who claims that Jesus Christ is the unique revelation of God and the unique means through which salvation is attained? If God was incarnate in Jesus, so that only through him could the Father be known, it would seem that here God has revealed the one way he provides for salvation. Hick's response is to deny the orthodox view of incarnation.[10] God's spirit can work in all persons, transforming them so that they fully manifest God. The incarnation is a metaphor describing God's activity in human lives. In Jesus (as well as in other great religious founders) we have persons who more fully realized the openness to being transformed to a Reality-centered life.

The center of religion, for Hick, is not doctrine but personal transformation. Hence he cautions that religious doctrines, such as the incarnation, should not be unduly emphasized. Neither should they be considered as true or false in the way in which we consider scientific beliefs to be true or false. Religious dogmas and historical claims are attempts to answer personal questions about human existence and experience of the divine. Consequently, they are true insofar as they succeed in changing our attitudes and life-patterns. Hence, though doctrines of the various religions might seem to contradict, when properly viewed as life-expressing truths they often do not. They simply express the diverse ways people from different cultures react to the reality they encounter.

In other words, Hick seems less concerned with theological truths (understood as propositions) than with the existential or life-changing aspects of religion. Religion is significant because it transforms human existence from self-centeredness to Reality-centeredness. Thus, exactly what one believes is not all that important; it is a mythic projection of one's own experiences, culture, and conceptual categories on Reality. For Hick, therefore, exclusivists' attempts to convert or sweep all into one religion's kingdom make no sense. What matters is that this Reality so interacts with us that we are transformed.

Critique of Pluralism

Pluralism is attractive; it accords well with our attempt to be open to and accepting of other persons without being judgmental. Yet this appeal often invokes the confusion between epistemological and ethical considerations noted earlier in this chapter. It is fallacious to affirm that making judgments about truth-claims or beliefs necessitates maltreating persons who hold differing beliefs. To answer the original question concerning what attitudes we should adopt toward other religions, we need to consider more carefully the epistemological and ontological questions raised in the previous section.

What, then, is at issue in this debate? The answer is, in part, the nature of religion. For many pluralists, the significant aspect of religion is its power to transform the individual, to move someone from concern with self to being Reality-centered. This being the case, religious beliefs and practices are important as means to transformation, but are not intrinsically significant. Thus, two people can disagree about a certain belief or practice and it makes no difference. Hick writes, "I hold that someone who differs from me about, for example, whether Jesus had a human father is probably (though not certainly) mistaken; but in holding this I am also conscious that he/she might nevertheless be closer to the divine Reality than I. This awareness is important because it has the effect of de-emphasizing such differences of historical judgement. They can never be more than penultimately important."[11]

Does religion make truth-claims about Reality? Pluralists respond differently to this question. For some, truth is not to be understood propositionally, as if propositions are true or false apart from the time, perspective, and individual who believes them.[12] Rather, truth must be seen humanly, in terms of what propositions and beliefs mean to individual persons, and this is both a historical and an existential matter. Truth is how reality appears to us at a particular time and place, in a particular historical perspective. Religious orientations "can be seen as less or more true in the sense of enabling those who looked at life and the universe through their patterns to perceive smaller or larger, less important or more important, areas of reality, to formulate and to ponder less or more significant issues, to act less or more truly, less or more truly to be."[13]

Other pluralists hold that religious adherents make truth-claims, but only about Reality understood phenomenally (that is, as Reality appears to them). Consequently, there can be no contradiction between religious claims. For example, the claims that something appears to me to be blue and to you not to be blue are not contradictory. They would be contradictory only if we both claimed that the object itself was the color each of us perceived it to be. Similarly, religious adherents speak about what they have encountered from their cultural-religious perspective, not from some external, objective, all-encompassing point of view. Hence, they cannot be said to be really contradictory.

Further, the language and concepts we use to approach Reality are not subject to the type of scientific verification that characterizes our ordinary experience. They are "linguistic pictures or maps of the universe, whose function is to enable us to find salvation/liberation. . . . They accordingly test themselves by their success or failure in fulfilling this soteriological function."[14] What Reality really is like can be verified only eschatologically.[15]

Hick does argue that we can engage in rational scrutiny of religious systems. The criteria to be used are internal consistency and experiential adequacy. But this only tells us whether particular beliefs should be held within a certain system; it does not inform us about any overall truth concerning the nature or structure of Reality. Indeed, one might wonder whether the religious pluralist can even go this far, for experiential adequacy suffers from the same cultural and personal subjectivity that religious claims faced in the first place. By invoking logical consistency, Hick imposes his particular rational structure on Reality and precludes those who, like Zen Buddhists, maintain that logical consistency is part of the bane of human existence that must be transcended.

More generally, one can object that the pluralists' contention — that truth-claims are both historically and culturally subjective and only about the phenomena — leads inevitably to skepticism. Unless we can speak about the Ultimate, not only cannot we know anything about the real elephant (using Hick's analogy), we cannot even be sure that there is an elephant. In fact, the lesson one might draw from Hick's elephant analogy is not that all the blind men were correct, but that none of them was correct. It was not a pillar, snake, or plough that they felt but an elephant, and to claim that it was either or all of these is plainly false. Hick responds that we must *postulate* the existence of an elephant—of a transcendent, noumenal Reality that encounters us. But unless we can say something about that Reality itself, what have we postulated? For any of the blind men to have postulated that what they really felt was an elephant, he must have known what an elephant was.

It is well and good to say that there is a Reality that meets us, but what is Reality? The very willingness of some pluralists to admit atheistic Marxism and naturalistic humanism into the camp of religions alongside and on equal footing with theism[16] suggests the seriousness of the problem. Muslims and Christians maintain there really is a God, the encounter with whom brings meaning to our lives; the naturalist holds that we can find meaningful existence apart from affirming or encountering the divine. But the rational claims of the two are very different. In the former, meaning comes from encounter with a personal God; in the latter it is self-created.

Pluralists such as Hick are faced with a dilemma. If we have no clear concept of God, if we are left with nothing to be said about God or the Ultimate as it is in itself, our religious belief more closely approximates unbelief and becomes relatively indistinguishable from atheism. If we can speak about God, then we can employ some consistent set of predicates to describe the properties God has. Hence, we have a content about which we can make claims, and we are not in the position of being completely blind. We can evaluate which of the blind men's claims, if any, are correct.[17]

Finally, we cannot reduce language about God to language about our experience. Even language about our experiences refers to something beyond those experiences. For example, as Peter Geach (1916–   ) has argued, "worship" is an intentional verb. Our worship is directed toward someone, and it does matter to whom this worship is directed. "People may succeed in relating their thoughts to the true God even though they have a partly erroneous view of his attributes. . . . However, there are limits to the possibility. . . . A sufficiently erroneous thought of a God will simply fail to relate to the true and living God at all."[18] Thus, persons can fail to refer to the correct party by not knowing enough about either the one they are actually intending or the one they should be intending. For example, someone in 1991 who is not up on American politics and who is enthralled by movie actors might claim to support the President. But we cannot conclude that since he supports the President he supports George Bush, President at that time. Such a mistake might be serious, particularly if they hold political appointments in which their ignorance could cost them their jobs. Similarly, one can fail to worship the true God through ignorance and this could prove costly, should God require that salvation depend upon worshipping the true god.

In short, it seems that a pluralist view such as Hick's is accepted not only at the extremely high price of skepticism, but in disregard of what believers think they are doing. At the same time, we cannot ignore the insight of pluralism — namely, that in some way not only can God be encountered through other religions, but that these religions can be a positive force in helping persons to discover and worship the true God and to lead upright lives. How, then, can we bring together concerns about truth with those of meaning and salvation?

Inclusivism

If we acknowledge that there are many different religious and life-transforming experiences, and that God might reveal himself or graciously act in various ways in diverse places, while at the same time we affirm that religious claims about Reality are either true or false, we might adopt what Hick terms *religious inclusivism*. On the one hand, in common with exclusivism, inclusivists hold that there is one absolute provision for salvation that is made known truly in only one religion. The way of salvation is open to people only because they meet special criteria revealed in one true religion, or are accounted righteous on account of a specific salvific act. On the other hand, in common with pluralists, inclusivists hold that God can be encountered and his grace manifested in various ways through diverse religions. Everyone can experience salvation, regardless of whether they have heard and acknowledged the basic tenets of the one true religion. Inclusivism thus extends beyond exclusivism because, though it makes exclusivistic claims for the absolute truth of one religion and what it accomplishes, it allows that adherents of other religions can be saved because of things specified by the true religion.

The Catholic theologian Karl Rahner (1904–1984) argues that persons can be saved only because a particular salvific event has occurred. Christianity is an absolute religion and cannot recognize any other religion as providing *the* way of salvation. It not only tells us of God's unique Word, incarnate in Jesus who died on the cross for all persons, but provides the social context in which Jesus Christ comes to persons. However, it is also true that God desires that all persons be saved. To accomplish this salvation, since Jesus's atoning, salvific work is objective, God can apply the results of Jesus's work to all human beings, even to those who have never heard of Jesus and his death or have never acknowledged his lordship. In this way God makes it possible for all persons, even those who are not within the context of historical Christianity, to be transformed and reconciled to God.

One might think of an analogous scenario. In a particular town a large number of poor people owe debts they cannot pay from their meager resources. But unless they pay their creditors they will be destroyed. A rich woman in another town, learning of their plight, deposits a large amount of money in their town bank, with the stipulation that this be used to satisfy the debts of the poor. Since the poor of the town cannot remove their debts without using these resources, the benefactor's funds are objectively necessary for relieving their plight. However, knowledge of her is not necessary to their liberation; even though they do not personally know their benefactor, they can use these resources to pay off their debts and transform their lives.

Rahner notes that though Christianity began historically with Jesus of Nazareth, it had a prehistory. In pre-Christian times there were many Israelites and followers of other religions whom the New Testament claims were justified or saved subjectively by their faith and objectively by the still-future obedience of Christ. We can apply what is said about the pre-Christian Jewish and non-

Jewish righteous to adherents of other religions. The appearance of Jesus is the point at which Christianity faced the Jewish people, requiring those who heard the gospel to take a position on it. That is, when Christianity became a historical factor in first-century Palestine, it became realistic to claim that salvation depended upon some response to the proclaimed gospel. But Christianity is not a real historical factor for many other cultures, where many have never heard a proclamation of the Christian gospel. Hence, people in these cultures remain in a position comparable to those of the pre-Christian era. Since God desires that all persons be saved, it is reasonable to think that God applies the same grace he applied to those of the pre-Christian era to those who have never heard about Jesus. The Spirit of God is at work in the lives of people who worship in other religions, though they do not recognize God's activity in Christian terms. Rahner terms these persons *anonymous Christians* because although they lack an explicit Christian faith, they consciously or unconsciously seek and worship God.

But if Christianity is the true religion, whereas others contain various admixtures of falsity, should non-Christians then practice their own religion? Rahner holds that religious faith is not solely an internal matter; a social form is necessary for salvation. This form will always be culturally embodied in the religion (including practices and beliefs) that that person embraces. Since different religions have different degrees of truth, they have different degrees of lawfulness—that is, abilities to facilitate a right relationship with God. But just as the theological impurity of pre-Christian Judaism did not prevent its adherents from encountering God in and through their religion, so the theological impurity of contemporary religions does not prevent adherents from finding God. Indeed, these religions can be the mediators of supernatural grace. It is not an all-or-nothing matter; supernatural grace can be manifested in various degrees in all religions. It is only that the New Testament delineates the definitive difference between right and wrong and the unique, salvific revelation of God in Jesus Christ.

This analysis might apply just as well to inclusivist advocates in other religions. Just as the Christian might speak of Christianity as the only true religion and of persons whose lives manifest the grace of God as anonymous Christians, so the Muslim might speak of the absolute truth of Islam and of Christians or Jews as anonymous Muslims. The Jew might see others as anonymous Jews, while the Hindu might see others as anonymous Hindus. Each could hold that though one particular religion is the absolute or true religion, there are significant religious truths in other religions as well. Other religions would then perceive—dimly, partly, and perspectivally—the truths that are found in clearer form in the one true religion. Since not all religious doctrines or practices in all religions are true, cross-religious criticism is in order.

But if persons can achieve salvation without knowing anything at all about a particular religious tradition, why then should one term them anonymous Christians, Muslims, or whatever? Indeed, why try to convert them at all? Why not simply encourage them to continue to live according to what they know and believe, so that they can in that light lead transformed lives? Rahner holds that bringing anonymous Christians to the knowledge of what their faith is truly about and the basis for that faith is a stage of the development of those persons' Christianity. "The reflex self-realization of a previously anonymous Christianity is demanded (1) by the incarnational and social structure of grace and of Christianity, and (2) because the individual who grasps Christianity in a clearer, purer and more effective way, has, other things being equal, a still greater chance of salvation than someone who is merely an anonymous Christian."[19] Other inclusivists might reply that it does matter that persons know the true basis of their salvation because, since liberation comes through knowledge, truth matters. Hence we have an obligation to enlighten them as to the objective basis of their transformation. In any case, the exclusivist content of inclusivism provides a basis for justifying proselytizing.

More seriously, given that there is a plurality of religions that hold themselves to be the absolute religion, how would one decide which makes the correct claim? Some feel it is simply a matter of determining the locus of unique divine revelation. Rahner and Barth are certain that God has come in Jesus Christ; Muslims hold that Mohammed gave us Allah's mature revelation. But this simply pushes the problem back. How do we adjudicate claims to divine revelation? Some have suggested that we can do this by evaluating the life of the claim-maker. But are we able to know enough about the individual religious founders to make comparisons that could establish the spiritual or moral superiority of one over the other? Is the moral life of Jesus superior to that of the Buddha? Others have appealed to the character of the tradition that grew out of the work of the founder, yet this is risky, for the history of each religion is strewn with events that both credit and discredit the teachings of the religion.

A different way of assessing religions appeals to criteria by which we can evaluate the religious systems themselves. To this approach let us now turn.

Criteria for Assessing Religions

One conclusion we might draw from the discussion to this point is that we must take seriously the contention that religions make specific truth-claims about reality. Some say there is a god; others not. Some assert there are many gods; others that there is one God. Some declare that God becomes incarnate; others not. Some claim that Jesus is God incarnate; others that it is Krishna. Some claim that Christ is actually present in the bread and wine of Holy Communion; others that the elements are symbolic only. Some accept Ali, Mohammed's son-in-law, as the first Imam and rightful successor of the Prophet; others do not. Some believe we should pray facing Mecca; others face the Wailing Wall. We could go on presenting contrasts. The point, however, is that there is good reason to think that religious believers are making truth-claims about Reality or (in some traditions) God's acts in history, and that these must be given their due place.

If they are making truth-claims about reality, it follows that specific beliefs are subject to rational evaluation. We can use the canons of logic, human experience, and perhaps trained intuition to establish probabilistically that some beliefs are true and others false. In fact, much of what has already transpired in this book is directed toward that end. Other claims cannot be tested (e.g., is Christ present in the bread and wine of the Holy Communion?) except in terms of the degree to which they are consistent with or implied by other relevant religious claims, and make sense. In any case, there are legitimate grounds for rationally evaluating many individual religious beliefs.

But probably we want to go beyond this. We want not only to claim that individual beliefs are true or false, but to be able to make comparative evaluations of religions themselves. In deciding whether to be a Muslim, Hindu, Sikh, Jew, Christian, or whatever, we would want to know whether that particular religious system is true, or more true than any other. This is more difficult, for religious systems contain many propositions, some of which are true and others false. Thus, one has to weigh not only individual statements, but whole systems of statements according to some criteria.

What criteria might be used to evaluate religious systems? Keith Yandell (1938–   ) suggests the following:

1. The propositions essential to that religion must be consistent with each other.
2. Knowing that the religious system is true must be compatible with its being true. If the truth of the system entails that we cannot know it is true — for example, if, like Mādhyamika Buddhism, it claims that all views are false — that is reason to suspect its truth.
3. The truth of a religious system must be compatible with what must exist for it to be true. For example, the claim that Ultimate Reality has no distinctions is incompatible with the claim that religious statements that affirm this are true and not false.
4. If the only reason for offering the religious system is that it promises to provide a solution to a problem, and it fails to do so, there is no reason to accept the system. For example, if a religious system was introduced to resolve the problem of pain and suffering, and it clearly did not accomplish this, there would be no reason to advocate that religious system.
5. Essential truths of the system should not contradict well-established data — for example, in the sciences or psychology.
6. Ad-hoc hypotheses to avoid evidence contrary to the religious system count against that religious system.
7. A system should be able to account for and explain broad reaches of human experience.[20]

To Yandell's criteria one might add:

8. It should satisfy some basic moral and aesthetic intuitions, and provoke and inspire persons to live more morally responsive and responsible lives.

Reflection on this list suggests that further thought is necessary about evaluative criteria. Are the above good criteria? Are there others? Can these criteria be applied to systems so diverse as religions?

This brings up one final issue: What is it that we evaluate when we evaluate a religious system? Although we have spoken of religious systems here as making propositional claims, at the same time it is wrong to view religious systems as consisting of impersonal, objective statements of religious beliefs accepted by all advocates of that religion. Religious systems are complex bodies that have grown and developed historically. What a Christian or Hindu believes today differs (for some, remarkably) from what first-century Christians or eighth-century Hindus held. This is not to say that these persons today are not Christians or Hindus, but they are Christians or Hindus not only because they embrace certain beliefs, but because they participate in a historical tradition that is Christian or Hindu. The tradition is not pristine; we cannot get back to the original founders and believe exactly what they believed and practice as they did. The tradition is cumulative and dynamic, social and personal. Hence, there is an important subjective dimension to any description of that religion.

Religions are embodied historically in cultures, and it is difficult to isolate distinctively religious beliefs from cultural ones (for example, is monogamy a Christian religious or a Western cultural prescription? Is Hinduism isolable from the caste system?). Religions are embodied in individual believers, and there are no two believers who hold exactly the same beliefs. Thus, we must not speak about the totality of the assertions made by an advocate of a religion, but about what might essentially describe that religion. Yet even here difficulties emerge, for what must a person believe essentially to be a Christian, Muslim, or Hindu? The diversity within each of these traditions bears witness to the difficulty of discerning a particular credal essence.

The claim that each religion is a strand in the religious history of the world is an intriguing notion. But even if there are generic religious concepts such as faith and God, these concepts should be not taken to mean either that every claim is true for the person who holds it (which is the relativist's approach to religion) or that every claim is true only in a phenomenal sense (which is Hick's pluralism). One can acknowledge that there is a universal religion in which humans have participated throughout history in the same way as one can affirm that there is a universal science in which persons have participated. In the latter case, not every avowed scientific belief is true, nor every practice sanctioned — alchemy, for instance, was indeed wrong-headed. Yet each scientist was grappling with reality, seeking to understand how it operated and what causal explanations best sufficed. Similarly, one can see humans grappling religiously with the God who comes to them, attempting to understand that Reality and apply it meaningfully to their own existence. Some of their beliefs are false; some of their practices wrong-headed. If there is a Reality, a God who operates in the world, encountering humans, it becomes as much an intellectual task to understand that Reality as an existential task to appropriate that Reality in our own lives.

STUDY QUESTIONS

1. Make a list of some of the differences between various religions you know about. Are these differences significant or insignificant? Defend your view. What criteria did you use to decide significance?

2. What is religious exclusivism? How might one defend this view? What critique might be given of this view?

3. How does the story of the blind man and the elephant help one understand religious pluralism? How might this analogy be turned into a criticism of pluralism? Would the story and its moral change significantly if the men were not blind, but only partially sighted?

4. What objections might be raised against Hick's pluralism? Why does he think personal transformation is more important than religious beliefs? What do you see as the proper relation between personal transformation and religious beliefs? Defend your view.

5. How is religious inclusivism similar to and different from both exclusivism and pluralism? How does Rahner defend this position, and what criticisms might be given of his view?

6. Compare and contrast pluralism with inclusivism on the question of whether religions make truth-claims about reality. What is the dilemma facing Hick on this issue? How might he respond to it?

7. Use the criteria suggested by Yandell to evaluate your own or another religious tradition.

NOTES

1. *Mu* is part of an ancient Zen *koan*, or saying. Literally it means "not, not having, or having nothing."
2. Philip Kapleau, ed., *The Three Pillars of Zen* (Garden City, NY: Anchor Press, 1980), pp. 237–39.
3. This is a central theme in Wilfred Cantwell Smith, *Towards a World Theology* (Philadelphia: Westminster, 1981).
4. Both are described in more detail in Smith, pp. 6–13.
5. John Hick, ed., *Problems of Religious Pluralism* (New York: St. Martin's Press, 1985), chaps. 3 and 4.
6. Karl Barth, *Church Dogmatics* I, 2 (Edinburgh: T. & T. Clark, 1956), p. 303.
7. Barth, IV, 1, p. 45.
8. "In whatever way men approach Me, I am gracious to them; men everywhere . . . follow My path." *Bhagavad-Gītā*, Eliot Deutsch, trans. (New York: Holt, Rinehart & Winston, 1968), IV, 11.
9. John Hick, *God and the Universe of Faiths* (London: Macmillan, 1977), p. 140.
10. Hick, *Problems*, p. 35; also John Hick, ed., *The Myth of God Incarnate* (London: SCM, 1977).

11. Hick, *Problems*, p. 89.
12. Smith, p. 190.
13. Smith, p. 94.
14. Hick, *Problems*, p. 80.
15. Even here there is a question, since there is little reason to think that the same epistemological difficulties that plague our present awareness would not still apply.
16. Smith, chap. 7.
17. Peter Byrne, "John Hick's Philosophy of World Religions," *Scottish Journal of Theology* 35, no. 4 (1982): 297.
18. Peter Geach, *God and the Soul* (New York: Schocken Books, 1969), pp. 110–11.
19. Karl Rahner, "Christian and the Non-Christian Religions," in John Hick and Brian Hebblethwaite, eds., *Christianity and Other Religions* (Glasgow: Collins, 1980), pp. 76–77.
20. Keith E. Yandell, "Religious Experience and Rational Appraisal," *Religious Studies* 8 (June 1974): 185–86.

SUGGESTED READING

Byrne, Peter. "John Hick's Philosophy of World Religions," *Scottish Journal of Theology* 35, no. 4 (1982): 289–301.

Hick, John. *God and the Universe of Faiths*. London: Macmillan, 1977.

Hick, John, advisory ed. *Faith and Philosophy* 5, no. 4 (Oct. 1988).

Hick, John, ed. *Problems of Religious Pluralism*. New York: St. Martin's Press, 1985.

Hick, John, and Brian Hebblethwaite, eds. *Christianity and Other Religions*. Glasgow: Collins, 1980.

Smith, Wilfred Cantwell. *Towards a World Theology*. Philadelphia: Westminster, 1981.

Yandell, Keith E. "Religious Experience and Rational Appraisal," *Religious Studies* 8 (June 1974): 173–87.

13

Religious Ethics:
The Relation of God
to Morality

It is important that you have the best information now available for fighting the AIDS virus, a health problem that the President has called "Public Enemy Number One." . . . I encourage you to practice responsible behavior based on understanding and strong personal values. This is what you can do to stop AIDS.

C. Everett Koop,
former Surgeon General
of the United States, 1981–1989

What are we talking about when we discuss ethics? As we shall see, this is a very complex question. But a basic distinction may help us get started. Let us assume that we want to engage in an ethical discussion about AIDS and college life. Some of the issues we might consider would be primarily *descriptive*. That is, they would relate to what college students or personnel *actually* believe or the way they *actually* behave. Would most colleges inform a student who had been assigned to share a dormitory room with someone known by those in student services to have the AIDS virus? Has the "AIDS scare" modified the sexual behavior of college students? Other issues, however, would be primarily *prescriptive* or *normative*; that is, they would center around what college students *ought to* believe or how they *ought to* behave. Ought college students to modify their sexual behavior in light of the AIDS epidemic? Should colleges disseminate information? Ought students be told when they are rooming with someone who has the AIDS virus?

Philosophers certainly do not deny that *descriptive ethics* is important. They realize that we cannot, for example, create proper public policies if we do not know what people actually believe and how they live. Most philosophers, though, feel such considerations lie primarily in the domain of the anthropologist, sociologist, or political scientist. On the other hand, philosophers continue to be very interested in· *normative ethics*. That is, they continue to be interested in the question of how people ought or ought not act, or whether certain activities are intrinsically good or bad. Moreover, philosophers are interested in a wide range of questions related to normative systems. Is it important for us to affirm normative ethical principles? What is the origin of the normative ethical principles we affirm? Under what conditions can such principles be rationally affirmed? Which set of normative ethical principles (hereafter simply referred to as *ethical principles*) is the correct one?

The Source of Religious Ethical Truth

There is no standard order in which ethical issues such as those mentioned above are discussed. But in the area of religious ethics a rather natural progression arises. Let us start with the fact that almost all of us affirm ethical principles related to almost every area of our lives. That is, we believe we have some understanding of how we, our family and friends, and even those with whom we will never have any direct contact *ought* to behave.

But what is the origin of the ethical principles we believe to be true? At one level an answer is readily available. We initially acquired the vast majority in the same fashion we initially acquired what we believe to be true about U.S. Presidents or proper nutrition or types of automobiles: from some respected authority. For instance, most of us initially believed it was wrong to disobey our parents or engage in certain forms of sexual behavior because of what our parents, teachers, and religious leaders told us.

What, however, is the *ultimate* origin of the ethical principles we hold to be true? Are they solely the product of human thought? Were they "created" by God? Do such principles originate in some source independent of both? Or are there multiple sources?

All of these options have their proponents. Even among religious believers, a wide variety of opinion exists. However, the vast majority of believers continue to claim that the basic ethical principles they affirm in some sense have their origin in God, as opposed to human thought or some source totally independent of both.

But what exactly does it mean to say that ethical principles originate in God? One option is to grant that the basic ethical principles we affirm are not a divine creation and yet deny that they are independent of God. To draw an analogy with the laws of logic may help. Consider, for example, the law of noncontradiction—the contention that something cannot be both what it is and what it is not at the same time. Few believers have thought this law to be totally independent of God, or something that God discovered. Furthermore, the scope of its actual application is held to be dependent on God. But few believers hold that this law was created by God, or that it somehow came into existence as the result of divine decree. It is, rather, normally thought to be an eternal truth that has always existed in the mind of God.

For instance, according to this line of reasoning, the fact that humans cannot be both alive and not alive in the same sense at the same time is not true because God decreed that it should be so. Rather the nature of reality (what is it to be alive or not to be alive) simply makes such a state of affairs an impossibility. But God *is* the one who decided whether any humans would actually come into existence and is, thus, the one who determined whether the logical truth in question would actually apply to the world as it is.

Some have suggested that basic ethical principles might reasonably be viewed the same way. Let us consider, for example, the widely accepted moral belief that it is wrong to inflict pain unnecessarily. We should not, we are told, view this ethical principle as independent of God in the sense that it is a principle with which God came in contact and that he determined from then on should guide all divine and human behavior. And, of course, if God had not created beings capable of experiencing pleasure and pain, this specific "truth" would have no relevance for our world. But this ethical principle did not come into existence as the result of some divine decree, nor can God do away with it at will. Rather, the fact that inflicting unnecessary pain is wrong is simply *inherent* in the very concept of any being who can experience such pain. Hence, much like the laws of logic, it is best viewed as having always existed in God's mind.[1]

Many believers, however, have not liked the idea of anything in any sense being independent of God or limiting divine activity. Thus, they have wanted to argue that the basic ethical principles they believe to be true have their origin *solely* in God in a stronger sense. One popular way in which this has been envisioned — by individuals often labeled divine command theorists — is to maintain that ethical principles find their inception in God's commands.

This does not mean, it is important to point out, that the commands themselves are seen as the *origin* of these ethical principles. God is not envisioned as mindlessly "uttering" statements that somehow magically become the basis for ethical standards the moment they leave "God's lips." God's commands are seen as an expression of God's will.[2] Just as a parent's command for a child to go to bed is best interpreted as an expression of what the parent wants the child to do, so too are God's commands best seen as an expression of how God wants us to live.

However, even given this clarification, a well-known challenge remains. If the ethical principles by which we are to live originate in the commands that express God's will, then it appears that we would be justified in doing anything God commanded. It appears, for instance, that even if God commanded us to kill innocent people routinely, or arbitrarily and capriciously commanded us to treat small children kindly one day but torture them the next, our obedience would be justified simply because God has said this should be done. And surely, argues the critic, this is unacceptable. Surely a rational believer would not affirm a theory about the origin of correct ethical principles that had *this* implication.[3]

One popular response has been developed by ethicist Robert Adams (1937–).[4] He wants to tie the origin of ethical truth to the will of God, but denies that the "believer is committed to doing the will of God just because it is the will of God." That is, Adams denies that the believer would always be required to be what God commanded solely because God commanded it. He grants, for instance, that it would not be wrong for the believer to refrain from practicing cruelty, even *if* God commanded it. This is so, we are told, because

God's commands can be viewed as worthy of obedience "only if certain conditions are assumed — namely, only if it is assumed that God has the character which [we] believe Him to have, of loving His human creatures."[5] Otherwise it would not be wrong to disobey him. Or, stated in more positive terms, Adams's response is that if we assume that God is a personal agent who loves his human creatures — an assumption Adams believes we can justifiably make — then we need not fear that those commands originating in the will of God will obligate us to act in a capricious, unloving manner.

Others have elaborated more fully on the important connection between God's commands and character. It is certainly true, they acknowledge, that God has the ability to command us to kill innocent people. God obviously can formulate the relevant concepts and could communicate the divine intentions to us. However, the divine moral will expressed by God's commands does not exist in a vacuum, nor is it dependent on some autonomous moral standard that has existed eternally in God's mind. God's will, rather, is an aspect of God's nature — that is, it is an expression of the type of being God really is. And once we understand the type of being God really is, it is argued, the criticism in question loses its force.

We must first realize that God is the all-knowing creator of everything. Thus, God knows exactly how all aspects of the divine creation function best. God knows, for example, exactly what will satisfy us individually and what will help us to live together harmoniously. Second, God does not just happen to be caring and loving most, or even all, of the time. God could not be unloving because God's essential nature is never-changing. God necessarily wills our individual and corporate fulfillment. Accordingly, God's commands could not be arbitrary and capricious in the way the critic envisions. God, for instance, could not command us to kill innocent children "just for the fun of it," since this would be inconsistent with God's nature.[6]

But could God not have been a different type of being, one who believed that lying, cheating, or killing innocent children was an intrinsically meritorious action? Possibly, some believers respond. However, the God we worship is not such a being. Thus, the criticism in question simply fails to apply, and, accordingly, it remains perfectly reasonable to maintain that God's nature is the ultimate origin of the ethical principles we believe to be true.[7]

The Authoritative Basis of Religious Ethical Truth

Even given that God's nature is the origin of ethical principles, a significant question remains: What gives the ethical principles that originate in God their authority? Why ought the believer to obey what God communicates? Or, as Alasdair MacIntyre (1929–) has recently phrased this question, "What conditions must be satisfied for it to be rational for someone to treat God's [ethical] beliefs as authoritative?"[8]

In reality, some believers may follow God's commands primarily out of fear, others out of love or the belief that it will generate the best consequences, and still others primarily because their culture has ingrained this desire or duty in them. However, as MacIntyre and others rightly point out, believers could not justifiably view the ethical principles originating in God as the ultimate ethical standard if they did not think that God were *perfectly good*.

What basis, though, do believers have for maintaining that God is good? Religious critic Kai Nielsen (1925–   ) contends there are only two possible avenues of response.[9] One possibility, we are told, is for believers to claim that God's goodness is a factual or evidential matter. That is, they might claim that God is good because God has, for example, given them a purpose for living or healed a loved one or offered guidance in times of need.

However, this will not do, Nielsen is quick to point out. We can claim that an individual possesses a certain characteristic only if we already have some understanding of the characteristic in question. For instance, to cite an example not found in Nielsen's writings, we can claim that a new acquaintance is friendly *only if* we already understand what it means for someone to be friendly. In a similar fashion, to return to Nielsen's argument, we can claim that God is good by appealing to the actions God has performed *only if* we already have in mind a standard of goodness by which God's actions can be judged. But if this is true, Nielsen concludes, then it can, of course, no longer be claimed that the ethical principles that originate in God provide the ultimate ethical standard. Rather, our own ethical intuitions must be acknowledged to be the ultimate standard.

The other option, Nielsen informs us, is to claim that the statement "God is good" is true by definition or, more correctly, to claim that "goodness" is a necessary defining characteristic of "God." God's attitudes (and actions) are then good simply because God possesses (or performs) them. But this response generates another question: Upon what basis do believers label the being they worship "God"? Or, to state Nielsen's question in a somewhat different fashion: How do believers know that the being from whom they have received those ethical principles which they accept as authoritative is actually God?

Believers, Nielsen points out, cannot justifiably claim that such a being is God simply because this being says it is good. The question then simply becomes: Upon what basis can the claims of such a being be believed? Nor, he argues, can believers claim that the actions of the being they worship are good, and thus that the being can justifiably be considered God, just because they believe this being is the omniscient, omnipotent creator to the universe. It may be true that it would be unwise not to follow the commands of such a being, but it is not impossible for an omnipotent, omniscient creator to be wicked. The only valid response, we are told, is for believers to admit that the being they worship is called "God" because they possess independent ethical standards of goodness with which the actions and attitudes of this being are consistent.

An analogy may help clarify this important point. Let us assume that someone declares the statement "All puppies are young" to be a definitional truth. This alone does not allow her to maintain justifiably that a dog which has just entered the room is a puppy. To make this claim justifiably, she must first determine whether the dog is young. And to do this she must already have in mind the characteristics that young dogs possess — for instance, oversized feet, an excitable personality and a certain type of teeth. Likewise, Nielsen is arguing, believers can claim that the being whose commands they follow is God and thus is an acceptable ethical authority only if they can determine (possibly in addition to other things) that this being is good. But this can be accomplished only if they already have in mind a concept of goodness by which this being can be judged. Thus, again, believers must admit that their own ethical intuitions are the ultimate ethical standard.

Is Nielsen correct? First, it must be emphasized that Nielsen's argument applies only to those believers who maintain that ethical truth originates totally in God — for example, in God's nature. His comments are not relevant to those believers (noted earlier) who maintain that, although ethical truth is in some sense dependent on God, it is also in some sense independent of him.

What, though, of those believers who hold that ethical truth *does* originate totally in God? Is Nielsen's argument compelling in this case? It appears that in at least one sense it is. It may well be true that many believers maintain that God is good because the attitudes and actions of the being in question are consistent with their own ethical sensibilities. That is, it may well be true that many believers generally judge God to be good by ethical standards possessed before this judgment is made.

But to grant Nielsen this much is somewhat innocuous. The crucial part of his thesis is his contention that the ethical criteria used by the believer to evaluate God's goodness constitute an ethical standard that is separate from, and more fundamental than, the basic ethical beliefs of the divine code-giver being judged.

However, it is not clear that the believer need grant Nielsen this point. The ethical criteria by which believers judge the goodness of God are only "separate" and "more fundamental" in the sense required by Nielsen if they are formulated by each believer apart from divine influence. However, Judeo-Christian theology, for example, has traditionally maintained that humans and the environment in which we function are both divine creations. More specifically, it has traditionally been held that the basic ethical principles that we as humans find ourselves affirming are actually divine in origin. In exactly what sense this is so, as we shall see, differs among believers. Yet if such principles are in any sense divine in origin, then believers need not grant in the last analysis that they judge God by an ethical standard that is separate from, and more ultimate than, God's. They can claim, rather, that they judge God by a standard that God has brought it about that they possess.[10]

To state the point differently, it appears that by affirming the "divine" origin of their own ethical sensibilities, believers can grant that they judge the goodness of God by their own ethical standards and yet justifiably deny that their own personally formulated ethical code is the final seat of ethical authority. They need not grant that the ethical standard in question is ultimately independent of God. They can still justifiably claim in a meaningful sense that the *ultimate* ethical authority resides solely in God.

Nielsen, of course, does not accept this religious understanding of the origin of humanity's basic ethical intuitions. But this is not relevant. Nielsen is not assessing the truth or falsity of the believer's beliefs concerning God's existence, attitudes, or actions. His contention, rather, is that believers cannot consistently maintain that their ethical decisions are based on a ethical standard ultimately independent of human thought, even if they make certain religious assumptions. However, this contention, it appears, can be countered successfully.

The Acquisition of Religiously Based Ethical Truth

Let us assume, then, for the sake of argument that believers can justifiably maintain not only that ethical truth originates in God but also that it is authoritative. This still leaves us with the question of how believers acquire this ethical insight.

Three distinct, although not mutually exclusive, methods of acquisition are mentioned most frequently. First, believers often claim that God has communicated ethical truths through some form of written revelation — for example, the Bible or Koran. Opinions differ widely on the extent to which God is thought to have been directly involved in the production of this revelation. Some believe God is directly responsible for every word, others believe God is responsible for the basic concepts, and still others believe that God is responsible only for helping to collate the most accurate human ethical insights. But many, if not most, believers hold that written revelation is a very important source of information about the ethical principles by which God wants us to live.

It is here, though, that conservative Jewish and Christian believers — those who believe the Torah or Bible to be a clear, direct communication from God — run into a well-known dilemma. The problem is that, at face value, some of the actions attributed to God appear to be ethically questionable. For example, in Numbers 31 it is God who declares that all members of an enemy tribe are to be killed by the Israelites, and then decides how to divide up the thirty-two thousand virgin girls who were not destroyed. And in I Chronicles 21, it appears that God has seventy thousand individuals killed solely to punish King David, and not because of any wrongdoing on their part.

Some conservative believers respond by separating the ethical principles by which God operates from those applicable to human behavior. God, it is argued, has created a consistent, thoughtful ethical standard for humans that, if followed, will bring about what God desires and the greatest fulfillment for all. But God is not bound by such a standard. God can do whatever he wants for whatever reasons he possesses, and such actions are ethically justifiable simply because he has performed them.[11]

Of course, this position generates obvious questions. If God operates by a different ethical standard, how can God remain the object of our ethical admiration? We might well obey a being who has created rules for us because we recognize that these rules maximize human fulfillment or because we fear the rule-giver. But could we truly admire a being who not only could, but did violate the most basic ethical concepts by which we have been told (and created to feel) we should live?

Most believers think the answer is no. They deny that two distinct standards exist. Of course, they grant, God has created some ethical tenets that apply only to humans. For example, rules related to the well-being of our physical bodies are not relevant to God because God has no such body. However, the basic ethical principles God has communicated to us are the same ethical principles that also "guide" God's activity. Accordingly, any seeming violation of these principles must ultimately be a problem of human perspective. If we could see the whole picture from God's perspective—if we were aware of all the contextual factors—we would see that everything God has actually said and done is consistent with God's nature, which is loving in the basic manner in which we understand the term.[12]

Second, some believers, in the "natural law" tradition of Thomas Aquinas (c. 1224–1274), continue to believe that human reason is capable of discovering divine ethical truth. According to this perspective, God is the ultimate source of all ethical knowledge. That is, God establishes the ultimate distinction between good and evil. However, as the result of being created in God's image, we as human possess the rational capacities to comprehend those aspects of this ethical standard that have been revealed in nature.

We have, for example, a natural tendency to preserve ourselves, to produce offspring, and to live in a social setting with others. From these principles, Aquinas would argue, we can deduce that God sanctions self-defense. And from the fact that we have a natural tendency to protect young children and the fact that we all desire to avoid pain, we can deduce that God does not sanction the killing of innocent children. The laws derived here are the laws of our natures, laws about how human beings are to act and be treated.

Thomistic natural law theorists are quick to point out that such ethical reflection is not a more trustworthy avenue for discerning ethical truth than written revelation. In fact, many have acknowledged that written revelation must be given precedence in the event of a conflict. But, although written revelation is *sufficient* for giving us God's basic ethical perspective, it is not always *necessary*. Human reflection, these thinkers observe, can discover much about God's basic ethical standards and their application to our daily lives.[13]

Finally, as has been implicitly stated, some believers also claim that some divine ethical truth is innate. All persons, they maintain, have been created in the "image of God," including God's "ethical image." And this means that our basic ethical intuitions—for example, the belief that we should not kill innocent children—automatically mirror God's basic ethical perspectives. As Gottfried Leibniz (1646–1716) and others rightly noted, such innate intuitions may require some external illumination before we become consciously aware of them.[14] We may, for instance, need to understand what a child is, and what killing means, before we become consciously aware of the fact that killing children is wrong. Moreover, not all available ethical insight comes to us in this fashion. Written revelation and reason are also necessary. But some of the basic

ethical principles we believe to be true were not "learned." We, as divine creations, were simply "born" with them.

There is, however, a seemingly serious problem that proponents of all three
of these modes of acquiring divine ethical truth must face. Why is there so
much ethical diversity among believers? That is, why do seemingly sincere,
knowledgeable believers differ significantly on so many issues related to human
thought and action? If believers have access to basic ethical truth, as they
claim, why is there not greater ethical consensus among them?

Some of this diversity can, of course, be explained by the diversity in
religious perspectives. Proponents of most religions do sincerely believe that
they have access to ethical truth through reason, inborn awareness, or written
revelation. But they are aware of the fact that not all "written revelations" offer
compatible or equally specific guidance on the same issues — for example, on
how we should behave sexually or how we should respond to those who treat us
wrongly. Moreover, they realize that many religious traditions maintain that
only adherents to that tradition have access to divine truth through innate
awareness or rational reflection. Thus, proponents of any given religion can
readily grant not only that some ethical diversity in the general religious community exists but that some is to be expected.

What can be said, though, about the significant amount of ethical diversity
that remains *within* various religions — for instance, within the Judeo-Christian
perspective? Believers can respond, in part, by appealing to the common distinction between basic ethical principles and their practical application. Let us
take the case of the conscientious parent who desires to respond appropriately
to his three-year-old daughter as she lies screaming and kicking because she
does not want to go to bed. There is little debate at the level of principle. The
conscientious father will believe he ought to respond in a just, loving manner.
But what does this mean? Should he scream and kick with her? Should he just
passively wait until she is finished? Should he try diversion? Should he pick her
up and take her to bed? The fact that he believes he ought to respond in love
does not, alone, give him the answer.

In other contexts, ethical diversity within a given religion can be explained by
differing factual assumptions. Abortion is a good example. Most people in the
Judeo-Christian tradition affirm the same relevant ethical principles: for instance, that taking an innocent life is wrong. What they differ on is whether the
fetus is sufficiently human to fall within the protective bounds of this principle.

Alternatively, let us assume we are discussing the nature of a good marriage. Most individuals will agree that certain characteristics are essential — for
example, that such a relationship should be characterized by mutually fulfilling
love. But the specific form of marriage that best exemplifies this ideal can
remain an open "factual" question. Some have argued that while monogamy
may best serve this function in Western cultures, polygamy may be most functional in those parts of the world where social service programs are not available for individuals in need.[15]

Or consider the question of government. Most believe that government is
necessary for protection and order. But to what extent ought government con-

trol our lives to fulfill these functions? Is government too greatly involved in economic affairs? Does government exercise too much control over our personal conduct? In all such cases, believers can again acknowledge ethical diversity, even among themselves, without denying that they have access to the authoritative source of ethical truth.

Even granting, though, that some diversity can be explained in this fashion, the basic tension remains. Some believers within given religious traditions differ on the *basic* "innate" or "rational" principles themselves. For example, some Christians believe it is never right to use life-threatening force while others believe this is justified in times of war or to defend an innocent person. And while some proponents of given religions have thought all humans have the right to political liberty—that is, the right to formulate the laws by which they are governed—other proponents of the same religion have thought it perfectly permissible to own another person, or for those of only one gender or economic level to control the lives of all others. Can diversity of this fundamental sort justifiably be viewed as compatible with the contention that the proponents of a given religion have access to authoritative ethical truth?

In response, many believers emphasize the important distinction between affirming *different* basic ethical principles and ranking the *same* basic ethical principles differently. Take, for example, the case of Christians who were hiding Jews in their houses during World War II. When the Nazis came to ask if Jews were within, some thought it right to lie while others did not. But the issue here was not primarily one of principle. All of the Christians involved thought it was their God-sanctioned duty both to protect innocent lives *and* not to lie. They differed on the question of which principle was properly to be given precedence in this case. Such value conflicts, many conclude, account for much of the basic ethical diversity among believers.[16]

Other believers hold that the human ability to identify divine ethical principles accurately has been severely damaged by "the fall"—that is, by a break in the relationship between humans and God that was precipitated by an act of rebellion by humans. Thus, they claim that although many of us at times are able to discern with relative accuracy the ethical principles affirmed by God, some of us will inevitably be unable to do so, or at least be unable to do so consistently.[17]

Finally, those believers who maintain that some ethical truth is "inborn" often emphasize the significance of cultural conditioning. It is one thing, they argue, to say that each human has some basic understanding of the divine ethical law, but quite another thing to say that such an understanding will always be consciously felt as predominant. Individuals are greatly influenced by their culture. If they are raised in a culture where slavery or cheating or lying is condoned, they will have a strong disposition to believe it is right to engage in such activities. They might have some vague feeling that such actions are wrong, but it need not be held that this "divine perspective" will always be most influential.[18]

Of course, even if all this is granted, pervasive ethical diversity among believers still leaves us with the following question: Which religious ethical standard most closely resembles God's standard? And, this surely *is* an *important* question in that much strife historically has been the result of individuals or groups acting on what they perceived to be the correct set of divinely sanctioned ethical principles. In fact, it is so important that it may well be true that the reality of such diversity stands as a good reason for believers to periodically reassess their ethical beliefs (and the behavior such beliefs generate). That is, such diversity may well stand as a real challenge to ethical dogmatism, especially in action.

But we must be careful to keep all this in perspective. There is diversity in the methods used by believers to acquire ethical truth and in the "truths" allegedly acquired. However, just as the reality of diversity in political opinion does not necessarily require us to become political relativists or skeptics, the reality of ethical diversity does not necessarily require us to become ethical relativists or skeptics. Ethical diversity ought to be recognized and considered as we put our ethical beliefs into action, but it does not follow from the fact that a believer acknowledges the reality of ethical diversity that he cannot justifiably claim that there exists any ethical truth, that such truth is divine in origin, or even that he has access to it.

The Significance of Religiously Based Ethical Truth

What does all this mean for those individuals who are not religious? If believers are correct in holding that ethical truth originates in God and that they have access to such truth, what are the implications for those who do not believe in God (or at least deny that ethical truth is in any sense dependent on God)?

Does it mean, for instance, that those who do not believe ethical truth is in any sense dependent on God cannot meaningfully communicate with those who do? On the basis of what has been said thus far, we can see that believers need not hold this to be the case. Most believers, as we have seen, do not claim that one must believe in God (or believe ethical truth is dependent on God) to be aware of any of God's basic ethical beliefs. Most hold, rather, that God has created *all* individuals with an "inborn" understanding of, or the rational ability to discover, certain basic ethical principles. Hence, such believers can maintain that the mutual possession of these principles allows for meaningful ethical dialogue between the two groups. The fact that nonbelievers do not recognize the "divine" origin of their basic ethical beliefs need not be viewed as altering this situation.[19]

However, a number of significant questions remain. For example, can a nonreligious person, or anyone else who does not believe ethical truth to be dependent on God, justifiably affirm ethical absolutes? That is, can someone who does not ground ethical truth in God justifiably claim that some actions are wrong (or right) for all persons at all times and places? As a matter of fact, of course, most nonreligious individuals do affirm ethical absolutes. The vast majority believe, for example, that innocent children ought, in principle, never to be tortured. But can such absolutes be justifiably affirmed? Most believers ground absolutes in an objective, external standard: God's nature. But if no God exists, then are not all ethical beliefs ultimately human in origin? And if this is so, then how can it be said justifiably that one human or group of humans has the right to dictate how all others *ought* to live? Does it not follow rather, as Jean-Paul Sartre (1905–1980) has said, that "everything is permissible if God does not exist?"[20]

In response, Nielsen argues that the "nonexistence of God does not preclude the possibility of there being an objective standard on which to base moral judgments." There are, he tells us, "good reasons, of a perfectly mundane sort, why we should have the institution of morality as we now have it. . . . Morality has an objective rationale in complete independence of religion."[21]

But what is this "objective rationale" that is "independent of religion"? Such objectivity, Nielsen tells us, is founded on ethical beliefs such as "happiness is good" and "all persons should be treated fairly." Such beliefs, we are told, are not only ethical principles that most persons intuitively know to be true, but are principles that, if put into practice, are normally most advantageous for all involved.

Suppose, however, that it is pragmatically advantageous for an individual to treat others unfairly—for example, to cheat on her taxes—and that she therefore does so. Or suppose that an individual claims to have radically different ethical intuitions—for example, claims that lying and stealing are right. On what basis can such persons be judged ethically wrong? Nielsen is aware of such difficulties. He admits that he cannot prove that happiness is good, arguing that he "can only appeal to our sense of psychological realism to persuade us to admit intellectually what in practice we acknowledge." And he admits that he cannot prove that fairness is always the most advantageous principle to employ, but argues that "to be moral involves respecting [human] rights."[22] Or, as he phrases this point in another context, unless such a principle is affirmed, there can be "[no] understanding of the concept of morality, [no] understanding of what it is to take the moral point of view."[23]

Such reasoning seems in one sense to beg the question. Fundamental to Nielsen's case is that we accept his "concept of morality" and "sense of psychological realism," but it is the acceptability of these very ethical intuitions that needs to be established.

In another sense, though, Nielsen's comments point the way to some very helpful distinctions. Nielsen is clearly not defining "objectivity morality" as it is usually defined by believers. For most believers, absolute (objective) ethical principles are nonexperientially grounded (*a priori*) statements that are true for all persons at all times in all places. For Nielsen, "absolute" ethical principles are experientially grounded (*a posteriori*) statements that ought, on the basis of rational considerations, to be affirmed *at present* by everyone. Thus, while most believers see "Thou shalt not kill" as a timeless truth affirmed by but not founded on human reasoning, Nielsen sees this ethical principle as a truth that all individuals ought to affirm, at present, on the basis of rational thought.

But if this is all that nonreligious individuals such as Nielsen have in mind when they claim to possess an objective ethic, then is not their ethical perspective quite relative in the sense of being conditioned by the obvious variations in human thought and the amount of relevant data being considered? In response, Nielsen is willing to admit that if ethical principles are solely the product of human thought, then they are to a certain degree relative in this sense. However, to maintain that ethical truth is relative can also be taken to mean that there is no objective basis for preferring one ethical perspective to another. It can be taken to mean, for example, that there is no stronger *objective* basis for favoring capital punishment than for opposing it. Rather, what is *right* in every case is solely a function of what each individual personally thinks is right. And Nielsen obviously does want to deny that his ethic is relative in this sense. He believes, as we have seen, that given the human desire for happiness, and given that there are good pragmatic reasons for believing that certain forms of behavior will generally help us reach this goal, nonbelievers do have an objective basis in some contexts for saying most people should behave in certain ways most of the time.

Some have argued, though, that to base ethical beliefs on common elements in human thought or experience is to confuse factual and ethical issues — to deduce unjustifiably that people *ought* to affirm certain ethical norms solely from the observable fact that such norms *are* affirmed. Nielsen is quick to respond to this charge. We cannot, he tells us, simply "deduce that people ought to do something from discovering that they do it or seek it any more than we can conclude from the proposition that a being exists whom people call God that we ought to do whatever that being commands." However, he adds, "we do justify moral claims by an appeal to factual claims, and there is a close connection between what human beings desire on reflection and what they deem to be good."[24]

Nielsen appears to be correct. The majority of philosophers agree that neither the religious nor the nonreligious individual can directly deduce an *ought* from an *is*. But it does seem that religious as well as nonreligious individuals justify their ethical claims at least in part by appealing to factual contentions — for example, by appealing to certain claims about the nature of God, natural human desires, or shared ethical intuitions.[25]

It appears, then, that there is a meaningful sense in which affirming a nonreligious basis for ethics does not necessarily lead to radical ethical relativism. It may be that nonreligiously based ethical norms must be somewhat relative to the context to which they apply, or must at least be more relative than religiously based norms. But to establish the total relativity of nonreligiously based ethics — to establish that ethical truth for the nonreligious person is nothing more than personal preference — it must be demonstrated that there exists no rational basis for humanity (all rational individuals) in general to affirm any given ethical norm, and it does not appear that this has yet been done.

But, even granting this fact, if ethical truth is solely a human invention — if there exists no ultimate standard of value apart from our human perspective — can life have any real meaning? Or, to state the question differently, is it at least true, as some believers have claimed, that belief in God is necessary if life is to have any significant purpose?

To answer this question, we must more clearly understand what believers have in mind when they claim that ethical relativism leads to "meaningless-ness." Most argue at the very least that the nonbeliever can posit no ultimate purpose for the universe as a whole. Hans Küng (1928–   ), for example, argues that "by denying God, man decides against an ultimate reason, support, and ultimate end of reality."[26] This reading, however, has limited significance. Al-though it may be true that some nonbelievers need to be reminded of the fact that a godless universe is ultimately nonpurposeful, thoughtful nonbelievers readily acknowledge this fact.

Some believers, however, have wanted to go further. They have wanted to argue that once the nonbeliever realizes that there exists no ultimate purpose for the universe as a whole, she will no longer experience any personal mean-ing. Rather, in the words of Küng, she will be exposed "quite personally to the danger of an ultimate abandonment, menace and decay, resulting in doubt, fear, even despair."[27]

Not surprisingly, however, most nonbelievers do not find this line of reason-ing compelling. First, while they grant that some nonbelievers may experience a loss of personal meaning when they come to recognize that there exists no ultimate cosmic meaning in a godless universe, they deny that this is the case for most people.

More important, however, nonbelievers argue that this type of "head-counting" approach to the question of personal meaning begs the question by its very nature. They do not deny that many believers have found in their own experience a significant tie between cosmic and personal meaning. They do not deny, for example, that many believers truly hold, with St. Augustine (354–430), that the human "heart" is restless until it finds its rest in God. In fact, many do not even deny that the believer is justified in maintaining that some such connection necessarily exists.

But the key philosophical issue, they point out, is not what the believer can rationally affirm; the issue is what the nonbeliever can rationally affirm. And here, they argue, the burden of proof clearly lies with the believer. What the believer must establish is not that she is justified in claiming that she would possess no personal meaning if there were no God or even that some nonbe-lievers also feel this way. What the believer must establish is that nonbelievers who deny cosmic meaning but still claim to possess personal meaning are not justified in maintaining this position. And this, most nonbelievers contend, the believer has not done. In fact, given that there appears to be no widespread scientific (psychological or physiological) or logical support for the claim that one cannot justifiably claim to have personal meaning if one denies cosmic meaning, most nonbelievers do not see how the believer could even attempt to establish such a connection in a nonquestion-begging manner.

Again, it appears that the nonbeliever is right, at least in the way he has identified the key issues. A nonreligious world-view may require some rework-ing of the traditional concept of personal meaning. Some nonbelievers may in fact no longer experience personal meaning. But it does not follow necessarily from this that nonbelievers *cannot* justifiably affirm an enduring sense of personal meaning. A separate argument is needed for this end, an argument that does not already assume the truth of what is to be proved.

Current Issues

Recently, philosophers have been giving considerable attention to what is called virtue ethics, and this has carried over into the religious realm.[28] To understand any aspect of this discussion, we must first bring to the forefront the well-known distinction between *what* a person does and *why* she does it. Consider, for example, the following situations.

Case A: One day while walking to the Post Office, Grandmother Smith trips on a crack in the sidewalk and falls. Tim is cycling past on his way to a ball game and sees what occurs. Because he is late, he momentarily considers riding on. But this thought is quickly replaced by his concern for Grandmother Smith's welfare. Thus, he stops, helps her up, and makes sure she is not hurt before continuing on his way.

Case B: One day while walking to the Post Office, Grandmother Smith trips over a crack in the sidewalk and falls. Bill, who is cycling by on his way to a ball game for which he is late, observes the event. But he has no intention of stopping. He is late for his game, but even more importantly, he dislikes Grandmother Smith. Thus, he is actually pleased that she has fallen. However, just as he is ready to leave the scene, he notices at a distance a person who looks very much like the pastor of his church, and he fears that this person has seen Grandmother fall and will see him riding away without helping. Thus, Bill stops, helps her up and makes sure she is not hurt before riding on.

The observable behavior in each case is identical. Grandmother Smith has fallen, and a young man has stopped to help. Hence, any ethical theory stating that ethical judgment should be based solely on observable behavior would have to consider the behavior of Tim and Bill as ethically equivalent. But for many of us in the Western ethical tradition, this would not be acceptable. We are happy with the "ethical output" in each case — we are glad Grandmother Smith has been helped. But our ethical assessment of Bill and Tim would not solely, or even primarily, be based on their observable behavior. It would be based primarily, or at least significantly, on our assessment of their "ethical input" — their motivation or intentions. And in this regard Bill and Tim do differ significantly. Tim wanted to help; Bill did not.

It is possible, however, to discuss this difference in ethical input in terms of either *duty* or *virtue*. In terms of duty, we might say that Tim's behavior is praiseworthy because he desired to act in accordance with the recognized ethical duty to help those in need, while Bill deserves no commendation because his actions were not motivated by this or any other relevant ethical duty. In terms of virtue, we might say that Tim alone deserves praise because his desire to help was an expression of a virtuous character trait — for example, benevolence.

Now of course, these two ways of describing ethical input are not mutually exclusive. In fact, it seems to many that both are necessary to a full understanding of ethical behavior. However, there has recently been a great deal of interest in whether we should view duties or virtues as the more basic or primary ethical concept. Those wanting to emphasize duty argue that it is because we have a duty to do something that our intention to do it is virtuous. That is, to state this point more formally, they argue that it is because we have a basic disposition to want to act in accordance with recognized duties that we can be said to have a praiseworthy character. In terms of our current illustration, this would be to say that Tim's desire to help Grandmother Smith is virtuous because he acted in accordance with the recognized duty to help those in need or because his behavior was an expression of his character, which is virtuous because of its tendency to act in accordance with recognized ethical principles.

Those wanting to emphasize virtue argue instead that we have the ethical duty to act, or refrain from acting, in certain ways because such duties are expressions of virtuous character traits. In terms of our illustration, this would be to say that Tim can be praised for fulfilling his ethical duty to attempt to help Grandmother Smith because this duty is the expression of his benevolent character. Still other philosophers see neither virtue nor duty as primary, but rather as two partially overlapping and mutually interdependent perspectives on ethics.

The relevance of this question for religious ethics should be obvious. The discussion of traditional ethical issues in this chapter has generally been couched in terms of ethical principles, which can quite plausibly be understood to be statements describing ethical duties. That is, it might appear from the tone of this chapter that to be ethical from a religious perspective is to act in accordance with the revealed rules (duties) that have their grounding in God. But the recent interest in virtue ethics has led some to conceive of religious ethics differently. They no longer conceive of ethical activity primarily in the terms of doing what God wants, or even wanting to do what God wants, but rather in terms of being the type of person God wants us to be.[29]

To help make this distinction clearer, let us consider the common religious belief that we should love one another. In the traditional framework of a duty ethic, the believer's primary task is to apply this principle to each aspect of daily life. Such a process, of course, is contextual. For instance, how one responds in love to a three-year-old throwing a tantrum or to an unhelpful store clerk quite properly differs from situation to situation. But in each case the believer's task is to determine consciously what would be the most loving response.

Under a virtue ethic, however, the situation is fundamentally different. The essence of ethical activity is not seen as conscious adherence to a set of duties. Specifically, the key to ethical living is not thought to be something that can be abstracted from the religious tradition and rationally applied to culture. The essence of ethical living is to *be* religious — for example, to be Christian or to be Jewish. We must become part of a tradition — a faith community — in which the character of this community — its intentions, desires, and values — become our own. We will then quite naturally find ourselves living as we should. Or stated differently, once we *become* religious, we will act in a proper religious manner. The development of a religious character is prior to the realization of one's religious duty.

This perspective also leads, not surprisingly, to a deemphasis on the traditional philosophical responses to ethical issues. For example, as we have seen, many believers have traditionally thought it important to respond to the problem of evil: Why does there exist so much seemingly unnecessary pain and suffering in a world allegedly created by an omnipotent, omniscient, perfectly good being? But in the words of one influential Christian "virtue ethicist," for a Christian to even attempt to answer this question "is a mistake." Evil is not a "metaphysical problem needing a solution" but rather a "practical challenge needing a response." And the appropriate response is a "community of care which [makes] it possible to absorb the destructive terror of evil that constantly threatens to destroy all human relations."[30]

Now, of course, there are many believers who think both "duty" and "virtue" approaches to religious ethics are important. But the emphasis on virtue ethics appears to be something that will have an impact on the nature of religious ethics for the foreseeable future.

STUDY QUESTIONS

1. What do you think most believers really mean when they say that ethical truth has its origin in God? Given this interpretation, are believers still open to the charge that God's commands could be arbitrary and capricious?

2. Do you believe that ethical truth originates solely in God? If not, what is its origin?

3. Why does Kai Nielsen believe that the religious person's ethical standard is ultimately based on his own ethical intuitions, not God's commands? How do believers respond?

4. Why does ethical pluralism — the wide variety of ethical perspectives — pose a challenge for religious ethics? Which of the responses discussed in this chapter do you find most convincing?

5. Is there any truth to the claim that, apart from belief in God, life can have no ultimate meaning?

6. Why do some claim that ethics must be totally relative if there is no God? Do you agree with Kai Nielsen's counter?

7. Those believers who consider the Torah or Bible to be a trustworthy source of information about God must grapple with the seemingly questionable behavior sometimes attributed to God in these texts. Which of the responses discussed did you find most convincing?

8. What is "virtue ethics"? Do you think either "virtue" or "duty" is the more significant ethical concept? Why?

9. Do you think that religious individuals behave more ethically than nonreligious individuals? If not, is the opposite true?

10. In what ways might the fact that a person is religious affect the way she responds to an ethical crisis? For instance, how might it affect the way she responds to the AIDS crisis?

NOTES

1. See, for example, A. C. Ewing, "The Autonomy of Ethics," in Janine Marie Idziak ed., *Divine Command Morality* (Lewiston, NY: Edwin Mellen Press, 1979), pp. 228–30.
2. William of Ockham, *On the Four Books of the Sentences*, book II, quest. 19, in Idziak, ed., pp. 55–59.
3. See, for example, Patrick Nowell-Smith, "Religion and Morality," *The Encyclopedia of Philosophy*, vol. 7 (New York: Macmillan, 1967), p. 156; A. C. Ewing, *Prospect for Metaphysics* (London: George Allen and Unwin, 1951), p. 39.
4. See, for example, Robert Adams, "A Modified Divine Command Theory of Ethical Wrongness," in Louis Pojman ed., *Philosophy of Religion* (Belmont, CA: Wadsworth Publishing Company, 1987), p. 527.
5. Adams, pp. 533–34.
6. Bruce Reichenbach, "The Divine Command Theory and Objective Good," in R. Porreco, ed., *Georgetown Symposium on Ethics* (New York: University Press of America), pp. 219–31. It should be noted that Adams is not necessarily in agreement with all aspects of this line of reasoning.
7. Adams, pp. 525–537.
8. Alasdair MacIntyre, "Which God Ought We Obey and Why?" *Faith and Philosophy* 3 (1986): 359.
9. Kai Nielsen, *Ethics Without God* (London: Pemberton, 1973), chap. 3.
10. E. J. Carnell, *Christian Commitment* (New York: Macmillan, 1957), p. 134.
11. See, for example, Gordon Clark, *Religion, Reason and Revelation* (Philadelphia: Presbyterian and Reformed Publishing Company, 1961), pp. 221–41.
12. Adams, pp. 525–37.
13. See, for example, R. E. O. White, *Christian Ethics* (Atlanta: John Knox Press, 1981), pp. 124–35; Garth L. Hallet, *Christian Moral Reasoning* (Notre Dame, IN: University of Notre Dame Press, 1983), pp. 83–84, 114–15; E. Albert, T. Denise, S. Peterfreund, *Great Traditions in Ethics*, 5th ed. (Belmont, CA: Wadsworth, 1984), pp. 106–25.
14. Gottfried Leibniz, *New Essays on the Human Understanding* (1765), book 1, chap. 1, sec. 5.

15. See, for example, Richard Purtill, *Reason to Believe* (Grand Rapids, MI: Eerdmans, 1974), pp. 91–98.
16. See Norman Geisler, *The Christian Ethic of Love* (Grand Rapids, MI: Zondervan, 1973), pp. 76–127.
17. See Mark Talbot, "On Christian Philosophy," *Reformed Journal* 34 (September, 1984): pp. 19–20.
18. John Hick, "The Philosophy of World Religions," *Scottish Journal of Theology* 37 (1984): 231–36.
19. Adams, pp. 535–37.
20. Jean-Paul Sartre, "The Humanism of Existentialism," in Burton Porter, ed., *Philosophy: A Literary and Conceptual Approach* (New York: Harcourt Brace Jovanovich, 1974), pp. 70–71.
21. Nielsen, pp. 48, 64.
22. Nielsen, pp. 86, 62.
23. Kai Nielsen, "On Religion and the Grounds of Moral Belief," *Religious Humanism* 11 (Winter, 1977): 33–34.
24. Nielsen, *Ethics*, p. 56.
25. Reichenbach, p. 230.
26. Hans Küng, *On Being a Christian* (Garden City, NY: Doubleday and Company, 1976), p. 75.
27. Küng.
28. See, for example, Alasdair MacIntyre, *After Virtue* (Notre Dame, IN: Notre Dame University Press, 1981); Stanley Hauerwas, *The Peaceable Kingdom* (Notre Dame, IN: University of Notre Dame Press, 1983).
29. Stanley Hauerwas, *The Peaceable Kingdom* and *A Community of Character* (Notre Dame, IN: University of Notre Dame Press, 1981).
30. Stanley Hauerwas, "God, Medicine and the Problems of Evil," *Reformed Journal* (April 1988): 19.

SUGGESTED READING

Donagan, Allan. *The Theory of Morality*. Chicago: University of Chicago Press, 1977.

Frankena, William. *Ethics*, 2nd ed. Englewood Cliffs, NJ: Prentice-Hall, 1973.

Gill, Robin. *A Textbook of Christian Ethics*. Edinburgh: TPT Clark, 1985.

McClendon, James W., Jr. *Ethics: Systematic Theology*, vol. I. Nashville, TN: Abingdon, 1986.

Outka, Gene, and John P. Reeder, Jr., eds. *Religion and Morality*. Garden City, NY: Anchor Books, 1973.

Quinn, Philip. *Divine Commands and Moral Requirements*. Oxford: Oxford University Press, 1978.

Veatch, Henry. *For an Ontology of Morals*. Evanston, IL: Northwestern University Press, 1971.

Yandell, Keith, ed. *God, Man and Religion: Readings in Philosophy of Religion*. New York: McGraw-Hill, 1973.

14

Philosophy and Theological Doctrine: Can Philosophy Illumine Religious Belief?

> I do not seek in order that I may believe, but I believe in order that I may understand.
>
> St. Anselm of Canterbury, 1033–1109

As we have seen, philosophers have always been interested in discussing basic religious concepts: God's existence and attributes, religious experience, evil, miracles. And there is an increasing interest in analyzing the relationship between religion and other disciplines: science, ethics, linguistics, and psychology. Historically, philosophers also thought it important to help clarify and defend specific religious doctrines — for example, the Trinity or Incarnation. Such use of philosophy in the service of theology has become less common in modern times, but in the last few years, many influential philosophers of religion have once again turned their attention to specific theological doctrines. Typically, these philosophers are not trying to prove or establish these doctrines philosophically. Rather, in the spirit of Anselm, they assume a particular doctrine as a given topic of religious concern and set about to analyze its meaning and assess whether it can be affirmed by a rational person.

In this chapter, five representative samples of this type of philosophical activity will be presented. Specifically, we will be considering Thomas Morris's examination of the Incarnation of God in Jesus Christ, Philip Quinn's reevaluation of the classical understanding of Christ's atonement for sin, William Alston's exploration of the meaning and implications of the "indwelling" by the Holy Spirit, Eleonore Stump's attempt to respond to the claim that petitionary prayer is actually a pointless activity, and George Mavrodes's analysis of various "models" of divine revelation.

Each of these philosophers happens to be a Christian and discusses the doctrine in question from within a Christian context. However, the discussions of prayer and divine revelation are also quite relevant to other religious traditions. It is also important to clarify exactly what it means to say that the views of these philosophers will be presented and considered. Our primary goal is not to engage in a critical dialogue. For instance, our primary goal is not to determine the extent to which we believe their work illuminates what we see as the crucial philosophical questions related to the doctrines in question. Our primary goal is not even to offer a *comprehensive* critique of what each has produced. We do briefly assess the work of each, and at the end of the chapter we consider some recent comments about the value and appropriateness of this sort of philosophical activity. But our *primary* goal is simply to *expose* the reader to a rather new, exciting emphasis in contemporary analytic philosophy of religion.

The Incarnation

> I believe in God the Father Almighty, Maker of heaven and earth; and in Jesus Christ his only Son our Lord.
>
> Apostles' Creed

Historically, one of the most fundamental tenets of the Christian faith has been the Incarnation: the belief that God became human in the person of Jesus Christ. Specifically, it has been held that Jesus Christ was both *fully human* and *fully divine*. However, some believers have even begun to question not only whether the Incarnation actually occurred but even whether it is possible. Could one person be fully human and fully divine at the same time? Is it still possible for a rational, well-informed, intelligent person to accept this doctrine?

Recently, Thomas Morris (1952–   ) has attempted to respond to this question.[1] His goal, he makes it quite clear, is not to prove that Jesus Christ was in fact fully human and fully divine, or even that all Christians ought to say so. His main objective, rather, is to demonstrate that none of the criticisms of this belief has to date been successful and, thus, that belief in the traditional doctrine of the Incarnation remains rational.

As Morris points out, the most common current criticism of the Incarnation is that it is an incoherent concept. To say that a property of a thing or person is essential is to say that the thing or person in question could not be what it is without this property. For example, having three sides is an essential property of any triangle; nothing without this characteristic can be rightly called a triangle. And being unmarried is essential to being a bachelor. Some married men might sometimes claim to be bachelors, but none can actually be a bachelor.

But the essential properties of being human, some critics are now arguing, are incompatible with the essential properties of being divine. Humans are, for instance, essentially limited in power, restricted in knowledge, fleshly, and liable to sin, while God is essentially all-powerful, all-knowing, without a fleshly body, and unable to sin. Thus, one person could never be fully human and fully divine at the same time. This is no more possible than it is for a figure to be both fully a square and fully a circle at the same time.

The key to countering this criticism, Morris tells us, is to understand the distinction between a thing being *fully* what it is and *merely* what it is. For example, diamonds and turtles are both *fully* physical objects. That is, both possess all the essential properties of being a physical object: mass, spatiotemporal location and so on. However, a turtle is not merely a physical object in the sense of being only a physical object. It has the properties of being animate and organic as well. In like fashion, we are told, an individual can be *fully* human without being *merely* human. An individual is fully human if she has all the properties essential to being human—for example, the capacity to exercise power, and the ability to formulate true beliefs and freedom of choice. Thus, Jesus, as well as we, can be considered *fully* human. And we are *merely* human in that we "possess all these properties *plus* some additional limitation properties as well, properties such as being less than omnipotent, less than omniscient, and so on." Jesus, however, was not *merely* human. He possessed all the properties essential to being human "but had higher properties as well, properties constitutive of deity." He was, for instance, all-powerful, all-knowing, and incapable of sin. Thus, Jesus was also *fully* God.[2]

But if Jesus was fully divine, does not this commit us to saying that he was all-knowing, all-powerful, and omnipresent as he lay crying in his crib? Are we not committed to saying that "the bouncing baby boy of Mary and Joseph [directed] the workings of the cosmos from his crib?" And does this not "sound just too bizarre for even a moment's consideration?"

The answer, Morris maintains, lies in reaffirming a distinction that Christians have held since the earliest times: that Jesus Christ, the God-Man, possessed "something like two distinct ranges of consciousness." The distinctively divine consciousness was all-knowing; it was aware of all that exists in the eternal mind of God. The distinctively earthly consciousness, on the other hand, "grew and developed as the boy Jesus grew and developed." This "range of consciousness, and self-consciousness, was thoroughly human, Jewish and first-century Palestinian in scope."

Moreover, Morris adds, the divine consciousness contained, but was not contained by, the earthly range of consciousness. That is, Jesus Christ's divine mind had full access to his earthly experiences. The divine mind knew, for example, exactly what would occur in the future. But the earthly consciousness did not have access to the divine mind—for example, did not know what would occur in the future. Thus, Jesus really was able to suffer temptation, doubt, and fear and experience real intellectual and spiritual growth.

In short, Morris maintains that although Jesus Christ was not two persons in one body, he was "one person with two natures, and two ranges of consciousness" and "in this doctrine," there is "no apparent incoherence whatsoever."[3]

There exists however, one other "major sort of objection" to which Morris believes he must respond. Both critics and "many prominent professors of Christian theology" have recently been emphasizing the fact that the doctrine of the Incarnation was originally developed within a prescientific perspective quite different from the one "modern scientifically minded people have today." Thus they have concluded that ancient religious claims, which may well have made sense in their original context, can rightly be said to "have lost much, if not all, of their plausibility in the modern age."

In response, Morris first chides Christians for being so quick to "relinquish or 'reinterpret' important doctrines on no better grounds than that those beliefs can appear to some secular critics to be somehow out of step with the march of science." However, he is willing to grant that occasionally an interesting challenge of this sort does arise. He considers, for instance, the "geocentric challenge." It seems clear that the doctrine of the Incarnation was formulated during a time when "it was believed by great numbers of people, including the best educated, that we human beings live in a relatively circumscribed universe, the entirety of which has been created for the benefit of human life . . . [and] around which all else literally as well as figuratively revolves." And in such a setting, of course, it would seem reasonable to assume that God would be so interested in earthly affairs that he would even appear among us. But, of course, we now know that we and our world are only a small, insignificant peripheral cog in a vast, complicated machine. Thus, the assumption that God would believe it important to become human and dwell among us loses much of its plausibility.

Morris, though, sees no reason to believe that God's attention and care cannot extend fully to every part of the universe, and thus views sheer size as an irrelevant consideration. Moreover, "it is simply wrong to think there to be a necessary link between spatial centrality and value." Accordingly, he concludes, "it is a bit surprising to find that a challenge to Christian belief which seems to have such widespread emotional appeal for critics has so little substance when examined closely."[4]

But if it is, then, possible for a rational person to believe in the Incarnation, *how* is it possible? On what grounds can a person be rational in maintaining that Jesus was literally God in human form? There is, Morris holds, no deductive or single inductive argument that can establish this fact. But, he asks, could there not be an innate human capacity that, when functioning properly, allows us to recognize God in various contexts? If so, then perhaps traditional Christians have just *seen* Jesus to be God Incarnate. That is, perhaps when Christians see the portrait of Jesus in the Gospels or experience what they take to be Jesus's presence in prayer or his transforming power in their lives, they simply find themselves believing that they are having experiences of God Incarnate. And from Morris's perspective, there is no reason to believe this is not actually the case. In fact, he feels it is perfectly reasonable to think this is so.

Of course, he acknowledges that, for belief in the Incarnation to remain reasonable, one must be able to formulate sufficient responses to challenges. But he believes he has shown that the significant challenges to date fail. Thus, he concludes that there is no obstacle to accepting the rationality of the widespread Christian assumption that Jesus is God Incarnate.[5]

Morris's comments certainly are unique and stimulating. Of course, for those who believe that limited knowledge or power is an *essential* property of any *fully* human person, Morris's arguments will carry little weight.[6] And because it is difficult to see how one would even begin to try to argue that there is a single *correct* conception of humanity, it is difficult to see how those who affirm a conception of full humanity different from Morris's could be proven wrong. However, Morris never claims to be arguing that all persons, even all Christians, must themselves acknowledge that belief in the Incarnation is rational for them personally. He is arguing, rather, that it cannot be said that no rational person can affirm this doctrine, and thus he need establish only that his understanding of what it means for someone to be fully human is not, itself, incoherent. Not all are convinced he has done so. However, almost everyone grants that Morris's contribution to the philosophical discussion of the Incarnation is significant.

The Atonement

> Having become the sin of all men, he washed away the sin of the human race.
>
> St. Ambrose, 339–397

Christians have traditionally held that we are born separated from God because of the sin of the first humans — Adam and Eve — and can be reconciled to God because of the suffering and death of Jesus Christ. But exactly what role did Christ's death play in reconciling humans to God? Why was it necessary? And exactly what was it intended to accomplish? These are the types of questions that Philip Quinn (1940–   ) has considered in some recent discussions. Specifically, he has been interested in analyzing Thomas Aquinas's position on these issues.[7]

Aquinas (c. 1224–1274) believed that the sin with which we are born has three effects on us. First, it stains our souls. We have a natural desire to turn away from God and attempt to satisfy ourselves in ways that are contrary to both reason and divine law. In short, we are born not wanting to think and act as we should. Second, we are born in bondage to the devil. That is, not only do we have our own natural tendency to think and act improperly, but the devil is also able to influence us strongly. And finally, our sin (both what we are born with and what we ourselves produce) deserves punishment because it is a transgression against the divine order of justice. In fact, since to be in sin is to have turned away from God, and turning away from God is the ultimate insult to God's holiness, eternal punishment is the only appropriate "sentence." Or, stated even more simply, eternal punishment is the debt we owe God because of our sin.

God could, Aquinas believed, justly have freed humans from the debt of sin without any restitution being required. Since God alone is the one who has been wronged by our sins, God could have pardoned us without exacting a penalty. In other words, God could simply have cancelled the debt much as a grocer might simply cancel a debt rightly owed for food purchased on credit by a customer. However, since we do in fact owe a debt to God because of our sin,

God is not unjust in requiring that the debt be paid. It must be admitted that this shows that God is *severe*, but it is within God's moral rights to require restitution, just as it is within a grocer's rights to demand payment from a customer.

The problem, as Aquinas viewed it, is that none of us can pay the debt for our own sin. We cannot collectively pay the debt for original (inherited) sin because no set of human acts can make up for the harm done to the whole of the human race by Adam's sin. Furthermore, we cannot individually pay the price for our own sins. We are finite, and, since God is infinite, any offense against God is infinite in magnitude. Thus, since God demanded that the debt for sin be paid and we as humans could not pay it, God's only option was to pay it himself, which was done through Christ's suffering and death. In fact, not only was Christ's death sufficient to pay the debt for all humanity, it was superabundant. That is, the dignity of Christ as an infinite being, the quality and amount of his love and the magnitude of the suffering he endured made his death a much *more* satisfactory payment than God's justice required.

Such an account of the atonement, Quinn is quick to point out, raises some obvious questions. For example, if Christ's suffering and death are not only sufficient but superabundant restitution for the sins of the whole human race, why does anyone need to suffer for his own sins? Why will anyone be in hell? Why do individuals suffer in this life?

Aquinas's answer, with which Quinn has no quarrel, is that although Christ's death was a sufficient payment, it must be appropriated by us. That is, to use a modern analogy, Christ's death functions much as does the power supply in a home. The power supply is normally more than enough to light all the lamps in a house. But the lamps will in fact be lit only if they are connected to the power source. In like manner, Christ's death was more than enough to pay our debt to God, but it will in fact function in this manner only if we make use of it, and the way humans come to appropriate or claim Christ's payment is through the sacraments — baptism, penance, and so on.[8]

But there are other questions to which Quinn believes Aquinas does not have adequate answers. First, Quinn is dissatisfied with the role the devil plays in Aquinas's account. According to Aquinas, remember, we are in bondage to the devil. To be more specific, Aquinas believed that God justly allows the devil to punish us for our sins, yet he also believed that the devil unjustly holds us in bondage because the debt for sin is owed to God, not Satan. But it is not clear to Quinn that Aquinas can have it both ways. Some have suggested that Satan serves as a sort of deputized punisher for God. But then it cannot be said that Satan is inflicting the punishment unjustly. On the other hand, if Satan's punishment is actually unjustly inflicted, then it appears that God cannot justly allow it. The most reasonable way of avoiding this type of dilemma, Quinn concludes, is to give up the belief that Christ's atonement in some sense ransomed sinners from Satan and to think of the atonement solely in terms of the payment of a debt to God.[9]

Quinn is also concerned about the seemingly harsh consequences of Aquinas's view. For instance, since only those who have appropriated Christ's death through baptism can have the debt for original sin paid, and the punishment for unpaid original sin is exclusion from God's presence, it follows for Aquinas that all babies who die unbaptized and all those who have never heard about God are eternally excluded from heaven. Quinn's suggestion is that we consider modifying the conditions under which Christ's atonement can be appropriated. Specifically, he is sympathetic to the view that Christ's payment automatically applies to those who, through no fault of their own, lack either the ability or the opportunity to demonstrate faith in Christ.[10]

Quinn is most troubled, though, by Aquinas's belief that *Christ's* death can be viewed as an acceptable payment for *our* debt. In Aquinas's day, Quinn points out, monetary compensation was common for crimes, sometimes even for crimes as serious as murder. And, of course, given such a model of compensation, the idea of someone paying the debt for someone else's crime makes good sense. But we no longer view things this way, we are reminded. We might, for example, allow that a mother can pay her son's fine. But if her son has been sentenced to spend time in jail, she cannot pay his debt for him. Even if she volunteered to spend the required time in jail for him, *his* debt would not have been paid. Of course, it is possible that he will not be asked to serve his sentence because of ill-health or a pardon. But even then his debt has not been paid. We are simply allowing the debt to remain unpaid. In other words, as Quinn sees it, our moral intuitions clearly tell us that the idea of one person actually absolving another person of his moral duty to pay for his crimes by volunteering to take his place no longer makes much sense.

Quinn is quick to acknowledge at this point that our moral intuitions are fallible and, thus, could be mistaken. "But if they remain stable under reflection," we are told, "we should trust them." And he believes that under reflection we will continue to be convinced that a just punishment for a serious crime cannot be totally transferred to an innocent person. Thus, he doubts that it is rational to accept the idea of Christ totally paying our justly incurred debt for us.[11]

But how then should we conceive of the atonement? Quinn offers us a "fable" to point the way to what he sees as a plausible modification of Aquinas's position.

> Suppose a great magnate makes his two sons stewards of the two finest farms on his estate. The elder son irresponsibly neglects and thus ruins his farm, but the younger son conscientiously makes his own farm flourish. As a result of his negligence, the elder son has come to deserve punishment at the hands of his father; it would be severe but just for the father to disinherit him if he does not restore the ruined farm to prosperity. Unfortunately, the elder son is not a good enough farmer to accomplish this task, though he could have prevented the ruin of the farm if he had tried.
>
> Then the younger son wonderfully intervenes. Moved by love for his brother as well as by devotion to their father and the welfare of his estate, the younger son undertakes to restore the farm his brother had ruined. This new undertaking requires tremendous sacrifice from him: he now has to maintain one farm and rehabilitate another. But the sacrifices so work upon the father's

heart that he is persuaded to be merciful rather than severe toward his elder son. He forgives his elder son for the damage he has done to the estate and does not disinherit him even though the elder has not himself repaired the damage.[12]

In this case, Quinn argues, there is still a sense in which it can be said that the younger son has paid his brother's debt. But it seems more accurate to say that the father was moved by his younger son's sacrifice to forgive the debt. And this, Quinn believes, is a plausible way to conceive of Christ's atonement. We do owe God a debt that God can justly demand us to pay but that we cannot pay alone. However, Christ's voluntary suffering and death for us has so moved God that God has decided not to be so severe with us. In other words, Christ's suffering and death does not pay our debt in whole; rather, it generates divine mercy. It leads God to forgive that part of the debt we cannot pay. Hence, Christ's suffering and death remain a necessary condition for reconciliation with God, as orthodoxy demands, but we need no longer view it as payment in full for our debt, which reason will not allow.[13]

Quinn is to be commended for the bold and innovative manner in which he approaches this complex doctrine. Some believers, of course, will be troubled by the "authority" Quinn gives to moral intuitions and rational argumentation. They will see in his comments a devaluation of the role of Scripture and tradition in the search for religious truth. Specifically, they will be troubled by his use of reason in interpreting Revelation. And other questions arise—for instance, if God was persuaded by the voluntary suffering of Jesus Christ on our behalf to be lenient with us, what are we to say about the voluntary suffering we do for one another? Does this, too, move God to leniency? But even those who disagree with his conclusions or methodology will be able to appreciate the new categories of discussion Quinn has unveiled. He has especially highlighted the important philosophical question of what constitutes just recompense.

The Indwelling of the Holy Spirit

> I believe in the Holy Ghost, the Lord, and Giver of Life, who proceedeth from the Father and Son.
>
> Niceno-Chalcedonian Creed

The process by which we appropriate Christ's payment for our sins and are then reconciled to God is called *salvation*. Christians, however, have not thought that things stop there. God does not want only to establish lines of communication with us: He desires us to become a different type of individual as the result of this relationship. We are, in biblical terms, to become "new creatures." We are to have our personality and character transformed into the type of individual God originally designed us to be. We are to become more loving, joyous, peaceful, tolerant. This process is called *sanctification*. And traditionally, it has been held that this requires the help of the third person of the Trinity: the Holy Spirit.

But how are we to conceive of this involvement? What role does the Spirit play in bringing about changes in a person? And just how is this accomplished? These are questions about which William Alston (1921–   ) has recently been thinking.[14] He dismisses as unorthodox the contention that the Spirit plays *no* active role in our transformation. Thus, the initial question for consideration becomes: "To what extent is the transformation wholly God's work and to what extent is a human response, human effort, human voluntary choice, assent, or cooperation involved?"[15]

Alston considers three perspectives. The first, labeled the *fiat model*, holds that all transformations within us are directly brought about by the Spirit. Just as we cannot save ourselves, we cannot renew ourselves. By a work of grace the Spirit simply makes us into the new creatures we are to be.

Alston does not deny that God could do things this way. In fact, he acknowledges that perhaps this is the way things are, "at least sometimes." Changes in Christians do sometimes seem to those transformed to be "a bolt from the blue." However, he believes there are good reasons for doubting that this is the way God normally works. For one thing, Christians have commonly believed that God created us to enter into a distinctively interpersonal relationship and "on the fiat model the inner working of the Holy Spirit is not distinctively interpersonal in character." Moreover, Alston asks, if God always turns us into saints directly by an act of divine will, why does such transformation often take so long or seem so incomplete? Of course, God could have reasons that we simply do not understand, he grants, but a more plausible explanation—and one that is compatible with the belief that we have a personal relationship with God—is that God does not always transform us by fiat, but, rather, that "human responses play a significant role in the process."[16]

This leads into a discussion of a second transformational perspective: the *interpersonal* model. From this perspective God goes about transforming us in much the same way we attempt to transform each other. Just as parents discipline, encourage, and care for their children, God calls us to repentance, chastises us for our failure, encourages us, makes new resources available to us, and energizes us with his love. But just as a loving parent does not *make* a child respond to such influence in the desired manner, God does not by fiat make us change into the type of person we ought to be. In both cases, what is sought is *voluntary* response. It is left up to the person being offered assistance to determine whether the desired response is forthcoming.

Alston is impressed with the role that human decision-making plays in this model. And he believes it can be shown to be compatible with much of what the Bible says about God's work in our lives. However, he feels that there is a significant inadequacy in both this and the fiat model. This inadequacy, we are told, "is simply that both models represent God as relatively external to the believer." God may *at times* change us by fiat, and it is useful to think of God attempting to call forth voluntary change in the way a parent attempts to transform a child. However, even in this latter case, the parent is normally working from without. The child might feel guilt or joy or peace as the result of parental activity, but the words or actions the parent uses to try to bring about such changes are normally external to the child.

But traditional Christian theology, Alston reminds us, has always held that the Spirit of God actually *dwells within* us. We are, as the Bible says, to be *"filled, permeated, pervaded* with the Spirit." Thus, we need a transformation model that captures this truth. That is, we need a model that explains how we are to conceive of this sort of indwelling and its workings.[17]

And Alston believes that such a model—the sharing model—is available. Biblical texts, he points out, lead us to maintain that when the Holy Spirit dwells within us, we actually come to "partake of, or participate in, the divine nature." We actually *share* in the divine life. This ought not to be taken to mean, Alston quickly adds, that we and God become one. Even though God is within, we still have sinful tendencies and the capacity to act on them. What it means, rather, is that there is "a breaking down of the barriers that normally separate one life from another."

Alston gives us a human analogy to help clarify what he has in mind. Two humans might have as much in common as possible. They might have "mutual liking, respect, regard, affection for each other" and "might share many interests, attitudes and reactions." But these two lives are still effectively insulated from each other by physical and psychological barriers. Each must still remain within her own body, each still has her own attitudes and reacts to life on her own. But let us suppose that these barriers are broken down, "perhaps by a neural wiring hookup." Then the "reactions, feelings, thoughts and attitudes" of one friend would actually be experienced by the other as her own and would influence her accordingly. "There would have occurred a partial merging of . . . hitherto insulated lives." Life-sharing would have occurred, and such life-sharing is how Alston views the relationship between us and the indwelling Spirit of God. We are actually connected with God in such a way that we are in some sense aware of God's love—God's loving attitudes and tendencies.

Moreover, Alston believes it is best to conceive of this type of sharing on both the *cognitive* and *conative* levels. That is, we both *know* to some degree what God believes is best or right, and we also feel *some inclination* to respond in the appropriate fashion. Now, of course, he cautions, we will have to conceive of all this in a manner that still allows for meaningful human freedom. Our connectedness to God cannot be so strong as to make our compliance to God's will inevitable; such compliance must still be voluntary. But such a life-sharing model, he concludes, is at least quite promising. It allows us to talk meaningfully about God's Spirit dwelling within us without violating biblical texts or human experience. God *is* within us. But God is still God and humans are still humans. In other words, as Alston sees it, this model rightly gives the Spirit a prominent *internal* role in any transformation and yet also "leaves the individual with a lot of work to do."[18]

Will Christians find this sharing model helpful or convincing? Of course, those Christians who do not share Alston's rather literal understanding of the biblical texts will want to couch any discussion of this topic in more allegorical or metaphorical terms. And those Reformed Christians who believe that God's control is undermined if humans can refuse to do what God desires will find the life-sharing model somewhat unappealing. But most Christians have wanted to hold not only that God is in some meaningful sense in control of this world but that humans possess meaningful freedom — that they can choose not to act in accordance with God's will. In short, most Christians struggle with the classic theological/philosophical question of exactly how the relationship between God's power and human freedom is to be understood. Alston's discussion demonstrates the relevance of this question for any interpretation of the working of the Spirit and points the way toward a possible resolution. Hence, most Christians should find his work to be a thought-provoking piece of philosophical analysis.

Petitionary Prayer

The effectual fervent prayer of a righteous man availeth much.

Holy Bible (KJV)

Christians (and the proponents of many other religions) frequently petition God in the sense that they ask God to bring about events that they believe might not occur without direct divine assistance. God is often asked, for instance, to soothe a troubled mind, or to help reconcile the broken marriage of friends, or sometimes even to do such things as calm hurricanes or heal diseased bodies.

But why exactly do Christians approach God in this manner? At first glance, it might appear that the answer is obvious. We often petition our human parents because we need help and believe they can offer assistance. Christians believe God is their "heavenly parent," so it seems perfectly reasonable to assume that they would petition God for assistance in times of need.

However, the situation is actually much more complex. Let us suppose that a college student, Fred, is in need of money for his school bills and calls home to ask his parents for help. And let us further suppose that he is able to convince his parents to send the money. In this case we can rightly maintain that Fred's petition was effective in the sense that it brought about something that otherwise probably would not have occurred. But what if Fred knows that the school has informed his parents about his bill, and what if they have repeatedly told him that they will meet his financial needs when they think it is best to do so? It then appears that a call by Fred is not capable of changing anything. It is *already* the case that his parents will do what they think is best. In fact, a call to his parents under these conditions could quite plausibly be read as displaying Fred's lack of confidence in his parent's integrity.

However, is this not exactly the situation in which believers find themselves with respect to God? If God is all-knowing, then God does not need to be informed by prayer of *any* problematic situation. And if God is all good, then God is surely willing to bring about anything that is really needed. Thus, it would appear that petitioning God is pointless at best or displays a lack of faith at worst. If what is requested is something that God—as an all-powerful, perfectly good being—believes should be brought about, then it will be brought about regardless of whether some believer has requested that it be done. On the other hand, if what is being requested is something God believes ought not be brought about, then it seems God will not bring it about regardless of whether a request is made. For example, if God believes that it is best for Mary to be healed, then it seems God will heal her regardless of whether someone asks him to do so, while if God believes Mary should not be healed, then God will not heal her in spite of any request that he intervene. In short, it appears that while petitioning humans can often change things, petitioning God cannot. Petitioning God, it seems, makes sense only if a believer does not have confidence in God—does not believe that God will automatically always do what is best.

Eleonore Stump (1947–) is one of a number of philosophers of religion who have been thinking seriously about this seeming dilemma.[19] She begins by looking at Thomas Aquinas's proposed solution, which she sees as the one "adopted by many theologians and theistic philosophers today." According to Aquinas, we do not pray in order to change God's will but for the sake of acquiring by petitionary prayer what God has disposed to be achieved by prayer. In other words, Aquinas acknowledges that prayer does not really change things in the sense that it motivates God to do things that would not otherwise be done. He holds, rather, that God not only determines *what* will occur but exactly how it will occur, and has chosen to use our petitions as a means to some of these ends—that is, has decided that doing some things in response to human petitions is better than just doing them directly. And for this reason, Aquinas concludes that such prayers are not pointless.

Stump, though, does not find this response adequate. She is perfectly willing to grant that God wants humans to pray and that God answers prayers, "but why should prayers be included in God's plan as causes of certain effects?" she asks.[20]

Accordingly, she sets out to sketch a new model for making sense of the common Christian belief that petitionary prayer not only is useful but also changes things in the sense of influencing God to do things that he would not otherwise have done. Indispensable to Christianity, she tells us, is the belief that God desires a loving *relationship* with humans. The Bible, for instance, often represents the God-human relationship as analogous to that between husband and wife or parent and child. But to conceive of the relationship between God and humans as one of true friendship is difficult, for how can there "be friendship between an omniscient, omnipotent, perfectly good person and a fallible, finite, imperfect person?"

Specifically, Stump sees a relationship between such different persons as facing two serious problems. First, when one person in a relationship is obviously superior in every way, it is easy for the other to become "simply a shadow reflection of the other's personality, a slavish follower who slowly loses all sense of his own tastes and desires and will." Hence, since God is infinitely superior in every way, it is easy to see how we could become completely dominated by God. Second, when there is a great discrepancy in the status and condition between two friends, there is a danger of both becoming spoiled. The superior will be tempted to "use the lesser as his lackey" while the less powerful will be tempted to depend on the other to meet his needs. In the case of a relationship between God and humans, at least the latter is a real possibility. Humans might well be tempted to let a "friend" such as God do everything for them.[21]

However, Stump believes that the institution of petitionary prayer can be understood as a safeguard against these dangers. She asks us to consider the relationship between a caring teacher and a needy pupil, Jim. It might be tempting for the teacher automatically to give Jim whatever help is needed without even being asked, or at least always to respond positively whenever asked. But the wise teacher knows that this is not best. She knows that Jim will quite likely become spoiled — that is, come to depend on, or even believe he is always entitled to, such help. She knows it is best to withhold help at times, even when it is requested.

And the same is true, Stump believes, with respect to a relationship between a loving God and humans. Just as the teacher wants to foster a meaningful relationship with Jim, God wants to foster a meaningful relationship with us. But just as Jim is in a position to become overly dependent on the teacher if all his needs are automatically met, so, too, are we in a position to become overly dependent if God automatically meets our needs. Thus, it makes sense to believe that God will not always do what he might desire to do for us *unless* we ask, and that even when asked, God will not always respond positively. This is best for our relationship in the long run.[22]

This does not mean, Stump is quick to point out, that God must at *any* given time or in any given situation *totally refrain* from interacting in earthly affairs until requested. God might still bring about much of what he generally thinks is best even if not requested to do so, but perhaps "not in the same amount of time or not by the same process or not with the same effect." Perhaps, for example, God would have brought it about that Augustine was converted even if his mother had not requested it, but not in such a way that he became "one of [Christianity's] most powerful authorities for centuries." In short, Stump wants her model of prayer to incorporate both a meaningful sense in which God is still in control and a meaningful sense in which our prayers do directly influence earthly affairs — that is, do change things.[23]

However, should not a loving human parent at least automatically do things for his child *if* the child suffers from a physical, mental, or cultural condition making the child unlikely to know she has a parent or that the parent sometimes responds to requests? In such cases, Stump believes that a parent and, thus, by analogy God, can justly fulfill the "child's" need without being requested to do so. But this does not mean, she adds, that God ought not at times bestow "benefits in response to requests" for those of us who do have a "normal" relationship with him.[24]

But what of those cases in which someone asks God to do something for someone else? To return to our analogy, what if John asks the teacher to help

Jim? Cannot John and the teacher be accused of meddling in such a case? They can, Stump believes, to the extent that Jim has not freely shared his problems with John. And even then, the most that the teacher can justly do in response to John's request is "to try to elicit from *Jim* in genuinely noncoercive ways a request for help." The same, she believes, applies to God. When asked by one person to help another, God can avoid the charge of oppressive meddling only if the person God has been asked to help comes to the place where he "has willingly shared his thoughts and feelings and the like with God."

Stump acknowledges that her petitionary model becomes even more problematic when applied to prayers related to the natural environment – for example, for prayers in which God is asked to keep earthquakes from hitting populated areas. But she believes that her account "is on the right track," that seeing petitionary prayer "as a kind of buffer between man and God" is the best way to preserve both the Christian belief that God is a loving, caring parent and the Christian belief that asking makes a difference.[25]

Will those who have struggled with the problem of petitionary prayer find Stump's model helpful? In one sense, most surely will. It seems quite plausible to hold that an earthly or heavenly parent ought at times not offer help until requested by the "child" in need. But Stump's model, by her own admission, is less clear on what sense it makes to petition God to help others – that is, to petition God to interact uninvited in the lives of others for their benefit. And some have argued that this is the very type of petitioning that generates the most serious questions about the usefulness of petitionary prayer in the first place.

Revelation

It is expedient to have . . . what God has revealed, in addition to the philosophical researches pursued by human reasoning.

Thomas Aquinas

Most believers have a healthy respect for human reason. They normally see our abilities to do such things as observe, hypothesize, test, deduce, and create as gifts from God that enable us to discover a great deal of useful information about our world. They are quite willing to grant, for example, that human reason has enabled us to conquer many dreaded diseases and produce inventions that have made life easier. And many are even willing to grant, as we have seen, that human reason can discover some moral and religious truth.

However, as we have also seen, many hold that some religious knowledge is not acquired by the use of reason but is revealed in some other way. It is often held, for example, that some information about how we can come to know God or how we ought to live is known only because it has been *revealed* to us by God apart from rational considerations. But what exactly are we to make of this concept of revelation? Is direct divine revelation of this sort possible? And if so, what forms might it reasonably be said to take? These are the types of questions with which George Mavrodes (1926–) has recently grappled.[26]

If we define revealed theology as that religious truth which lies beyond the range of reason, then, as Mavrodes sees it, three distinct models of revelation emerge. First, there is the *Causation Model*, within which "revelation" is used to label what has traditionally been called *innate knowledge*: religious truth that could not have been acquired from our ordinary encounters with the ordinary world. To claim that some religious knowledge is innate in this sense, we are told, can be understood in two ways. One can claim that the believer has the type of innate knowledge described in Plato's Socratic discussion (in the *Meno*) of a slave boy and geometry. Socrates begins to converse with a slave boy who has had no exposure to geometry. But in response to persistent questions by Socrates about the areas of various squares, the boy begins to display a rather sophisticated knowledge of this subject matter, a phenomenon that Plato explains by arguing that the boy was "born" with this knowledge in the form of a dormant memory that was simply brought to consciousness by Socrates' questions.

In a similar fashion, Mavrodes explains, believers such as Descartes have held that certain types of religious information—for example, the concept or idea of God—are in our intellect when it comes into existence.

But there is, he informs us, another way in which believers have held that religious information can be innate. John Calvin, for example, apparently did not believe that God has directly implanted in us the idea of the divine. What he seemed to believe, rather, is that God has implanted in the human intellect the natural disposition to believe that there is a God, a disposition activated by a variety of natural sensations—for example, by "seeing the blazing beauty of the sky on a clear night."

Is it *possible* that we acquire religious content in either of these innate fashions? Of course, Mavrodes grants, if one believes there is no God, then one will rightly hold that no such revelation can occur. But if there is a God, he contends, then there appears to be no good reason to deny that one way in which people might come to have certain beliefs about God is that God simply causes them to have such beliefs, either by "implanting" the beliefs or by creating us with the natural tendency to form such beliefs under the appropriate conditions.[27]

Mavrodes then turns his attention to what he labels the *Manifestation Model* of revelation. The key to understanding this model, we are told, is the distinction between *claiming* that something is the case and manifesting or exhibiting this fact. Bill might, for example, *claim* that he can speak English by passing Mary a note that says this is so. But Bill would manifest or exhibit this ability by actually speaking English in Mary's presence. Applied to divine revelation, this allows us to distinguish between God's claiming (revealing) that he exists—for example, by bringing it about that this is written in the Bible—and God's *manifesting* (revealing) his existence by allowing us to have "something like an *experience* of God, a sort of perception, or quasi-perception, of the divine presence."[28]

Mavrodes's first task here is to specify further the types of manifestation this model might include. In almost all such cases God is clearly the revealer, but many things can plausibly be said to be revealed, sometimes by the very same act. Just as "the eavesdropper, when he steps from behind the drapery, may with equal propriety be said to reveal *himself*, to reveal *his* presence, and to reveal *that he is there*," there is no reason to think that God could not by some act—for instance, by making himself present to us in a time of need— reveal *himself*, his *presence* and that he is *there or that he is good*.

But even if a person believes that God exists and can reveal himself and information about himself in this fashion, how is she to know that she has really experienced a manifestation of God? "What is it about an experience that warrants *that* belief?" Mavrodes explores two possibilities. Perhaps we have a way of recognizing God's presence that is analogous to the way we recognize a friend's presence without being able "to describe that way in any satisfactory and illuminating manner." Or perhaps we have no *way* of recognizing God's presence in the sense that we recognize it by doing something else— for example, consciously or subconsciously utilizing some line of reasoning. Perhaps it is simply a basic cognitive act. That is, perhaps we simply have the spiritual capacity for recognizing God, just as we have the physical capacity for recognizing trees. And if we are "God's creatures, it also seems plausible . . . to suppose," Mavrodes concludes, "that this capacity, if [we] indeed [have] it, is part of His endowment to [us]."[29]

Finally, Mavrodes turns to the most prominent model of revelation: the *Communication Model*, within which God is viewed as revealing himself by *speaking* with us in much the same sense we speak with one another. And here Mavrodes's strategy is basically to respond to criticisms or potential misunderstandings.

Some have argued that communicating with humans is beneath the dignity of God. But to this Mavrodes replies simply that "if God in fact speaks to men and women, then . . . so much the worse for any conception of the divine nature with which such speaking is incompatible." In fact, he doubts that this type of revelation need even be restricted to important theological and religious truth: It is "a real possibility . . . that God is just not as spiritually minded as are some theologians."

Others have argued that divine revelation might somehow damage human autonomy. After all, if we are spoon-fed important information by the author of truth, what need is there for us to utilize our own powers of thought? But again Mavrodes is not impressed. First, it seems obvious to him that many reject what God reveals. And even in those cases in which divine communication is accepted as such, "there seems to be no appreciable damage to human autonomy and initiative." Perhaps, he acknowledges, if God were to reveal every important fact to us, our natural human activities might be inhibited. But God only reveals some things. And just as we need not suppose that the autonomy of chemists is damaged by the fact that they rely on the accuracy of the labels on the bottles of chemicals they utilize, we need not suppose that the autonomy of believers is damaged by the fact that they rely on *some* important divine information about fundamental aspects of reality.[30]

Finally, Mavrodes takes up the question of whether God *can* in fact communicate to us personally through other persons or things — for example, through stories in the Bible or events in our lives or the lives of others. Specifically, can God communicate more to us personally than we might receive simply by taking the relevant stories or events at face value? The answer, he believes, is yes. In fact, he thinks this may be the work of the Holy Spirit.

But what reason other than the testimony of others do we have for believing that such mediated communication actually occurs? We do in fact have little to go on, he grants, as long as we ourselves never hear (or recognize) the voice of God. But if we do hear that voice, "then we can make our own stab" at determining how God's voice has come to us.[31]

There certainly appears to be much of value in what Mavrodes has done. The first step in any philosophical analysis is to clarify the meaning of the concepts in question, and no other philosopher has recently attempted to clarify in such detail the various meanings of "divine revelation." On the other hand, there are other important philosophical issues that Mavrodes has chosen not to consider in detail. What is the proper relationship between reason and revelation? How does one identify a divine revelation as such? Moreover, there is one important issue that is not discussed at all. Almost all religions believe that God has revealed himself to us in the ways Mavrodes indicates. However, the revelations of the major religions do not simply differ in many ways, they are at points clearly incompatible. Even within the same religious perspective significant revelatory differences appear. For example, some conservative Christians clearly find God revealing in Scripture that it is always wrong to use life-threatening force or that one must be baptized to be "saved," while others find just the opposite. In fact, wars have been fought over such issues. Why is this so? What does this say, specifically, about the plausibility of believing that any one of us has actually received a divine revelation or that we have interpreted it correctly? Responses are available, but it would certainly be interesting to know Mavrodes's thoughts on these questions, and perhaps we shall if he continues to work on this topic.

Doctrine and Interpretation

As we stated at the beginning of this chapter, the philosophers currently under consideration are not trying to *prove* or *establish* the Christian doctrines they discuss, but rather to *analyze* their meaning and determine whether a rational person can affirm them. And this is surely an important goal. That is, it is important for all Christians to understand what the doctrines they hold actually mean and to identify the conditions under which they can justifiably continue to hold them. It is important as well for those who are not Christian believers to be able to understand the logic and import of the doctrines.

There remains, though, a related issue for philosophers of religion to consider. What has been clarified and defended in almost every case in this chapter is the classical (traditional) interpretation of the doctrines in question. However, all of these doctrines are currently subject to a wide variety of interpretations within the Christian community. Views on the Incarnation, for example, range all the way from the traditional claim that Jesus Christ was fully human and fully God to the contention that Jesus was a man who received divine insight to the highest degree humanly possible. Views on scriptural revelation range from the claim that God directly dictated every word to the contention that the Bible at best contains the most illuminating human thoughts about God to date. And views on the Atonement range all the way from the traditional claim that Christ died to "pay the price for sin" to the claim that Christ's death was a moral example of what divine love can lead one person to do for another. Accordingly, it would appear that knowledgeable Christians cannot concern themselves solely with clarifying and defending a given interpretation of any of these doctrines. It appears that at some point they need to consider the question of which interpretation is actually most worthy of clarification and defense.

However, some have argued that philosophers of religion fail to acknowledge this fact — that is, they often fail to acknowledge that they are defending or clarifying *one interpretation* of a Christian doctrine. Rather, they imply by the way they use the term *Christian* and their comments about the meaning of Scripture that they are discussing *the* correct Christian perspective. And, accordingly, they often fail to consider the most fundamental question that arises in this context: Are there good reasons to believe that the perspective being clarified and defended is the best option available, or at least one that deserves to be defended?[32]

Now, of course, it is questionable whether this stands as a valid *criticism* of the classical philosophers discussed in this chapter. They might reply that although they are well aware of the fact that many viable Christian interpretations of the doctrines in question exist, they have simply chosen to concentrate their efforts on the clarification and defense of one well-known, historically important Christian perspective. But the critics' *general* point would appear to be helpful. If Christian (or other religious) philosophers really desire to concern themselves with specific theological doctrines, it does seem important that they at some point not only clarify and defend a given perspective on a doctrine but also discuss why such a perspective is actually worthy of defense in the first place.

STUDY QUESTIONS

1. Try to state in your own words the distinction Thomas Morris draws between an individual being *fully* human and *merely* human. Do you think this distinction resolves the problem it is intended to address?

2. Do you believe that Jesus Christ was fully human and fully divine? If not, *could* any person have both of these properties simultaneously?

3. Philip Quinn's moral intuitions tell him that one person cannot, by volunteering to take someone's place, absolve that other person of her obligation to pay for a crime. Do you agree? Why?

4. What is your response to Quinn's own model of Atonement?

5. Compare and contrast William Alston's three models of how the Holy Spirit interacts with humans.

6. Do you agree that Alston's "sharing model" seems to be the most appropriate analysis of the work of the Holy Spirit?

7. Many believers maintain both that God is in total control of earthly affairs and that prayer changes things. Can both beliefs justifiably be affirmed at the same time?

8. What do you think of Eleonore Stump's "solution" to the problem of petitionary prayer? Can you think of other ways in which believers might respond?

9. Compare and contrast George Mavrodes's three models of Revelation. Which one seem to you to be the most significant?

10. Do you believe there are many different written revelations that come from God? Why is the same written revelation often subject to so many different interpretations? Should this fact bother the religious believer?

NOTES

1. Thomas V. Morris, "Rationality and the Christian Revelation," in *Anselmian Explorations* (Notre Dame, IN: University of Notre Dame Press, 1987), pp. 213–241; *The Logic of God Incarnate* (Ithaca, NY: Cornell University Press, 1986).
2. Morris, pp. 219–22.
3. Morris, p. 224.
4. Morris, p. 229.
5. Morris, pp. 239–41.
6. Two representative critiques of Morris on this point can be found in Bruce Reichenbach, *Christian Scholar's Review* 16 (September 1986): 77–79; and Eleonore Stump, *Faith and Philosophy* 6 (April, 1989): 218–23.
7. Philip L. Quinn, "Aquinas on Atonement," in Ronald Feenstra and Cornelius Plantinga, Jr., eds., *Trinity, Incarnation and Atonement* (Notre Dame, IN: University of Notre Dame Press, 1990).
8. Quinn, pp. 164–65.
9. Quinn, pp. 167–69.
10. Quinn, pp. 169–71.
11. Quinn, pp. 171–74.
12. Quinn, pp. 174–75.
13. Quinn, pp. 175–76.

14. William P. Alston, "The Indwelling of the Holy Spirit," in Thomas V. Morris, ed., *Philosophy and the Christian Faith* (Notre Dame, IN: University of Notre Dame Press, 1988).
15. Alston, p. 124.
16. Alston, p. 135.
17. Alston, p. 132–37.
18. Alston, p. 147.
19. Eleonore Stump, "Petitionary Prayer," *American Philosophical Quarterly* 16 (April 1979): 81–91.
20. Stump, p. 86.
21. Stump, p. 87.
22. Stump, pp. 87–88.
23. Stump, p. 89.
24. Stump, p. 89.
25. Stump, pp. 88–90.
26. George I. Mavrodes, *Revelation in Religious Belief* (Philadelphia: Temple University Press, 1988).
27. Mavrodes, pp. 73–74.
28. Mavrodes, p. 75.
29. Mavrodes, pp. 105, 106, 109.
30. Mavrodes, pp. 116, 125–26.
31. Mavrodes, pp. 130–52, 153.
32. See, for example, James Keller, "Reflections on a Methodology for Christian Philosophers," *Faith and Philosophy* 5, no. 2 (1988): 144–58.

SUGGESTED READING

Alston, William. "Christian Experience and Christian Belief." Alvin Plantinga and Nicholas Wolterstorff, eds., *Faith and Rationality: Reason and Belief in God*. Notre Dame, IN: University of Notre Dame Press, 1983.

Baillie, John. *The Idea of Revelation in Recent Thought*. New York: Columbia University Press, 1956.

Basinger, David. "Why Petition an Omnipotent, Omniscient, Wholly Good God?" *Religious Studies* 19 (1983): 25–41.

Daujat, Jean. *The Theology of Grace*. Vol. 23 in Henri Daniel-Raps, ed., *Twentieth Century Encyclopedia of Catholicism*. New York: Hawthorne Books, 1959.

Goulder, Michael, ed. *Incarnation and Myth: The Debate Continued*. Grand Rapids, MI: Eerdmans, 1979.

James, William. *The Varieties of Religious Experience*. New York: Modern Library, 1902.

Jantzen, Grace. "Incarnation and Epistemology." *Theology* 83 (May 1983).

Lampe, G. W. H. *God as Spirit*. Oxford: Clarendon Press, 1977.

Morris, Thomas. *The Logic of God Incarnate*. Ithaca, NY: Cornell University Press, 1986.

Quinn, Philip. "Christian Atonement and Kantian Justification," *Faith and Philosophy* 3 (1986): 440–62.

Young, Robert. "Petitioning God," *American Philosophical Quarterly* 11 (1974): 193–201.

15

The Continuing Quest:
God and the Human Venture

Oxford philosopher J. L. Mackie (1917–1981) writes:

> It is my view that the question whether there is or is not a god can and should
> be discussed rationally and reasonably, and that such discussion can be re-
> warding, in that it can yield definite results. This is a genuine, meaningful
> question, and an important one—too important for us to take sides about it
> casually or arbitrarily. Neither the affirmative nor the negative answer is obvi-
> ously right, but the issue is not so obscure that relevant considerations of
> argument and evidence cannot be brought to bear upon it.[1]

These words begin Mackie's book, *The Miracle of Theism*. As the title suggests, Mackie takes it to be astonishing—or, to speak in hyperbole, "miraculous"—that theism has endured for centuries as a credible idea in the minds of
intelligent people. For him, when the arguments and evidence are fairly evaluated, it is more reasonable to believe that theism is false than that it is true.

Mackie echoes the judgment of numerous influential philosophers, both
past and present: Lucretius (c. 99–55 B.C.), David Hume (1711–1776), Friedrich Nietzsche (1844–1900), W. K. Clifford (1845–1879), Bertrand Russell
(1872–1970), Antony Flew (1923–), William Rowe (1931–), and many
more. On the other side, there have been equally distinguished philosophers
who think that, when all of the relevant considerations are weighed, it is indeed
rational to believe that theism is true. The names of Augustine (354–430),
Anselm (1033–1109), Aquinas (c. 1224–1274), René Descartes (1596–1650),
Richard Swinburne (1934–), William Alston (1921–), and Alvin Plantinga
(1932–) merely begin the list of creditable theistic philosophers.

As we have seen throughout this book, a host of important issues constitute
a full-scale discussion of theism: the significance of religious experience, the
viability of arguments for and against God's existence, the question of whether
rational argument is relevant or necessary to the acceptance of theism, the
problem of how religious statements are meaningful, the difficulty of making
sense of the concept of miracle, and the extent to which the plurality of other

religious belief systems affects the appraisal of theism. These considerations provide a basis for an informed opinion about the overall acceptability of theism. Of course, one's overall opinion of theism can be placed in an even larger context when one realizes the connection of issues in religion with those in other areas of philosophy and with general world-view considerations.

The Intellectual Process

All of the issues surrounding the appraisal of theism — religious experience, miracles, evil, and the like — are of enduring and almost universal concern. They are not raised and finally answered at a specific point in the history of thought, such that all of those who come later can simply memorize the correct response. Instead, these issues embody the sorts of themes and questions that every generation must raise and ponder for itself. And in every generation, each thoughtful person must face these issues along with all of the other pressing intellectual challenges that confront him. While no one will arrive at an answer to these questions that puts a halt to all future discussion, deliberating about the issues and adopting the best position one can find are stages of a very worthwhile intellectual process.

Fortunately, we are not without help in our intellectual investigation of religion. Great thinkers of past and present have left a legacy of thought and opinion for us to build upon. They have helped to clarify the main problems, to show where burdens of proof lie, and to detect dead ends. We need the wisdom of past and present, in addition to the best thinking we can bring to the subject, in order to make progress on the enormously important issues related to religious belief. Throughout the present study, we have attempted to draw from the wisdom of past and present in order to elucidate the issues, identify the options, and find the most reasonable positions.

Throughout this text we have been engaged in a great dialogue, which has been carried on for centuries and will continue as long as people raise philosophical questions regarding religious belief. The intellectual process we have entered — the process of argument and counterargument, of carefully considering alternatives, and of trying to gain insight into the issues surrounding religious belief — is an ongoing one. This very text stands as a refutation to all those who say that human reason cannot penetrate matters of religion, as do all of the classic and contemporary works in the philosophy of religion. All important issues in human life must be subject to reason. This holds for beliefs associated with a particular theistic religion, beliefs drawn from theistic religions generally, or beliefs held by other, nontheistic religions. If religious beliefs are not subject to the earnest, objective approach of reason, then prospects for the human enterprise are bleak indeed.

We commend the method employed in this book — broadly, philosophical analysis — on the merits of the results obtained in the discussion of religious topics, as shown in the preceding pages. But if rational analysis is appropriate, are there *limits* to the philosophical investigation of religious belief? The answer here depends on precisely how one takes such questions. If the question is about psychological limits, the answer may well be yes. Along these lines, we may even ponder just how far we can continue the rational investigation. Obviously, each individual or personality-type will have some idiosyncratic limitations. Cultural background, family upbringing, religious convictions, capacity for abstract thought, and the like will surely produce real limitations for each person. There may come a point at which a given person simply says that he can press the investigation no further.

Yet if the question is meant to ask whether there are "theoretical" (or perhaps "logical") limits to the rational investigation of religious belief, then the answer must be no. There is no fixed terminus or predetermined point at which investigation must stop. Granting that certain individuals reach their own idiosyncratic limits, one of the lessons of history is that when someone declares an absolute limit to thought in some area of human endeavor, someone else goes beyond it. No person or group can prescribe for someone else the limits to her rational search.

We are all aware that some people claim that the sacredness of the subject makes it disrespectful or blasphemous to analyze religion, or that it encourages unwholesome doubt. Others argue that the vastness and mystery of God, Brahman, Nirvāṇa, or some other Ultimate Reality is inaccessible to finite human minds. But while the subject matter may be deemed sacred, every respectable religion recognizes and encourages responsible thought. Indeed, the major world religions have long histories of debate and discussion of their key doctrines and themes. Besides, nothing encourages intractable doubts as much as forbidding free and open inquiry. Even if God is beyond our thoughts in certain very significant ways, rational investigation is simply an inquiry into *concepts* and *beliefs* about God. It is the enterprise of trying to make our thoughts about God and related subjects clear and coherent, informed and reasonable. God may well be infinite, but concepts and beliefs about God are not infinite and are entirely open to rational investigation.

To maintain confidently that the intellectual process cannot be blocked or preempted in the examination of religious belief is not to say that it is in any way infallible or complete. The fate of humanity seems to be that of bringing our best thinking to bear upon the problems we face, realizing full well that our results are tentative and incomplete, and that we may have to revise and move ahead cautiously. Yet this process is all we have. Even if some revelation is true or if a certain religious vision is valid, its credentials still must be rationally evaluated, and must either stand or fall in the light of arguments and evidence. The recognition of our own fallibility, as well as the strong proclivity of some religious dogmatists to claims of infallibility, suggests to us that the hope is brightest for progress in the appraisal of religion when we strive hard for objectivity, fairness, and tolerance.

Philosophical Activity and Religious Faith

Although many will admit that religion is subject to rational appraisal, some would insist that the results of philosophical inquiry are irrelevant to authentic religious faith. The opening words of Pascal's Memorial (dated November 23, 1654) make a strict distinction between "the God of Abraham, God of Isaac, God of Jacob," on the one hand, and the God of the "philosophers and scholars," on the other. For Pascal (1623–1662) and many other people, even if the existence of God could be validly inferred from acceptable premises, it would be of merely academic interest. Deeply religious people typically claim that they already live in a dynamic relationship with God and thus that rational argument and other intellectual exercises are patently beside the point. The proper response to their claim runs along two lines.

First, it is certainly right to distinguish carefully between philosophical activity on the one hand and vital religious faith on the other. *Philosophical* interest in God is simply different from *religious* interest in God, a different mode of human activity. In general, we can say that engaging in rigorous analysis and argument is neither a necessary nor a sufficient condition for a healthy religious faith. Philosophical understanding is not a *necessary condition* because a person may not have the mental ability to engage in the sophisticated intellectual study of religion — and thus cannot produce any persuasive argument, say, for the existence of God — and yet may clearly possess a robust religious faith.

Second, another person may be quite skilled in philosophical matters, able to advance creditable arguments in favor of God's existence, and not have religious faith at all. She might be intellectually persuaded, for example, that Christianity is true and yet not commit herself to or find herself in relation to the God worshiped in that religion. Likewise a person might be intellectually persuaded that Hinduism is true and yet not be personally devoted to Brahman. The same holds for all who merely assent to the truth of other religions. Thus, the philosophical examination of religion is not a *sufficient condition* for faith either.

While the rigorous philosophical examination of religion is neither necessary nor sufficient for religious faith, we must not suppose that faith is entirely divorced or separated from rational thought. It seems, rather, that religious faith (conceived as trust in a divine being and the like) is predicated on at least some minimal amount of thought — and perhaps on more thought than some might initially suspect. The thought with which we are concerned here, of course, takes the form of belief that a statement or proposition is true. Many beliefs make up a religious believer's set of intellectual commitments, conscious or unconscious.

As we have seen, displaying faith in God involves having certain beliefs about God and his ways with the world. Granted, an ordinary religious believer may not be fully conscious of his own beliefs or may not attend to those beliefs when acting naturally as one of the faithful. But those beliefs are present nonetheless, and much the same general rules and constraints for reasonable believing apply to them as to other human beliefs. This fact is often seen when some religious believers more consciously desire to probe and make sense of their beliefs. They feel the need to maintain their own intellectual integrity, to have their beliefs be faithful to both *logic* and *fact*. Their religious faith is not, as Bertrand Russell once remarked, "believin' what you know ain't so."

Ultimately, whether or not religious believers are aware of the beliefs that underpin their faith, the beliefs can nonetheless be abstracted and systematized for philosophical study and reflection. Philosophy of religion applies standard methods of analysis and argument as well as the insights from metaphysics, epistemology, and other fields of philosophy to these abstracted beliefs. Of course, this means that such concerns as consistency, coherence, and correspondence to the facts really do pertain to religious believing, and that matters of plausibility and truth are relevant. But then it is possible for religious believers, wittingly or unwittingly, to violate these intellectual concerns.

This is true not only of religious believers, but also of nonbelievers who fail to recognize the intellectual or belief component of faith. Nonbelievers can mistakenly characterize faith as a purely emotional response or as socially conditioned behavior and thus fail to perceive the underlying beliefs that are appropriately subject to intellectual investigation. Thus, anyone—believer or nonbeliever—considering the viability of a religious perspective must maintain a conscientious respect for the intellectual standards that philosophy employs. It is this kind of rational consideration that figures prominently in the decision as to whether a religious faith is sensible and warranted or confused and misguided.

Where Do We Go From Here?

In a sense, we have just scratched the surface of philosophy of religion in the preceding chapters of this text. Each issue we have treated could be pursued in much more depth and detail. Or, as one moves beyond the standard core of issues presented here, other fascinating topics arise and provide material for further consideration of *classical theism*. For example, the problems surrounding divine action in the world would be interesting to pursue in light of the theistic concept of God and our ordinary concepts of agency. And issues such as the relation of church and state would not lie outside the purview of philosophy of religion. So, the task of pursuing the standard issues beyond what has been done in this text remains as enormous as it is rewarding.

There are still other kinds of topics for philosophers of religion to treat— topics that pertain more specifically to the doctrines and beliefs unique to given historic religions. Many key theological conceptions within Christianity—such as creation, heaven, hell, and forgiveness—need further philosophical attention in the vein and spirit of our Chapter 14.[2] And, although this occurs only rarely among current philosophers of religion, it would be enlightening to apply philosophical analysis to important religious activities. Within Christianity, say, liturgy and Holy Communion appear to be fertile ground for philosophical attention.[3]

Another area for philosophers of religion to explore is the problem of dialogue and interaction between philosophy and theology. The whole problem of dialogue between philosophers and theologians occurs, in part, because of differences in how the assumptions and methods of their two disciplines are conceived.[4] Traditionally, tension arose because theologians used revelation as the final authority and arbiter in religious matters, whereas philosophers recognized only reason. A more contemporary controversy revolves around the use of modern logical techniques and conceptual analysis by philosophers, and the insistence by theologians that such methods cannot do justice to human experience and history. Although insulation of the two fields of theology and philosophy continues in many quarters, there are signs that some thinkers are attempting to break down old barriers.[5] It appears that the whole issue of how to find grounds for theological-philosophical dialogue will be in the forefront for some years to come.

While many theologians, particularly those associated with historical theology and biblical exegesis, have avoided contact with academic philosophy, other theologians have consciously shaped their perspectives around certain philosophical concepts. These "new theologies" range from process theology (which makes use of process metaphysics to shape its religious perspective) to liberation theology (which essentially adopts a Marxist point of view on the nature and function of religion). Feminist theology and environmentalist theology, among others, also supply the substance for much philosophical thought and reflection.

The philosophical scrutiny of other major religious conceptions offers one more direction for further study and reflection. For example, the general *pantheistic* conception of the Ultimate, together with all of its logical implications, could be studied just as we have here studied the philosophical issues related to the classical theistic conception. Among other things, the logical coherence of the pantheistic conception of deity could be explored, just as we explored here the coherence of the theistic conception.

On the other hand, a specific nontheistic religion — its particular beliefs and living practices — could be a fruitful object of philosophical scrutiny. It would be wholly appropriate for a text analogous to this one to be written, say, on the religious beliefs emerging primarily from Hinduism. In this text, Hindu pantheism (or panentheism) was mentioned from time to time for the primary purposes of comparison and contrast with Western theism. A more complete treatment of Hindu beliefs would, for example, discuss the precise shape of the problem of evil as it arises for Hinduism. Also, the implications of the Hindu belief system for human morality could be traced out. Fundamental Hindu theological conceptions, such as karma and Nirvāṇa, could be analyzed and their logical structure clarified.[6]

It is possible to provide a careful, philosophical treatment of the beliefs of any other world religion following the approach used in this book. Of course, one complicating factor that is of great philosophical interest itself is that each major religion has its own philosophical tradition, a tradition that may not endorse the same approach we have used. A notable example is the Hindu philosophical and theological tradition denying that the laws of Western logic apply to beliefs about the Ultimate, Brahman, or its manifestations in Śiva and Viṣṇu.

Ideally, the serious study of religion will lead one eventually to other disciplines: anthropology, sociology, and psychology. The additional perspectives that these other disciplines offer on the complex reality of religion allow the philosophical scrutiny of religion to be relevant and informed. In fact, the whole question of the bearing of these other disciplines on religion or on the philosophy of religion is itself a philosophical question.

It seems patently safe to say that the standard issues in philosophy of religion will continue to be discussed by serious thinkers. The perennial problems offer an almost inexhaustible supply of possibilities for research and reflection. And, of course, new strategies and approaches provide countless permutations on old issues, and then themselves become part of the standard fare in philosophy of religion. Add to this the fact that virgin territory always remains to be pioneered, opening to us new and important problems for consideration. What we have in philosophy of religion, then, is a dynamic and growing domain of discussion.

Those interested in the important problems related to theistic belief can participate in an ever-stimulating and helpful discussion by following the developments in the philosophy of religion. We cannot always predict the outcome of historic issues, nor can we anticipate the direction of future debates. However, to sense the seriousness of the rational appraisal of religious belief and to understand its value is to take a large step toward being able to navigate religious issues and to fulfill one's intellectual responsibilities. As Aquinas said, we must adopt the posture of always being willing "to inquire, in a rational way, into the things human reason can disclose concerning God."[7]

STUDY QUESTIONS

1. Discuss the kinds of attitudes appropriate to the fair and objective discussion of religious beliefs.

2. After engaging in the analysis and appraisal of religious belief throughout this book, how would you assess the reasonableness or the truth of classical theistic belief?

3. In light of all you have read so far, try to make the best case you can for theistic belief.

4. In light of all you have read so far, try to make the best case you can against theistic belief.

5. What topics in the philosophy of religion covered in this book would you be interested in pursuing more thoroughly?

6. What topics in the philosophy of religion not covered in this text would you be interested in pursuing?

7. What issues in fields related to the philosophy of religion would you be interested in pursuing?

8. In what ways, if any, has studying the issues presented in this text changed your approach to religion?

NOTES

1. J. L. Mackie, *The Miracle of Theism* (Oxford: Clarendon Press, 1982), p. 1. Also see pp. 11–12 for a further explanation of the title of the book.
2. Fred Freddoso, *The Existence and Nature of God* (Notre Dame, IN: University of Notre Dame Press, 1983).
3. Nicholas Wolterstorff, "The Remembrance of Things (Not) Past: Philosophical Reflections on Christian Liturgy," in Thomas P. Flint, ed., *Christian Philosophy* (Notre Dame, IN: University of Notre Dame Press, 1990), pp. 118–61. The volume in which this essay appears is devoted entirely to exploring the philosophical ramifications of a variety of Christian ideas (e.g., the effects of sin) and practices (e.g., creedal affirmation).
4. Notice the differences between theology and philosophy assumed in such pieces as Gordon Kaufmann, "Evidentialism: A Theologian's Response," *Faith and Philosophy: Journal of the Society of Christian Philosophers* 6, no. 4 (1989): 353–77; Maurice F. Wiles, "Review of *The Logic of God Incarnate*," *Journal of Theological Studies* 38 (April 1987): 272; Thomas V. Morris, "Philosophers and Theologians at Odds," *Asbury Theological Journal* 44, no. 2 (1989): 31–41; William J. Abraham, "Oh God, Poor God," *The American Scholar* (Autumn 1989): 557–63.
5. One piece of evidence that there is some interchange is the conference on "Philosophical Theology and Biblical Exegesis," at the University of Notre Dame, March 15–17, 1990. Theologians and biblical scholars are also starting to invite philosophers to speak at their professional conferences (e.g., American Academy of Religion, Society of Biblical Literature). Another piece of evidence of the contact between philosophy and theology is the Cornell Studies in Philosophy of Religion series of scholarly monographs and the Library of Religious Philosophy series from the University of Notre Dame Press. The Society of Christian Philosophers continues to sponsor conferences and seminars on topics related to theology. *Faith and Philosophy: Journal of the Society of Christian Philosophers* continues to seek dialogue with major theologians (e.g., see the October 1989 issue which is devoted entirely to the topic of the Bible and philosophy).
6. For an example of how the philosophical examination of concepts in a nontheistic religion might be carried out, see Bruce Reichenbach, *The Law of Karma: A Philosophical Study* (London: Macmillan, 1990).
7. Thomas Aquinas, *Summa Contra Gentiles*, trans. Anton C. Pegis (Notre Dame, IN: University of Notre Dame Press, 1975), 1, 9, n. 4.

SUGGESTED READING

Alston, William P. *Divine Nature and Human Language: Essays in Philosophical Theology.* Ithaca, NY: Cornell University Press, 1989.

Audi, Robert, and Wainright, William, eds. *Rationality, Religious Belief, and Moral Commitment: New Essays in the Philosophy of Religion.* Ithaca, NY: Cornell University Press, 1986.

Freddoso, Fred. *The Existence and Nature of God*. Notre Dame, IN: University of
    Notre Dame Press, 1983.
Mackie, J. L. *The Miracle of Theism*. Oxford: Clarendon Press, 1982.
Plantinga, Alvin, and Nicholas Wolterstorff, eds. *Faith and Rationality: Reason and
    Belief in God*. Notre Dame, IN: University of Notre Dame Press, 1983.
Ross, James. *Philosophical Theology*. Indianapolis: Bobbs-Merrill, 1969.

Name Index

Abraham, William J., 45n.8, 177
Adams, Robert M., 91, 237–38
Alston, William P., 17–19, 27–28, 119, 127–30, 134n.21, 150–51, 201–4, 254, 262–64, 274
Ambrose, St., 258
Anselm, 10, 51, 70–74, 89, 254
Aquinas, St. Thomas, 35, 56, 62, 74, 78, 138–40, 148–51, 190, 193–94, 242, 258–60, 265, 267, 274, 280
Aristotle, 86, 190, 194, 211
Augustine, St., 13–14, 21, 30, 51, 59, 62, 107–8, 248, 266, 274

Badham, Paul, 188, 193n.3
Baier, Kurt, 193
Barth, Karl, 154n.28, 201, 222–24, 230, 233
Basinger, David, 46n.23, 172n.12
Basinger, Randall, 134n.25, 172n.12
Bodon, Margaret, 165–66
Borowitz, Eugene, 92
Bradley, F. H., 4
Braithwaite, R. B., 146, 148, 154n.19
Broad, C. D., 189, 194
Brunner, Emile, 154n.28
Buber, Martin, 200–202
Buddha, the (Siddartha Gautama), 85, 125, 230
Bultmann, Rudolph, 39, 177, 193
Byrne, Peter, 234

Campbell, Keith, 194
Carroll, Lewis, 49
Cartwright, Nancy, 98, 114n.16
Chisholm, Roderick, 122–23
Clifford, William K., 34–35, 45n.15, 274
Collingwood, R. G., 208
Copernicus, 196–97

Coulson, Charles, 203
Craig, William L., 75, 90

Darwin, Charles, 200
Descartes, René, 37, 120, 124, 161, 268, 274
Dilthey, Wilhelm, 208
Dostoevsky, Fyodor, 92

Emerson, Ralph Waldo, 30

Flew, Antony, 96–97, 141–43, 154–65, 274
Forman, Robert K. C., 31
Foster, Michael B., 211–12, 266
Francis, St. (of Assissi), 126

Gadamer, Hans-Georg, 47n.18
Galileo, 196, 211, 214
Gaunilo, 71–72, 89
Geach, Peter, 227, 234
Griffin, David, 110, 170–71
Gutting, Gary, 123

Hare, Peter, 97–98
Hare, R. M., 142–43
Hartshorne, Charles, 58, 73, 89n.10, 109
Hasker, William, 114n.22, 134n.25
Hawking, Stephen J., 90
Heim, Karl, 203
Hempel, Carl, 208
Hick, John, 74, 90, 108–9, 143–44, 193–94, 221, 223–28, 233–34
Hofstadter, Douglas, 184, 194
Holland, R. F., 157–58, 166
Hudson, Donald, 146
Hume, David, 80, 90, 157, 160–64, 274
Husserl, Edmund, 46n.17
Huxley, Julian, 200

283

General Index